A description of the East, and some other countries. ... By Richard Pococke, LL.D. F.R.S. Volume 3 of 3

Richard Pococke

ECCO

PRINT EDITIONS

A description of the East, and some other countries. ... By Richard Pococke, LL.D. F.R.S.
Volume 3 of 3
Pococke, Richard
ESTCID: T031684
Reproduction from British Library
For additional holdings, please see N66300. Vol.2 is in 2 parts, with separate titlepages, pagination and register, and imprint reading: printed for the author, by W. Bowyer. 1745.
London : printed for the author, by W. Bowyer; and sold by J. and P. Knapton, W. Innys, W.Meadows, G. Hawkins [and 6 others in London], 1743-45.
2v.,plates : maps ; 2°

Eighteenth Century
Collections Online
Print Editions

Gale ECCO Print Editions

Relive history with *Eighteenth Century Collections Online*, now available in print for the independent historian and collector. This series includes the most significant English-language and foreign-language works printed in Great Britain during the eighteenth century, and is organized in seven different subject areas including literature and language; medicine, science, and technology; and religion and philosophy. The collection also includes thousands of important works from the Americas.

The eighteenth century has been called "The Age of Enlightenment." It was a period of rapid advance in print culture and publishing, in world exploration, and in the rapid growth of science and technology – all of which had a profound impact on the political and cultural landscape. At the end of the century the American Revolution, French Revolution and Industrial Revolution, perhaps three of the most significant events in modern history, set in motion developments that eventually dominated world political, economic, and social life.

In a groundbreaking effort, Gale initiated a revolution of its own: digitization of epic proportions to preserve these invaluable works in the largest online archive of its kind. Contributions from major world libraries constitute over 175,000 original printed works. Scanned images of the actual pages, rather than transcriptions, recreate the works *as they first appeared.*

Now for the first time, these high-quality digital scans of original works are available via print-on-demand, making them readily accessible to libraries, students, independent scholars, and readers of all ages.

For our initial release we have created seven robust collections to form one the world's most comprehensive catalogs of 18th century works.

Initial Gale ECCO Print Editions collections include:

History and Geography
Rich in titles on English life and social history, this collection spans the world as it was known to eighteenth-century historians and explorers. Titles include a wealth of travel accounts and diaries, histories of nations from throughout the world, and maps and charts of a world that was still being discovered. Students of the War of American Independence will find fascinating accounts from the British side of conflict.

Social Science

Delve into what it was like to live during the eighteenth century by reading the first-hand accounts of everyday people, including city dwellers and farmers, businessmen and bankers, artisans and merchants, artists and their patrons, politicians and their constituents. Original texts make the American, French, and Industrial revolutions vividly contemporary.

Medicine, Science and Technology

Medical theory and practice of the 1700s developed rapidly, as is evidenced by the extensive collection, which includes descriptions of diseases, their conditions, and treatments. Books on science and technology, agriculture, military technology, natural philosophy, even cookbooks, are all contained here.

Literature and Language

Western literary study flows out of eighteenth-century works by Alexander Pope, Daniel Defoe, Henry Fielding, Frances Burney, Denis Diderot, Johann Gottfried Herder, Johann Wolfgang von Goethe, and others. Experience the birth of the modern novel, or compare the development of language using dictionaries and grammar discourses.

Religion and Philosophy

The Age of Enlightenment profoundly enriched religious and philosophical understanding and continues to influence present-day thinking. Works collected here include masterpieces by David Hume, Immanuel Kant, and Jean-Jacques Rousseau, as well as religious sermons and moral debates on the issues of the day, such as the slave trade. The Age of Reason saw conflict between Protestantism and Catholicism transformed into one between faith and logic -- a debate that continues in the twenty-first century.

Law and Reference

This collection reveals the history of English common law and Empire law in a vastly changing world of British expansion. Dominating the legal field is the *Commentaries of the Law of England* by Sir William Blackstone, which first appeared in 1765. Reference works such as almanacs and catalogues continue to educate us by revealing the day-to-day workings of society.

Fine Arts

The eighteenth-century fascination with Greek and Roman antiquity followed the systematic excavation of the ruins at Pompeii and Herculaneum in southern Italy; and after 1750 a neoclassical style dominated all artistic fields. The titles here trace developments in mostly English-language works on painting, sculpture, architecture, music, theater, and other disciplines. Instructional works on musical instruments, catalogs of art objects, comic operas, and more are also included.

The BiblioLife Network

This project was made possible in part by the BiblioLife Network (BLN), a project aimed at addressing some of the huge challenges facing book preservationists around the world. The BLN includes libraries, library networks, archives, subject matter experts, online communities and library service providers. We believe every book ever published should be available as a high-quality print reproduction; printed on-demand anywhere in the world. This insures the ongoing accessibility of the content and helps generate sustainable revenue for the libraries and organizations that work to preserve these important materials.

The following book is in the "public domain" and represents an authentic reproduction of the text as printed by the original publisher. While we have attempted to accurately maintain the integrity of the original work, there are sometimes problems with the original work or the micro-film from which the books were digitized. This can result in minor errors in reproduction. Possible imperfections include missing and blurred pages, poor pictures, markings and other reproduction issues beyond our control. Because this work is culturally important, we have made it available as part of our commitment to protecting, preserving, and promoting the world's literature.

GUIDE TO FOLD-OUTS MAPS and OVERSIZED IMAGES

The book you are reading was digitized from microfilm captured over the past thirty to forty years. Years after the creation of the original microfilm, the book was converted to digital files and made available in an online database.

In an online database, page images do not need to conform to the size restrictions found in a printed book. When converting these images back into a printed bound book, the page sizes are standardized in ways that maintain the detail of the original. For large images, such as fold-out maps, the original page image is split into two or more pages

Guidelines used to determine how to split the page image follows:

• Some images are split vertically; large images require vertical and horizontal splits.
• For horizontal splits, the content is split left to right.
• For vertical splits, the content is split from top to bottom.
• For both vertical and horizontal splits, the image is processed from top left to bottom right.

A

DESCRIPTION

OF THE

E A S T,

AND

Some other COUNTRIES.

VOL. II. PART II.

OBSERVATIONS on the ISLANDS of the
ARCHIPELAGO, ASIA MINOR, THRACE, GREECE,
and some other Parts of EUROPE.

By *RICHARD POCOCKE*, LL.D. F.R.S.

LONDON,
Printed for the AUTHOR, by W. BOWYER.
MDCCXLV

CONTENTS

OF

VOLUME the Second, PART the Second.

BOOK the First.

Of the Greek iflands of the Archipelago

BOOK the Second

Of Afia Minor

CHAP

CONTENTS.

BOOK the Third

Of Thrace and Greece.

BOOK

CONTENTS.

BOOK the Fourth.

Obfervations on fome parts of Europe.

BOOK the Fifth.

Obfervations on Germany, Bohemia, Hungary, Iftria, and fome parts of Italy.

BOOK the Sixth.

Geographical Obfervations.

CONTENTS of the PLATES

O F

VOLUME the Second, PART the Second.

CONTENTS.

E R R A T A.

Page	Line	for	read
11	38	Romans	Roman
11	45	iflands. Vicaadı	iflands, Vicardt,
35	14	if m	into it
44	19.	fourth	fourth of December
59	25	eaft	weft
67	1	Caria	Lydia
72	36	Leodicea	Laodicea
78	11	Apamea, Cibotus	Apamea Cibotus
79	9	mark	a mark
83	42	Trogitis	Trogitis, though it does not feem to be that lake,
90	36	The antient Halys	which falls into the Halys
90	30	Halys	river
50	56	weft fouth weft	eaft fouth eaft
91	1	Sebiftiopolis	Sebaftia
92	39	Sagum	Sagari

Page	Line	for	read
93	2	eaft	weft
104.	29	Berbreri	Berbieri
110	5	are	is
120	5	all	of all
158	40	Coronei	Chæronea
162	18	Parthenon	Parthenion
162	21	emblifhed	embellifhed
172	14	Saron	Sciron
172	28	Sciro	Sciron
175	39	weft	eaft
188.	1	incifum	incifus
190	3	folio	longifque anguftifque folius
192	6	Cytiffus	Cytifus
192	6	latifolius	latifolius
207	27	aqueduct O.	aqueduct O
222	30	facrifty	facrifty
236	10	deferved	defervedly

Directions to the Bookbinder.

Put Plate XXXVII at pag 6. Part II.

A
DESCRIPTION

OF

The *EAST, &c.*

BOOK the First.
Of the GREEK iſlands of the ARCHI-
PELAGO.

CHAP. I.
Of the iſland of SCIO.

I Embarked on board a French ſhip at Canea on the firſt of October, one thouſand ſeven hundred and thirty-nine, and ſailing in ſight of moſt of the iſlands, landed at Scio on the fourth The iſland of Scio is now called by the Greeks Kio [Χιο], the antient Greek name of it was Chios [Χιος], it was firſt called Ætalia in very antient times, and alſo Maſtic, on account of the great number of maſtic trees that were in this iſland It is ſituated to the weſt of that large promontory, which makes the ſouthern part of the bay of Smyrna which is to the north, and the north part of the bay of Epheſus Where it is neareſt to the continent, it is only eight miles diſtant, the north part of it is all mountainous, and is diſtinguiſhed from the other parts of the iſland by the name of Epanemeria [The upper quarter], there are notwithſtanding ſome fine ſmall vales in that part The mountains extend to the ſouth weſt, and end with low hills to the ſouth, on which moſt of the villages of Maſtic are ſituated To the weſt of the mountains, about the middle parts of the iſland, there are alſo ſome villages of Maſtic, and likewiſe of Epanemeria, theſe extend to the north weſt corner,

the other villages in that quarter being to the north. The whole
island is about thirty miles long, and fifteen broad, and is computed to
be ninety miles in circumference, though Strabo makes it one hundred
and twelve miles and a half, which may be true if it were measured round the bays and harbours. This island was taken by a Genoese, called Simon Vignosius, and was mostly governed by the family
of the Justiniani from Genoua. The Turks became masters of it in
one thousand five hundred sixty-six, the Christians remaining in possession of the castle till one thousand five hundred ninety-five, when the
Florentine galleys under Virginio Ursinio, making an attempt to recover
the island were repulsed, and the Christians dispossessed of the castle.
About forty-five years ago the Venetians took this island, but held it
only six months, and were forced to yield it again to the Turks, leaving only about thirty soldiers in the castle, who were soon subdued by
the conquerors This island has only one city in it, which is commonly
called Scio, and by the natives, by way of eminence. The place or city
['H Χωρη], it was antiently called Chiepolis. This town is situated
about the middle of a shallow bay on the east side of the island ; to the
south of it is that fine country called the Campo, and a narrower strip
to the north called Livadia Within this bay there is another small one,
which being defended to the east by ruinous peers, and having a light
house on each side, makes the port of Scio, into which the shipping
enter when they are unloaded , and there is a good road without for the
largest ships to ride in. The castle is to the north of the bay, which is
about half a mile in compass , it is inhabited only by Turks and Jews,
and is often a place of confinement for state prisoners who are sent from
Constantinople ; and when I was there the late vizier landed from
Rhodes , but it is esteemed a good omen when they are brought nearer
to Constantinople To the north of it is Palaiocastro, or the old town,
so that probably the antient city was on the north side of the port. The
chief part of the present city is on the west side of it, and is separated
by gardens from the old city, which is mostly inhabited by the lower
rank of people Though the streets are narrow, yet the town is well
built, there being many fine houses in it of hewn stone, inhabited by
the Italian families who remained here, and by the rich Greeks; many
of which were built in the time of the Genoese government. The Greeks
have a great number of churches in the city, which are remarkable for
the skreen, or partition of wood before the altar, which is of fine carved
work One of the churches is a beautiful fabric, with galleries supported by pillars, and was built a little before the Venetians took the island ;
the old and new city together are about two miles in circumference without the walls

The Campo, or plain of Scio to the north of this town is a very beautiful country, about two leagues long, and a league broad, but it consists entirely of country houses and gardens walled round, great part of
them are groves of orange and lemon trees, and the houses are so near
to one another that it appears like the suburb of a town , and from the
sea it looks almost like one continued city The plain country to the
north and south is about four leagues long, and a league broad in most
parts, and in some more : There are also in it several gardens of mul-

5   berry

berry trees for filk worms; thofe that are the moft beautiful have a walk in the middle, and to the right and left from the houfe, with fquare pillars on each fide, and feats built between them of hewn ftone; the pillars fupport a trellis-work, which is covered with vines, and on the fpaces on each fide there are groves of orange and lemon trees: Some have chapels in their gardens, with a family vault under them. Here almoft all the people of the city retire in the fummer, and as conftantly return to the town in winter, they go alfo out of the town to their country-houfes when there is any plague; and the fpring before I was there, when there were fuch terrible earthquakes, many went out of the town; but found that it was more fecure to ftay in the city, where the houfes being contiguous, fupport one another better againft the fhock To the fouth and fouth weft part of this country are the villages of the Campo, but thefe, as well as moft of the others in the ifland, which are fixty in all, are really like towns; the houfes are built together, and confift of feveral narrow ftreets, having gates at the entrance, and many of them a caftle in the middle, efpecially the villages of Maftic; which manner of building in the country feems to have been introduced as a defence againft the incurfions from the continent, which were often made when this ifland was not under the fame government On a hill to the fouth of this plain there is a large convent called faint Minas, from it one afcends to the hills on which there are one and twenty villages of maftic, all which except four are together on the fouth fide of the plain, one of the four is on the hills to the weft, and is called faint George It produces no maftic, but enjoys the privileges of the others, as being the guard to three villages that are to the weft of the mountains, for thefe villages have great privileges, they pay no rent, only a certain quantity of maftic to the grand fignor, which I was informed is yearly five thoufand and twenty okes of four hundred drams each, and they are fubject only to an aga placed over them, are permitted to have bells to their churches, being all Chriftians, and may wear white fafhes to their turbants At the firft village there is a guard to hinder any one from entering during the feafon when they make maftic, unlefs they have an order from the aga. The maftic tree, or as it is fometimes called the lentifk, in Arabic Carice, they fay, is of two forts, the wild and the domeftic tree · What they call the wild I have feen in great abundance in Syria, efpecially in the Holy Land, and in Cyprus and Candia, it bears a fmall red berry, which they affirm the domeftic does not, it is a large fhrub, I have feen it fifteen feet high, they affirm that they obferve a male and female fort of the domeftic kind The wild produces maftic, but not fo good as the other, and of this the female, which has larger leaves, and is a brighter green, produces the beft maftic, and that which comes firft from all of them, is better than that which drops afterwards, when the tree has loft its ftrength On the ninth of July they make holes in the rind acrofs the trunk with an inftrument called Timetti, it is like an awl, except that it has two edges, and the point of it is an eighth of an inch broad, they fweep the ground, and throwing water on it, tread it even to make a fmooth floor, in three days the gums begins to run, and they let it lie and dry for about eight days, it is then hard

enough

enough to handle, and they take it up, it continues running all the month of Auguſt, and drops alſo in September, but then it is not good, the fineſt and beſt is called Flhſcari, and ſells for two dollars an oke, the reſt from a dollar to a dollar and a half, and if they have a greater quantity than the tribute which they are to pay to the grand ſignor, they may have a licence to ſell it, notwithſtanding I have reaſon to believe that moſt of it is ſold clandeſtinely, that their tribute may not be increaſed I have been told that water, in which the wood of this tree has been boiled, is good againſt the gout, and that the wood of it has been clandeſtinely procured by ſome perſons, in order to ſend it into ſome parts of Italy for that purpoſe. The maſtic was formerly ſent to Venice, but is now exported only to Conſtantinople and Smyrna, it is chewed only by the Turks, eſpecially the ladies, who uſe it both as an amuſement, and alſo to whiten their teeth, and ſweeten the breath, on which account it is much uſed by thoſe of the grand ſignor's ſeraglio, it is alſo put in bread, and is ſaid to have a very good taſte, the whiteſt and cleareſt is the beſt, but after a year it turns yellow, tho' it is thought it does not loſe its vertue They ſometimes cut the wild ſort, but I have great reaſon to think, though they ſaid otherwiſe, that the difference between the wild and domeſtic is, that they take off the flowers from the domeſtic, which would produce fruit, in order to make the tree give a greater quantity of gum, and of a better quality, not to mention that their cutting it early may prevent its flowering, by enervating the force of the tree I obſerved on the domeſtic tree a ſort of a black dried flower, like that of the male aſh, which, they ſay, is ſometimes on all the trees, both male and female, though I imagine it to be the flower only of the male The maſtic muſt not be made in any other parts of the iſland, and, if I do not miſtake, the making of it is prohibited throughout all the grand ſignor's dominions, and it is actually made no where elſe, though it was formerly, for Dioſcorides ſays, that the maſtic of Scio was the beſt in the world, which probably may be owing to ſome art they may have to keep it from blowing and bearing fruit After I left that part of the iſland, I was informed that at one of the Maſtic villages called Kalamoty, on the ſouth weſt part of the iſland, there was lately diſcovered a ſubterraneous building, ſupported by pillars

I went to viſit two convents further to the ſouth, and was ſhewn a ſpot of ground, near a winter torrent, about two miles in compaſs, which, they ſay, after a great flood, ſunk down in ſuch a manner that the trees and houſes were overturned, and I ſaw the marks of this accident ſtill remaining, which, one would imagine, muſt be owing to ſome cavity under ground, the flood looſening one ſide, which ſupported it There are three ſmall convents, and a nunnery this way, I did not ſee them all, but I was at a large nunnery near a village called Calimati, they build or buy their apartments, half going to the head convent of Neamone, and half to the relations of the deceaſed, they cannot profeſs before they are twenty-five years old, and they may take the vow after that age without probation, they are admitted by the abbeſs, and have no allowance, but live on their fortunes, or labour, for they have a dimothy manufacture in this convent, They may go out when they

pleaſe,

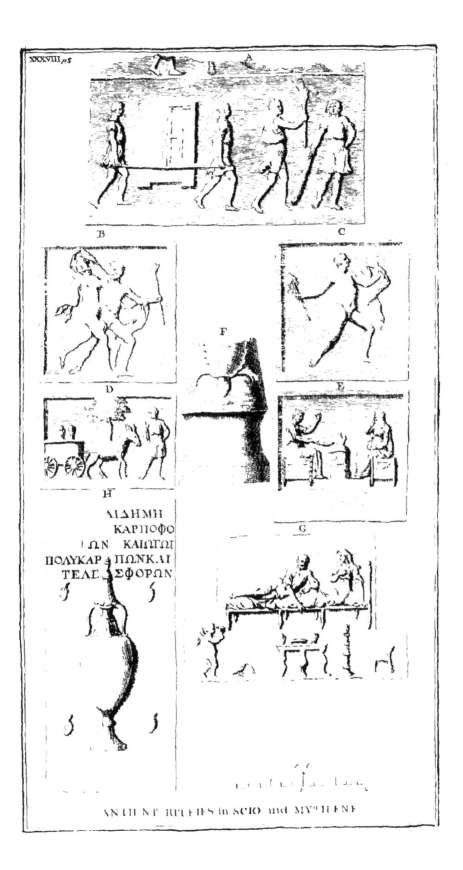

ΛΙΔΗΜΗ
ΚΑΡΠΟΦΟ
ΩΝ ΚΑΙΩΤΩΙ
ΠΟΛΥΚΑΡ ΠΩΝΚΑΙ
ΤΕΛΕ ΣΦΟΡΩΝ

ANTIENT RELIEFS in SCIO and MYTILENE

pleafe, as they often do, and live fome months in the houfes of their friends, the gates are open, and all have accefs, and that without any fcandal, and to gratify a ftranger for a fmall piece of money they will fing in their churches a form which they call a Paraclefis, fome live in the convent without ever taking the vow, or at leaft not till fuch time as there is little danger of being induced to break it   There are in this nunnery fome old women, who live on the charity of the others, and of thofe who come to it.

Going from the villages of Maftic, we came to a place called Sclavia, it was formerly much inhabited by the Genouefe, moft of whom went away with the Venetians, and there remain now only a few poor Roman catholic families of Genouefe extraction, who have a fmall church, there are two of their magnificent houfes remaining, with a very fine fountain before one of them   At a village called Carchiofè I faw over the church a very antient alt relief of our Saviour's triumphal entrance into Jerufalem, the fculpture is but indifferent   I faw feveral reliefs here, two of which are reprefented in the thirty-feventh plate at B C, and in the plain I faw D and E over the doors of fome houfes, under the latter, there is an imperfect Greek infcription

We went northward between the mountains, and turning weft came to the large convent of Neamone, about two leagues to the weft of the city, it is fituated on a hill in the middle of the mountains   This convent was founded, or the church built by the emperor Conftantine Omonomilos, his picture, and that of his emprefs Thea, are in feveral parts of the church   The convent is large and irregularly built round an oblong fquare court, and two or three fmaller   In the middle there is a church which is efteemed one of the fineft in the Archipelago, it originally feems to have had two porticos, to which a fmaller has been added, and a tower that has deftroyed the beauty of the front, the door cafes are all of jafper or fine marbles, and on each fide of the outer one there is a column of the fame, the eaft fide of it within is wainfcotted with jafper and beautiful marbles, the fecond portico is painted, and the arch is adorned with feveral figures in mofaic   In the outermoft are the reliques of three faints of the place kept in a red jafper cheft. The church itfelf, which is the choir, is a fquare of about thirty feet, excepting the part within the fkreen of the high altar, the whole is adorned with pillars, and wainfcoted and paved with jafper, and the moft coftly marbles, and on the dome and upper parts are reprefented hiftory pieces of our Saviour in mofaic, finely done for thofe times They fhew fome reliques, much efteemed by the Greeks, as the thumb of St John Baptift, the fcull of Timothy, a bone of St Luke and St. George, and a piece of the crofs   The abbot is chofe for two years, and no woman can enter the convent, they keep, at leaft in public, the old inftitution of eating no meat, there are two hundred perfons in the convent, twenty-five of which are priefts, fifty ftavioforoi, or crofs bearers, who are thofe who have taken the ftrict vow, and ought never to eat flefh, and four or five of the Megalofkema, whofe vow is fo ftrict that they can have no employ in the convent, or elfewhere, and though they ought to have no property, yet this is permitted, becaufe they are obliged to pay their poll tax   They admit employers here for a fum of money, who may go and live on their own farms, and are entitled to a certain portion of bread and wine, though absent, so that the convent is served, either by hired servants, or such as labour five or six years to be admitted caloyers without money, or by such caloyers as have offices, by which they gain something for themselves

In the way from the convent to the town there is a hill called The marble table [Μαρμάρου τράπεζα], out of which, they say, the jasper was taken that is employed about the church Strabo observes, that there is a vein of marble in the island, and Pliny says, that the first jasper was found here, it is a fine red sort, and the winter torrents near the city having brought down several pieces of it, they have taken those stones to pave the streets, and there are several other curious marbles found in the beds of those torrents I went to see two of the three fountains on the sides of the mountains, which are conveyed five or six miles to the city, and passed a valley on an aqueduct built with arches

From the city I made a voyage round part of the island, the plain to the north of the city is called Livadia, and is near two leagues long, there is a small village in it called Eretes, which might give occasion for the mistake of a certain author, who mentioning a place here of such a name, says, that the Sibyl Erithræa was born there, whereas she was of the city Erythræ, on the opposite continent At the end of this plain, and toward the south end of the bay, is that great piece of antiquity, which is called Homer's school, it is near the sea side on the foot of a mountain called Epos, it is a part of the rock that sets out beyond the rest, the surface of which is hewn into a seat all round, which I take to have been a figure of many unequal sides, as represented in the thirty-eighth plate at A, though it is commonly said to be round, it is indeed much broken and defaced, and the side next to the sea is fallen down, within this seat there is a cube three feet above the floor at D, and on the side next to the sea there is a mezzo relievo of a person sitting, and a smaller figure on each side as represented at B, that in the middle may be supposed to be Homer, and those on each side two of the Muses The heads of the figures are broken off, except of the lion behind, for on the three other sides are reliefs of an animal, that behind is a lion passant, the other two have the heads broke off, and are very much defaced, but seem to be lions, by which may be represented the fire and force with which this poet wrote Many think that Homer's verses were taught here, and it is not improbable, when so many places contended for his birth, that the people of Chius should cause this place to be hewn out in memory of him, and here they might at some certain times rehearse his verses to his honour About two or three leagues further north is a bay called port Delfin, which I thought might be Janum, mentioned by Strabo, till I came to Lina mentioned below in another place, opposite to this are the islands called Sperm adori, and in Greek Egonuses, which stretch almost to the mouth of the channel, they belong to Scio, and are inhabited only by herdsmen The north west cape of the island, is that which Strabo calls Posidium, which, he says, comes near to the promontory of Argenum of Erythræ, though the

diſtance which he mentions of ſixty ſtadia ſeems to be a miſtake for a
hundred and ſixty, as it is computed twenty miles   Oppoſite to the
mouth of this channel is Mytelene, the antient Leſbos, computed to be
about forty miles diſtant.   About a league to the weſt of the north eaſt
part of Scio, now called Laguardia, is the deep bay of Fana, which
is wide at the opening, but narrower towards the end, and is ſheltered
by an iſland called ſaint Margaret   Here Strabo ſays there was a grove of
palms, and a temple of Apollo, the weſt wall of which is ſtill ſtanding,
it is four feet thick, and at the diſtance of every three feet there are two
layers of brick, the entrance of it fronts to the eaſt ; it was about ſeventy five feet long, and thirty-five broad, as well as I could diſcover
from what remains of the foundations   I ſaw ſome pieces of grey marble about it, which appeared to have been joined with iron cramps
This inner part of the bay has a fine beech on the weſt and ſouth ſides
for boats to come up to, and ſeems to be the placed called Notium by
Strabo, which he ſays is a fine ſhoar, and may have received its name
from its ſituation to the ſouth ſouth weſt, that wind being called Notia :
He ſays, it is three hundred ſtadia diſtant from the city by ſea, but by land
only ſixty, which is another miſtake for a hundred and ſixty, it being
computed eighteen miles   This is now called the bay of Cardamilla,
from a village of that name near it   In this part of the iſland, to
the north of the city, and along the northern ſhoar, there are fourteen
villages, it is the part called Epanameria, with the eight villages mentioned to the weſt of the mountains   A rivulet called Sclavia runs into
the ſea about a league to the weſt, its ſource comes from the foot of
the mountain, and runs on a bed of white marble with a reddiſh caſt :
This country called Nagoſe or Naoſe, without doubt from a temple near,
ſome ſmall ruins of which are now to be ſeen, from the beſt judgment
I could make, it was fifty five feet long, and thirty-five broad, the
pieces of marble which are very large, ſeem to have been poliſhed, and
it appears as if there had been two ſteps all round, there are no ſigns
either of pillars or pilaſters   This temple Tournefort ſuppoſes to have
been dedicated to Neptune, who had amours with a nymph here   He
conjectures that this fountain of water is that of Helena, mentioned by
Stephanus, and, as he obſerves, Vitruvius ſpeaks of a fountain in this
iſland, the waters of which make people mad, in which he was probably
miſinformed, there being not ſo much as any tradition that there ever
was ſuch a fountain   This place is oppoſite to port Sigri in Mytilene
We went on weſtward, came to a ſtream, and walked along the ſide of
it to a poor village called Aio-Thelene, on a high hill   We went to ſee a
grotto on the ſouth ſide of the hill under it, which is more famous for
a fooliſh ſuperſtition of the Greeks, than for any thing that is very curious in it, over it there is a church, and within the grot, which has
ſome petrifications in it, made by the droppings of the water, there is
one of thoſe pendant petrifications, from one part of which the water
continually drops, they ſay, that it formerly dropped from another
part of the ſame ſtone, which is now broken, theſe, they tell their de-
votees, are the teats of the Virgin Mary, that the water is milk, and that
no body muſt drink of it but faſting, and give the pilgrims ſome little
ſtones of the petrifications, which, they ſay, are good againſt a fever when
boiled

boiled in water   The water of the rivulet below never fails, and they have small eels in it called Mungri, which is the only fresh water fish in the island   If we suppose that saint Thelena is a corruption of Helena, we may conjecture that this is her spring, mentioned as above by Stephanus   We walked two miles almost as far as the north west cape of the island called Melano, and went to a village of the same name, this is the old promontory of Melana, and the city of that name mentioned by Strabo, might be where the village is, though there are no signs of antiquity   The governor of saint Thelena sent an express to this village to give advice of our arrival, according to their custom   Going about three leagues further to the **south,** we came to Volisso, where the country of Ariousa seems to begin, which was so famous for its wines, it extended for three hundred stadia in length, and is said to have produced the nectar of the ancients, the Chian wine is praised by Horace and Virgil, and we have an account that Cæsar used it in his triumphs, and this spot still produces very good wine

Vol (o

Volisso is said to have had its name from Bellisarius, whom they call Vellisarius, and say, that he came here with his armies, and built the castle; and I find there is an author who gives an account that he was imprisoned in it   Volisso is about two miles from the sea, on the side of the hill on which the castle stands, which was defended with round towers, there is a church in it dedicated to saint Elias   About two leagues south of this place is the convent of Diefca, dedicated to saint John Baptist, situated in a very retired place on the side of the hills, which extend a great way to the west, and make a cape called Pelaro, at the angle of the bay there is a village of Mastic, to the south of which there are several other villages along the western shoar   This land makes a sort of a large bay with the land of Volisso to the north, but there is no port, and it is much exposed to the west and south west winds   These mountains extend to the east to mount Elias, which is the highest hill in the island, and was antiently called Pellineus, to the west of these mountains is the country of Volisso, full of small hills, with little fruitful vales between them, where they make good wine, much silk, and preserve a great quantity of figs   From the high lands I discovered what they told me was Monte Santo, but I rather took it to be Stalimene   And here we saw Sciro, the Negropont, Andros, and Tine   The villages of Volisso and Perich, which is one of the villages of Mastic, are exempt from all ecclesiastical jurisdiction, except that of the patriarch of Constantinople

CHAP. II.

Of the natural hiſtory, cuſtoms, trade, and government of Scio.

A Great part of Scio conſiſts of rocky mountains and hills, and even the ſoil of the plains is but poor, and naturally fit only for trees, but they are very induſtrious, and the inhabitants beſtow great labour on it The greateſt part of the mountains are of a lead coloured marble, ſtreaked with white, they have alſo about the city and plain ſome quarries of a reddiſh free ſtone, it being a rocky ſoil The air of Scio is conſequently very good, but the great communication it has with other parts is the cauſe that they often have the plague, they alſo feel thoſe earthquakes which do more damage on the neighbouring continent There are ſeveral winter torrents, but very few rivulets that run all the year, however they have a great number of fine ſprings, and find water almoſt in all places where they dig, that of the plain of Scio is not reckoned ſo good as the water of the rocky countries

The ever-green oak, the pine, the wild maſtic tree, and the caroub, are the only trees that I obſerved growing wild, except a very few common oaks, but by improvement they have all ſorts of fruit trees, and the mulberry-tree for their ſilk has a great place among them, they have alſo the terebinth-tree, the rind of which they cut to let the turpentine run out upon ſtones, which they place under it, they call it Crementina, and by the Druggiſts it is called Terebintina, and Turpentine, and does not dry to a gum, but is preſerved in vaſes, it is eſteemed the beſt that is made, tho' the tree is very common in Syria they have cotton here for their own uſe, and a very ſmall quantity of flax, and ſome corn, but not ſufficient for the conſumption of the iſland, there being much corn imported from the continent of Aſia, and ſometimes from Alexandria The herbage here is ſo ſcarce, that they give their cattle the cotton ſhrubs to eat when the cotton is gathered, and preſerve the dried leaves of the vines for them in winter

They have no ſort of wild beaſt, except foxes and hares Mules are generally uſed throughout the iſland, and they ſell ſome of them at great prices, the humble aſs ſerves the poorer ſort of people, there being only a few of the top families in the city who uſe horſes, they have no wheel carriages The want of herbage makes all ſorts of meat very dear except goat's fleſh, which they have on the mountains, but ſheep are ſo ſcarce, that in the villages of Maſtic, every family almoſt has a domeſtic ewe for breeding, which follows them about like a dog They have now no domeſtic partridges that come at a whiſtle, but great plenty of wild ones of the red ſort

Beſides the original natives, there are here ſome noble Greek families who retired from Conſtantinople, when it was taken by the Turks, they have alſo ſeveral Genoueſe families on this iſland, but only thoſe of the name of Juſtiniani and Grimaldi, who are noble and rich, of the former there are about ten families This iſland is rich, and exceedingly well peopled,

pled, infomuch that every thing is twice as dear as it is in Candia, they compute that there are a hundred thoufand inhabitants, of which half are in the city, and in the villages about the plain, and of thefe three thoufand are Roman catholics, who are all of Genouefe extraction, and call themfelves Italians   There are about forty families of Jews in the caftle, and five thoufand Turks, the reft are all Greeks, there being no Turks in the villages   The Greeks have a bifhop, whom they call metropolitan, and the Romans have one likewife, who is chofen by the pope out of fix natives of the country, nominated by the chief people among them, as they informed me, though I find the prefent, who is the firft fince their churches were deftroyed on the Venetian invafion, was put in by the pope without any nomination   They have about fifty Roman priefts, who celebrate according to the Latin rite, fome few of them have been educated in Rome, and all the Roman catholics of fafhion fpeak Italian very well   The government here has cor-rupted the language in the city in fuch a manner, that the country people talk by much the purer Greek   In the convent of Neamone, and in the city, there are priefts that teach the old Greek, thofe who underftand it are reckoned to fpeak the beft modern Greek, and often ufe old words, and if they would come into the cuftom of ftudying the antient Greek in all parts, it might be a great means to purify and im-prove the modern language

Character   As to the genius of the people they are induftrious, and fharp in ac-quiring, but luxurious and extravagant on the days when they have re-pofe from their employs   They are very dextrous in managing affairs, and one may make a conjecture of their capacities from a reafon a Sciote gave me why they had fo few Jews there, which was, becaufe the peo-ple were too fharp for them   The Greeks and Roman Catholics have a great averfion to one another, and thofe of one profeffion are not Chri-ftians in the judgment of the other, the Francifcans of propaganda fide, and the Capuchins, have a fmall convent in the city, the former under the Dutch protection, and the latter under the French, to whom they are chaplains   There are in the ifland three nunneries and eight convents

Drefs   The drefs of the men here is much the fame as that of Candia   The youth and people of fafhion, when in the country, wear trowfers, with fhoes and ftockings   The garments of the ladies come but a little be-low their knees, and they are dreffed all in white, even to their fhoes, except that their coat is often of damafk, or fome other coloured filk, but without fleeves, they wear a head drefs, which is particular to the Sciotes, it is of a ftiffen'd fine muflin, made fo as to ftand up very high, extends out far on the right fide, and is called a Capafh, they are very fair and beautiful, and the men alfo are comely   The women are not fhy, but have a certain air of affurance and fimplicity that feemed to befpeak their virtue, for they appeared to me to be modeft women, and though I have heard general reflections made on them, yet I was affur-ed that the character of their being otherwife is owing to fome inferior people among them, who go out of the ifland chiefly to get into fer-vices   Their open manner of behaviour feems to be owing to fome cer-tain cuftoms they have, for vifiting is not in fafhion, but the houfes in

the

the ftreets having all ftone feats before them, the women of beft fafhion, as well as the vulgar, on Sundays and holidays, fit almoft all day
in the ftreets, and the men come and ftand by them, and hold a converfation, or they difcourfe with one another In the villages the men and
women dance together in the public fquares, and the mothers and the
virgins fit round till midnight, and enjoy the converfations of their
neighbours It feems to be a cuftom continued from the antient Greeks,
among whom dancing was looked on as a great perfection, whereas with
the Romans it was hardly confiftent with the character of a modeft woman Though there is no jealoufy, yet the men hardly ever go into
the houfes of any that are not relations, and not often even to thofe,
the women alfo rarely go into one anothers houfes, as they enjoy
converfation in this public manner, nor is it the cuftom to make any
invitations to entertainments, not even of ftrangers, much lefs to lodge
them in their houfes The women fpin filk, and do other bufinefs at
home, never ftirring out, but on Sundays and holidays The Franks
have little trade, and no merchants here, but the French have a conful, and one of Genouefe extraction is conful both to the Englifh and
Dutch

The chief trade of the ifland is an export of manufactured damafks Trade
and other filks, to carry on which they import yearly from Tine, and
a place near Salonica, about twelve thoufand okes, their own produce
of raw filk not being fufficient They fend thefe manufactures to Conftantinople, Smyrna, and other parts, the natives paying only a duty of
half per cent whereas foreigners pay five, every oke of raw filk brought
into the town pays fixteen medins duty, and all that is exported a
medin a pike. Another great export is lemons and China oranges.
Their import is oil from Candia and Mytilene, both for lamps and eating, and wine from Ipfara and Mycone, though they have much good
wine here, but it is not fufficient for their ufe, they import corn from
Afia The public revenue arifes from the cuftoms, and from the poll
tax of fix to ten dollars a head, according as it is fixed on the villages,
except the villages of Maftic, in which they pay only three dollars,
alfo there is a fmall rent paid for lands, and the governor pays in the
whole about three hundred purfes, and raifes four hundred, that is between forty and fifty thoufand pounds

This ifland was ufually governed by a pafha, who was generally a dif- Government
graced perfon, and the Chriftians had five deputies, two of them Roman
catholics and two Greeks, who had great power, decided all civil caufes
between Chriftians, and could apprehend ill Chriftian offenders, fend
them to be judged by the cadi, and require them either to be fent out
of the country, or executed, but about twenty years ago the deputies,
on fome pretence, were carried to Conftantinople and imprifoned, and
then a mofolem was fent inftead of a pafha, and in the place of deputies
they have only, as they have in other iflands Vicudi, I fuppofe a corruption of vicini, they have thefe in the fame manner as the deputies,
but with lefs power, however they can remonftrate, and if the mofolem
does any thing unlawfully, they can move the iflan to the cadi, but if
that officer and the other governor are united they can do little, however
the cadi often calls them to be prefent at any difputes between Chriftians,
and

and they are frequently made referees in many cafes between them at this time, and lately they caufed a governor to be removed and punifhed, however the governor, on the leaft pretext, will fine, which is the punifhment for thofe that are rich, and render themfelves obnoxious One of the Juftiniani is always one of the two Roman vicardi, and often one of the Grimaldi, and one of the richeft Greeks, their office continues for one year, and is very troublefom, they name their fucceffors. When they had deputies the people paid no rent for their lands, and the deputies could levy money for their public expences, but when the deputies were laid afide, a valuation was made of all the lands, and a fmall rent fixed on them The moft any one pays does not amount to above fix or feven pounds a year, and fometimes a poor village does not pay more For in fome of the inland mountainous parts, where they are very poor, they live by trucking every thing, cannot fell the wine they have, by reafon of the difficulty of carriage, and raife what money they muft have, by their little flocks of fheep Every village is governed by a vicardi, who fometimes is the parifh prieft, and is appointed yearly in the fame manner, his office is much the fame as that of the head vicardi, to fend offenders to the cadi, and alfo to levy all public taxes, or to affift in it The cadi of the ifland is fent every feven or eight months from Conftantinople, his jurifdiction extends to Gefmè on the continent, he fends his deputy about to all the villages to refide in each eight or ten days, in order to decide difputes, but principally to raife money by fines for offences.

CHAP III

Of the ifland of IPSARA.

WE failed from Voliffo for Ipfara in about five hours, which, they fay, is forty miles diftant, though I conjecture that cape Melanon is but twenty miles from the north eaft point of Ipfara, Strabo computes it to be only fifty ftadia, though if he had faid a hundred and fifty, it would be nearer the true diftance, our boatmen looked out very fharply to fee if there were any Maltefe in the port of Ipfara I faw the ifland of Andros to the fouth, Schiro to the weft, and the cape of the Negropont, called cape Diro, which is the old promontory Cephareus, and was famous for the fhipwreck of the Greek fleet We arrived at Ipfara, called by Strabo, Pfyra, [Ψύρα] who fays, it had a city of the fame name, but he is miftaken in the circumference of the ifland, for it is computed to be eighteen miles round, whereas he makes it but forty ftadia or five miles The ifland is high and rocky on the north and eaft fides, and is about fix miles long and three broad, on the fouth fide there are two bays, in that to the weft is the fmall ifland of faint Demetrius, which has its name from a chapel on it, within which there is a good port to anchor, and the Corfans fometimes

ride

ride there in bad weather, but oftener at the uninhabited island called Antipsera, which is before this bay, and is about three miles in circumference. Between the two bays there is a small beach at the bottom of a very shallow bay, which is made by two rocky heights, on that to the east is the chapel of saint John Baptist, and a deep cistern sunk into the rock and foundations of what seem to have been walls of a castle, the rock on which it stands being very high, what they call the castle is situated on the western height, and is enclosed only with the walls of their houses, and has but one entrance, it is about a quarter of a mile round. The present town is on a gentle descent on two sides of the castle, probably on the spot of the antient city, and may be half a mile in circumference, the houses are low, and ill built most of them consisting only of one floor. In the castle is the principal church of saint Nicholas, near which I found three or four antient reliefs, and a short Greek inscription or two of no importance. There are some reliefs also in the church of saint John, and on a house near it, there is another church in the town, at a little chapel by the sea side, called saint Luke, there is a Greek inscription, in which the antient name of the people is mentioned. They say that there are thirty churches in the island, tho' in going the whole length of it I could see but thirteen, and as there are no Turks in the island, they have bells to their churches. I went to the north end to see the poor convent of the virgin Mary, which belongs to the city, and has only three caloyers in it. The island consists of a flaty stone, with several veins of white marble in it, the high mountain to the north, on which the chapel of saint Elias is situated is mostly of a grey marble, there is also here a bastard crumbling granite of a red colour, a little resembling porphyry. They have good springs, but no herbage, the ground being covered only with several dwarf shrubs, they have no trees that grow naturally, and only a few figs, which they plant, they have a small quantity of cotton and corn, and are supplied from Asia with the latter, the great produce of the island is a very good strong red wine, which they export to Scio, the old wine sells for about a halfpenny a quart, and the new for half that price, the south and middle parts of the island consist of small hills, and two little plains on the two bays, and all of it seems to be excellent soil, the sides of the mountains in many parts are improved with vineyards, they use oxen for the plough, and asses for burthen and riding, and they have some sheep and goats. The people, who are all Greeks, are computed to be about a thousand, two hundred of whom pay the poll tax, they live all in the town, but have huts in the country, where they stay during the busy seasons of the year, they are said to be brave couragious men, and have freed themselves from the dread of the Maltese, by sallying out, and killing some of those that made a descent, and taking several of them prisoners, and since that time they have never disturbed them. The men wear a sort of sandals made of raw hide, and tied with thongs round the foot and ancle. The women have a veil or towel, that comes over their heads, and is brought round the neck, and sometimes they put it over the chin and mouth, but they expose their breasts in a very indecent manner, which seemed rather owing to an ignorance of decorum, than out of lewdnefs; they have neither phyfician, chirurgeon, nor lawyer. They are governed here as at Scio by three vicardi, but all of them are labourers, the cadi of Scio fends his deputy to this ifland in his progrefs to decide their difputes They pay two purfes a year to the captain pafha or lord high admiral, to whom all the iflands belong which are not governed by a pafha or mofolem, fo that Cyprus, Rhodes, Candia, Negropont, Scio, and Mytilene, do not belong to the admiral In eccle-fiaftical affairs they are fubject to the patriarch of Conftantinople, as all the iflands are where there are no bifhops The patriarch has a lay vicar refiding here, who is alfo over Voliffo and Perieh in Scio; his chief bufinefs is to fend people to the bifhop of Scio to be ordained; they pay thirty dollars a year to the patriarch, which is received by the vicar of Scio, and they have only five priefts in the whole ifland They have no trade but the export of their wine, and the import of corn, and the few other neceffaries they want, as it is an open bay, they draw up their little barks and boats to the land. The fame day I arrived I went to fee the convent on the other fide of the ifland, and, as I returned, fome countrymen who were eating bread and fifh, called to me to take part with them, and they feemed much pleafed with my compliance I lay in my boat, but as it rained, and the wind was contrary, the next day I removed with all my baggage into the chapel of faint Luke at the port On the eve of faint Luke they performed devotions in the chapel, the women or children brought fmall wax candle, and a plate or bafket of boiled wheat, on which either raifins, or the infide of pomegranates was ftrewed, fome alfo brought cakes of bread, when the fervice was finifhed, all but the boiled wheat was diftributed to the people in or near the church On the feftival they brought lenfigs and brandy, which were given to the people in the fame manner, all which feems to be fome remains of the antient cuftom of having all things in common, and eating their bread together in finglenefs of heart

We failed for Mytilene, but put in the firft evening at Cardamilla in Scio, where I pitched my tent, and lay all night, and the next evening arrived at the port of Mytilene.

CHAP

An ANCIENT MARBLE CHAIR at MYTILENE

CHAP. IV.

Of the ifland of MYTILENE, the antient LESBUS.

THE ifland of Lefbus, fo often mentioned by the Greek hiftorians, is now called Mytilene, from the old name of its capital city, which it ftill retains. The Lefbians were formerly famous for their fleet. They were at firft under kings, and then became a republic, governed by a council of the fuperior rank of people, and by an affembly of the common people, whofe decrees are feen in fome infcriptions ftill remaining in the ifland. At one time fome perfons of greateft intereft ufurped a fort of tyrannical power over their fellow citizens, among thefe was Pittacus, one of the feven wife men, who, out of a public fpirit contrived to get all the power into his own hands, and then reftored to his country their antient liberty. Thucydides gives a particular account of the oppofition the people of Mytilene gave the Athenians, who fubduing them, made a decree to cut off all the people of that city, but a party in favour of the Mytilenians afterwards prevailing, they repealed that decree, the account of which arrived before the former was executed [*]. Mytilene, the antient capital of the ifland, was fituated on the fpot of the prefent city of that name, which is called alfo Caftro, it is on the north fide of the ifland towards the eaft end, and is only feven miles and a half from the moft eaftern point of the ifland, which was antiently called cape Malia, which diftance was probably computed to the head of land, which makes the bay of Mytilene, where the eaft end of the ifland begins, for the whole eaftern point feems to have been called cape Malia. The old city appears to have been built on the plain near the fea, and on the fide of the hill to the fouth of it, and to have extended along the plain to the eaft of that hill. There was an ifland before the city about a mile in circumference, which was well inhabited, and is now joined to the land by an ifthmus, which may be about a furlong wide, and of much the fame length, and they have ftill a tradition of its being an ifland, there was a port on each fide of it, as there is at this time, that to the fouth eaft was defended by two moles, of which there are now fome ruins, the entrance is between them. The other port to the north weft was defended by a mole, of which there are ftill great remains, the port to the fouth is now only frequented by large fhips. The city was formerly very large, and one fees in all parts of it many fine pieces of grey marble, which are remains of the antient buildings, and feveral imperfect infcriptions, and at the entrance to the palace of the bifhop, there is a very curious antient chair cut out of one block of white marble, the views of which may be feen in the thirty-ninth plate. Pittacus, one of the feven wife men of Greece, was of this city, and fo were Alcæus and Sappho the poets, and alfo Theophanes the hiftorian, who had the honour to enjoy the friendfhip of Pompey the great, and his fon was made procurator of Afia by Auguftus. The prefent city is on the neck of land that leads to the peninfula, and on each fide of it on the fhoar, and likewife to the

fouth,

* Strabo x. i. 618.

south, it extends up the side of the hill, it is about a mile in circumference, and is well built   The castle is on the top of the high rocky
peninsula, and is near three quarters of a mile in compass, consisting
of the old and new castle which are contiguous, but have their distinct
governors and bodies of militia, they are inhabited only by Turks,
and Franks are not permitted to go into them   The ruins of the old city
extend a considerable way to the west   I was told that there are in the
castle the arms, and cypher or name of one of the emperors Palæologi,
and that there is a stone coffin in a mosque, which, they say, is the
tomb of Sappho.   If this castle was built by the Greek emperors, it is
probable that it was much improved by the Genoese when they were in
possession of the island.   As well as I could be informed the island was
at that time the property of a family of the name of Catinisi, who were
lords of Lesbus, and it is said when the city was besieged by sultan Amurath, a lady of one of these Catanisi, sallied out at the head of the citizens, and raised the siege   There are in the city a great number of
Greeks, three or four Greek churches, and only a few families of Armenians   The French have a vice consul here, who has a chapel and
chaplain in his house, and there are two or three French factors of the
merchants of Smyrna   The English also have a Greek vice-consul.
The bishop has the title of metropolitan, though I could not find that
he has any jurisdiction over the other bishop, both being put in by, and
immediately subject to the patriarch of Constantinople   In this city, as
well as in some other parts of the Archipelago and Greece, they have a
priest who has studied at least the literal Greek, preaches, and has the
title of Didaskalos and Logiotatos [Most learned], which latter is given
to most of the priests   The person here in that character had studied several years at Padoua   As they are generally envied by the other ignorant priests, so they are commonly drove from one place to another
   They have a great trade in this city in building large ships and boats,
with the wood of pine, which they use even to the keels of the ships;
they bring the timber from the continent, there being no place there secure from the Corsairs for the building of them   These vessels are very
light, and last for ten or twelve years, it being a timber full of rosin,
and said to be much more durable than that of Europe   They use also
iron nails in building, and instead of crooked timber, they saw the
wood to the shape that is necessary for building   As to the other
branches of trade, it is the same here as throughout the whole island, and
consists in a very great export of oil of olives to France, and to many
parts of the Levant, which latter is carried on by small vessels or boats
They have also very good scamony and althea here, and I saw a great
quantity of alkermes, but they do not make any use of it   They have
likewise an export of tar extracted from their pines
   On the twenty-second of October, I set out to make a tour round
the island, in company with some gentlemen of the French nation,
and under the protection of a janizary   The island is mountainous,
one chain of hills that are mostly rocky, consists chiefly of marble,
and runs the whole length of the island, another crosses it towards the
west end, the whole island abounds much in hot baths   We went
along the north side of it, and observed that the ruins of the old city
                                                               extended

An *AQUEDUCT* in the *ISLAND* of *MYTILEN*

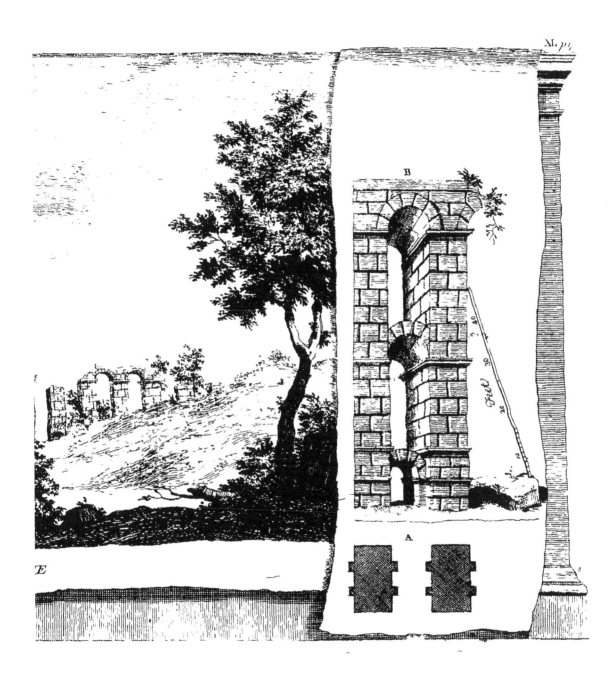

B

A

E

extended a confiderable way to the weft, and there are marks of the
city wall which was carried up the hill   Going about two miles from
the city, we came to a hot bath, which is little frequented; the waters
are warm, and have no particular tafte. We went in between the mountains, about a mile to the fouth, where there are remains of a very magnificent aqueduct of grey marble rufticated, built acrofs the valley, as reprefented in the fortieth plate.   A, is the plan of one of the arches, and B, an
elevation of it by a larger fcale, the upper arches are turned with brick · The
water having run a confiderable way on the fide of the hills from the fouth
weft, paffed thefe arches, and then went in channels round to Mytilene.
Returning into the road along the north fide of the island, about two leagues
to the weft of the city, there are hot baths near the fea; they are rather
falter than the fea water, and are now much ufed for bathing, as it appears they were by the antients; there are great ruins of buildings
about them, particularly of a colonade leading to them from the
fouth, the pedeftals of which remain, there are alfo feveral infcriptions
about this place   A little beyond the baths there are remains of a caftle of
the middle ages built with fquare towers at the corners, in which there
are feveral pieces of marble of the antient buildings.   Beyond the middle of the island is a large head of land, which I take to be the promontory Argenum of Ptolemy; to the eaft of it there is a bay, near
which is a village on a hill called Manoneia.   I conjectured that the
village Ægirus was about this place, and that from this bay to the bay
of Pyrrha was the narroweft part of the island, which, Strabo fays,
was only twenty ftadia, though it feems to be much more; oppofite to
this cape is the deepeft part of the bay of Adramyttium, in which there
are a great number of islands, called now Mufconifi, and of old Heca-
tonnefi, that is, the isles of Apollo, Hecatus being one of his names:
Some fay there were twenty, others forty of them; one of them
called Mufconifi, in diftinction from the reft, has a town of Greeks on
it, and perhaps it may be the island Pordofelena of Strabo; all the others
are now uninhabited, but I was informed that one of thofe near Mufconifi was formerly frequented by herdfmen for pafturage, and that there
are fome figns of an antient bridge to it.   This may be the island
which Strabo mentions before the town of the island of Pordofelena, for
there was a town in it of the fame name then deferted, and a temple dedicated to Apollo   Near the land of Mytilene there are three or four very
fmall islands, called the Tockmack islands, I fuppofe, from a village of
that name in Mytilene, which is near thofe islands.   The people of
the island fay, that the village of Tockmack is the neareft place on this
fide to Caloni, which is on the bay that was called Pyrrha by the antients, but they affirm that thofe places are four hours diftant, that is,
about eight miles   On the north weft cape of the island is the town
of Molivo, about four miles to the caft of it, on the fhoar, are the
ruins of a bath, and on the beach below, there is a fource of hot water
which feemed to have a taft of fulphur, and about half way between
this and Molivo, there is a fmall bath in repair, the waters of which are
warm, but have no particular tafte

Molivo is the antient Methymna, it is built up the fide of the hill it
that high point of land, which makes the north weft corner of the

island   Methymna was computed to be thirty-three miles and three
quarters from Sigrium, and seven miles and a half from the shoar of the
continent, though it is now computed to be eighteen miles over, and
it cannot be much less, the town is a mile in circumference, on the
summit of the hill there is a castle, about half a mile in compass, which
is inhabited by Turks, who have here their several bodies of soldiers with
their agas, as at Mytilene   From the castle westward the ground declines,
and makes a sort of a plain spot at the very point, on which one sees
some little signs of the old city Methymna, particularly the foundations
of the city walls on the south side of the hill, and the ruins of a large
strong tower or castle over the present little basin on the south, which is
made by art for small boats , it is probable that the city extended from
the end of the point, about half a mile, to that steep ground on which
the present town stands   There are not above two hundred Christians
here, who have three churches, for it is in a manner a Turkish town
The bishop of Methymna resides at Caloni, and the Greeks are so very
ignorant, that they imagine Caloni was Methymna, because the bishop
retains the old title   In this city the famous musician Arion was born,
who is said to have been carried on a dolphin: Terpandrus also was of
this island, who added three strings to the lyre, which before had only
four , the Lesbians having been formerly very famous in the art of music   The head of land on which Molivo stands, together with a small
point of land to the south, makes a bay to the south east, and there is
an island before it, which is a defence to the harbour , this is the port of
Molivo for large ships, where they often load with oil , it is also called the
port of Petra, from a village of that name which lies on it, and seems to have
its name from a high rock in the middle of the town, which is inaccessible
every way, except on the north side, and being enclosed at top with a
wall, about a hundred yards in circumference, they deposit in it all their
valuable effects, when they apprehend any danger from the Corsairs
They have also a chapel there to the Virgin Mary, and a church in the
town, there being a considerable number of Christians in this little place
We travelled on to the south, mostly on the sides of the hills near the
sea, and came to a narrow peninsula, it is a strong situation, and I expected to have seen some ruins on it   On each side of the isthmus, there
is a very good port called Calas-Limneonis [The Fair Havens]   Further on there is another smaller peninsula, about which there are many
ruins, particularly a wall on the north side of a rivulet, this seems to be
the antient Antissa, which was between Sigrium and Methymna   It is
said to have been formerly an island , and some on this account conjecture that this was the antient name of Lesbus', the inhabitants of this
place were sent to Methymna, from which time the ruin of the antient
city may be dated'   We came to a large village of Turks called Ido-
ni , there is a nunnery about two miles to the east of it, it a place
called Peribole, in which they have a manufacture of stuffs made of
silk and flax   About this place some accident happening to the mule on
which the slave rode, and which I had bought in Candia, he chose to walk,
and lost his way, so that we could hear nothing of him, but the next

' Ruins of the middle part   Plinium   Livy liv 31   Plin Hist liv 5,
Plin   Antissa folio   Plin Hist liv 5 c   Strabo l 63
& Ovid Metam l' 15 ver

day

day I sent the janizary in search of him, who brought him to me just as I arrived at Mytilene. The slave said, that towards night he was about an hour from the sea, and met some people, who conducted him to the aga of their village, who sent a man with him the next day to Caloni, where he was carried to the bishop, who designed to send him to Mytilene, when the janizary found him. But the janizary, in order to get money out of me, said, that he went to several places, according to the account he got of him, but coming to the village where the slave lodged the first night, he met with the men who brought him to that place, they offered to conduct him to the slave for a reward, which being agreed on, they carried him to Caloni, where, as he said, they had placed him, that they might get something by him, and that he might not fall into the hands of the aga.

The promontory of Sigrium, now called cape Sigri, is the south west point of the island, the port of Sigri is made by a small cape to the north, and by an island before it. To the east of it there is a convent on a very high rocky mountain, to which the ascent is very difficult, it is called Upselo monasterio [The high monastery], and is a very cold situation. The hills all this way, as far as port Caloni, are rocky and barren, and afford a very unpleasant prospect to a traveller. A league to the east of this mountain there is a large village called Eresso on the side of a hill, it is mostly inhabited by Christians, and from it one enters into a plain by the sea on the south side of the island. In the south east part of this plain there is a small hill, on which the antient city of Eressus stood, placed by the antients two miles and a quarter from cape Sigri, though it cannot be less than two leagues. The top of the hill is of an oval figure, and there are great remains of the wall that encompassed it, and of a round tower at the east end. I saw near it an entablature of white marble, in the frieze of which there is an imperfect Greek inscription. I observed several large cisterns under ground, and there appears to have been a considerable suburb round the hill, at the foot of which I saw a wall built of stones of five or six sides each, a sign of great antiquity. From this place I travelled northward between the mountains, and turning to the east passed through a village, about two leagues to the north east of it we came to the gulph of Caloni, and to a narrow part of it, which is about a league from the entrance of the bay. Just without this narrow part there is a small island, on which there is a ruined church, and on the west side, on the heighth near the ferry, are remains of a wall which was built to support the hanging ground, it is likewise built of stones of five sides. This gulph of Caloni extends to the north in between the land at least four leagues, and is about a league broad, being shut in by a narrow entrance not a mile over, and would be a very good harbour, if there was depth of water, at the further end of it is a small town called Caloni, near which I was informed that there is a convent and a nunnery, the latter is of the same kind as those in Scio, I was informed that there is a small convent to the north east of Eresso. The antient Pyrrha must have been on this bay of Caloni, a great part of the country on the east side of it is now called Peri, where I concluded from the bricks and tiles which I saw scattered about the field, that there had been some antient buildings, but as the greatest part of that city

W 1

was deftroyed by the incroachment of the fea, it cannot be expected that there fhould be any great remains of it [d] This golph muft be what Strabo calls the Pyrrhean Euripus, from its refemblance to a narrow ftreight between two lands; and here the land muft be narroweft, as he fays it was from the Pyrrhean Euripus to the other fea near the village of Ægirus He fays Pyrrha had been deftroyed, and that it had a port, from which, that is from the north eaft corner of it, Mytilene was only ten miles diftant, though it cannot be lefs than fifteen, as it is now computed. The country to the eaft of this bay for about two leagues to the mountains abounds with corn, and is called Bafilika, there are in it five or fix villages, which are' moftly inhabited by Turks There are fome baths here of very hot waters, which are now frequented, as they appear to have been formerly from the ruins that are feen about them They ufe the waters for bathing, and alfo drink them, tho' they have found falt in them, there feems alfo to be a compofition of iron and fulphur in them, and I believe, a very fmall degree of copper, they are very purging, and much efteemed for removing dangerous obftructions and fcrophulous diforders Near thefe baths are fome other hot waters not frequented, which probably are of the fame nature Further to the eaft towards the mountains there is a fmall convent of the virgin Mary From this place the road goes through the middle of the ifland to the north eaft over the mountains to Port Iero, or, as it is called by the failors, Port Oliviere. The entrance of it is near to the eaft end of the ifland, and opens to the fouth eaft; it is a large bafin, encompaffed with hills covered with wood, the entrance is fo narrow that it is not feen from within; fo that the port appears like a large lake, it is about two leagues long and near a league broad, the water is very deep, and it is one of the moft beautiful ports I ever faw, the fhips often come into it to be loaded with oil On the fouth fide of it there are feven or eight villages, called the villages of Iera, retaining the name of the antient city Hiera, fpoken of by Pliny, as deftroyed, and neither Strabo nor Ptolemy make mention either of the town or port. To the weft of thefe villages, and of the harbour, there is a fmall convent at a place called Quatrotrito, which belongs to the bifhop of Mytilene, and is a fort of a countryhoufe for that prelate To the fouth weft of it, on the hills, there is a large rich village called Aiaffo, it has a great revenue from the oil of the olive trees that grow on the mountains, and pays no other rent for the lands, but a certain quantity of tar every year for the ufe of the grand fignor's naval armament, they make it of the pine trees that grow on the mountains. On the north fide of the port there are hot baths, probably of a limeftone water, for they have no tafte From this place the road goes over the hills about two leagues to Mytilene I obferved on a hill near the town feveral round ftones of the pyrites kind Among many other great men of this ifland were Theophraftus and Phanias, the Peripatetic philofophers, and difciples of Ariftotle, the former being efteemed by Ariftotle himfelf, the moft eloquent of all his fcholars, on which account his great mafter gave him that name, and

[d] Pyrrha haufta eft mari Plin Hift v 9

decided

decided a controversy in relation to his succeffor, by calling for two forts of wine, and giving the preference to the Lesbian.

This ifland is governed by an officer called a Nafir, who receives all the revenues of it, which arife from a fifth part of the produce of the ifland from Chriftians, and a feventh from Turks And this officer appoints agas over a certain number of villages. The two cities of Mytilene and Molivo are governed each by its mofolem, and have a cadi for adminiftring juftice. The foil of this ifland is very rich, tho' there is but little of it improved, infomuch that they have not corn fufficient for their own confumption, the people, efpecially the Greeks, being very flothful, and fupported by the produce of their oil, which requires but a little labour only at one feafon of the year, for the women and children gather up the olives as they drop, which being ground by horfe mills, are preffed with large fcrew preffes, which they have for that purpofe, and the oil is put into fkins The women have no better character for their chaftity, nor the men for their fobriety, than in former times As this ifland is fo near the continent, it is much infefted with robbers in the fummer, who come over in fmall boats, attack people in the road, and if they apprehend any danger, return to the continent with their booty, or lie lurking in the woods.

CHAP. V.

Of the ifland of TENEDOS.

AFTER I had been at Conftantinople I went from the Dardanels to Tenedos. This ifland was called by the antients Calydna, and there are two iflands to the fouth of it, which are now called by the fame name; it was alfo called Leucophrys The antients fay, that it was five miles from the continent, but now it is computed to be nine, thirty from Imbrus, twenty from cape Jenichahere, or Sigeum, and ninety from Mytilene; it is five miles long and four broad. The antients computed it to be eleven miles and a quarter in circumference. The city of this ifland was reckoned among thofe of Æolia, and it is faid to have had two ports, one of which, I fuppofe, is the port now frequented, and the other is to the weft of the caftle clofe to the town, which is expofed to the north wind. The Grecian fleet that came againft Troy lay here, but it was not then efteemed a good port The road for fhipping towards the continent is looked on as very fafe There was a temple here to Sminthean Apollo, which probably was in the fine efplanade before the caftle, where there now remain fome fluted pillars of white marble, which are about two feet and a half in diameter The only town on the ifland is fituated towards the north eaft corner of it, in which there are two hundred Greek families, and three hundred Turkifh, the former have a church and three poor convents in the town, and are under the bifhop of Mytilene The caftle is a large high building, on a little rocky cape between the two ports, having a large efplanade to the land, it is very probable that this caftle, or fome part of it, may be the remains of the granaries that Juftinian built to preferve the corn which was brought from Ægypt from being fpoiled, in cafe the fhips which were bound to Conftantinople fhould be detained by contrary winds. The country about the town is rocky and unimproved, and the Turks will not permit them to cultivate that quarter; but on the north fide there is a fmall fpot well improved. This ifland belongs to the captain bafhaw, and only maintains the janizaries of the caftle, the chief export is good wine and brandy. I made a very fhort ftay in this ifland, and lay on board an Englifh fhip, which was in the road.

CHAP. VI.

Of the ifland of LEMNOS.

Imbrus

FROM the road of Tenedos we failed to Lemnos, paffing to the fouth of Imbrus, which is thirty miles from Tenedus, and is fituated to the fouth weft of the cape, that is at the entrance of the Dardanels, this ifland was facred to Mercury, and has on it five or fix villages, in two of which there are caftles. There are filver mines towards the fouth part of the ifland, but the ore requires fo much lethargy of lead to be mixt with it, that it does not anfwer the expence.

The high ifland called Samandrachi is to the north weft of it, which at firft had the name of Samos, and afterwards of Samothrace, or Samos of Thrace, to diftinguifh it from Samos of Ionia. If I miftake not, there is only one town or village in it, the ifland was facred to Cybele, and fhe is reported to have lived in it for fome time. It is faid that Jupiter had three children here by Electra, grand daughter of Atlas, namely, Dardanus, who founded the Trojan kingdom, Jafion who had Corybas by Cybele, from whom her priefts were called Corybantes, and Harmonia the wife of Cadmus. Perfes, when he was defeated by the Romans, fled to this ifland.

Lemnos

We landed on the eaft fide of Lemnos, at a bay well fheltered every way, except from the eaft, there are two villages near it called Odopole and Calliope. This ifland is called Lemnos by the Greeks, and by the Italian mariners Stalimene, from the Greek expreffion Eis tè Lemno, when they fpeak of going to this ifland. Lemnos was firft inhabited by a people of Thrace, then by the Pelifgians, and afterwards by the Athenians, until it became fubject to the Romans. Great part of the ifland is hilly, but the plains and valleys are fruitful, produce great quantity of corn and wine, and fome filk and cotton, which they manufacture at home, making a fort of fluff of filk and flax mixed, which is much ufed for fhirts, and is called meles, and a fort of filk like gauze, very light and tranfparent, called brunjuke, which is much ufed by the ladies for their under garments, they alfo export butter and cheefe made of goats milk, efpecially the latter. They have a ftrong middle fized race of horfes, which are remarkable for walking faft

                     This

This island is noted for the Terra Lemnia, called both by the Greeks and Turks The holy earth, it is said to have the same natural vertue as the Terra Sigillata of Calabria, confequently it is not carried into Chriftendom, but is only ufed in the Levant This earth was in efteem among the antients, who attributed the vertue of it to Vulcan's falling from his horfe on the fide of the hill where it is found, by which his thigh was broke, a fable which is thought to have its rife from a fuppofition that they firft practifed here the art of working iron The Greeks, and even the Turks imagine that it has a miraculous vertue, when it is taken before the fun rifes on the fifteenth of Auguft, which with them is the day of the afcenfion of the Virgin Mary, for this purpofe the Greeks and Turks, with their magiftrates, affemble at the place, which is called Aiokomo: A prieft performs a fervice about half an hour long, one of the laity among the Greeks killing a fheep, which the Turks carry away and eat, the Greeks not eating flefh at that time, then a man digs the earth, and throws it out, the waiwode and cadi take eighty okes, each near three pound weight, which they fend to the grand fignoi, in order, as I was informed, to make the cups out of which he drinks, and the people take what they pleafe This earth is dug on the fide of a low hill, which is to the fouth weft of Cokino port, and to the north of the port called the Golph The hole they have made is not large, as it lies near the furface, the earth refembles pipe clay, there are three thick veins which are white, and two fmaller that are red, the latter is moft efteemed; the people carry it home, and make it into balls, and feal it, as they have occafion, with a feal on which the Turkifh name of it is cut, and when it is taken at other times, they think it has not fo great vertue

About a league to the eaft of Caftro, the chief town of the ifland, there are hot baths, which they call Thermè, the waters are lukewarm, and feem to run on a limeftone. I was told alfo, that under the caftle there is an allum water, which I did not fee On each fide of the port where I landed there is a falt lake, that to the north dries up in the fummer, is called Alke-Limne [The falt lake], and leaves a cake of falt, which they purify for the ufe of the ifland, the other which they call the Mill-lake is not fo falt, and is of no ufe. To the north of this poit there is a large cape called Ecatokephale [The hundred heads], where there is a port of that name, on which I was told there are remains of an antient city called Palaiopolis, but I have reafon to think I was mifinformed, and that Palaiopolis is on a head of land to the north of Cokino port, which I faw from the place where the earth is dug, and is to the weft of Ecatokephale, becaufe travellers mention a ruined city at Cokino, as the antient Hephaftia To the fouth of thefe places, and of the road which leads to Caftro, from the port where I landed, there is a fine port called Golpho, which is near twenty miles in circumfeience The entrance is fo narrow that the bay appears like a large lake; to the eaft of it there is a town called Madrou, where there is a caftle; and to the weft of it is a large village called Sarpè

The chief town Caftro on the weft of the ifland is about a mile in circumference, and probably the antient city Myrina was on this fpot, to the weft of it there is a high rocky cape, on which there is a caftle very ftrongly fituated, there are about eight hundred families in the

town,

town, and the number of Greeks and Turks is near equal: The Greeks have three churches, and their bifhop refides here, who has an income of about four purfes a year. The waiwode has this island as an hereditary feud, paying about nine purfes a year for it to the captain bafhaw, or high admiral, who, whenever he comes this way, makes him pay confiderably more, on pretences that he has permitted corn to be exported contrary to law, or the like, which the waiwode is very well able to bear, making, at leaft, fifty purfes a year advantage by this island. A cadi and janizer aga refide at this place, and the feveral military bodies are here, which are in moft other towns. There are fixty villages in the island, feven monafteries, and about feven thoufand Greek families, and three thoufand of the Turks. About thirty miles to the fouth of Lemnos I faw the fmall island of Strati, which is uninhabited. I could get no information of a volcano in Lemnos, which is mentioned by the antients, nor of a labyrinth, that is faid to have been in this island.

CHAP. VII.

Of the ifland of SAMOS.

FROM Mytilene we went to Smyrna, and from that city to Segigieck, Ephefus, and Scala Nouva, where we embarked for Samos.

Samos
Its name

This island, when it was inhabited by the Carians, was called Parthenius, it afterwards had the name of Anthemus, it was then called Melamphylus, and laft of all Samos. It was computed to be feventy five miles in circumference, and is fituated to the north weft of the promontory Trogylium in Ionia. The two eaftern points of the island, were computed to be but feven ftadia from that promontory, though both the one and the other cannot be much lefs than a league from the continent, the furtheft to the weft was called Pofidicum, or the promontory of Neptune. The weft part of the island is the cape and mountain formerly called Ampelus, which now has the name of Carabichtes, and the cape is called cape Fournos from the oppofite islands; this mountain ftretches through the whole island to the eaft. So that Samos is hilly, and like all the other islands, is very rocky, it runs naturally into wood, of which there are all forts that grow in Afia, except that I did not obferve the cyprefs tree on this island.

Samos was under the Perfians and Athenians, and fometimes was governed by its own tyrants, or kings, of thefe one of the moft famous was Polycrates, with whom Anacreon lived, who often mentions him in his poems. Pythagoras was of this ifland at the fame time, but out of a diftafte of the tyranny that reigned in it, he travelled to Ægypt, Babylon, and at laft to Italy, where he died, after having improved all thofe countries by his excellent philofophy. Among the Athenian citizens, who were fent to this ifland as a colony, was the father of Epicurus, that philofopher was educated here and in Teos, and afterwards went to Athens, where he was cotemporary with Menander the comedian

We

We firft landed at the port of Vahti, which is a bay that lies open to^{Vahti} the north eaft, and is a good port when there is not a very ftrong northerly wind The town is fituated about half a mile from it to the fouth, and is built up the fide of a hill, there are in it about five hundred houfes, and fix churches, with a bell to each of them, as all the churches in the ifland have. The whole town confifts of Greek Chriftians, of whom there are about two hundred fouls. The convent of St Mary is near a league to the north eaft of this place. The town of Vahti lives by fifhing, and by an export of wine, which is very good, efpecially a white mufcadine fort, like that which is fold with us for Greek wine, of which the beft fells for about a half penny a quart

From Vahti I went two leagues towards the eaft end of the ifland; the paffage between it and the continent of Afia is called the boghas, that is the mouth, or ftreight of the paffage One of the eighteen towns, or villages of the ifland called Palaiocaftro is in the way to it   To the north of it is the port Cafonefi, and a fmall ifland in it of the fame name, lying open to the north eaft To the eaft of this is the fouth eaft point of the ifland, there are two little bays to the weft, which are open to the fouth eaft, and are excellent harbours The two points of the northern port appear to be the lands which are neareft to the continent. The fouthern point commands a fine view, and there are ruins of a very ftrong tower on it, which was probably defigned to guard the coaft. From this point, they fay, an iron chain went acrofs to the oppofite fide, though it is not eafy to conjecture what end it could anfwer, unlefs it were to receive a tribute from fhips that paffed that way. On both thefe bays there appears to have been a village, each of which had a church, one of them called St Mary's, has two or three marble pillars in it lying on the ground. To the fouth weft of the point, on which there are ruins of a tower, is another cape, and beyond that a fmall bay, to the weft of which there is a cape, which I take to be the promontory of Neptune, and oppofite to it is an ifland called by the antients Narthekis, and over againft that is the northern point of the promontory Trogylium, the fouthern part extending fomewhat farther to the weft; being, as Strabo obferves, the neareft land to Greece, at the promontory of Attica, called Sunium, from which it is one hundred and thirty two miles and a half · Oppofite to this point is the fmall ifle Trogylium There is a little bay at cape Neptune, and to the weft of it is the antient^{Antient port} port of the city of Samos, now called the port of Tigani, which is the^{and city} harbour of Cora, the capital town of the ifland, near a league from it, a plan of which, and of the old town may be feen in the forty-firft plate The bay is fmall, and it is a very bad port, being expofed to the fouth winds, from which little boats are fheltered by a fmall head of land R, and yet the fea runs fo high that in winter they are not fecure from damage An artificial mole B now ruined, was built from the bottom of the bay, extending towards the head of land, which made the narrow entrance of the antient harbour, as it does now of the prefent This, though it does not now feem to be a great work, yet it may be the remains of that mole which was efteemed one of the wonders of Samos, and is faid to have been two hundred and fifty paces long The port within feems to have been filled up, and the sea has loft on the weft fide, for there is a flat C, about a hundred paces wide, to a broad ruin D, which being an inclined plain, seems to have been the foundation for fteps down to the fhipping, which might come up to this place when the port was kept clean and open, and the fhips might lie there fecure from all winds when the pier was entire   Thefe fteps were on the eaft fide of that high land, which is to the weft of the port, and feems to have beem the fortrefs of the city towards the fea, it is a low rocky hill, about five hundred paces broad from eaft to weft, and a hundred from north to fouth, the remaining part to the north being flat, the middle part of it rather higher than the reft, is a hundred feet fquare, and appears to have been very ftrongly fortified with a wall and foffee, and at a fmall diftance from it on one fide there is a fally port G, cut down through the rock to the fea   There are great remains of very ftrong works towards the fouth, and on the weft fide is the bed of a winter torrent H, which might fill a bafon for fmall galhes   To the weft of this torrent there is a plain fpot I, full of pieces of columns, which feem to be the remains of a forum   The old city Samos extended about eight hundred paces beyond this to the weft, the plain being about a quarter of a mile wide to the foot of the hill, which was called mount Ampelus   The weftern walls L extended up the fteep fide of this hill, and on the top of the hill to the brow on the other fide, along which the northern wall was continued to the eaft of the hill, where turning to the fouth, oppofite to the middle of the bay, it croffed a rivulet at M, to another low hill at N, which feems to have been much inhabited, and going along to the north fide of it, it turns down to the fea to the pier in the middle of the bay at O, north of this enclofure N, I faw fome broken marble coffins, fome of which were covered with the ufual lids, and others with large ftones laid acrofs   The city walls are cafed infide and out with white marble, being filled up within with fmall ftones', they are ten, twelve, or fifteen feet thick, according to the ftrength of the fituation, and at the top are covered with very large hewn ftones, they are built with fquare towers at about fixty paces diftance, unlefs where the hill is fo fteep, as to make them unneceffary.   The walls do not feem to have been above fifteen feet high, but are the moft beautiful I have feen, and fome parts of them on the top of the hill are entire   Below at P there are remains of a theatre, the feats of which were not built on arches, but on the fide of the hill, it was two hundred and forty feet wide, and the fpace for the feats was eighty feet wide, it is built of white marble, and there are remains of an arch ten feet wide in the front of it   The walls are built in a very particular manner in the front, as may be feen in the plan E, in the forty-feventh plate, the ruins appeared in that manner, though probably there was an entrance in the front   It is a ruftic building, the ftones being rounded fo as to make a fegment of near a quarter of a circle, and towards the lower part of every tier are knobs at certain diftances, which make it look more ruftic, they might be hewn fo in order to command the ftones in placing them

Towards the weft fide of the town there are ruins of two or three very confiderable buildings, which are fo deftroyed that it is impoffible to judge of what nature they were, and there are many walls to the weft of them,

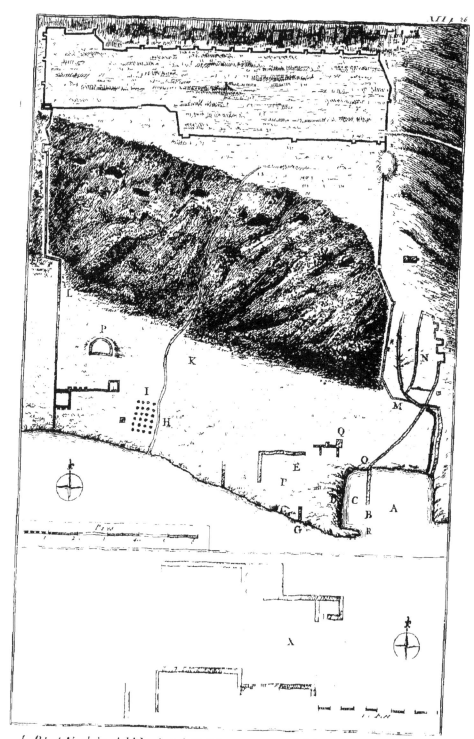

A PLAN of the CITY of SAMOS and of a BUILDING in it

them, especially several arches, like those which are now built in the east for shops, it is said that formerly they served for that purpose, and probably there was a town here in the middle ages, which might continue till the islands were taken from the Christians, when they might move farther from the sea, not to be exposed to the insults of the Corsairs. To the west of these there is a large pond made by a wall that confines the waters which comes from the hills, it does not seem to be a very antient work, but possibly may have been designed for a mill, as there is a mill race from it on a wall, which extends to a building, where, they say, there formerly was one. In this part there are likewise two or three small ruined churches, and to the north of the port at Q, there is a considerable ruin of a building of hewn stone, with two or three tiers of brick, at the distance of every four feet, which, they say, was a church and palace, probably the cathedral, and at this time there is a small church within it, dedicated to St Nicholas, the plan of which, as it seems to have been built, is seen at X. The hill over the lower city is of white marble, and there are several grotts in the side of it, which were the quarries of the city. The inhabitants were at great expence to bring water to the town by an aqueduct, the remains of which are seen all along the sides of the hills for a league to the west, having its rise at or near the river Imbrasius, the channel for the water was made on a low wall, except in a very few places, where there are remains of some arches over a valley on the east side of the city; these arches were at least sixty feet high, and above them, on the other hill, are a great number of grots, which were quarries, and are cut in like galleries, or as large square piazzas, supported by square pillars of the natural rock, these were doubtless dug in order to build the aqueduct, over which they are, and also for the use of the city, being a free stone, and more easily worked than the marble. As I went one day to visit these grottos alone, some shepherds, who were feeding their flocks on the hills, called to me, but as I did not understand their meaning, I went on. I had been informed that they found salt in some of these grottos, and my curiosity led me to taste the earth in several of them. I learnt afterwards that a man who died of the plague at the port, about three weeks before, was buried in one of the grottos, and that the shepherds called to me in order to prevent my going into them.

About half a mile to the west of the old city the hills retire to the north, so as to make the plain on the sea about two miles wide, and a league long from east to west. I take this plain to be the Heraion of Strabo, to which, he says, the suburb of the city extended, and not the temple of Juno, or the cape to the west of it, as some have apprehended, for the temple of Juno being at the south west corner of the plain, the ground to the east of it would be a very wet situation for a suburb in the winter, as it is for the most part a morass, so that it is most probable that this quarter to which the suburb of the city extended was situated here, and had its name from being the nearest building this way to the temple of Juno.

The temple of Juno was another of the wonders of Samos, and it was a very extraordinary building, both with regard to its size, and the manner of its architecture, it was built near the sea, fronting to the east,

Temple of Juno

a plan

a plan of it may be seen in the forty second plate at A ². Several of the bases and pedeftals remain on the north fide, though they are almoft buried in the ground, and likewife a part of one of the columns; and on the fouth fide there is almoft an entire fhaft remaining. The pillars were built of feveral round ftones laid one on another, as reprefented in the two half pillars B and C, where the extraordinary bafe and plinth are likewife fhewn· The bafe of the pillars of the portico are reprefented at C, which are different from thofe of thofe of the fides B The cufhion of the latter is reprefented in large at D, and of the former at E, in that at E the fpace between the large flutes has another flute on it; the pillars are of white marble, and the bafes of grey. One of the fhafts, which feems to be entire, confifts of feventeen ftones, from two feet to three feet and a half thick, thefe ftones are moved every way out of their places in a very extraoidinary manner, as if it were the effect of an earthquake, I faw part of two round capitals of grey marble, I found that one of them was four feet five inches diameter, but as the pillars are five feet fix inches, it feems probable that they belonged to pillars on the infide of the temple, they feem to have been Doric capitals, what remains of one of them is reprefented at F. This temple was famous for a great number of fine ftatues. I faw part of a large one of grey marble, the head and legs of which were broken off, and it appeared to be a work of no mean hand At fome diftance to the north weft of the temple are three fmall hills, to the weft of which there are great figns of buildings In a ruined edifice, which feemed to be of the middle ages, there is a fmall relief of a man, probably defigned for Hercules, having thefe letters under it ΑΛΚΕΙΔΗ. About half a mile to the weft of the temple there is a rivulet, which is the antient Imbrafius, on which, they fay, Juno was born, under a white willow, and there are a great number of thofe trees on it, which grow up in a fpiral form to a great height. This river comes from the mountains, and runs near a village fituated on them, called Baounda, where there is a red earth, of which it is fuppofed the antients made the earthern ware, which was famous here, and, if I miftake not, was firft invented in Samos, the pipes of the aqueduct were made of it: I faw fome of them from fix to eight inches in diameter, and alfo in Cora others of ftone, bored thorough, and about the fame fize The river runs below by a ruinous village called Milo, which is almoft forfaken by reafon of the injuries they have received from the Corfirs

The third wonder of Samos was a canal cut through the mountains to convey the water of a river on the north fide of it to the city, which muft have been near half a mile long, this is mentioned by Herodotus I could not meet with any information about it, only they talk much of grots that go under ground to the old city, but I could not find any grot that I could fuppofe was for that purpofe, and if there was fuch a canal, it muft have been made before they had invented the way of carrying water on aqueducts round the hills, which could have been very eafily done in this place As I was leaving Samos, I copied fome fragments of inferiptions juft dug out of the ground from a wall, on the outfide of which there was a portico, it is the remains of the large building mentioned towards the weft end of the city, one of the in-

fcriptions

² In front of this building in the plan ought to have been placed to the caft

PLAN of the TEMPLE of JUNO at SAMOS,
and a VIEW of the COLUMNS.

scriptions seemed to be to the honour of a person who had gained the prize in some games to Apollo

The capital of the island, called Cora, is at the north west corner of the plain, on the side of a rocky mountain, it is a poor ill built place, having more the aspect of a country village than a town, it has notwithstanding about twelve small churches in it, and two hundred and fifty houses, there are some imperfect inscriptions and broken reliefs there, which are mostly about the churches, I saw a defaced one of a naked youth with a dove in his hand, of a very fine sculpture   About a league to the east of this place, towards Vahti, is the village of Mytilene, there is a curious relief in the wall of the church a little defaced, which seems to be sepulchral, and has on it the name of the person, Apollonius, who probably was a physician, for one of the figures has a leaf in the hand, which I saw also in another relief, and it resembles very much the leaf of an herb that grows among the rocks in this island, and is called Pascalifa; it is much used there at this time for several disorders, being of a purging quality *.   At some distance to the west of this village is the highest mountain of the island called Carabounieh [The Black Hill] which seems to be the Cercetus of the antients   They have a white earth in Samos, which has something of the nature both of pipe clay and fullers earth; they call it Gouma, and as they use it for washing they call it Gouma saboni, [soap earth] they have the same in Milo, the women and children eat it, as well for amusement as for a sort of nourishment, but as it makes them drink much water, it is thought that it causes a swelling of the spleen, and also dropsies · This probably is one of those white earths of Samos used by the antients in medicine.   Julap and scamony grow here, I have been informed that the latter is not the best; and they do not collect the julap for sale   The people in Samos are much given to revelling and drunkenness, and are very poor, they till their own lands, and have no servants but their own children, the ladies of the highest rank in Samos, even to the governor's wife, go to the fountain for water, and do every kind of work

They have little trade, except an export of wine and raw silk, the trade latter is sent to Scio to be manufactured there to the value of about eight thousand dollars a year, they also export some corn, though contrary to law, and are generally obliged to import afterwards for their own use   In some of the grots I mentioned they find salt, as they have kept their cattle in them at night during the winter season, it is supposed that the salt, which is in the dung of the animals, in time, by the moisture of the place, makes a coat of salt on the surface of the earth, this the Greeks take clandestinely, that the Turkish governor may not deprive them of that benefit, or raise money on them, they call it a sal nitre, and I was informed that it is used also to make gunpowder, they have salt pans in the plain of Cora, and export the salt they make in to the continent   They also send out a great quantity of the timber of the pine tree to build ships and boats, especially to Patmos.   At the north west part of the island there is a small town called Carlovasi, from which they carry wine and oranges to Segigieck, there is no harbour there, but three leagues to the west is a port called Sitan

* The reliefs A and G in the thirty-eighth plate are in Samos, I and H in Lesbus

Lands

The lands of this island belong to the mosque in Constantinople called Tophana jamesi, they measure them once in seven years, by a measure which is a single pace, and for forty square paces they pay about ten or twelve medins a year, each medin being three farthings, the whole revenue that arises from the land amounts yearly to about twenty-two purses In the eighteen villages and towns of the island there are twelve hundred and sixty that pay the harach, or poll tax, which amounts to twenty purses more, and the Turkish governor makes about ten purses of what they call Avanias, which are fines on deaths, and for crimes, for this is the profitable way they have of punishing, even murder, unless a Christian happens to kill a Turk, though the few Turks that are here stand in fear of the Christians

Government

The island is governed by a Turkish waiwode and cadi, the former having the care of the revenues, and the latter administers justice in the capital, and goes round to the villages four or five times a year for that purpose The aga also has a servant in some of the principal villages, who is a sort of governor, they have likewise a Christian governor called the aga, who is a man of the greatest interest, is chosen by the people, and generally remains in the office for life, he has a great influence on the people, and the waiwode and cadi seldom do any thing of importance, unless he is present to give his advice The waiwode continues in office for seven years, paying a certain yearly sum, and makes the most of it. This is the regular government of the island, but about three years ago a troop of banditti Christians from the Morea and other parts, to the number of about fifty, came into the island well-armed, raised money on all the villages, murdered several people, and among them the Christian aga, some galleottes were sent against them, and they were dispersed, except about twenty, who submitted to the government, and pretend to have a liberty to carry arms, and in reality govern the island in every thing, in which they are pleased to interfere, they marry themselves by force to the richest parties, and being dispersed through the villages do what they please, and have a captain at the head of them, maintaining themselves by the money they have raised, and this small number of men render the island very unhappy, the Turkish governors themselves standing in awe of them, and no one has courage or resolution to oppose them

The bishop of Samos resides in Cora, there are five monasteries in the island, but no nunnery, there are only three or four priests in each of them, and a sufficient number of caloyers to till their lands.

C H A P. VIII
Of the ifland of PATMOS.

FROM Samos we failed to Patmos, which is one of the iflands, called by the antients Sporades, it is in the Icarian fea, directly fouth of thofe fmall iflands, which are between Nicaria and Samos Patmos is computed, by the modern Greeks, to be forty miles round, tho' the antients fpeak of it only as thirty, and it does not feem to be fo much On the eaft fide there is a deep bay, and on the weft two fmall ones, which make the north and fouth part of the ifland peninfulas The neck of land which joins them is not above a quarter of a mile broad The town was formerly on the eaft fide of the ifthmus, but the people removed to the hill on the fouth for fear of the Corfairs, and built a town about the convent, which is on the fummit of the high hill

There is a fmaller convent about half way up the hill, it is called Apocalypfe, in which there is a grot, now converted into a church, where they fay St John lived when he was banifhed to this ifland, and where they affirm he writ the Revelations, it is nine paces long and four wide, cut entirely out of the rock, except on the north fide, where it opens to the chapel of St Annè, and in the middle there is a fquare pillar, which feems defigned to fupport the rock To the eaft of this pillar there is a crack which goes all acrofs the grotto, by which they fay the Holy Ghoft fpake to St John when he writ the Revelations and the Gofpel, for the monks fay, that, according to the teftimony of fome of the fathers, he wrote the Gofpel here as well as the Revelations They fay he was feventeen years in this ifland, which feems to be a miftake for as many months, becaufe it is agreed by the learned that he was here but eighteen months, for he returned to Ephefus when the exiles were fet at liberty by Nerva This convent is a fort of novitiate, or feminary, fubject to the great convent, and is governed by a profeffor, whom they call Didafcalos, who has a mafter under him They teach the antient Greek, which they call Hellenike, phyfics, metaphyfics, and divinity They ufe the grammar of Conftantine Lukares of Conftantinople, and the logic of Theophilus Corudaleos, both printed in Venice, and the phyfics and metaphyfics of the latter in manufcript, and the divinity of Georgius Quinchius of Scio, which is likewife in manufcript, they teach in a large fchool, the mafter inftructs the children in the grammar, and the head profeffor teaches logic, philofophy, and divinity I was prefent at their lectures, one of the fcholars read, and the profeffor explained it This fchool, and the prefent profeffor who governs it, are efteemed the beft in all the eaft, they have about fifty fcholars who come from different countries, and the greater part lodge in the two convents, though fome of them are in the town

The fituation of the town and great convent, which are on the top of the hill, is fomething like that of St Marino The convent refembles a caftle irregularly built, but the fmall church is very neat, it was

Gro of the Apocalypfe

Univerfity

Convent

I

founded,

founded, as I am informed, by the emperor Alexius Commenius; they have two large bells in it   The abbot is chosen once in two years; there are in all two hundred members belonging to the convent, but there are only twenty priefts, and about forty caloyers in the monaftery   They have a fmall library, furnifhed with fome of the beft printed books, moftly the Greek fathers   The oldeft manufcript I faw there is a collection of the works of fome of the Greek fathers, which as I conjectured might be a thoufand years old , they have alfo the Pentateuch, with the comments of divers perfons, and they told me that they had one with the hiftories painted in it in the fame manner as the curious manufcript which belongs to the archbifhop of Smyrna   There are two or three hermitages dependant on the convent, and the whole ifland belongs to it, as well as all the fmall ifles to the eaft of it   From the top of the convent I faw moft of the iflands of the Archipelago   There is a nunnery in the town, dependant on the convent, which was founded by one of their abbots , it is inhabited by about thirty old women who live by their induftry

Town   There are feven hundred houfes in the town, but only a hundred and fixty perfons that pay the poll tax, except thofe that belong to the convent, who are about two hundred, moft of the inhabitants being natives of other places   The convent pays two purfes yearly to the captain bafhaw for the ifland

Government and t ade   Though the abbot has all the power , yet for the government of the people there are four vicardi for life, who are generally fucceeded by their fons   The inhabitants, who are all Chriftians, are mariners, or fhipwrights , for the ifland is a barren rock, and every thing is brought from without   The only export is cotton ftockings to Venice, to which city their fhips frequently go   They have a few gardens, and make a little poor wine that will not keep above a month , they have good water, it is a very healthy ifland, and there has been no plague in it for forty years paft, fo that one fees many old people , for they are careful to guard againft infection, by making veffels perform quarantine which come from infected places.   The people here are much civilized by the commerce they have abroad , they are immediately fubject to the patriarch ; and there are three hundred churches in the ifland.

THE BLA

PONTVS

EVROPE

THRACE

Ghaltzer

Emine
C. Emine
Mesempria
Anchialos
Burghas
Turus
Tzinghiane
Sozopolis
Octapolis
Kerdevro
Athmani
Rumé
Niada
Ercos
Midia
Yedi Cumlar

Bosphorus
Cavat
C. Bithynia
C. Psytha
Chile

Rodosto
CONSTANTINOPLE
Scutari
Chrysopolis
Aghra
Artace
Bogagic
Herpe
Thynias Daphnusia

Pendoz
Selivri
Panidos
Heraclee
Prin
Lesbi
Chalcedon
Pagnik
Gebsé
Pella
P.Wahonum
Ilagicie
Cirau Attacus
Nicomedia
Kisken Limene
R.Calpas
Diopolis

MARMORA SEA
I.Marmora
Count
B.Imir
Caramount
Debrendek
Adacui
Kechan

BRITH

Kamara
Careboli
Sardacur
Lapsaki
Entropa
C.Stellan
Rania
Artace
L.Aalosunno
Besbicus
Tolonay
Armosa
Gemblock
Lipa
Sabanjah
Jeropati
L.Salanrah
Gawey
Protomacre
Laryah
Handake
Micleno
Hispania

LITTLE
MYSIA
Dardanelles
Missaea
Dardanum
Panormio
Fenatin
Douta cut-y
Magraas Guel
Kruso
Port
Montenie
Boursa
Pealia
Karanick cui
L.Oenbara
Lanick
Nicaea
Knick
Ascanius
Menuchakere
Bugherlu
Chioslee

I

TROAS
B.Tzembrluk
Balanois
Scamander
Aidun
Eskitepe
Mguv Sophia
Lesmoke
Trojanopolis
Adrame
Bellicasar
Sungrulu
Carabick
L.Ibelhont
L.Ienichahor
Expat
Wellecnni
E.Mihalisha
Leffkeu
Laltus
Itimter Han
Agrilium
Eski Shahar
Dorylaum

Y
N
I
A

PHRYGIA
GREAT
MYSIA
Hyrcanus Campus
Hermonchi
Pordoselena
Scunta
Synnus
Dagsu
Nagsu
R.Gabus
T

Lectum
C.Bace
Musconesi
Assmaa
Atamout
Pergamus
Corogoulee
Culembee
Alydda
Krayak
Cutarise
Cotiaum
Angur
Ancyra Phrygia

MITIL ENE
C.Jorge
Tenedos
Canu
P.Janoti
Gryniun
Sandall
Syrink
Ca
Cuma
Aesar
Thyatira
L

Sancta Gemell
Midaium
G R E

A
MAP OF
ASIA MINOR

German 0 Miles
Italian 0 Miles
English 0 Miles
French Leagues

T. Jefferys del et sculp

CK SEA

EVXINVS

Carambis
Gede
Theuthrania
Ravi-Ianan
C. Chinax
Debiliath
Thea
Inebol
Avon
Kiltaik
Ununi
Tios
Sarion
Oksene
Gholimli
Tzakroz
Cromna
Myiad
Kiedrin
Cytorum
Kisatili
Kanak
Hsari
Stephane
Sinop
Sinope
R. Zibscus
Kivul
Talbelti
Kersedeu Heraclea
Kabasacal

PAPHLAGONIA
Changreh
Kepler Aghaii
Galorum
GALATIA
PONTVS
PONTVS
POLEMONIACVS
Nehritzan Hervetis
Tatara Armutoeh Hervetis
OCAN
R. Thermodon
Samson
Onti Palem
CAP

Borla
Geredy
Baunder R. Geredeu
Cherkes
Amadmani
Chosletti
Show Hamam
K'ss dje Hamam
Aangalar
Tocia
Osmancik
Androcia
Mascnari
Amafia

Sarilar
GALATIA
Tetuch
Niterimalk
Harakaki
Serirkifsar
Pipeck
Caranikifsh
Angoura
Ancyra
Ania Therma
Beybazar
Insti

O   L   E
Aamana
Kenaer
Dio csasarea
R. Esby
Hadjee Bertas
Baseronelti
Beram Hagilech
Romkusha

CAPPA
Asrlur
Gumeshac
Megaludag
Tocat
Neccorhria
Seuris

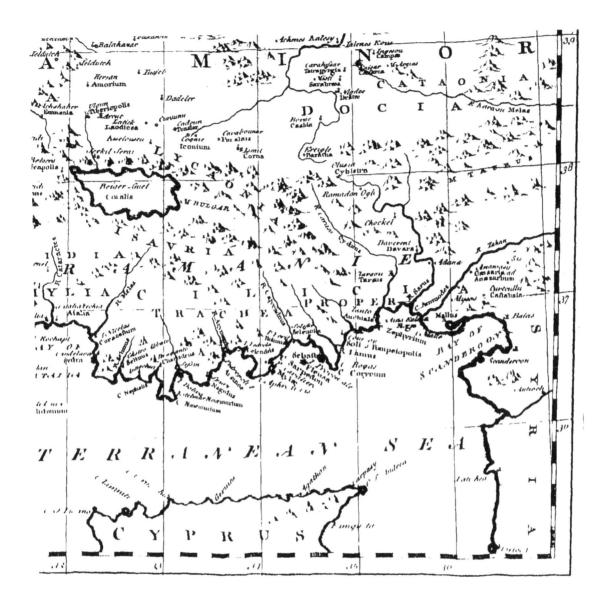

A

DESCRIPTION

OF

The *EAST, &c.*

BOOK the Second.
Of ASIA MINOR.

CHAP. I.

Of ASIA MINOR, and IONIA in general; and of the city
of SMYRNA.

THAT part of Asia, which has the Euxine and Mediterranean seas Asia Minor
on three fides of it, was called by the antients Asia Minor, and
by the easterns Natolia or Anatole, that is, the eastern country
with regard to Greece and the islands. The western part of it was distinguished by the name of Asia on this side mount Taurus, which was
bounded to the east by the river Halys The eastern part, beyond, and
about mount Taurus consisted of Pontus, Cappadocia, Cilicia, Pamphy-
lia, Lycia, Pisidia, Isauria, and Lycaonia On this side of the Halys
to the north was Paphlagonia, Galatia, and Bithynia, all the other
parts, which took in the whole the western coast was Asia Proper, in
which were the two Phrygias, the two Mysias, Æolia, Lydia, Ionia,
Caria, and Doris Almost all these were colonies of the Greeks, who
established free cities here, at first, in some measure, subject to the mother city from which they came; but afterwards they were governed successively by the Persian and Greek monarchs For some time Bithynia,
Paphlagonia, Lydia, and Caria had their kings, as well as Pontus and
Cappadocia The kings of Syria likewise, after Alexander, had foot-

ing in Afia Minor ; and Philetærus, general of Lyfimachus, laid the foundation for the kingdom of Pergamus, which he left to Eumenes, and fo it defcended to the two kings of the name of Attalus; the laft of which made the Romans his heirs, who delivered thefe countries from the tyranny of the kings of Syria, and left their kings and cities to enjoy their ufual liberties ; but the people favouring fome difturbances that were made, the Romans reduced the whole country into the form of a province, and governed it by prætors, among whom were Sylla, Lucullus, and Quintus the brother of Cicero. Auguftus made it a proconfular province, from which time it was called Proconfular Afia. Bithynia and Paphlagonia, after their kings were depofed, made another province.

Ionia.   Ionia was in the kingdom of Pergamus, famous of old for its twelve free cities, which were united together in council, and forces for their common defence· They were colonies from Athens, and faid to be built by Ion the Athenian, and from him this country had its name It was bounded to the north by Æolia, where Phocæa, and part of the river Hermus were its utmoft extent ; to the eaft it was bounded by Lydia, as it was on the weft by the fea, and to the fouth it extended beyond the Mæander to the promontory Poffidium, having Caria for its boundary that way. It is faid that the parts near Caria, as far as Ephefus, formerly belonged to the Carians ; and the northern parts, with the ifles of Chius and Samus, were inhabited by the Leleges ; but both being drove out by the Ionians, retired into Caria Androclus, fon of Codrus, king of the Athenians, was head of the colony of the Ionians, and built Ephefus, where his family enjoyed the empty title and honour of kings The other cities were built or improved by different perfons, who brought colonies to them. The capitals of the iflands of Samos and Chius were among the twelve cities, the other ten were Phocæa, Clazomene, Erythræ, Teos, Lebedus, Colophon, Ephefus, Priene, Miletus, and Myus.

Smyrna   We embarked at Mytilene, and landed at Smyrna. The Smyrnæans feparating themfelves from their brethren the Ephefians built Smyrna on the fpot, where the prefent city ftands, and by the intereft of the Ephefians were taken into this body, and made the thirteenth city of Ionia. The people of Smyrna firft inhabited a part of Ephefus; their name is derived from Smyrna an Amazon, it is not mentioned, whether they were defcended from her, or left their country under her conduct This city is towards the fouth eaft corner of a deep bay, great part of which to the weft is covered by the cape of Carabournou, which extends to the north, being a high mountain, and is part of the antient mount Mimas Over againft the mouth of the river Hermus, there is a bank of land which runs to the fouth, and is fuppofed to be made by the current of the river, oppofite to this there is a point, on which a caftle is built, to command the entrance of the port, the fhips being obliged to fail near it, by reafon of that bank of fand. This bay is three leagues wide at the weft end, about a mile from the fouth fide of it there is a fteep rocky hill, divided by a narrow vale from the hills to the eaft The caftle of Smyrna ftands on this hill, which extends about half a mile to the weft towards the fea I conjectured that the city of Smyrna in Strabo's time was on this hill, and on the plain to the north and weft of

it,

it ; and that what he calls the Smyrnean bay was that part of the gulph which is towards the fouth eaft corner ; for there were two antient cities   To the north of this hill there is a fmall bay, which is now called the Old port, to which all the fmall boats go . This I conjecture was the port that could be fhut up of the fecond antient city.   In this part there is a narrow plain fpot between the caftle and the fea ; the prefent town is fituated on it, and extends up the fide of the hill , the river Meles runs to the eaft and north of that hill, and is faid to have paffed near the city walls.   Twenty ftadia from this, there was another bay, on which Strabo fays the old city of Smyrna ftood . I take that to be the bay which fets in to the eaft, about half a league to the north of the prefent city, which by the Englifh is called Pegg's hole, extending near to a fine fource of waters called the baths of Diana, that fall it in a fmall ftream, about them there are fome fmall figns of buildings. This place is about the middle of the bay, which extends near a league and a half further to the north, having to the eaft a fine fruitful plain two leagues long, in which there are five or fix very pleafant villages. The Lydians deftroyed the antient city, and the Smyrneans for four hundred years lived near it in villages, till Antigonus and Lyfimachus rebuilt the city on the fpot where it was in Strabo's time , it extended a little more to the fouth than the prefent, further up the hill, and not fo far to the north   Dolabella befieged Trebonius in this city, and put him to death, being one of the accomplices in the affaffination of Julius Cæfar, and he did great damage to the city for taking part with Trebonius   About half a mile fouth of the old port, and on the fouth fide of a part of the caftle hill, which extends to the fea, there are fome remains of the walls of the fecond city, with a mole running out from it into the fea, and fome other parts of the wall, as defcribed below [*].   The town might be about four miles in compafs, and was of a triangular form ; it feems to have extended in length about a mile on the fea, and three miles on the north fouth and eaft fides, taking in the compafs of the caftle, which is very large, being not lefs than three quarters of a mile in circumference , the length of it is about twice the breadth , it is a very indifferent building, and ftands on the remains of a ftrong caftle, the walls of which were of the fame kind of architecture, as the city walls on the hill ; it is all in ruins, except a fmall part at the weft end, which is always kept fhut up.   One of the gateways of white marble has been brought from another place, and in the architrave round the arch there is a Greek infcription of the middle ages: At another gate there is a

[*] The city wall went up what they call the windmill hill, on the top of which there are foundations of a fmall caftle , from this hill the wall runs about a furlong to the north, turns again to the eaft, and goes up a fummit of the hill, which is to the fouth of the Circus, from which turning north, and going eaft of the Circus, it afterwards turns to the eaft for a little way, and fo joined the fouth weft corner of the caftle   the northern wall begin from the north weft corner of the caftle, defcends the caftle hill to the north weft, in which direction I fuppofe it went to the fea, through the middle of the prefent town, near the Armenian ftreet, where there are fome remains of a wall built of very

large hewn ftones, in which are cut feveral rough lines or letters, many of them in this fhape V, which has exercifed the learning of antiquarians to find out for what purpofe thofe lines were made   Some think that it was defigned for the initial letter of Vefpafian's name , though poffibly thefe lines might be made in the quarries from one ftone to another, to fhew how they were to be placed in the building   Indeed the walls above are built in a different manner of rufticated ftone, which is not fo large ; fo that this might be a later building, being in the ftyle of the work that was executed under the firft Greek emperors

coloffal

coloſſal head, ſaid to be that of the Amazon Smyrna; it is of fine workmanſhip, and the treſſes particularly flow in a very natural manner. Smyrna was one of the fineſt cities in theſe parts, and the ſtreets were beautifully laid out, well paved, and adorned with porticos both above and below; there was in it a gymnaſium, a library, the Homerium, which conſiſted of a portico, temple, and ſtatue, dedicated to Homer: For of the ſeven cities which contended for the birth of that great poet, it has been almoſt generally thought that Smyrna has the beſt title to that honour There was alſo here a temple of Mars, a circus, and a theatre, and yet there is now very little to be ſeen of all theſe things; the reaſon is that the new city is built on the ſpot of the antient one, and moſt of the materials of it have been removed to ſerve for the modern buildings, and they are even now continually digging under ground for the ſtones The ſpot on which the theatre ſtood, at the foot of the hill towards the ſouth end of the town, is all built upon: One ſees very little of the circus, except the foundations; it was hollowed down into the hill, not far from the ſouth weſt corner of the caſtle. At the north weſt corner of it is the tomb of St. Polycarp, who was here expoſed to wild beaſts, and torn to pieces by them. It is ſaid that great diſorders had been committed here by the Greeks at the time of his feſtival; and that a cadi laid hold on this pretence to get money, ordering that, in caſe any Chriſtians came to it, the community of Chriſtians ſhould be obliged to pay ſuch a ſum, but as he could not obtain his end, he put up a ſtone turbant on it, as if it were the tomb of ſome Mahometan ſaint, by which he thought to have his revenge in preventing the Chriſtians from ever reſorting to it again, which hitherto has had its effect. There is a tradition that the cathedral church of the archbiſhop of Smyrna was built on the north ſide of the circus, which ſeems probable, there being ſome ruins that look like the remains of ſuch a building; and to the ſouth eaſt of it there is a fabric of three rooms, which had a portico before it, the pillars of which are taken away. This ſeems to be the building mentioned by ſome travellers, in which the council of Smyrna was held, it having been probably the ſynod room of the archbiſhop, whoſe houſe might have been between this and the church. There are remains up the ſide of the hill of many vaults and paſſages for water, and there are ſeveral arched vaults under houſes, the entrances to which are well built, of large hewn ſtone Theſe vaults, doubtleſs, belonged to the houſes of the old city As they have no good water in Smyrna, the antients were very careful in making aqueducts, in order to ſupply the town with water, and the old aqueduct, which is now ruined, is undoubtedly very antient [b].

The

---

[b] There are ſome hills to the eaſt of the caſtle hill, and about a league to the eaſt of it there is a narrow vale between the hills, where there is water, which probably was brought from that vale round the hills to the city The firſt ſigns of the aqueduct are about a mile to the eaſt of the valley, in which the Meles runs, and to the eaſt of the caſtle, there is a wall which runs along on the height of the hill, higher or lower, according as the ground lies; this wall goes near the vale in which the river

Meles runs, the aqueduct was then carried along the ſide of the hill, and croſſed the valley, where the high arches are all deſtroyed, except ſome part of the wall on the ſide of the hills, and ſome remains of the arch over the river, it was then probably carried along the ſide of the hill to ciſterns under the caſtle; the ſide of the caſtle being higher than the aqueduct could poſſibly be raiſed In this manner it ſeems to have ſupplied all the parts about the caſtle, and probably the lower town likewiſe The wall is

not

The present town of Smyrna makes a very fine appearance from the water; it is about four miles in compass; the streets are narrow and not well laid out, there are in it two fine kanes, which are built round courts, and being covered with cupolas, make a very handsome appearance, they have also beautiful besesteens, or shops, which are arched over The upper parts of their houses are built with unburnt brick, in frames of wood plaistered over: Those in the street next the sea have courts and gardens behind them, extending to the sea side; they build these houses on three sides of a court, with a gallery of communication to the several apartments, their warehouses are below, and the dwelling house above On one side of the garden they have a long wooden gallery covered over, which leads from the dwelling house to a sort of a pleasure house over the water. This makes the situation of them very delightful, and there is a quay all along the sea side, to which the small boats come up and load at their doors

It is thought that there are near a hundred thousand souls in Smyrna; of these there are seven or eight thousand Greeks, two thousand Armenians, and five or six thousand Jews, who all have their particular streets, in which they live together. The Greeks have three churches, the Armenians one, in the cemetery of the latter are several inscriptions, and some pieces of antiquity The Franks or Europeans have their particular street, in which they enjoy great privileges, and lock it up every night The English, French, Swedes, Dutch, and Venetians have their consuls here; the English and Dutch have chapels and chaplains. The Franciscans, Capuchins, and Jesuits have their respective convents In the Franciscan monastery an apostolical vicar of that order always resides Both the Armenians and Greeks have their archbishop, who, if I mistake not, has only the bishopric of Phocæa under him, which seems to be united to Smyrna as there is no bishop in it The Greek metropolitan has a very fine manuscript of the Pentateuch,

not built with arches, for there is only one arch across the road that goes to the south, and three or four arches near it, where I discovered the channel of the aquæduct in the wall, which was made of large square stones, one stone being let into the other, and a round channel is worked through them, what is very particular, this pipe is laid in the wall a very little above the ground, though the wall is built much higher, and in many places where the wall was broke, I could see no sign of the pipes, not even at top, which I therefore concluded run mostly along the ground, except where the ground is low, and yet in all parts the wall is built high I saw also many pieces of earthen pipes, and one in the wall three or four feet above the ground, which might be a channel from some other source, but it is not easy to conjecture for what purpose the wall should be built so high, unless there was a channel at the top to convey water to higher places, though as the wall is built so thick at the passage of the road with buttresses on each side, and also some towers to it further to the east, one would be inclined to think that it was designed as some sort of defence against the incursions of enemies To the south of this there is another aquæduct

over the vale just under the castle; it is new built, with three rows of arches, one over another, towards the bottom of it there are remains of an old rusticated wall, after the manner of the city walls, which shews that in antienter aquæduct had been there A little to the south of this there is a place which they call the Homereum, and say, that the temple of Homer was there, tho' there is no sign of any antient building A mile to the south there are two aquæducts close to a third which crosses the same valley, each having three rows of arches, one over another, one of them is new built, the other, which is a very bad fabric, is older, they convey great bodies of water from a place to the south east, where several old artificial channels meet, and not being all conveyed to the city, they form a little river, which towards Segecui, falls into the Meles Near the abovementioned aquæduct there are remains of the paved road to Ephesus, which was made of very broad stones, there are also ruins of a gateway and wall, which crossed this road from the castle hill about a mile from the castle itself; this wall extended to the opposite hill, and was without doubt built to defend the pass.

supposed to have been wrote about the year eight hundred, with a large comment on it, it is on parchment exceedingly well written, and adorned with several paintings, which are well executed for those times. The great number of Franks who are settled here, make Smyrna a very agreeable place, and there is no want of good company, they live in a very sociable manner, and are particularly civil to strangers

Smyrna, and a considerable territory about it, belongs to the validea or sultaness mother. A waiwode, who has the more honourable title of mololem, has the care of the revenues, but the cadi is the principal governor here, in whom the chief power resides, there being no pasha over this district The city had been much distressed two or three years before I was there, by the rebellion of Soley Bey, whose army ravaged the whole country, threatened to plunder the city, and raised thirty purses of money on them, the Europeans removed most of their effects aboard the vessels in the harbour. The magistrates built gates to the town, planted cannon upon them, and for a pretence to raise money on the city, began to make a little fossee round on the hill, and to build a flight wall, great part of which has since fallen down, and the city and merchants found the effects of this blockade more sensibly, in a loss of their trade, the caravans not being able to travel in safety in order to bring goods for exportation The city, which has been alarmed on account of many earthquakes which have happened, was greatly terrified by a shock which happened in April, 1739, that overthrew several houses, many persons were killed in their beds, and there was not a house in Smyrna but what was shattered in a most miserable manner, and the people so terrified, that they slept in huts in their gardens and yards almost all the summer, and many retired altogether from their houses, both for safety and convenience

Trade   The trade of Smyrna for its export to Christendom, is more considerable than any port of the Levant, it consists chiefly of very rich goods; such as raw silk, Turkey carpets, but more particularly the fine goats hair or mohair of Angoura, with which our camlets, prunellos and buttons are made, they export likewise a great quantity of raisins to England, under the pretence of a privilege they have by our capitulations of loading so many ships for the king's table, they export also a great deal of unwrought cotton, and a small quantity of muscadine wine, for which this place is famous, as well as for the drier virgin white-wine. The import is chiefly woollen cloth, lead and tin, in the first the English have been very much supplanted by the French in all parts, except at Constantinople and in Ægypt, where the great people always use the English manufactures, because they are the best They import glass from Venice, and manufactured silks from other parts of Italy, they have also also another export to Italy from Vourla Segigieck, and some other small ports, of what they call Valinea, which is a large acron, they use them in Italy for tanning instead of bark, the cup also, as I have been informed, is used in some parts, especially in Holland, to mix with their gauls in dying black, being a cheaper commodity, and in some measure answers the end of gauls, from these two ports they sometimes export oil to France for making soap, and for working their cloths

To

To the fouth eaft of Smyrna there is a fine plain, and on the north fide of it is a pleafant village called Bujaw, where the Europeans have country-houfes, gardens, and fields planted with cyprefs trees, in the middle of this plain there are feveral canals which fupply the city by the aqueducts, and the river Meles runs to the fouth part of it, beyond which towards the foot of the mountains is the village of Segicui, where there are likewife fome country-houfes belonging to Europeans To the north of the city, there is a coffin of white marble in a garden, with an infcription on it, which fignifies that it was the tomb of a perfon of the name of Fabius Maximus, who died at twenty-one years of age In the way to the plain in which Bonavre is fituated, not far from the road, is that great fource of water called the baths of Diana ; the waters are warm in winter, and near them there are many foundations of buildings, and feveral arches of great antiquity, which doubtlefs belonged to the antient baths There are ruins all the way from the city to this place, and fo far probably the moft ancient city of Smyrna extended At the village of Bonavre there is a Turkifh burial place of great extent, from which one would conclude that it had been a confiderable town, and it is faid, that all the patents of the grand fignor for confuls, make them confuls of Bonavre and Smyrna, as if it had been a place of trade, though it is a league from the fea. In thefe burial places there are a great number of columns, pieces of entablature, and other ftones of antient buildings, fo that it is probable there was a temple in this place, and I found by a Greek infcription that there had been a church here On the fide of the hill more to the weft, and near the corner of the bay there are feveral very antient fepulchres, the plaineft fort confifts of a raifed ground in a circular form, either of ftones hewn out, or laid in a rough manner, in thefe there are generally two graves funk into the ground, made of hewn ftone, and covered over with a large ftone. The others are circular mounts from twenty to fixty feet in diameter, which are walled round with large rufticated ftone to the heigth of the mount There is a room within under ground, and fome of them are divided into two apartments The walls are all of very good work made of a fort of a brown baftard granite of the place, wrought every way very fmooth, infomuch that the joints are as fine as thofe of polifhed marble Round at the top is the plain cornifh ufed in the antient Ægyptian buildings, and thefe alfo, like the others, are covered with long ftones. One of the former fort being opened by fome Englifh, they found an urn in it. Towards the eaft part of the plain there are two villages called Norlecui and Hadjelar, in which likewife fome Europeans have their country-houfes At the Turkifh burial place of the latter there are feveral ftones of antient buildings, and fome imperfect Greek infcriptions, as well as in moft of the burial places of the villages here, fo that it is probable there were antiently villages in thefe places, which had their temples to their Sylvan, or country gods. Thefe two plains, with part of the neighbouring hills, were probably the territory of the Smyrnæans.

CHAP.

CHAP. II.

Of VOURLA the antient CLAZOMENE, SEGIGIECK, and the antient TEIUS.

I Went by sea from Smyrna to Vourla, which is a village a league to the south of a bay of the same name, on which there is a castle built to command the entrance to the port of Smyrna. This place is on that large promontory which is made by the high mountains of Carabournou, among which was mount Mimas of the antients, so often mentioned by the poets, which Strabo says was between Clazomene and Erythræ, which is on the west side of this great promontory, and so is not, as some have taken it to be, that mountain between Vourla and Smyrna, which by reason of two high points is called The Brothers This port of Vourla is computed to be eight or ten leagues from Smyrna, and is that bay, which with another to the south made the Isthmus so frequently mentioned by the antients, as having on the north side of it the territory of the Clazomenians, and on the south that of the Teians, and has that peninsula to the west which was the country of the Erythræans; consequently the port of Vourla must have been the port of the famous city of Clazomene, which was one of the twelve cities of Ionia; but Kelilman, a village on the east side of this bay, has been taken for this city by some travellers, from a similitude of the name, altho' it is without the Isthmus, and in a place where there are no ruins Strabo also mentions eight small islands before the city, which are directly before the port of Vourla, and though it is true, that there are very few signs of the city in this place, yet the ground is covered with antient brick and tiles, which are a proof that some considerable city formerly stood there But what makes this place without all doubt to be the site of the antient Clazomene, is the island of saint John, about a quarter of a mile from the land, it is half a mile in circumference, there are remains of a broad causeway leading to it, and tho' it is almost destroyed by the sea, yet they pass over to the island on foot This must be that island to which the Clazomenians retired for fear of the Persians, and joined it to the continent by the causeway, at the end of which there are some signs of an old wall, and a small arch, and there are two or three pieces of antiquity remaining at Vourla European vessels are often loaded with raisins and oil of olives at this port, where there is only a mosque and a custom house

The town of Vourla is a league to the north north east of the port, and is situated on two rising grounds, on one of which the Christians live, of whom there are about five hundred houses, the Turks inhabit the other part of the town, the Christians have two churches, and the archbishop of Ephesus has a tolerable house here, and resides for two or three months in the year at this place, which is in his diocese Strabo mentions a steep place at the beginning of the Isthmus, which was the division between the Erythræans and the Clazomenians, and that Chytrium was be-

hind

Clazomene (margin)
Vourla (margin)

hind it, where Clazomene was at firſt built, and then he mentions the city of his time, before which, he ſays, there were eight iſlands In order to underſtand this, it muſt be obſerved, that, to the weſt of the bay of Vourla, there is another narrow deep bay, called the bay of Sharmn, between the two bays and the plain of Vourla, there is a ſteep rocky chain of hills, which I take to be the ſteep ground mentioned by Strabo, it extends to the bottom of the bay of Sharpan, where probably Chytrium was ſituated, which is the more likely, as this bay is about a league and a half deeper to the ſouth than the bay of Vourla, ſo that this muſt have been the bay that made the Iſthmus, mentioned by Strabo as ſix miles and a quarter broad from the ſouthern bay of Teius to this place Whether or no the city of Clazomene might extend acroſs any part of the high ground, ſo as that an iſland or two in that bay might be ſaid to lie oppoſite to it, is very uncertain, and rather too forced an interpretation of Strabo, and I ſhould rather think that he was miſtaken in the number of iſlands ſituated before Clazomene, for there are but five in that bay, and a rock, which might formerly be larger, and reckoned as an iſland That which is to the north weſt of St John's iſland is called Chicelle, between them is the rock before mentioned, and to the north weſt of this is the iſland Neuſle, to the weſt of which there is a larger iſland called Vourlah, which is known to Europeans by the name of the Partrige iſland; to the weſt of this there is an iſland ten miles long, called by the Turks Kiuſlin, and by Europeans the Long iſland, it was antiently known by the name of Drymiuſa, and was given by the Romans to the Clazomenians, when they made Clazomene a free city, and ſome large arched ciſterns in it, are a proof that the iſland has been conſiderably inhabited Between Clazomene and Smyrna was the temple of Apollo, which probably was at a village about eight miles from Smyrna, to the ſouth of the caſtle, where I ſaw about the burial place of the Turks a great number of pieces of marble and fine columns A mile to the eaſt of this place are the hot baths mentioned by Strabo, they riſe at the foot of the mountains on each ſide of the bed of a ſmall ſtream, over which there are ruins of a conſiderable bridge, as there are on one ſide of the antient baths, the waters are very hot at the ſources, they have no particular taſte, but by a red ſettlement on the ſtones, and by a yellow ſcum on the top of the water, I concluded that there is in them both iron, and ſulphur, they are much frequented for bathing at a certain time of the year by the common people Between mount Mimas and Erithra, Strabo mentions a village called Cybelia, and the promontory of Melæna, which is probably that to the north of the great bay oppoſite to Scio, at the bottom of which Erithra ſtood, the place now has the ſame name, and is famous for giving birth to the Erithræan Sibyl I was informed that there are ſome marks there of the antient city Between Teos and Erithra, rather nearer to the former, the ſmall town of Era was ſituated Mount Corycus was near Erythre, which Strabo deſcribes as a mountain ſtretching itſelf from north to ſouth, under this mountain to the ſouth of Erithre was the port Caſyſtes, probably that which is now called Gelme, between which and Scio there is a great intercourſe, then followed the port of Erithræ, and feveral others in that bay, which have not at prefent fufficient depth of water for the fhipping e

The inhabitants of this part of the country having a bad character, we could not go to vifit thofe places, but went from Vourla fouth eaft three leagues to Sevrihiffar About half way in this road there is a Turkifh burial place, there is one alfo at Erecui, another at a ruined village called Guzelhiffar, and one near the town of Sevrihiffar, in all which burial places there are feveral pieces of marble and columns, and imperfect infcriptions, which are a proof that there were fome antient buildings in thofe places, particularly at Erecui is the famous infcription, which is called the Curfes of the Teians, and this place may poffibly have its name from having been part of the territory of Eræ At Guzelhiffar there are alfo feveral famous infcriptions relating to the alliances of the Teians Antient writers mention that there was a wood above Clazomene dedicated to Alexander, and that games were performed there by the whole community of Ionia, which were called the Alexandrian games, and from Strabo's account this fpot feems to have been towards the fouth fide of the Ifthmus, becaufe in fpeaking of the breadth of it, he fays, that from the Alexandrian fpot to the fteep ground at Clazomene, it was fix miles and a quarter broad, fo that it is poffible thefe buildings might have fome relation to thofe games, or might be different temples dedicated to Bacchus, who was worfhipped in thefe parts

Sevrihiffar   Sevrihiffar is a large country town, fituated on three heights, there are very few Chriftians in it I faw feveral imperfect infcriptions and

Segigieck   fragments of antiquity about it The town of Segigieck is a league to the fouth weft of it, it is built within a caftle, about half a mile in circumference, and has a very fine fecure harbour d

Teos   Half a league to the fouth of it are the ruins of Teos, now called Bodrun, and on the fouth fide of one of the hills, within the city, are remains of a theatre, which is partly built againft the fide of the hill, the plan of the lower part of

---

e Here are feveral iflands called Hippi by Pliny The Romans granted it privileges to this city on account of its fidelity to the republic during the war in thefe parts Strabo fays, that beyond Coryce was the fmall ifland Halloneus, probably towards the north part of the promontory Argenum, which was the north weft point of that promontory, which is now called cape Corbouron on the weft fide, or rather a hundred and fixty ftadia been the Pofthium in the ifle of Chius

f The little bay which runs the coaft, extend to the north, then winds round to the fouth and eaft, and the land feems in fuch a manner that it appeared like a bafin, concerning which I am the more particular, becaufe it may be the port Cheradis, mentioned by Strabo as north of Teos, who would not eafily be deceived in this particular, as one who had feen the fituation of the port of Teos which he thefe to the fouth and fouth eaft, for the ruin of the antient Teos extend about a mile eaftward to its port, which was at the fouth weft corner of the bay that made the Ifthmus, to

the north of which bay Sevrihiffar is fituated This Ifthmus of the great promontory feems to have been called Chalcis, probably from the antient inhabitants of it, and to have belonged to the Erithraeans, Teius, and Clazomenians, who were diftinguifhed on this Ifthmus by the name of Chalcideus I traced the wall of Teos from its port along the north fide of it up two fmall eminences, from which they turned to the fouth weft, and were carried along on the top of another little hill, which is to the north of the theatre, where I had reafon to think there had been a gate of the city, as it is the great road to the north and weft from this part The wall was built down to the valley, and I fuppofe was carried acrofs the hill to the fouth weft, as far as the other fide, to the bay without the port of Segigieck fo that Teos had the fea to the fouth and fouth weft, though the principal part of the city feems to have been in the vale, extending to the fea between that hill and the fmall hill, which are mentioned to the north, on which the city wall was built

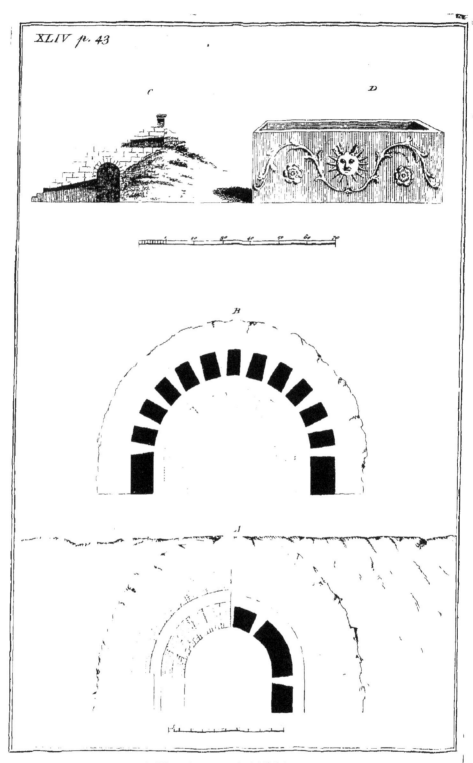

A THEATER at TEOS

it may be feen in the forty-fourth plate at A, together with a view of
the feats, as they may be fuppofed to have been   B is the plan of it,
as it was at the firft gallery, in which the plan of the lower part is
dotted out   C is the fection of the whole, and as the hill was higher towards the middle, fo the feats feem to have been carried up higher, as in
in the theatre at Ephefus, and there was doubtlefs an entrance to them
from the top of the hill, and the wall was built up higher than the gallery, probably to fhelter the people from the weather   It is very pro
bable that from the top of this wall the covering of the theatre was
ftretched, but I could not judge whether it was of the fame height all
round   To the fouth eaft of the theatre are great ruins of a temple, but
all the walls are thrown down   Any one might conjecture that this was
a temple to Bacchus, the deity of the place, as I found it to be, by an
imperfect Greek infcription at it, this temple was an oblong fquare,
built of very large ftones of grey marble   Some of the fine Ionic capitals remain, and moft beautiful pieces of entablature, richly adorned
with fculpture in the higheft tafte   To the fouth eaft of this temple
there are two arched rooms on a hanging ground, which might ferve
for refervoirs of water, the walls which fupport the ground are built
with arches.   Further on to the eaft, and near the theatre, there is an
oblong fquare enclofure, which appears to have had turrets round it
At firft I thought it might have been a public place, or a citadel, and
feeing at one corner fome feats made in the theatrical manner like fteps,
which feemed to be part of a fmall circle, I imagined it might be an
odeum, or fome other place for a fmall auditory, but obferving that
all round within the thick wall there were great ruins for the breadth of
thirty feet, like thofe of a theatre, I concluded that the whole muft have
been defigned for fome public fhews   Towards one corner there are foun
dations of an oblong fquare building, which probably was erected after
the antient building was deftroyed   The towers might ferve for afcents
from without, and there might be femicircular tiers of feats in them, as
I obferved in fome   On the outfide of the north eaft corner of this
enclofure there are feveral pieces of marble fluted pillars, and beautiful
entablatures, fome of which were unfinifhed, but I could fee they were
of the Corinthian order, it is probable that they worked the ftones here
for the building, which I could perceive had been cafed with marble, and
I faw likewife a pediment of an entrance to the building, but it is not
to be wondered at that all the ftones of the fabric have been carried
away, as it is fo near the fea   The fhape of this building is not fo proper for a circus, and having feen juft fuch another at Ephefus, to which
there feemed to have been a canal from the lake near the temple of
Diana, made me conclude that both the one and the other might be a
naumachium, there being a river near this of Teos, which on occafion
might be turned into it.

The port of Teos was on the weft fide of the bay, and defended
from the fouth wind by a mole extending about a furlong to the eaft,
and was near thirty paces broad, there are remains of the ftone work
about it, and it feems to have been made by hollowing out a bafin
within it, which is now choaked up, but as there is a fmall rivulet
which runs into it, by the help of floodgates, it might have been made

a very

a very advantageous fituation for fhipping. About a mile to the north of Teos there is a high rocky mount, and on the weft fide of it a fmall lake in a deep bafin, which, as the people imagine, feeds all the fountains about the country, to the fouth of this there is a hollow ground, where there are near twenty large pieces of grey marble, each of which is cut out into feveral fteps, they are of fuch a fize that it would be very difficult to move them, it feems as if other pieces had been cut off from them, and yet, that part of them at leaft, was defigned for fome building, for on one of them I faw thefe letters Loco IIII, as if it were to fhew the part of the building they were defigned for Teos is placed by the Tables twelve miles from Smyrna, which feems to be a miftake for twenty-two, for it is computed to be nine hours from that city, and Ptolemy places it fixteen minutes both to the fouth and weft of it, tho' both thefe diftances feem to be rather too little This place is famous for the birth of the lyric poet Anacreon There are alfo about this place feveral infcriptions, which contain the alliances of the Teians

I was recommended to a perfon of Vourla, who received me in his houfe, fhewed me every thing in that neighbourhood, and went with me on the fourth to Sevirhiflar, where we could not meet with any accommodations, and fo we came on to to Segigieck, and I lay every night on board a Dutch fhip, being recommended to the captain of it, for there was no convenient place in the town for ftrangers I went out every day to fee the antiquities of Teos and the neighbouring places There were many remarkable places in this country to which I could not go with fafety. Myonnefus was to the eaft of Teos, fituated on a height on a peninfula Lebedus was fifteen miles to the eaft of Teos, which feems to have been on a fmall bay within the great one, the two bays are divided by the ifland Afpis or Arconefus, which I take to be the long ifland about the middle of this bay, which ftretches to the fouth weft, and is now called Carabafh [The black Safh] from fome imaginary refemblance Some feditious people of Teos having fled to Ephefus, were fent by Attalus to Myonnefus, and began to fortify that place in oppofition to the Teians, but on their applying to the Romans, they were received at Lebedus, which was then very thinly inhabited. Fifteen miles further to the eaft was Colophon, which probably was on the fmall bay, which is to the north weft of the bay of Ephefus, for it was but feven miles and a half in a direct line from that city, that is, probably from its port at the mouth of the Cayfter, but it was fifteen miles if they failed round by the bay This is one of the places which contended for the birth of Homer To the weft of it was mount Corac̄ius, and a little further weft was the ifland of Diana, which might be a fmall ifland near the fhore towards the north eaft corner of the great bay which is to the weft of the fuppofed Colophon, concerning which ifland Strabo relates in extraordinary fuperftition.

C H A P.

CHAP. III.

Of Scala Nuova, and Ephesus.

I Embarked on the ninth at Segigieck on board an open boat for Scala Scala Nuova, and arrived there in the evening. This town is situated on the side of a rising ground over the bay of Ephesus, at the distance of three leagues west south west of Ephesus; it stands on the north side of a head of land that stretches to the west. The port is defended against westerly winds by a small island, which has a tower on it, but it is somewhat exposed to the northerly wind. The town or castle, as it may be called, is about three quarters of a mile in circumference. To the north of it there is a large suburb, in which are some of the principal bazars or shops, the Christians live on the side of a high hill to the west, they have about two hundred houses; there is one church in the town, and another in a ruinous condition on the top of the hill, which is called saint Elias. The archbishop of Ephesus, to whom I was recommended, lives at the church in the town. He told me there were formerly thirty-two bishops in his province, but at present he has not one diocesan under him. The castle here belongs to the high admiral, who puts in a governour. The town is under an aga subject to the pasha of Guzelhissar. This place is a mart that supplies all the neighbouring countries, and Samos with rice, coffee, flax and hemp imported from Ægypt, coarse woollen cloth from Salonica, cotton and callicoes from Smyrna, and many other things from other parts, and they export corn to Samos, and the neighbouring islands. They have vineyards in great abundance about the town, but the wine is not very good, tho' Ephesus was formerly famous for wine, but they dry a great quantity of raisins, which they export to Ægypt. It was late in the evening when we landed at Scala Nuova, and three of the janizaries went with me to the house of the archbishop of Ephesus. They stand so much in awe of the soldiers, that my conductors were first had in to the archbishop and entertained by him, and in the mean time I was served with a collation in another room. When the janizaries were gone I was introduced to him. He was a venerable old man, and dressed like the Greek priests, except that he had on a red mohair scarf. The next day I took lodgings in the kane, and by the help of some other persons to whom I was recommended, I procured a proper Turk to go with me to Ephesus.

We arrived at the village of Aiasolouk, to the north east of the ancient Aiasolouk city of Ephesus, where I lodged in a kane, which served also for a stable, Ephesus there being sophas and chimneys all round for the convenience of travellers. The Turk that conducted me made me sensible that it was necessary to make presents of coffee to two of the governors in the castle, and I spent three or four days in this place, viewing the antiquities, not without being molested at night with large caravans that were going from Smyrna to Guzelhissar. The prophesy in the Revelation, that the candlestick should be taken from this place is so literally fulfilled, that there is not so much as one Christian within two leagues of the place

There is a plain towards the sea about a league broad, extending to the north east corner of the bay, where the great promontory begins, which extends westward to Scio At a little distance from the sea this plain widens in a circular form, and there is a narrow vale to the south, which extends about half a league in between the mountains, and at the north east corner of the great plain is the entrance to that narrow vale between the hills through which the Cayster runs This river makes a great number of windings as it passes through the plain, and particularly towards the south west part of it, where it winds so much like the Mæander, that the Turks call it, The little Mandras Whether the mouth of the river is any way obstructed, as it seems to have been in Strabo's time, or that the lakes have not a proper vent, especially that which is near the temple of Diana, or that the fosses are filled up, by which the waters were drained off, whatever is the reason of it, a great part of the plain, especially to the south of the river, is a morass, and hardly passable after great rains On the west side of the plain I saw those lakes mentioned by the antients, one of which was called Selenusia, that belonged to the temple of Diana, but was taken from it by the kings, I suppose, of Pergamus, and restored again by the Romans These lakes brought in a great revenue, doubtless by the fish they produced , at one of them was the temple of the king, said to be the work of Agamemnon, and I observed a high ground to the north of the river towards the lakes, which seemed to have had some building on it, that possibly might be this temple To the north west of the lakes mount Galesius stretches away to Colophon Where the plain begins to widen into a circular form, there is a hill on each side , that to the north of the Cayster, I take to be the hill through which, according to Dr Smith's account, there is an extraordinary way cut in the rock , that to the south is near the high mountains which encompass the plain This mount had the name of Prion, and afterwards of Lepre , it has two summits a and b, as represented in the forty-fifth plate , there is a hollow ground between them c, part of the east wall of the city was on the highest summit of the hill at d, and was carried along the south side of the hill at c, it crossed the vale in three places at f, was built at g up the side of mount Corissus, and was then built along the height of it for about a mile to the west at h, and turning to the north west for half a mile at i, and afterwards to the north east at k, it crossed a little hill at l, on which is the tower m, called the prison of St Paul, which is a building with Gothic arches, from that tower it descends to the lake P, which is to the west of the temple of Diana O This famous temple is about a furlong to the west of the first mentioned hill of Lepre, the wall then turns north at p, going by the lake to the west of the temple, and turning to the east at q, it is carried along upon a little eminence, and so passes north of that building r, which is near the circus s, beyond which it turns for a little way to the south at t, and goes up the hill, crossing it as mentioned before This was the situation of Ephesus when it was in its glory The part of the town K, at the foot of mount Corissus, was called Aspera The whole compass

Ephefus, its was

A PLAN of EPHESUS and of a BUILDING in that CITY

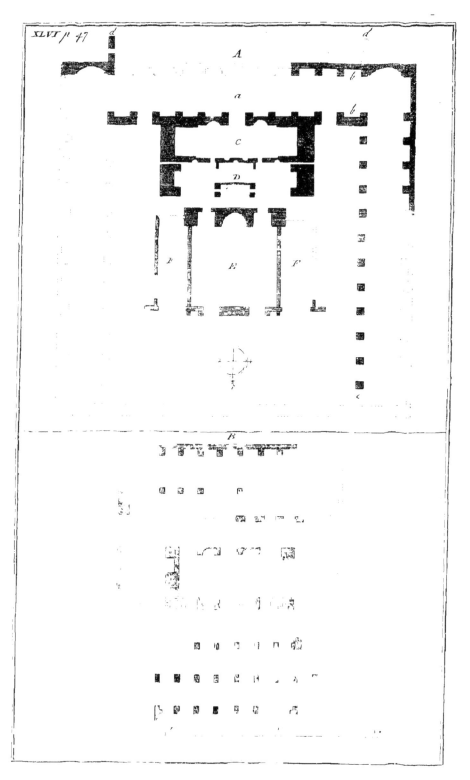

PLANS OF BUILDINGS AT EPHESUS

of the walls which I traced, are about four miles, they are built in a ruſtic manner, are caſed with hewn ſtone, and defended by ſquare towers, in ſome parts the walls remain almoſt entire, in others one ſees the foundations only, which are ten feet thick

Before Epheſus was ſo large a city, it had changed its ſite more than Its hiſtory once The Leleges and Carians firſt built a city here, probably on mount Lepre, theſe being almoſt diſpoſſeſſed by Androclus, he with his people ſettled at the ſouth eaſt foot of mount Lepre, about the place where, I ſuppoſe, the Gymnaſium was afterwards built at u, and alſo on the ſide of mount Coriſſus The part behind mount Lepre was called Opiſtholepria, and the quarter between the hills was that which was inhabited by the Smyrnæans, and was called in diſtinction from other parts, the city of Smyrna The Smyrnæans ſeparating themſelves from the Epheſians, ſettled where Smyrna now is In the time of Crœſus, the Epheſians left this higher ſituation, and came down to the plain, about the temple of Dana. Lyſimachus, one of the generals of Alexander the great, built the preſent walls, called the city Arſinoe from his wife, and was obliged to make uſe of a ſtratagem to bring the citizens back to the more advantagious high ſituation, by ſtopping privately the public ſhores, and ſo in a manner overflowing the low ground And by the ruins one may ſee that the lower parts of the hill were inhabited every way, and likewiſe much of the weſt part of mount Lepre, there ſeems alſo to have been a ſuburb on the ſouth ſide of Lepre, and near a mile from the ſouth eaſt corner of it, to that hill, about which the preſent village of Aiaſalouk is ſituated at w, on the hill x there is a Turkiſh caſtle, round the top of the hill there are great ruins of thick walls built of brick, with many ſmall arches, which ſeem to be of the time of the Greek emperors, though it might have been inhabited before as a ſuburb of Epheſus

To the eaſt of mount Lepre they had their burial places I ſaw there Antiquity a very large marble coffin, with an imperfect inſcription on it, and I had reaſon to think that they had alſo grots cut into the rock for depoſiting their bodies, there are ſeveral arches all round the hill, on which it is probable they built their houſes, and on ſome of them are ruins of an aqueduct, for I ſaw the channel in which the water ran It is probable that this part alſo was encloſed with a wall that might extend to the cayſter, and on the low ground between the hill and the village of Aiaſalouk, there are remains of many ſquare pillars, made of ſingle ſtones laid one on another, on which it is probable they turned arches, and built their houſes on them. I ſuppoſe the ruin u, at the ſouth eaſt corner of the hill, was the Gymnaſium, which ſeems to have been in Gymnaſium that place, where formerly there was a building, probably of the ſame nature, called the Athenæum, there are great and magnificent remains of it; the ſpot near this was called the Hypaleum, probably becauſe there was ſome plantation of olives there, a plan of the great remains of this building may be ſeen at A, in the forty-fifth plate, it is a very ſolid fabric, the outer walls are of brick and ſtone, there being four or five tiers of each alternately, the inner walls are built of large ſtone, on which the arches of brick were turned A gallery or portico ranged all round, that to the ſouth at a, had on each ſide large arched niches b b,

which

which in the outer wall were continued all round, and there is within a colonade c on each fide. From the front of this building at A there is an entrance to a ftately room C, which leads to another D, and that to a third at E, on each fide of which there was another apartment F. All this was doubtlefs cafed with marble, as the temple of Diana, and fome other buildings of Ephefus appear to have been. At the fouth eaft corner of this building a wall d extends a little way to the fouth, with an entrance through it, which made me think that the wall fuppofed to have been built at the eaft foot of mount Lepre joyned on here, and that it was continued on to mount Coriffus, for I faw fome ruins that way of a wall, and alfo heaps of ruins like towers. There are alfo remains of a ftone wall, at fome diftance to the fouth, which probably enclofed a court before the Gymnafium.

On the fides of mount Lepre and Coriffus, as well as in the valley between them, there are ftill great ruins to be feen of the antient city, where, I fuppofe, that part of the city, antiently called Smyrna, ftood, and continuing on to the weft, the fouth part of mount Lepre is hollowed in by cutting away the rock, and before this are remains of the front of a theatre at y, which I fhould conjecture to be the new theatre, as it muft have been built after the great theatre, which is near the temple of Diana, becaufe by the remains of it, it appears to have been built in a very elegant tafte, a plan and view of it may be feen in the forty feventh plate at B, C, three arches of hewn ftone remain entire, within which are built niches with a fhell at top, and over each there is an oblong fquare window. When Antony extended the privilege of the afylum of the temple of Diana, as far as two bow fhot, which is fomething more than two ftadia, and thereby took in part of the city, and probably the great theatre, the citizens might at that time build this theatre, in order to avoid being molefted with the company of thofe who took refuge there. A few paces further to the weft, there are remains of a femicircular building Z, which feems to have had feats in it, made like fteps, as in theatres, and is built in a ruftick manner with pilafters on the outfide at equal diftances. This might poffibly ferve for an odeum or theatre for mufic, a plan of it may be feen at F in the forty feventh plate. A little further on there are great ruins as of a ftrong gateway, and of walls extending from it on each fide up the hills at K, which probably was built to defend the city againft the people of the afylum, when their privileges extended fo far. Beyond this, at the foot of mount Lepre, there are very imperfect remains of a ftrong brick building, a little further is the fouth weft corner of the hill, and to the weft of it is the plain, in which are the ruins of the temple of Diana, and feveral other public buildings; the theatre I, is near oppofite to it, at the fouth weft corner of the hill, the Circus S, being near the north weft corner. When all thefe buildings were ftanding, they muft have made a moft glorious appearance, for few cities have had the advantages of Ephefus for building, mount Lepre and Coriffus being rocks of ftone and marble, fo that they had nothing to do but to dig out the marble, and roll it down to the places where they defigned to build. The like to the weft of the temple of Diana, was probably a fort of port, into which they could bring all thofe fine marbles, that

were

5

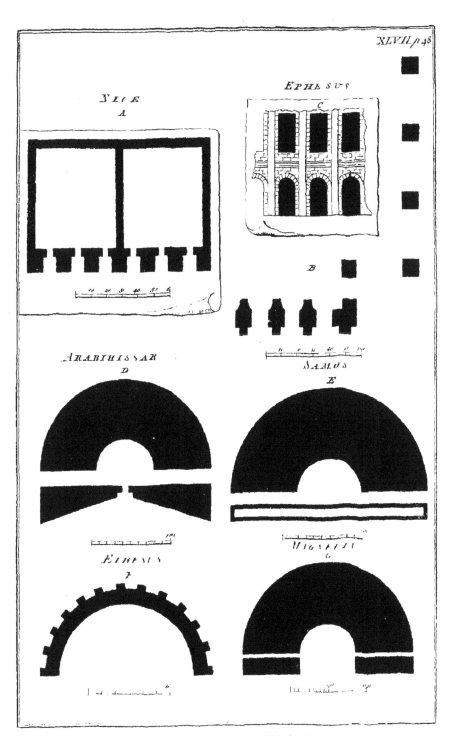

NICE
A

EPHESUS
C

B

ARABIHISSAR
D

SAMOS
E

EPHESUS
F

MIGNESIA
G

REMAINS of ANTIENT THEATERS

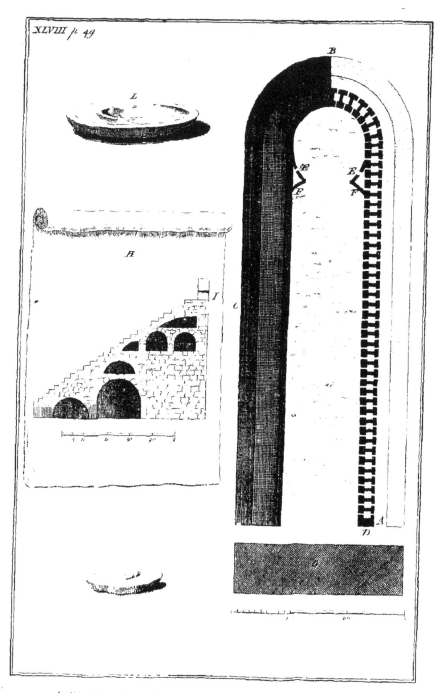

A PLAN and SECTION of the CIRCUS at EPHESUS

were the produce of foreign countries, close to the very spot they built on, which made this quarter so proper for their public buildings, and being full of them, the city did not suffer much in permitting it to be an asylum   The plain A, which is to the west of mount Lepre, is about a quarter of a mile broad from east to west, and half a mile long; at the north east corner of it there is a small rocky hill B, between which and the Circus, there was a road or street c, paved with large stones, many of which are eight feet long and four wide; to the east of this road, was the Circus S, and north of it another large building   There is a plan of the Circus in the forty eighth plate[a]   On the north side it is built on a gallery A, the seats on the south C, being built up the side of mount Lepre, there are arches to the north in a line from D, in order to support the lower seats, these make so many apartments, above them there were three more tiers of arches on which the seats were built, as may be seen in the section H.   I could not find out any staircases, and I rather think that they descended to the seats from the hill on the south side, and went round on the gallery at top, or ascended by the seats from the bottom   The outside wall was of large rusticated hewn stone, and, what is very particular, towards the end of the Circus, there is a wall E, built with a large entrance in the middle, which with the end of the Circus makes a circle, and from it to the west other walls F are built, which taking in the wide entrance in the middle is near a semicircle. Whether or no these were carceres from which the coursers started, or whether it has been erected since it was used as a Circus, I will not pretend to determine, the wall is not built in the best manner   The end of the hill G, to the west of the Circus, and of the road, appears plainly to have served for the spectators, and to have had seats on it; and on the top of it there is a fine Ionic entablature, which made me conclude, that the ornamental parts of the Circus were of that order. Round the top of the Circus at I, there are arched windows or entrances about forty feet apart, and three feet wide, which might serve for the people to enter from the side of the hill, and also to give air, if they covered the place when they exhibited their sports.   To the south west of the Circus there is a well turned arch at D, in the plan of Ephesus, which seems to have been an entrance to some building, round at the spring of the arch, and in the two fronts it is adorned with the cornish of the Ionic order, which were probably taken from the Circus, as well as the white marble, with which the arch is built   It appears that some narrow building had been carried on to the east of it, but whether for a church, or for what other use I could not conjecture   On the stones of this arch are several pieces of inscriptions, which, as they are put together without any order, have puzzled the learned to explain them, on a supposition, that the letters originally followed one another in the order, in which they are seen in this place   There is also a relief of a person on horseback, with his garment flowing behind, before the horse there is a cypress tree, a serpent is represented twining round it, which with its head makes at the horseman, and a dog at the tree, is in a posture is leaping towards the ferpent. To the north of the Circus there are remains of a very large and magnificent building r, with a road or ftreet between it, and the Circus; the ground is raifed on each fide of the road, as if there had been fteps there, or fome other buildings, the ruins of which have raifed the ground, efpecially on the fide of the Circus, and I faw feveral pedeftals on each fide of the road   The great building mentioned to the north of the Circus was raifed on high arched rooms, which open to the north, where, I fuppofe, the city wall run ⋅ To the north of it the ground is very low, and poffibly a canal might be cut from the river to this place, and they might land their goods before thefe arched places, which might ferve for warehoufes; and the magnificent building above might be a forum for the merchants of this city, which was the greateft mart on this fide mount Taurus . This building feems to have confifted of large pillars of hewn ftone, on which arches of brick might be turned, a plan of it may be feen at E in the forty-fifth plate ; in the middle the architecture is different, where it is probable there was a ftatue, there appeared to have been a wall on the north fide of this building, probably to fecure it from the cold wind   Beyond this to the eaft there is a high ground, which extends near as far as the Circus; this ground was fupported by the city wall, which went near the end of the Circus, and one of the city gates was, without doubt, between this high ground and the Circus.   Going to the fouth along the plain, I obferved a large bafon fifteen feet diameter at F ; it is of one ftone of red and white marble, and is fhaped within in a particular manner, as it is drawn at K, in the forty-eighth plate, and, as I remember, is fomething like that of St. Victor at Marfeilles, and doubtlefs was ufed for facrifices, though they have a tradition that St. John baptized in it   This vafe lies on the ground, which has grown up round it, though doubtlefs it was fomewhat raifed, and a vafe of fuch great weight muft have been placed on a ftrong foundation to fupport it . Near this vafe there are remains of a fmall femicircular building for fome large ftatue   To the weft of this there are ruins of a ftone building G, which I concluded was a church, becaufe the eaft end of it is femicircular, and to the weft of it there is a brick building of the fame kind H, with large open arches on each fide, a plan of it may be feen in the fiftieth plate at X, and probably it was defigned for the fame ufe as the other.   Returning to the large bafon, and going along to the weft of mount Lepre, we came to the remains of a very confiderable building at L, moftly built of brick, a plan of it may be feen at B in the forty-fixth plate. It is poffible this might be fome public building belonging to the people of the afylum, it may be their forum, as it very much refembles the building I have already defcribed near the Circus   Between this and the temple of Diana there is a hollow ground, in which there is fome water, this might antiently ferve for a bafon   Further fouth at I, is the great theatre facing to the weft, and hollowed into the hill, a plan of it, and a view of the feats may be feen in the forty-ninth plate at A and B ², a fection down the middle is reprefented at F², and another at D, at the end of the feats, which is taken as it

² Thefe ought to have been reverfed

would

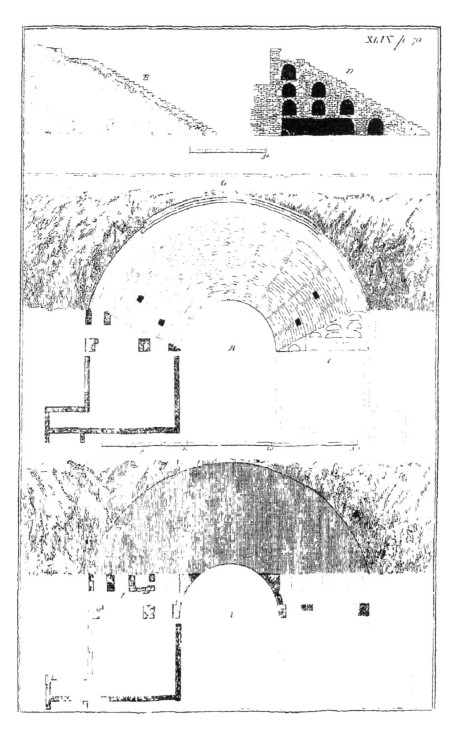

A THEATER AT EPHESUS

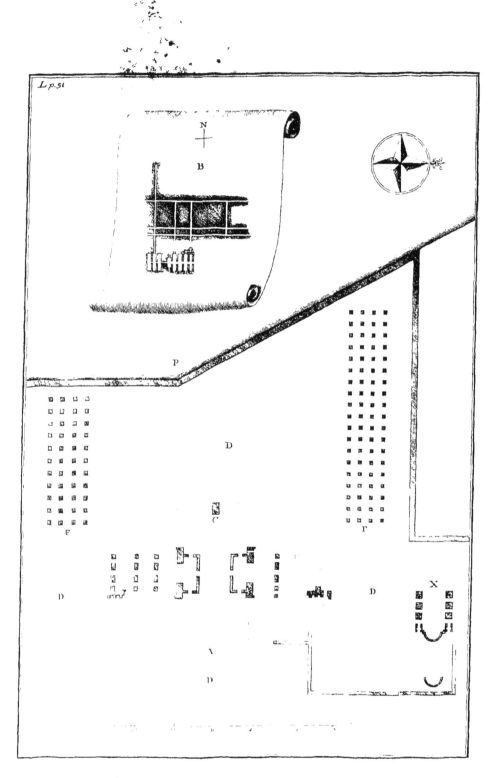

A PLAN of the TEMPLE of DIANA at EPHESUS

would appear at F, it had two entrances on each fide, and the feats of
it were carried up the hill to a great height, and continued up the back
part of it at G, feveral feet higher than on the fides; there feem to have
been but four vomitoria; fo that the greateft part of the fpectators muft
have either defcended from the hill into the theatre, or afcended from
the bottom   By the manner in which the ground lies, one may fee that
there have been great buildings to the weft of the theatre, and to the
fouth of them there is a fquare M, which is funk down, and has a hanging ground all round within, as if there had been feats, which gave me
reafon to conjecture that it might have been a naumachium, and particularly, as I obferved, to the weft a hollow ground, like the bed of
a canal, extending towards the lake near the temple of Diana, by which
the water might be let into the bafon   There feems to have been a colonade round at the top of the feats, and I faw feveral rough pedeftals,
and pillars of grey granite lying about the place, and a broken
capital, which was either of the Corinthian or compofit order: Near it,
on the foot of mount Coriffus, there is a fmall heap of ruins at N, in
which there are fome of the fineft pieces of architecture I ever faw, the
columns are fluted, and meafured thirty feet in length; the entablature
is cut in very large pieces of marble, and adorned with carvings, which
fhew it was of the Corinthian order   By the beft judgment I could make
there were only four columns, which probably fupported a pavilion, under
which fome coloffal ftatue (perhaps that of Diana of Ephefus) might be
placed, and as it was probably at the end of the ftreets, and commanded all thefe buildings, it was a very advantageous fituation; and I obferved in a line from the road or ftreet, at the end of the Circus, fome
columns of grey granite ftanding, as if they had formed a colonade on
each fide of a ftreet, which paffed to the eaft of the ftone bafon of the
great building near the theatre, and of the naumachium, and croffed
the ftreet that went under the pavilion, and continued along eaftward
to the hills.

The temple of Diana is fituated towards the fouth weft corner of the The temple of Diana.
plain at O, having a lake P, on the weft fide of it, now become a morafs,
extending weftward to the Cayfter. The plan of this temple may
be feen in the fiftieth plate. This building, and the courts about it, were
encompaffed every way with a ftrong wall; that to the weft on the lake,
and to the north was likewife the wall of the city, there is a double
wall to the fouth, and within thefe walls were four courts D, that is, one
on every fide of the temple, and on each fide of the court to the weft,
there was a large open portico or colonade E, extending to the lake, on
which arches of brick were turned for a covering The front of the
temple A was to the eaft. The temple was built on arches, to which
there is a defcent, I went a great way in till I was either ftopped by
earth fallen down, or by the water, they confift of feveral narrow arches
one within another B is a plan of what I faw of them. It is probable
they extended to the porticos on each fide of the weftern court, and
ferved for foundations to thofe pillars This being a morafsy ground,
made the expence of fuch a foundation fo neceffary, on which, it is
faid, is much was beftowed is on the fabrick above ground, it is probable

bable alſo that the ſhores of the city paſſed this way into the lake   I ſaw a great number of pipes made of earthen ware in theſe paſſages; but it may be queſtioned whether they were to convey the filth of the city under theſe paſſages, or the water from the lake to the baſin, which was to the eaſt of the temple, or to any other part of the city   In the front of the temple there ſeems to have been a grand portico at A   Before this part there lay three pieces of red granite pillars, each being about fifteen feet long, and one of grey, broken into two pieces, they were all three feet and a half in diameter, there are four pillars of the former ſort in the moſque of Saint John, at the village of Aıaſalouk   I ſaw alſo a fine entablature; and on one of the columns in the moſque there is a moſt beautiful compoſit capital, which, without doubt, belonged to it   There are great remains of the pillars of the temple, which were built of large hewn ſtone, and probably caſed with marble, but from what I ſaw of one part, I had reaſon to conclude that arches of brick were turned on them, and that the whole temple, as well as theſe pillars, was incruſted with rich marbles · On the ſtone work of the middle grand apartment there are a great number of ſmall holes, as if deſigned in order to fix the marble caſing   It is probable that the ſtatue of the great goddeſs Diana of the Epheſians was either in the grand middle compartment, or oppoſite to it at C.

To the north of the forum I ſaw an old channel, which made me think that a canal might be brought from the Cayſter to that part, and ſo along by the city walls to the lake, by which means they could always command the water for their boats and ſhipping, if this really was the port.

The preſent village of Aıaſalouk appears to have been a conſiderable Mahometan town from the great number of moſques about it, which are moſtly built with cupolas.   The tradition of two or three churches, that particularly of the ſeven ſleepers with their grot near it R, ſhew that old Epheſus was inhabited before the Saracens conquered this country, though the large moſque of Saint John at the village is falſly ſaid to have been a church, the front is of white marble poliſhed, and it is a ſtately building covered with lead   An aqueduct of many arches at T, which ſeems to have been built in the middle ages, goes from the eaſtern hills to the caſtle, there are ſeveral inſcriptions on it, and over the old caſtle-gate there are two very fine reliefs

All the way from Epheſus to Scala Nuova (which is ſouth ſouth weſt of it) one ſees on the ſide of the hills to the eaſt, another antient aqueduct, it conſiſts of a very low wall on which the channel was made for the water: There are remains likewiſe of two parts of the aqueduct acroſs two valleys, that which is neareſt to Epheſus is the longeſt, it is in a fine vale, about two miles from the city walls, the arches, which are low, extend about a furlong in length . As they are ill built of rough ſtone, I concluded that the old aqueduct had been ruined, and that this might be a building of the middle ages, to the north of this aqueduct one ſees ſome ruins, and particularly on an advanced ground, which ſuppoſing this to be Pygela, might be the temple of Diana Munychia, built by Agamemnon   This ſituation of Pygela agrees beſt with the order

of

of Strabo's account, who goes from that place to the port of Panormus and the temple of Diana, and then to Ephesus For afterwards, as if returning towards the sea shoar, he mentions Ortygia as near the sea, where there was a fine grove, through which the rivulet Cenchrius ran , this possibly might be to the west of those hills, on which the south wall of Ephesus was built, between which and another hill to the south, there is a small bed of a winter torrent, which passes also by Pygela, and possibly might be the Cenchrius There are several fables of this place in relation to the delivery of Latona, the mother of Apollo and Diana, and of the nurse Ortygia, who gave occasion to the name of it. Mount Solmissus, which was over the grove, I suppose to be the hill to the south of it, and to the west of the road , on this, they say, the Curetæ stood, and frightened Juno with their arms, who lay in wait to disturb Latona at the time of her delivery, being envious of her happiness, in bringing forth two such children as Apollo and Diana , a story that would be well worthy of the ridicule of such a pen as Lucian's Continuing in the road to Scala Nuova, I saw the other part of the aqueduct on the south west side of the same vale, there being a hill in this vale between these two parts of the aqueduct, I could see no sign of arches in it, being only a solid wall, with a channel towards the bottom of it arched over , this channel is four feet high, and two wide , the ground here is rather high , but whether this large channel is a part of the other aqueduct, or more antient, and that another channel run on the top of the wall, joining to the other parts of the aqueduct, in order to convey the water to the higher parts of the city, may be difficult to determine, only, I observed, that the wall, though of rough stone, is well built, and seemed to be very antient Crossing over a hill, we came to another vale which leads to a little bay, within which there is a small lake . To the south of this bay there are some ruins on a hill, and a high wall, which has two or three arches in it, crosses the road ; it seems to have been an aqueduct to convey the water to this town or village, from the aqueduct of Ephesus, which runs near it on the side of the hill This place is about two miles from Scala Nuova, thought to be Neapolis, which probably was somewhere near it, and, as I supposed, might be on the small peninsula near the town ; for they have a tradition that this town is not above two hundred years old, and it is not unlikely that the town of Aiasalouk or Ephesus declined on the trade taking a turn this way.

About sixteen miles to the south of Scala Nuova there is a Christian village called Changlee, to which I did not go , it is supposed to be the antient Panionium, where the meeting of the twelve cities of Ionia was held, and a solemn sacrifice performed to Neptune Heliconius, in which the people of Priene presided , it was at the foot of mount Mycale, to the north of which was mount Pactyes in the Ephesian territory There are some ruins at an uninhabited place called Sapso, which is also the modern name of that mountain , this is supposed to be Priene, the native place of Bias, one of the seven wise men The country at the foot of mount Mycale, which was nearest to Samos, belonged to that island, and so did the city Neapolis, by an exchange with the Ephesians for Marathesium

CHAP. IV.

Of Guzelhissar, the antient Magnesia, on the Mæander.

AFTER our return from Ephesus we went to Samos, I stayed there sometime waiting for a passport from Constantinople, and returning to Scala Nuova, where the plague raged at that time, I set out on the thirteenth of February for Guzelhissar, which is twenty four miles south east and by east from Scala Nuova. Having travelled twelve miles we came to the east side of the mountains, which extend from north to south, and joyn to mount Sapson, which is opposite to Samos. These mountains must be the antient Pactyes, mentioned as stretching from the territory of Ephesus to mount Mycale, to which the mountains Mesogis joyned, being those which run from east to west on the north side of the Mæander, as mount Latmus does on the south of it. We lay the first night in a coffee-house at Jermanseik, which is nine hours from Scala Nuova. Having passed the mountains, we came into the fine plains of the Mæander. This river rises in Phrygia at the mountains of the Celeni, and runs into the sea at Priene. The southern hills come very near it, but the northern mountains in many parts are at the distance of two or three leagues. At first it runs in Phrygia, then divides Lydia from Caria, and afterwards is the boundary between Caria and Ionia; it is well known that the many extraordinary turnings of this river has given the name of Mæander to all such sort of windings.

Guzelhissar [The Fair Castle] is the antient Magnesia on the Mæander, which Strabo describes as on a plain spot [a], at mount Thorax, but it was on a hill level at the top, about three miles in compass, having a steep hanging ground all round, it is indeed very plain ground, except that on the east side there are some eminences, from which there is a very steep precipice down to the deep bed of a stream that runs to the east of the present city, which is at the south foot of the hill. Magnesia was about half a league from the Mæander, and is described as nearer to the river Lethreus, which probably is a large stream about two miles to the west, that runs between the mountains Mesogis, and, I suppose, rises at mount Pactyes, as it is described. The situation of this place is very delightful, commanding a view of the fine plain of the Mæander, which is broad towards the west, the view extends to the sea, and from the height I saw the Agathoniff islands, which are near Patmos. Mount Thorax is to the north, which is covered with snow. The foot of that hill extends to the city, being divided only by the bed of a torrent. Adjoining to that mountain there is a situation of the same kind, except that to the north it is contiguous to the hill, and is not altogether so strong. What adds to the prospect of this place, is a most beautiful enclosed country to the south and west, and the fields are planted with fig and almond trees, the

I   modern

modern city also adds to the beauty of the view, which being large, and there being courts and gardens to the houses, improved with cypress and orange trees, and some of the streets also planted with trees, it makes it appear like a city in a wood, and round it there are a great number of gardens, divided into squares, by rows of orange-trees in a more regular manner than is commonly seen in these parts. This is one of the first of those cities between Ephesus and Antioch on the Maander, which were of a mixed race, and not properly Ionians, being composed of Lydians, Carians, and Greeks, for anciently the people were ranked according to their different tribes, till the Romans divided the country into diocefes, which consisted of such a number of neighbouring cities as could most conveniently go to the city where the conventus or meeting for distributing justice was held, by which they broke that union which was among particular cities, by taking away all distinctions of people, and united them very politically all together under the Roman government. The Magnesians were of Greek original, and thought to be Delphians, who inhabited the mountains Didymi in Thesfaly. Magnesia, probably a city still older, which might be in another situation, was destroyed by the Treres of Cimbria, and was afterwards possessed by the Milesians. There was a flight wall round the city, only four feet thick, as they were so well defended by nature. On the hills to the east there were many buildings, now entirely destroyed, and probably they had there a strong fortrefs. There are figns of many great buildings all over the city, but they are ruined in such a manner, that, except two or three, it is difficult to judge of what nature they were. Towards the south east corner of the city there are very imperfect remains of a theatre, hollowed out of the hill to the east, which by its height, I judged could not have lefs than fifty degrees of feats, all that remains of it is an arched entrance on each fide. Near the theatre there is an aqueduct under ground, by which water is conveyed to the present city, as it was, without doubt, to the old one. The water is brought from the mountains at some distance, and crofles a narrow vale on some high arches. To the west of the theatre there are a great number of large pieces of marble entablatures, and other remains of buildings. Here the Armenians have an altar and a burial place, and there might have been a church on this spot built with the materials of fome other great edifice, which seems to have been there. Further west, at the Jews burial place, there are more ruins, and to the west of that, there are two or three very thick walls, which are not of the best workmanship. To the north also there are remains of the east end of a large church, and a furlong more to the east are very great ruins, which feem to be of some magnificent large palace. At the foot of the eastern hills are several arched rooms. On the north fide of the city there are ruins of a very grand temple, which must be that of Diana Leucophryne, and was the largest in Afia after the temples of Ephefus and Didymi, and though it yielded to Ephefus in its riches, yet it exceeded it in its proportions, and in the exquifite architecture. It appears to have been arched underneath moftly with large hewn ftone, the principal front feems to have been to the fouth, where there are remains of a colonade, which may be feen at A, in the fifty first plate, it feems, to be a portico made with a particular fort of pillars, often feen in thefe parts, which may be either called oval, or confidered as a femi-circular pilafter on two fides of a fquare pillar, which fets out about an inch beyond the pilafters, a plan of one of them, reprefented at large, may be feen at B At the Francifcan convent of Trinita de Monti in Rome, there are likewife two oval capitals, a plan and drawings of which may be feen in the fifty fecond plate[b], and in the Maffimi palace at Rome, there are two modern pillars of the fame figure as thefe of Magnefia On the north fide there are three very maffive entire arches, which are about forty feet high; the work over them is brick, from which an arch feems to have been turned to the fouth, probably to three other arches of the fame kind, to the weft of thefe, at fome diftance there, is a thick wall, which probably enclofed the whole, and to the north of them are arches under ground, over which there might be a portico. On the fouth fide of the hill, in the way to the prefent town, there are fome walls which appear to have belonged to a very magnificent build-ing of great extent, and I obferved among them fome pieces of pillars of verd antique, and at this place, and in another part of the town I faw the ca-pital of a fquare pilafter, which is of a particular kind, as reprefented at C. On one fide of this building there are two or three rooms; a plan of the building may be feen at D, in the fifty-firft plate In the fide of the hill there are many fepulchral grots to the eaft The prefent city is to the weft of the ftream I have mentioned before; it extends up the fide of the hill to the north, and is encompaffed with very flight walls, it has a large fuburb to the fouth, and another to the eaft. The other fide of the rivulet is inhabited moftly by Chriftians, the Greeks and Armenians have their churches there, and the latter a bifhop, who, I fuppofe, is archbifhop of Ephefus The town is not lefs than four miles in compafs, and the ftreets broader, and better laid out than commonly are feen in Turkifh cities There are alfo many Jews here, and it is a place of great trade, efpecially for cotton, and cotton yarn, which are fent to Smyrna, and exported to Europe They have alfo manufactures of coarfe callicoes, and their merchants are generally rich, it is likewife a mart for all fuch things as are imported from Europe, Ægypt, and other parts, for the ufe of the country, for fixty miles eaftward, near as far as thofe parts that are fupplied from Satalia, and other fouthern ports There are alfo feveral great families of Turks who live here, many of them are Beys, a title they give to fons of pafhas, thefe have their eftates about the city The pafha of this country refides here; fo that altogether it is one of the moft confiderable places in Afia.

[b] Thefe drawings were procured by the learned and accurate abbot Revillas of Rome

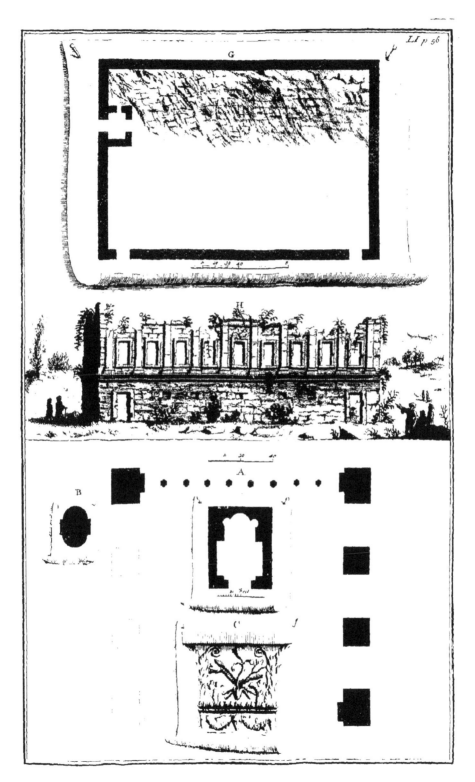

OVAL CAPITALS OF ROME

CHAP. V.

Of CARIA in general, and of the antient ALABANDA.

FROM Guzelhiſſar I croſſed the Mæander on the fifteenth into Caria   The Carians were firſt called Leleges, inhabited the iſlands, and were ſubject to Minos, they poſſeſſed themſelves of the continent, which belonged both to the Leleges and Pelaſgi, and were drove out of it by the Greeks, Ionians, and Dorians   The river Mæander is here about half a furlong broad ; it is a rapid ſtream, and the bed of it was at this time full, the rivulet at Guzelhiſſar, and ſome others that run into it overflowing, make the country a moraſs for a mile from the Mæander   There is a large cauſeway acroſs this low ground, and even that is overflowed in winter   The banks of the Mæander are ſloping, and they croſs it on a ſort of a boat, like a ſledge in ſhape of a half lozenge, the ſides of it not being above a foot high : They tie vine boughs together, which are about an inch and a half diameter, and from ten to fifteen feet long, which are fixed acroſs the river, a poſt in the boat reſts againſt it, and keeps the veſſel from being carried down by the ſtream, and by the help of this three men pull the boat from one ſide to the other   About half a mile lower the river China, which is a very conſiderable ſtream, falls into the Mæander on the ſouth ſide of it ; it riſes in the ſouth eaſt part of Caria beyond Aphrodiſias, and paſſing thro' the valley which is near Stratonicea and Lagena, turns to the north a little before it falls into the Mæander   Between theſe two rivers there is a chain of mountains, which, though rocky, afford fine herbage for ſheep and black cattle, in which this country abounds. About eight miles further eaſt we croſſed the China on a wooden bridge, which is built on nine or ten large ſtone piers, and is about three hundred feet long   We went a league further to Salaſhar, to a miſerable kane, no better than a ſtable, where it was difficult to lie free from dirt and water, the caravan lodged without with their baggage, and made fires. On the ſixteenth we went about a league and a half between little green hills, and came to a ſmall fertile plain about a league over, it is encompaſſed for the moſt part by high hills, this country is called Carpouſley, it has in it five or ſix villages, and is governed by an aga under the ſangiac of Smyrna, as it belongs to the waladen or ſultaneſs mother. The aga was not there, ſo I delivered my letter to his deputy at the village of Demerje

On the ſouth of this little plain there are ruins of an antient city, Alabanda. not mentioned by any modern writer, and exactly anſwers to the ſituation deſcribed of Alabanda   The founder of it is ſaid to be Alabandus whom they worſhipped as a God [*], and in the Roman diviſion of the country, Mylaſa was made the head city of a juriſdiction, and the judicial conventus was held here   The town was ſituated on the eaſt ſide of a very high hill, and on a little hill to the eaſt of it,

[*] Cicero De natura Deorum

it was encompassed with strong walls, cased with hewn stone within and without, and filled up in the middle with rough stones; in the casing of the wall one tier of stones lies flat, and another is set up an end alternately; and in some places this casing is fallen down, and the middle part is standing, the most easy ascent is from the north side by a paved way of very large stones of an irregular shape, having the town wall on the right. About a third part of the way up the hill, there are great ruins of a most magnificent palace, to which there was an entrance by a colonade, leading to an oblong square court, to the right of this there was a portico of twenty oval pillars of the same kind as those already described, they are of a very rustic order, and the capital is more simple than the Tuscan. Under it there were apartments with entrances from without, and over that another colonade, which is almost destroyed, as the floor of the grand gallery that belonged to it is entirely ruined, this gallery seems to have had a colonade all round. Opposite to this, on the west side of the court, there appear to have been three artificial terraces, or galleries, one above another, with colonades to them, and small apartments within them, and above this is another plain spot, where there appear to have been great buildings. Ascending the steep hill, another third part of the way we came to a beautiful theatre, which for the most part is hollowed into the hill, and all but the front is entire, a plan of it may be seen in the fifty-third plate at A, and a section at B. On each side there is an arched entrance at a, and moreover on the east side there is an arched way b, which seems to have served for a passage towards the top of the hill, and there is a wall carried southward from the theatre, as a defence to the summit of the hill. The top of the hill is level, and there is a little rocky mount in the middle of it, on which I saw the foundations of a circular building; and to the west of this mount there is a square building entire, which probably was designed for a house of pleasure, from this the wall seems to have extended to the south, and then turned eastwards down to the low hill. From the south west corner there was another wall which was carried about a furlong south to another summit of the hill, where there are remains of a strong oblong square castle, and adjoining to it to the south are the walls of a smaller castle. On the little hill, or rising ground below, are remains of two buildings, one like a square castle, with a round tower at each corner, the other is built like a palace, with several doors and windows, these buildings are of a red granite in large grains, all the mountains here abounding both in the red and grey sort, and probably, if quarries were dug down, many beautiful veins might be found. To the south of the city, at the foot of the hill, there are a great number of sepulchres made in different manners, some are hewn down into the rock like graves, others are cut in the same manner into small rocks that rise up above the ground, some are built like pedestals, with two or three steps round them, and covered with large stones, as represented at E, in the fifty third plate. I saw others like an oblong square rock above ground, without any visible entrance, but by a small hole that appears to have been broke in, and one would imagine that there was some passage cut under ground to them. There are also several of them which are small buildings about eleven feet square, a plan

and

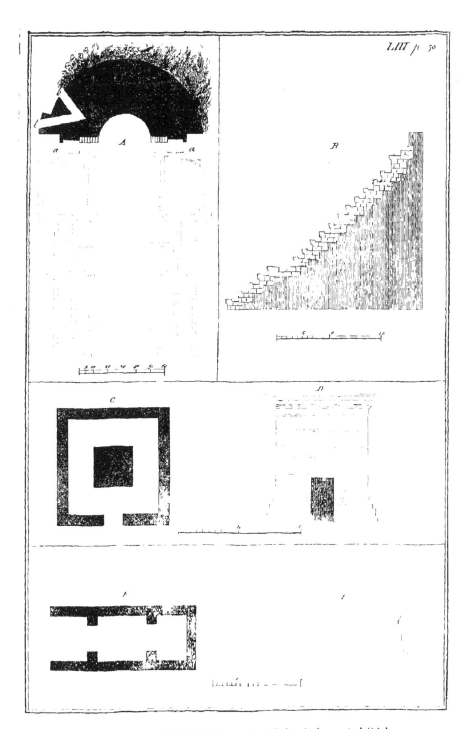

A THEATER and SEPULCHRES, at ALABANDA in CARIA

and view of one may be seen at **C, D**, in the same plate, some have a bench of stone round within to lay the bodies on, others are built with two or three rooms, as at **E**, but the most beautiful are square buildings of very fine mason work channelled, with a cornish at top, a basement at bottom, and another cornish about three feet higher, some also have two square pillars within, and all of them have two or three steps round them

From the south east corner of the plain we ascended southwards about three miles to the top of mount Latmus, where they say there are not only wolfs, wild boars and jackals, but also tigers and bears, there is a plain on the top of the mountain about a league broad. Here we staid all night, and made large fires to defend ourselves against the wild beasts, as well as the cold, and I reposed under the shelter of a large rock of granite, part of which lay hollow to the ground. There are many herdsmen on these mountains, and they have begun to plough some of the plain parts, making enclosures with large trees laid round the fields. There is a low, easy descent from the mountain into that vale of Caria, in which the city of Mylasa stood, which is now called Melasso by the Greeks, and Millels by the Turks. This vale is about four leagues long and a league broad, towards the west it winds a little to the south, turns again to the west at Mandaleat, about two hours or four miles from Melasso, that place is more infested with scorpions than any other in these parts, insomuch that several die every summer by the sting of this animal, the sea at Joran, the antient Jassus, is five or six miles to the east of Mandaleat. To the south of the hills which bound this valley, there is another vale which extends to the bay on which Myndus was situated, not far from Halicarnassus, and to the south of that there is another bay opposite to Stanchio, made by cape Ciu to the south, on which Cnidus was situated, at the south west corner of Asia Minor.

CHAP. VI.

Of MELASSO, the antient MYLASA.

MELASSO, the antient Mylasa, is situated at the foot of a high mountain about the middle of the south side of the plain of Caria. Strabo seems to be mistaken in saying, that Physcus was the nearest sea port to Mylasa, for Melasso is twenty four miles from Marmora, about which place Physcus must have been situated, whereas

* Attenations, quoted by Strabo ... miles Physke to chun he's od fifty, miles from Tralles andi muft have been about Marmora, where they now call aul for Rhode, Physcus having been opposite to that island, but by the most exact computation I could make it is not above sixty miles, and the map makes it about a degree. The same author computes the distance from Tralles to Physcus by Alabanda and Legence, by which will be understood the distance

... into the countries out of cities, and not the cities themselves, because I agree, either it is not, or China, seventeen to the east of Alabanda, so that there seems to be some great error, probably in the transcript, imagining it is not to be above them he's mile from Physcus, and above fifty from Tralles, for it is not above twenty mile from the latter, or fifty from Physcus, so that the number of miles computed by Strabo, seem to be double of what they really are

Cshideb,

Caff'deh, which is at prefent the port of Melaffo, is not above ten miles from it, and feems to be the place mentioned by Paufanias at that diftance   The Greeks are grofly miftaken, in imagining that Melaflo is the antient Miletus which was at Palat, near the mouth of the Mæander. I could not trace the city walls of Mylafa, but on the weft fide there is a magnificent gate entire, of the Corinthian order, which may be feen in the fifty-fourth plate   The old city feems to have extended chiefly to the eaft of the prefent town, what has been taken for the city walls is evidently nothing but the enclofure of fome public buildings, which were moftly on a rifing ground towards the weft end of the antient city, where the prefent town, or rather large village is fituated There feem to have been two antient temples to Jupiter in this city, one properly belonging to the people of Mylafa, dedicated to Jupiter Ofogus, the other of Carian Jupiter in common to the Carians, Lydians, and Myfians   That to Jupiter Ofogus, I fuppofe, was fituated on the fummit of the rifing ground on which the city ftood, where there are remains of a large enclofure, part of the prefent town is built about it, and to the fouth there are two fluted Ionic pillars ftanding, each confifting of five ftones   The members of the bafe are fluted like thofe of the temple of Juno in Samos, but in a much finer tafte, one of thefe pillars may be feen at A, in the fifty-fourth plate   On the north wall of the enclofure there is a beautiful fluted Corinthian pillar, with an infcription on it to the honour of Mænander, there is a drawing of it at B in the fame plate To the fouth of this there is another enclofure, and to the weft of it are fome fmall remains of a theatre, built of white marble, which appears to have been a very beautiful fabric   At fome diftance to the eaft of the temple, in the gardens belonging to fome houfes, there are ruins, which I have reafon to believe belonged to a prætorium, or fome other public building, from an imperfect infcription I found on a wall, which feemed to be of a public nature   At the foot of the hill to the fouth eaft are remains of a long colonade, like the avenue to a building, and near it there is part of a thick wall built in the antient manner with ftones of five fides, which appears like a city wall, but not feeing any figns of a wall extending from it, I took it rather to be the enclofure of the building to which that colonade belonged   The magnificent gate of the city, reprefented in the fifty-fourth plate, is adorned with pilafters of a particular Corinthian order, which appears to have been much ufed in Caria; they had likewife a fingular manner of fluting the bafe of the Ionic order   This Corinthian order confifts of one row of leaves, about half the length of the capital, the upper part being fluted to the abacus, and in fome I have feen the abacus itfelf fluted, and likewife capitals entirely fluted without leaves, which feems to be rather in a Gothic tafte   To the fouth of this gate there are remains of an aqueduct, which has no marks of antiquity, but the antient aqueduct feems to have been carried the fame way, and it may be probably on the city walls, for to the north of this gate, there is a fmall low hill, near which there paffes an antient aqueduct which conveyed the water acrofs the plain, and ended at a fmall hill towards the other fide of it   Moft part of this aqueduct feems to have been deftroyed, and rebuilt, but not in the beft manner, I faw in it feveral pieces of entablature of the Doric order, taken from the ruins of

fome

A CAII II MYLASA

The TEMPLE of AUGUSTUS and ROME at MYLASA

some building Where the ground is low, there are two rows of arches one over another, the upper arches being double the number of the lower To the east of this there are remains of another colonade, which seems to have led to the town, on this side I saw some marble coffins, and near the city there are three or four very massive buildings, which seem to be of the middle ages, they are raised on large open arches, and seem to be remains either of palaces of the middle age, or it may be of reservoirs of water

But the great curiosity of Melasso is a temple which was built to Augustus and Rome, and is a most exquisite piece of architecture, a plan and view of it may be seen in the fifty-fifth plate The temple itself was very small. In the front there is a portico of the composite order, and on the other three sides an Ionic colonade At the entrance of the temple, on each side of the door, there is a foundation of large stones a, on which probably there were pedestals for the statues of Augustus and Rome The pillars are fluted, and the temple is raised on a basement, the cornish of which is only to be seen, there is also a sort of plinth about it that ranges round like a step, and has three faces like an architrave, as it appears at A , every particular pillar has likewise a plinth, and the base is fluted, as mentioned above The frieze is adorned with tripofes, bulls heads, and pateras, the cornish and the pediments at each end are very richly ornamented with carvings. What the architect seems to have designed as an ornament to the building, may be rather looked on as a bad taste, that is, putting the composite order in the front, when the other three sides are Ionic The capitals are indeed fine, except that the curled leaves, and the abacus seem rather to project too far at the corners, in proportion to the size of the capital. About two feet below the capital there are four festoons round the shaft, but what is most particular, and has the worst effect, is a work like a capital on the base of the pillar, the shaft resting on it in a sort of a socket, from which the leaves turn outwards, this is executed in a particular manner, as may be seen in the drawing The top of the leaves are broken, from which one might at first conjecture that the pillars had fallen down, and had been set up again on old capitals, but by examining the work, I saw that the pillars were made so originally. This building, when Christianity prevailed, was doubtless converted either into a church, or some other public building, for on the stones of the temple I saw several defaced inscriptions, with the cross on them

About half a mile to the west of the town there is another very extraordinary building, a plan and view of which may be seen in the fifty-sixth plate, it cannot very properly be called a temple, for it consists of twelve pillars on a basement, with a front every way of four pillars, supporting an entablature, on which there is raised a very grand covering of large stones laid across in four tiers one over another, every tier setting in so as to make a sort of a cupola within, which on the outside appears like four steps, in manner of a pyramid The whole soffit is finely carved with flowers in lozenges The corner pillars are square, and the capitals of them are represented at A , the others are oval, as at B, and are such as have been described at Guzelhiffar , two thirds of the

shafts are fluted   There is an entrance through the basement on the
west side at C, and within there are four square pillars to support the
floor above, which is composed of large stones; the plan of the lower part
is marked with dots, there are two steps round the building   I conjecture that this was a very magnificent altar of the Taurobole kind,
and what induces me to think so, is a round hole in the pavement about
eight inches in diameter, which below lessens to three inches, under which,
I suppose, the sacred person stood, that the blood of the sacrifice might
run on him, after which he wore the garment till it dropped from him,
a ceremony which rendered his person most sacred among the Heathens   I
saw afterwards exactly such a hole at Stratonicea in a large altar made
like a bason, which doubtless was for that purpose, and another at
Eleusis, there is also a bason of the same kind at Ephesus, called St
John's font, but if there was such a hole it has been filled up, there
was an arched place under it, now almost full of earth, a drawing of
these and of that of Eleusis may be seen in the forty-eighth plate   There
is another of this shape, as observed before, in the abbey of St Victor
near Marseilles, which is supposed by many to have been an altar, but
I do not know whether there is any hole in it.   Prudentius indeed describes this sacrifice as performed on boards, through which the blood
run on the person who was destined to this honour; but possibly this
might be the original way of performing the sacrifice, which probably
was afterwards improved, though it might always be continued in the
same manner in some places   All which is submitted to the judgment
of others, being founded only on conjecture, and on the tradition that
a vase of this kind at Marseilles was an altar   It appears by a groove
on each side of the pillars, which is four inches broad, that this building was enclosed on three sides, and probably with stones set up an end,
but it was open on the north side where the hole is, that side also
fronts the hill, from which the people might behold the ceremony   If
there were any ruins near, I should have thought that the temple of Jupiter Carius was here, which at first was at a village separate from the
city, so it seems Strabo ought to be understood in speaking of this place,
though this small pavillion, when enclosed, might possibly be called a
temple   I saw in the town the fine altar at C in the fifty-fourth plate
In a wall near a bridge there is a fine relief, which seemed to be part
of a frieze, it was a Cupid, holding on each side a festoon loaded with
fruit, which looked like peaches, on one side was a medusa's head, and
there seemed to have been one between every festoon   As to the temple
of Jupiter Labrandenus, it was sixty stadii from the city, on the hills towards Alabanda, and there was a paved way to it, this might be on a
hill which I saw in the way to Eskihissar, the top of it is encompassed
with a ruined wall, and is about that distance from Melasso to the north
east   Opposite to it on the hills, on the other side of the plain, there is a
ruined Mahometan town called Puttshin, it is very strong by nature on
three sides, being situated on a hanging ground over the plain, there
is a castle in it, which was repaired as a defence against Soley Bey, and is
naturally very strong   I saw here some steps up the rock like the seats
of a theatre, but in a strait line, which together with a marble pillar,
much resembling porphyry in the colour, but not so hard, are the only

remains of antiquity which I saw there. It may be carrying my conjectures too far to suppose that Mylasa was in very antient times, either here, or on the opposite hill before mentioned, and so to account for a quotation in Strabo, that Mylasa was situated on a strong hill, at which he seems much to wonder, when the city in his time was in the plain. The present town of Melasso is small and ill built, but there are two very good kanes in it, there is also a large old mosque that seems to have been a church, and a new one in a very good taste, it is the residence of a sangiac, who is not a pasha, and so has only the title of aga. The country produces the best tobacco in Turkey, except that of Latichea, and exceeding the tobacco of Salonica, this, together with cotton and wax, is the principal trade of the place There are about thirty Greek families here, who live together in a kane, and in one house, a room of which serves for their church; the Armenians live in the same manner, who are not fixed here, but come and stay at some seasons on account of merchandize. I was recommended here to the great aga, who received me as civilly as I could expect without a present, which he seemed to look for from the physician at Guzelhissar, who recommended me to him; but he gave me leave to see every thing, and promised me a letter to Paitshin A Greek priest, to whom I was recommended, was of no service to me, being afraid to send any one to accompany me, so I went every where with my own janizary, the aga's son came sometimes, and talked very civilly to us, and the aga sent a relation of Mahomet with me to Paitshin.

CHAP. IX.

Of ESKIHISSAR, the antient STRATONICEA, of LAGENA, and ALINDA.

I Set out on the twentieth of February for Eskihissar, and crossed the mountains to the north east about twelve miles, there are two or three little plains on the hills, and a ruined church, where, they say, there was a Christian village

Eskihissar is a poor village built on the ruins of Stratonicea, which was inhabited by a colony of Macedonians, both the situation and inscriptions, that mention the temple of Jupiter Chrysio cus, which was here, prove it to be that city It is on a level spot between the hills, which opens to a large plain, in which the river China runs By the ruins of a very grand enclosure to the north east of the town, and from the inscriptions there, I concluded that the famous temple must have been in that place, tho' I could not trace out the foundations of it At the north part of the enclosure, there is a grand gate of a plain architecture, there was a double row of large pillars from it, which probably formed the avenue to the temple, and on each side of the gate there was a semicircular alcove nich, and a colonade from it, which with a wall on each side of the gate might make a portico, that was of the Corinthian order,

fifty

fifty paces to the north of the wall there are remains of another colonade, which feemed alfo to have made a portico with a wall to the
north of it   This temple was in common to all the Carians, where
they met to facrifice and confult about the commonweal, in which the
cities had votes in proportion to the number of their villages, and it
was called the Chryfaorean meeting   To the fouth of this at fome diftance, are ruins of a building of large hewn ftone, it is twenty-five paces
wide, and feems to have extended about a hundred paces to the town
wall, fome part of which is built in the fame manner   I conjectured
by an infcription on the wall that it might be a temple of Serapis
To the fouth of this on the fide of a hill, there is a large theatre, the front
of which is ruined, there are in all about forty feats, with a gallery
round in the middle, and another at top   In this and many other
theatres, I obferved the inner half of the breadth of the feats to be cut
down about half an inch lower than the outer part, the feats are generally about two feet fix inches broad

The people of this place, though all Mahometans, were very civil
and obliging the firft evening, and an empty houfe being allotted me,
many of them came and fat with me, brought medals, were very ready
to affift me in my defign, and to fhew me every thing   When I was
going to fee the theatre, the deputy governor came to me, and told me,
that the theatre was on his ground, and afked me what I would prefent
him to fee the antiquities. I gave myfelf no trouble about his demand,
but examined it thoroughly   When I returned to the town, the aga's
man came, and told me, that the aga was arrived, and defired to fee
me, when I came to him, he afked me, what was my bufinefs, which I
told him, and that I had a firman or paffport, he faid, it was the pad-
fhaw's or grand fignor's firman, and not the pafha's, and therefore he
would not regard it, but if I would make certain prefents to him and
his cadi, I might view what I pleafed   I gave him to underftand, that
by vertue of my firman I could fee the antiquities, and that he muft anfwer it, if any harm happened to me there   I left him, and purfued
my obfervations as before   Some people came from the aga, but I
fhewed no fear, which I knew by experience was the beft way.   There
was an infcription on an old ruined houfe, which I had a defire to copy,
and the poffeffor of it demanded a fequin for his permiffion, however,
I went in the afternoon, and began to copy it, though the janizary re-
fufed to go with me, fo that I was accompanied only by my flave, the
man that owned the houfe foon came to me, and, to pacify him, I
told him I would pay him when I had done, but not being fatisfied, I
gave him what he demanded, with which he feemed well pleafed, and
put his hand to his mouth and forehead, as a mark of gratitude and
fidelity   The deputy came foon after, made figns to me to go away, but
not regarding him, he began to difturb me, on which I pulled out my
firman, and ordered the flave to hold it, he went to take it out of his
hand, but when I laid hold of it, and held it faft, he feemed to be very
cautious not to tear it, forbore ufing any violence, and foon after went
away   Whilft I was abfent the aga came to the houfe I was lodged in,
and talked to the janizary, who informed him that I was gone to a private houfe by the permiffion of the owner, and affured him that I would

not

not go any more abroad I ordered every thing to be got ready for our departure The aga fent word that he defired to fpeak with me, and when I did not go to him, he faid he would not permit us to go away, and threatened particularly to detain the janizary We mounted our horfes, and the janizary, *contrary to my repeated orders, was for going to him again as we paffed by, and left us for that purpofe,* but thought better of it, and returned to us: We put on pretty faft; the janizary, and guide to whom the horfes belonged, frequently looking back in the utmoft confternation, left they fhould fend after us, and injure us fome way or other But the aga could not have ftopped us, without bringing himfelf into trouble, for the guide and horfes were of another pafhalic, fo he could not meddle with them; I was no fubject, and the flave was my property, and if he had ftopped the janizary, a detachment would have been fent by the janitzer aga at Guzelhiffar to have delivered him, and would have levied damages and expences on the village.

We defcended from Efkihiffar Oppofite to it towards the north on the other fide of the vale, in which the China runs, there is a village called Aharer; and to the right on another fide of the plain at about a league diftance, is the village of Bopeck. They go to market from Efkihiffar to Gulfuk, which is about fix hours. Mulla, where the pafha of the country refides, is about fifteen hours from Efkihiffar We went a league to the north, and afterwards about two leagues to the weft, and afcended near a league to a village called Lakena; about a mile from it on the top of the hill, there is a ruined caftle, ftrongly fituated by nature, but it did not feem to be a very antient place, nor do they find medals in that part. The name however would incline one to conjecture that it might be Lagenæ in the territory of Stratonicea We were here conducted to a houfe built by a public fpirited Turk for the reception of ftrangers, where he conftantly prepares lodgings and provifions for all comers : He feemed to be a good man, and was there to receive us, he fupped and fpent the evening with us, and on our going away the next morning, the twenty-fecond, he feemed much pleafed when I expreffed my gratitude, and told him, I fhould be glad to fhew him the fame hofpitality in England.

We went about two leagues north to the river Paieflu, which runs into the China, and croffed the hills to the weft for three leagues, to one of the villages called Akfhoureh; we went on a league to the weft between low rocky hills, by the fide of a rivulet, which we paffed on a bridge, and faw the remains of an old aqueduct acrofs the river, confifting of one arch, which feems to have conveyed the water from a rivulet that runs from the hills. We came into a very fine plain, and croffed it, travelling northwards two miles to the village of China, China which is fituated near the eaft end of the plain, and to the fouth of the river China I lodged here in the coffee-houfe, and when the people knew my bufinefs, they informed me of the antiquities of the place, and half the village accompanied me up the hill, laughing and jefting with much good humour; and afterwards many of them came and fat with me in the coffee houfe The top of the hill had been fortified, and I faw there two or three fepulchral grots, I obferved alfo a ciftern built above ground in two oblong fquare compartments, and cafed

Lagenæ

with brick As there are so many antiquities, I should rather take this to be Lagenæ, where there was a temple to Hecate, in which there were yearly very considerable meetings, and it is very probable that the old name of the China was Lagena, that the town and country had its name from it, and that when Lagenæ is mentioned in the way from Physcus to Tralles, the country is meant and not the town

Arabihissar Alinda

From China, we crossed over to the south side of the plain, and came to the ruins of an antient city called Arabihissar, which may be Alinda, the place of residence of Ada, queen of Caria, who had nothing left her by the Persians but this city, and probably her kingdom was confined to this small plain, but this queen going to meet Alexander, gave her city to him, and adopted him for her son, who left the place under her government, and afterwards restored all Caria to her [a].   The city was on two high hills; from one of them the eastern walls went down to the plain, and were carried on to the north for near half a mile, then turning to the west for a quarter of a mile, passed to the north of a remarkable building, which I shall mention, they then turn to the south, and go to the top of the other hill, from which they come down on the east of it, and join the walls on the first hill.   On the south side of this hill there is a theatre, a plan of which may be seen in the forty-seventh plate at D, the inside and the front are almost entirely destroyed, there was an arched entrance into it on each side near the front; and I observed that the wall in the front of the theatre was built in a very particular manner, as represented in the drawing   In the plain towards the south side of the city there is a building, a plan and view of which may be seen in the fifty-first plate at G, H, the grand front was to the south, and from the plainness of the base, I suppose it was of the Doric order   There are heaps of ruins within on every side, except to the front, as if there had been seats, built after the theatrical manner like steps, which is a reason to conjecture that this place served for some public meeting; there appears to have been a grand colonade to it from the east, and probably there was another from the west, both running parallel with the front, there are many ruins about this building, which seems to have had an enclosure round it, and between it and the hill are ruins of a strong built church.   All these works are of a brown sort of granite, which is not beautiful.

From this place we went about a league south west in the plain, crossed some low hills to the west, and came again to the bridge over the China, which we had passed to Melasso, and returned to Guzelhissar the same way we came; I was here recommended to a Sciote, a physician settled in this city, who assisted me in every thing which lay in his power, and conducted me to the moselem or governor, to whom I had a letter, who treated me with much civility, and offered to send a man with me to Sultanhissar and Nasley

[a] The supplement to Quintus Curtius, Strabo xiv p 657 and Ptol. v 2

CHAP.

CHAP. X.

Of Tralles and Nysa in Caria.

I Set out on the twenty-eighth of February from Guzelhiſſar, and went ten miles eaſtward to a village called Sultanhiſſar, near which on a height at the foot of the mountain the antient town of Tralles *Tralles* was ſituated, it was divided into two parts by a ſtream that runs in a very deep bed This city is ſaid to have been built by ſome Thracians and people from Argos, there are appearances in it of very great buildings, eſpecially two in the higheſt parts of the city; that to the eaſt ſeems to have been a large temple, and the other a caſtle to defend the aſcent, with ſome large public building adjoining to it On the eaſtern part alſo there are remains of a grand portico of two rows of pillars round an area, which is about a hundred paces ſquare, and on the eaſt ſide of the weſtern part is a theatre, built on the ſide of the hill, and fronting to the ſouth, it is very large, and ſeems to have had fifty degrees of ſeats in it, there are arches above it to the weſt, which probably belonged to ſome grand building, and further weſt there are ruins of a ſuburb, extending a conſiderable way, where the ground is not ſo high.

We went the ſame evening to a town called Naſlee by the Greeks, and *Naſlee* Naſſalee by the Turks, which muſt have its name from the antient city Nyſa, that was at ſome diſtance between the hills to the north I ſaw in the way between Sultanhiſſar and Naſlee many ſtones of antient buildings, ſet up in the Turkiſh burial places, which may be the remains of the temple of Pluto and Juno, that were at a village called Acharaca, where there was alſo a grove dedicated to Pluto, and an extraordinary cave called Charonium, the air of which in ſome parts was good for ſeveral diſeaſes, though in one ſpot it was mortal to any animal that breathed it I could learn nothing concerning this cave, only on my departure I was informed that there is a cave there, which went a great way under ground. I was here recommended to the aga, and to one of the Greek church

To the north of Naſlee the high mountains of Meſogis retire to the north, and form a ſemicircle, in which there is a ridge of high ſandy hills that run from eaſt to weſt. About half a mile in between theſe hills are ruins of ſome antient town, which, I ſuppoſe, to be Nyſa or *Nyſa* Nyſa, ſaid to have been inhabited by people of Lacedæmon in extraction, there are very little remains of it, except ſeveral well built arches, moſtly under ground, it appears that the city was on both ſides of a ſtream, as it is deſcribed On the weſt ſide of it there are remains of a building, which ſeems to have been a temple On a very high ſummit of the hill, over the city, there are ſome walls, which may be Aromata, ſaid to be on the mountain over the city, this place was famous for good wine The town of Naſlee being new, and the hills being ſo ſandy, without any ſtones for building, ſeems to be the reaſon why there is ſo little to be ſeen of this city, in which there was a theatre, gymnaſium, forum, and ſenate houſe. The village of Maſtaura was probably near

I the

the city; for there is one now which is at the entrance in between the hills, called Maftauro, and thefe ruins, from the village near, are called Maftaura-Kalefi [The caftle of Maftaura]. I met with an infcription, in which mention is made both of a perfon of Maftaura, and alfo of the Nyfeans. Strabo fays, there was a place called Limon, thirty ftadia from Nyfa, going acrofs mount Megofis to the north, where the Nyfeans, and the people of fome neighbouring places had their meetings, that there was a cave near it, which went to that of Acharaca, and that fome thought this place called Limon, was the meadow Afius, mentioned by Homer. Strabo is very particular concerning thefe parts, having ftudied here under Menecrates. Some fay faint Gregory Nyffenus, brother of faint Bafil, was bifhop of this place; I know not on what authority, for the place of which he was bifhop was Nyffa, probably the city of that name on the weftern bounds of Cappadocia; and the people of this place writ themfelves Nyfeans [Νυσαεῖς] and not Nyffenians

Six miles to the eaft is a large village called Iack-Cui, which poffibly might be Biula, another village mentioned by Strabo. The prefent town of Naflee confifts of two parts, half a mile diftant from each other, that to the north is the place where the market is held, and where they have their fhops, it being ufual in fmall places to hold the markets at fome diftance from the town or village, probably for the greater fecurity of their families, and there being two kanes here, and fome houfes as well as fhops, it is grown into a fort of town called Naflee-Bazar, as the other is called Naflee-Boiuke [Great Naflee]; there are three or four hundred Armenians, and about thirty Greeks, who live in the kanes, and are merchants.

CHAP. XI.

Of ANTIOCH on the Mæander, and APHRODISIAS in Caria.

I Set out from Naflee on the fecond of March, and went about four miles fouth to the Mæander: The river being neither large nor deep in this part, has only a flight wooden bridge over it. About a mile to the fouth of the Mæander, directly oppofite to Naflee, there is a ruined place called Arpas-kalefi, which probably is either Cofcinia or Orthopia, which were great villages on the fouth fide of that river, it is walled round, and fituated on a hill over a little plain between the mountains to the fouth. Turning to the eaft, we ftopped at the houfe of the great aga of this country, who was taking the diverfion of hawking. We went to him, and he defired us to go to his houfe: When he came home, he ordered a man to go with me to Geyra. We went to a village two leagues further to the eaft, it is at the entrance of a narrow vale that extends fouthwards between the hills. To the eaft of this place there is a low hill which ftretches from eaft to weft, and is called Innichere, on which there are ruins of the walls of a town,

and

and a great number of arches under ground, I take this place to be Antioch on the river Mæander, which is mentioned as south of the river, and that there was a bridge over it near the city, the territory of which was on both sides of the river, it was formerly famous for figs, in which the country on the other side of the Mæander still abounds as far as Guzelhissar. The rivulet which runs from the valley to the east, is probably the Orsinus mentioned by Pliny, as washing this town. This place is remarkable of late, as it was the spot on which the famous rebel Soley Bey Ogle was cut off in the year one thousand seven hundred and thirty-nine, with four thousand of his followers, by about forty thousand soldiers of the grand signor. Going about eight miles to the south along this narrow vale, we left to the west a town or large village called Carajesu, which belongs to the Bostanjees, and is so defended by the deep beds of mountain torrents that Soley Bey could not make himself master of it. There are some Christians in the town. Turning to the east, and going four miles in a plain, which is about two leagues long from east to west, and a league broad, I came to a village called Geyra, towards the east end of it. This place is situated on the spot of the antient Aphrodisias. The walls are about two miles in compass, of an irregular triangular figure, the east side of the town being very narrow; they seem to have been for the most part destroyed, and rebuilt out of the ruins of the antient fabrics, which appear to have been very magnificent, there are three gates of the city remaining, one to the west, and two to the east. In the middle of the city there is a small hill, in the side of which there was a theatre, now almost entirely ruined, there are remains of an arched entrance to it, about the middle of the north side, and of some arches at each end of it, on which the seats were probably built. The very summit of the hill seems to have been a fortress, for this hill, and some public buildings near, appear to have been enclosed with a very strong wall, cased with small hewn stone, which might be designed for the greater security of their gods, and their treasures. To the north west of this hill are remains of a building, which I take to have been a temple built to Aphrodisia or Venus, from which this place might have its name, and I collected from an inscription, that there was some goddess particularly worshipped here. This temple is built something after the manner of that of Ephesus, with large piers of hewn stone, on which, it is probable, arches were turned, and by the holes in the stones, the building appears to have been cased with marble, it may also be concluded from some remains near, that this temple was of the Corinthian order. About a furlong to the north east, there are ruins of another most magnificent temple, which I conjectured was dedicated to Bacchus, from an inscription there mentioning a priest of Bacchus, and from a relief of a tyger, and a vine, which I saw among the ruins. The walls of it are destroyed, and the stones were probably carried away to build the town walls, but there are two magnificent rows of fluted Ionic pillars of white marble, which are almost entire, there are nineteen on each side, four feet in diameter, and about five feet apart, each consisting of five stones, there were five entrances at the west end, three of which are to the middle part between the pillars, and one on each side, from the front there was a colonade of Corinthian pillars of grey marble, one

foot fix inches in diameter, but it could not correfpond with the magnificence of the lofty temple, there was a door place at each end about
thirty paces from thefe pillars, with which it is probable another colonade ranged, and fome paces further at the eaft end, there are two
fluted Corinthian pillars of grey marble, two feet in diameter, which fupport an entablature   It is probable that a row of pillars went all round
at this diftance, and I have great reafon to think, that between thefe
and the temple, there were continued colonades of Ionic pillars two
feet and a half in diameter, two thirds of which were fluted, for there
are a great many of thefe pillars ftanding, particularly to the fouth   I
concluded that there were above fifty from eaft to weft, and between
twenty and thirty from north to fouth, by fupplying fuch as had fallen
down between others that were ftanding, and on all fides I faw remains
of fuch pillars extending to the theatre and the other temple, all
which were probably covered, and made fpacious fhady walks for the
great number of people that reforted to this place to their public
games, as it appears they did by fome infcriptions there; and when
it was all entire, it muft have made a moft magnificent appearance   The
middle part of this temple had been converted into a church, there
being a femicircular wall at the eaft end built in a different manner
from the reft.   On the north fide of the temple of Bacchus there is an
altar of grey marble, like that at Ephefus, refembling a large bafin with
a hole through it in the middle, cut exactly in the fame manner as that
in the pavilion before mentioned, near Melaffo.   A furlong to the
north weft there is a Circus, which is femicircular at both ends, it is
entire within, had an entrance at each end, and confifted of twenty-five
degrees of feats   The city wall is built againft it, in which there are fome
very fine capitals of that fort of Corinthian order which was ufed in Caria
Towards the eaft end of the Circus there is a femicircular wall, very ill
built, like that of Ephefus, which makes a circle with the eaft end,
which confirms the conjecture that it was not originally in the Circus,
poffibly the Chriftians might make fuch an enclofure, and ufe it for a
church   In the walls of the city, towards the fouth weft corner, there
are fome very fine reliefs, which feem to have been part of a frieze;
they are moftly cupids or winged perfons, encountring the giants with
fpears, bows and arrows, the latter are reprefented below with two fer-
pents inftead of feet, turning up like the tails of Tritons   At one end
Jupiter in a fmall figure has one under his feet, and is levelling his
thunder at another, a perfon near is drawing a bow at them, and
there is a trophy near Jupiter.   There are a great number of marble
coffins in this place, fome of which are fluted, others have figures of
perfons round them in mezzo relievo, with pilafters on each fide, and
there are infcriptions on fome, two of them which are in the beft tafte,
and are fet in the wall near the top, have on one fide two feftoons
of very excellent workmanfhip, in one they are fupported in the middle by a naked perfon, in another by a body wrapped up like an Ægyptian mummy   I found an infcription here, which calls Antioch a colony, and another makes mention of the Plarafenfes, as united with the
Aphrodifians, though I cannot find any fuch people fpoken of by antient
authors.   The village is a poor place, the Turks here make a very ftrong

I   well

well flavoured white wine, and drink of it very plentifully. These vines may be of the race of those which they had here when they were worshippers of Bacchus. It is probable they formerly had some staple commodity here, and that they bestowed great expences on their public games, in order to make people resort to a place which was so much out of the way, for I found by a curious inscription, that great number of cities, even as far as the Euphrates, were partakers of their sports, and in another there is a sort of table of the fees or salaries due to the several officers who were employed about the games

At Geyra I went to the house of the aga, a venerable old man, who was one of those public spirited Turks that entertains all strangers I went out every day to see the antiquities, and in the evening the inhabitants of the village came and sat with us; they were a very squalid poor tribe of people, among whom I should not have thought myself safe if I had not had a letter from the great aga I set out on the seventh on my return to Naslee; the first night I was generously entertained by a Turk at a village called Chislic, and arrived the next day at Naslee.

CHAP. XII.

Of LAODICEA on the Lycus.

WE set out from Naslee on the ninth of March, and went eastward near the Mæander. About sixteen miles from Naslee the hills on both sides come near the river, and opening again gradually, about three leagues farther there are several sources of hot water rising on the south side of the river, and in the very bed of it, which exactly answers to the description of Carura, a village on the bounds of Phrygia and Caria, which was formerly full of inns, for the convenience of travellers, and of those who frequented the waters, which are only bathed in, and not used for drinking This place, as well as the country about it, was, and is still much subject to earthquakes. Strabo observes that a whole company of people that lodged here were swallowed up by an earthquake in the night Opposite to it, on the side of the hill, is another hot water, from which, a smoak or steam arises as from the others, the hills are of a red colour, so that probably they contain some iron ore Two leagues further the river first begins to run near the southern mountains, and so continues till it falls into the sea We crossed it in this place on a wooden bridge, the hills open, and make a large plain four leagues wide every way, in which the river Lycus falls into the Mæander Towards the south east part of this plain is a town called Denizley, situated on a low hill, the old town was destroyed about twenty five years past by an earthquake, in which twelve thousand people perished, the town extended also to another rising ground south of it After the earthquake the people began to live at their gardens and farms, and there are only very mean shops in the town,

Carura.

Denizley

which

which are built of unburnt brick and boards There are about forty Armenians here, who live moftly in a kane together, there are alfo feveral Greeks The country near the town is much cultivated with vineyards, they make raifins of the grapes, and a fort of fyrup like treacle, which they call Becmefs, and it ferves on all occafions inftead of fugar. There was a temple of the month Carus between Laodicea and Carura, and a famous fchool for the ftudy of phyfic, which might be at this place, where I faw fome ftones which had marks on them of the antient workmanfhip To the fouth and eaft of Denizley there are very high mountains covered with fnow called Dag-Baba [The father of mountains], they run eaftward from the neigbourhood of Geyra, and turning to the north, bound part of the eaft end of this plain, they then extend again towards the eaft, and from that corner a chain of low hills runs to the weft, and joins other hills, which extend to the high mountains further to the weft than Denizley, among thefe low hills, a league directly fouth of Denizley is Efkihiffar, the old Laodicea on the Lycus, one of the feven churches, which is frequently mentioned in the Revelations, and by St Paul in his epiftle to the Coloffians, whofe city was near unto it Thefe high mountains are the antient mount Cadmus, and where they begin to bound this plain to the fouth the hills end, which had run all along from the fea to the fouth of the Mæander, and, I fuppofe, were all comprehended under the name of mount Latmus.

Laodicea on the Lycus

The ruins of Laodicea are on a low hill about half a mile long, and a quarter of a mile broad, to the fouth of it there is a narrow vale, which is to the north of the plain and the Lycus, that runs in a deep narrow bed about half a mile from the town. The city was diftinguifhed by the name of this river, from others of the fame name, by the title of Laodicea on the Lycus To the eaft there is a fmall rivulet that may be the Afopus, which is faid to fall into the Lycus at this place To the weft there is another fmall ftream, which is probably the Caprus, for Pliny fays, that it was wafhed by thefe two rivers, the latter appears to have been a confiderable ftream from four large piers of a bridge, built of hewn ftone, which are now to the eaft of the river, fo that probably its courfe has been diverted another way by earthquakes The top of the hill, on which Laodicea ftood, is fomewhat uneven, entirely uninhabited, and appears like a green field, except where there are remains of antient buildings. It was at firft an inconfiderable city, and began to flourifh after the time of the Roman conquefts in thefe parts; and notwithftanding its miferable defolation, there are remains in it of very great buildings

Antiquities

The eaftern part of the hill is lower than the reft, and towards the north eaft corner there appears to have been an entrance up to the city, and a gate, for there are ruins of a building on each fide of the way, which feems to have been a tower to defend the entrance, and in order to ftrengthen the place on this fide a fecond wall was built acrofs At the weft end there feems to have been another entrance between two heights The north weft corner is the higheft part of the hill, and there are foundations of walls, which probably were thofe of a fortrefs, as it is the ftrongeft fituation in the whole city Further eaft between this building and the theatre, I fuppofe there was another entrance, as there

was

was on the oppofite fide to the fouth, a little more to the weft than the
Circus, where there is now a road acrofs the hill   There are remains of
three buildings along the middle of the hill, two of them appear like temples, built with large piers, on which arches were turned, the whole was
cafed with marble ; and part of one of the piers is ftill covered with white
marble ; in the eaftern building I faw an Ionic entablature , the
other, which is to the weft of them, was an oblong fquare building,
which for the moft part feems to have been open, and had a colonade
on each fide, there being great remains of an entablature, and no figns
of a wall, except at each end , it is fifty feet wide, and a hundred and
eighty paces long   The Circus is on the fouth fide of the town, and
appears as if it was hollowed down into the hill , it is not much ruined,
the area within is three hundred paces long, and ninety feet wide
There are twenty three feats remaining, and the ground probably has
covered two more, the ufual number being twenty-five   There was an
arched entrance at each end eleven feet wide   Towards the eaft end of
the Circus are remains of a very grand building with doors from it,
leading to the galleries round the top of the Circus, I faw in it two pillars about a foot and a half in diameter, which appeared to me to be of
oriental jafpar-agate, and if fo, muft be of great value   There was an
enclofed area to the north of it ; on a lower ground to the weft of this
building, there are remains of a colonade leading to it   North of this
are the ruins of a building like a theatre, which, from the dimenfions,
I take to be an odeum, or mufic theatre. I could fee but eight degrees of feats, though I have reafon to think there were twenty , the
diameter between the feats was but feventy-feven feet and a half, and
the fpace which the feats took up on each fide was thirty feet ; fo that
the whole diameter was a hundred and thirty-feven feet fix inches: There
were three entrances in the front, that in the middle was twenty feet
wide, and the other two twelve, and were divided by two piers about
fix feet high, on which there were two Corinthian pilafters on every
fide , there is a relief of a head in the middle of the capital inftead of
the rofe   I fhould conjecture that a couplet of pillars was erected on
each of them, as well as on two others, on the fides of the narrow entrances, they were probably of the compofit order, for I faw near this
place a compofit capital, finely wrought, reprefenting a vafe covered
with leaves, and fruit round at the top of it like peaches, inftead of
eggs and darts   From the carvings which I faw about the building, it
appears to have been adorned in the higheft manner

On the north fide of the hill there is a theatre, fronting weftward to
the ftreet that led into the city, there are no remains of the front of it,
and the feats are broke down at both ends, the other parts are not
much ruined, being built up the hill, the diameter of it within the
feats is fixty feven feet, there were about forty-three degrees of feats,
and eleven defcents down from the top, which are two feet wide, and
the uppermoft are about fifty-five feet apart ; thofe defcents are made by
dividing each feat into two fteps   To the eaft of this is a very grand
theatre, the feats being about three quarters of a circle, it feems to
have ferved for the ufes of an amphitheatre, and fo probably did moft
of the theatres in the eaft, for I do not remember ever to have feen in

these parts what is properly called an amphitheatre, that is, an entire oval, or round building This theatre is every way cut out of the hill, except the part to the front, which opens to the north, the area within the seats was about a hundred and ten feet in diameter, there were fifty degrees of seats above the podium, or gallery at the bottom, which is fifteen broad, and is now only four feet above the ground, there are seventeen descents, like those in the other theatre.   There seems to have been much art bestowed on the front, which was of the Corinthian order used in Caria, there was a descent down from it of above twenty feet, and, as well as I could judge, the steps made a circle with the seats of the theatre, to which I imagine they might join; for the entrance being eight feet wide, the wall thirty-five feet on each side of it, is built like a pedestal, and makes a segment of a circle, the die of which pedestal or basement was richly adorned with reliefs From this there extended on each side, in a strait line, a colonade of square pillars, nine in number, covered with semicircular pilasters, being about two feet thick, and five feet two inches apart, this seems to have been a grand portico on each side of the entrance Before the front there lies a statue of a woman ten feet long, the drapery of it is very fine, the garments being long, almost covered the feet, and three feet below the neck the vest hangs over, as if tied about the loins, and six inches lower the garment hangs over again in the same manner, the whole is beautifully executed, the head seems to have been of another piece, there being a socket for it to go in, and probably it was of a more costly material.   At the south west corner of the city there are some small ruins of a church, in which are fragments of a pillar or two of dark grey marble of the Cipolino kind.   Below the church to the south are remains of many stone coffins, where it is to be supposed they deposited their dead.

Aqueduct   There being no water on this hill, the city was supplied by an aqueduct, which run along the side of the hills from the south, and conveyed the water from some streams which come from mount Cadmus, it was carried through a valley on some arches, which are now ruined, and crossing a hill, partly on the ground, and partly on arches, it was carried through the vale, and up the hill on which the city stands. The water runs in a channel two feet in diameter, bored thro' stones, which are about three feet square, being let into one another, and the reservoir of water seems to have been at the end of the grand building over the Circus, for a wall remains there, which is incrusted with petrifications from the droppings of the water.   Strabo says he was informed, that the waters of Laodicea were of the nature of those of Hierapolis in making these petrifications, which is also seen in the arches and pipes, the latter have an incrustation on the inside three or four inches thick, and the arches are loaded with this rock work Strabo also takes notice that the sheep about Laodicea are exceedingly black, which is very true, three parts of them being black in all the country from Naslee to this place, and some of them are black and white like the Ethiopian sheep

CHAP. XIII.

Of HIERAPOLIS in Great Phrygia.

OPPOSITE to Laodicea, about a league to the north of the
river Lycus, are the remains of Hierapolis, mentioned by faint
Paul, in his epiftle to the Coloffians, which had its name from
the great number of temples that were antiently in the city, it is now
called Pambouk-Kalefi [The Cotton Caftle] It is fituated on a flat
fpot on the foot of a mountain, the walls of it extending up the fide of
the hill, and is about a mile and a half in circumference This city is
placed by Ptolemy in Great Phrygia, though Strabo fpeaks of it under
Lydia, among thofe cities which were of a mixed race. Philadelphia,
now called Allacfhahar, which is about thirty miles to the north, was
in Lydia Tripolis, which was between Hierapolis and Philadelphia, is
placed by Ptolemy in Caria; and on a medal publifhed by Spanheim,
it is called Tripolis on the Mæander; fo that probably it was on the
north fide of this river, where it runs between the hills, and as Laodicea, on the fouth fide of the Lycus is in Caria, and Hierapolis in
Phrygia, it is probable that the country between the Lycus and Mæander
was in great Phrygia. Tripolis is put down in the Tables as twelve
miles from Hierapolis in the road to Philadelphia, and, I fuppofe, it
was at Oftraven, which is about that diftance, where I was informed
there are fome ruins. Tripolis was no inconfiderable place, for there are
feveral medals of it found in thefe parts Between Hierapolis and Philadelphia was the country called Catakekaumenè, reckoned to be a part
of Myfia, or Mæonia, it was a fandy burnt foil, producing only vines;
it is fuppofed to have fuffered by Vulcanos, and was computed to be
fixty two miles long and fifty broad

At a fmall diftance to the eaft of the walls of Hierapolis there is a
deep bed of a winter torrent, over which there are ruins of a bridge
built on the rock, which feems to have ferved for an aqueduct, and to
have confifted of two arches, one over another, twenty-five feet wide
At the afcent between this and the town there are fome ftone coffins
and fepulchral buildings, moft of the latter are fmall, having a door at
the end, and a pediment in front, fo that they appear like little temples, within them about half way up, are ftone benches to lay the bodies on, which were alfo depofited under them, one of the fepulchral
monuments, which is more grand than the reft, confift of a wall built
to a rifing ground, and adorned with five pilafters, fupporting a grand
entablature, on the other fide the ground is as high as the entablature,
on which there is a Greek infcription, two of the fpaces between the
pilafters, half way from the top, are cut in holes in figures of lozenges
and half lozenges, like windows, though there does not appear to be
any apartments within, nor is there any vifible entrance

At fome diftance from the weft fide of the town there are a great
number of fepulchral buildings, and ftone coffins, extending for half a
mile A hundred and fixty paces, from the weft gate of the city
there

there is a colonade of pillars two feet fquare, on which there are femicircular pilafters ; it extends a hundred and fifty paces, and leads to a building which is in a bad tafte, and I fuppofe to be a triumphal arch, from an infcription over it, in honour of fome emperor, it confifts of three arches, and a round tower on each fide of it To the north and fouth there are two or three fmall buildings, and feveral others in a line from them towards the eaft, they extend about a hundred paces to the remains of a very magnificent church, to which there is no entrance on that fide I conjecture that thefe buildings are alfo fepulchral The church is built with large piers, on which there are arches turned, as in the antient temples ; and from this building the fepulchres extend weftward, fome of them are built like thofe already defcribed ; others like large fquare pedeftals ; and the tops of feveral of them are covered with ftone coffins, of which likewife there are a great number. I faw alfo two or three circular enclofures with an oblong fquare room built under ground like thofe near Smyrna, and covered over only with three long ftones, and fo are many of the other buildings, fome being worked like an arch, others like a roof, ending in an angle at top, on many of thefe there are infcriptions, but being built of a free ftone, they are for the moft part defaced There are alfo ruins of another magnificent church to the eaft of the hot waters.

Theatre

On the fide of the hill which is to the north of the city, there is a very beautiful theatre, which fronts to the fouth, and is the moft perfect I have feen, for though the front of it is a little ruined, yet fo much remains, that one may judge in what manner it was built, it had thirteen arched entrances, five of which opened to the front of the area, and four on each fide in the femicircle There is a gallery round the theatre, above which there are twenty-five feats, and I fuppofe that there were as many below it, tho' the ground is fo much rifen, that there are but few to be feen at prefent· The theatre is not entirely hollowed into the hill, and there are two entrances from the gallery on each fide near the front to the arches on which the feats are built, and from one of them on each fide, there is a defcent down to one of the doors in the front, and there are feven defcents down the feats from the top, as defcribed in fome other theatres, the door frames within, which are of white marble, are beautifully carved, and there are fragments of fine reliefs cut on white marble, in which combats are reprefented, which confirms the conjecture that the theatres ferved for fuch diverfions, as well as for acting.

Warm waters

The warm waters here are the greateft natural curiofities in Afia, they rife to the fouth of the theatre in a deep bafon, and are very clear They are only tepid, have the tafte of the Pyrmont waters, but are not fo ftrong, and muft have in them a great quantity of fulphur, they do not drink them, though I could not perceive either falt or vitriol in the tafte of them to make them unwholefom. The fprings flow fo plentifully that they make a confiderable ftream, it is obferved by the antients that thefe waters were excellent for dying, and that the roots of the trees at this place give a tincture equal to the fcarlet and purple, and now there are fhrubs growing about the hill, the roots of which are incrufted

crufted with a petrification of thefe waters, which might be ufed in dying   The water now runs in channels about three feet wide, which
are incrufted on each fide to the thicknefs of about half a foot.   The
fide of the hill, where the water runs, is covered with a white incruftation, and the channels which conveyed it through the city into the plain
are entirely filled up, as well as the arches of the aqueduct, all appearing like the folid rock, and I obferved towards the brow of the hill
fome hollow parts, where the rain water has fettled, round which there
are partitions of a white fulphurous incruftation, probably occafioned by
the motion of the water in windy weather, and in fome parts there are
little heaps, which appear like white falt, but are folid ftone   In
one part, where the water runs down the hill, it forms a moft beautiful
hanging petrification like rock work, the fide of the hills below appearing
as white as fnow, and poffibly they might call this place Pambouk-Kaleſi
[The cotton caftle], from the refemblance of its whitenefs to that of cotton   There are ruins of walls, and a colonade round the bafon of water, and remains of porticos, and other buildings about it: And to
the north of the water there is an oblong fquare building, which feems
to have had an open colonade to the bafon ; it is built in a very particular manner, as if it was defigned for the reception of ftatues, and is
without doubt the temple of Apollo mentioned by Photius, as built near
the lake or bafon.   To the fouth of the waters there are great remains
of moft magnificent baths, confifting of a large court, with a portico
of fquare pillars at each end. Thefe pillars, and fome others which I
faw, are very curious; they refemble the Jallo Antico, or that of
Siena, and feem to be a natural compofition of pieces of marble, and of
this yellow petrification: This mixture may be accidental, or might have
been made by putting marble in places where this water run, in order to
be enclofed by this curious petrification   The rooms for the baths to the
fouth of this area are very fpacious, and covered with arches   Another
great curiofity here was what they called Plutonium, a cave, out of
which a vapour exhaled, that was mortal to animals, like that at Pier-
mount, and, I fuppofe, for the fame reafon, the waters here being of the
fame nature   They promifed to fhew me this place, but brought me to
a deep hole full of water near the bafon, which was more ftrongly impregnated with the mineral, but it had no manner of effect on a bird which I
put on the water   They fay the water is exceedingly deep, and that formerly it was noxious   If it agreed with the fituation defcribed by Strabo,
I fhould have thought that this was the cavern, and that it had been filled
with water, by a fpring breaking into it, but as he defcribes it under the
brow of the hill, in a fquare enclofure of about half an acre, it might
be a place to the fouth weft of the baths, where, below the brow of the
hill there is a high wall, which runs from the hill to the fouth, and
then turns to the weft, the water having been diverted to it, probably on
purpofe to cement the building, which looks like the natural rock, tho'
when I was on the fpot, as this did not occur to me, fo I did not examine into the truth of it, and if it was here, it is probable the hole is
either filled up, or that fuch a vapour does not at prefent proceed from
it, as it is a thing that is not known.

I went from Denizley to fee Laodicea and Pambouk, having taken up my quarters there in one of the moft private coffee-houfes   The officer here came to demand the harach, or yearly tax upon Chriftians, on which I produced my firman, which, according to cuftom, was carried to the cadi, who faid, if I would pay him a fum, amounting to about as much as the harach, I fhould not be obliged to pay that tax, and, on my refufal, he gave orders that I fhould not be furnifhed with horfes to go on, upon this I applied to the aga, who did me juftice, and was fo generous as not to accept of a prefent which I fent to him as mark of my gratitude.

CHAP. XIV

Of Colosse, Apamea Cibotus, and Synnada, in Great Phrygia.

FROM Denizley we continued on our journey to the north eaft, and went by a large ftream called Sultan Emir, which I take to be the river Cadmus, it runs near that corner of the mountains, from which the hills of Laodicea begin, and falls into the Lycus, about a league to the eaft of that city.   At the bridge where we paffed over the Lycus there is an antient well built kane, called Accan; it is of white marble, and was doubtlefs built out of fome antient ruin.   I faw a head of a ftatue in the walls, a relief of Medufa's head, and another ftone with a relief on it of two dragons   Mount Cadmus turns here to the eaft, and runs fo for about fix miles, at the northern foot of it there is a rock with a caftle on it, which with a village below it, has the name of Konous   This was the ftrong hold of Soley Bey, where he generally refided, and had eleven cannon for his defence. It is thought to be Colofsè, mentioned as near Laodicea, to the inhabitants of which city faint Paul's epiftle to the Coloffians is addreffed All over the plain there are fmall channels made for the water to pafs, which are now dry, but they are incrufted like thofe of Pambouk, they are on a high ground over the vale, which extends to the hills   This high ground in one place makes a femicircle over the valley, and the bed of a river, which runs in it, acrofs this fpot there is a row of ftones fet up an end for about half a mile, which could not be for defence, for there are no ruins of a wall, but finding to the north of them graves made in the ground, with ftones like thefe, fet up an end at them, and fome little pillars crowned with pyramids, I conjectured that fuch tombs were likewife under thefe, which might be made in a line in this regular manner   To the fouth of thefe and of the rivulet there is a high fquare piece of ground, which feems to have been regularly laid out for a fortification, the banks all round being like a hanging ground, and there is an afcent to it on the north fide, over which there is a raifed work, it is a plain fpot, on which there are no ruins, and the people

Colofse (margin)

speak

speak of it as an unfinished fortrefs, which, if Colofsè was near, might be defigned for a place of defence, though I could not be informed of any other ruins here.

A little further the hills run for about two leagues to the north, and then turning eaft again, they are the fouthern bounds of a fine vale about a league wide, and four leagues long, in which poffibly the town Themifonium might be fituated. On the fouth fide of the above mentioned hills there are waters like thofe at Hierapolis, rifing on the fide of the hill, and running down in the fame manner, they incruft it with a white petrification, and on the oppofite fide there are other hot waters. We came to the foot of the high hills to the north of this vale, where there was an encampment of Turcomen, who breed camels and other cattle, they fpoke kindly to us, but we were fenfible that we were in great danger from them. When we afcended the woody mountains, the janizary looked pale, and owned he never was in fo great a terror, for thefe Turcomen, when they attack people, fhoot from the woods, and travellers are wounded or murdered without feeing any enemy. We croffed over the high hills to the north eaft, and came to a village, where we were conducted to an uninhabited houfe, and two green heads foon brought us a hot fupper, and I treated the village with coffee. On the fifteenth we went on in this fmall plain, which leads to the north weft into the great plains of the Mæander, which are from two to three leagues wide, and above twenty miles long, the Mæander runs along on the weft fide of them for about twelve miles, and goes in between the hills, going, as I fuppofe, about fouth weft, and comes into the plains of Laodicea, and, it is probable, that between thefe hills were the ruins of Tripolis, as well as that lake, which Strabo mentions between Laodicea and Apamea. The Mæander runs to the weft, at the diftance of eight miles from the norh end of the plain, turning fouth when it comes near the weft fide of it, it before runs through a plain joined by this, which extends to the eaft, that plain is about two leagues wide, and four long, at the eaft end of it there is a high hill, and a village called Dinglar, where the Mæander rifes, and, as they fay, falls down a hill from a lake at the top of it, where, as I was informed, there are fome ruins, but could not have the opportunity of a caravan to that place, having travelled fo far in fafety without company. Strabo fays the Mæander rifes from a hill of the Celæni, where, according to Livy, there was a ftrong fort. Metropolis feems to have been between this place and Apamea. Going over the Mæander, where it croffes the large plain, we lay at a village on the north fide of it, and having travelled eight miles, came to a town called Iſhecleh under the hills which are at the north end of the plain, and, according to Pliny, had the name of Sigma. This place is fituated at the rife of a river, which muft be Ceere the antient river Marfyas, now called Ochiſuſe, and confequently this Apamea Ci muft be Apamea Cibotus. A more delightful fcene cannot be imagined bound than the rife of this river, which flows out of the foot of the mountain in eight or nine ftreams, fome of which are huge, the water is very clear, and all the ftreams foon unite, and run through the plain into the Mæander. The place is fo pleafant that the poets fay, the nymphs, taken with the beauty of it, fettled on the rock over the rife of this river. Here alfo

they

they fix the famous contention in the art of music between Apollo and Marſyas   Theſe fables Strabo ſeems to place at the riſe of the Mæander, and Quintus Curtius alſo deſcribes the riſe of the Mæander, and applies it to the Marſyas, in ſaying that it riſes from the top of the hill, and falls down the rocks with a great noiſe.   On the whole it is probable Celæne was here on the hill, and Apamea on the plain, and being a place of great trade, the ſuburbs of it might extend near as far as the Mæander, and ſome authors might chuſe to diſtinguiſh it as being on the Mæander, which was a noted river, and when that river is ſaid to riſe at Celæne, it muſt be underſtood of the mountain of that name, though Strabo ſeems to place the town Celæne at the riſe of it, which, by a ſmall correction, may be underſtood, that Celæne was ſomewhere on that mountain.   There are many difficulties in relation to the account, which different authors give of the riſe of theſe rivers, and of the towns about them, the greateſt is to reconcile the account they give of them as riſing from the ſame ſources, as they ſeemed to be fourteen miles apart, but Maximus Tyrius, who was on the ſpot, ſeems to reconcile them, for he ſays, that they riſe from the ſame fountains, which by others are called a lake over the head of the Mæander, ſo that we are to ſuppoſe that the Mæander riſes at the lake, and that another ſtream is loſt under the hills, and afterwards comes out here at the foot of them   There are many pieces of pillars, and wrought ſtones here, and ſome few inſcriptions, but moſt of them are imperfect   At the ſouth ſide of the the town there are foundations of ſome large buildings, where they lately dug out a ſtone, on which there is an inſcription that mentions the council and people   Over the town is a very high ſteep hill, on which are ſome little remains of the antient fortreſs, which was ſo ſtrong by nature, that the people of the town going to it for refuge, Alexander the great could not take it, and the people agreeing to ſurrender if Darius did not come to their ſuccour in ſixty days, Alexander thought proper to wait ſo long to have it on thoſe terms   It was a ſatisfaction to buy at this place the medals of that great man, though I had them before, ſuppoſing they might be left here by his army   The ſecond name of this city ſeems to have been Cibotus, and Antiochus Soter king of Syria founded Apamea, and brought the inhabitants of Celane to it, which probably was on the hill over the preſent town, and he called the new town Apamea from his mother, which, to diſtinguiſh it from other cities of that name, had the name of Apamea Cibotus.   Poſſibly the paſſage of Strabo may be corrupted, which mentions Apamea at the mouth of the Marſyas, which ſhould have been ſaid to be at the riſe of it, becauſe he ſays immediately after, the Marſyas riſes at the city, runs through it and the ſuburbs, and falls into the Mæander, and Curtius ſays, that, after it has paſſed the city, it was called the Lycus   This place has often been deſtroyed by earthquakes, and I felt one there which continued a conſiderable time   Strabo ſuppoſes that they were antiently worſhippers of Neptune, and had their name from his ſon Celænus by Celæno   This river produces great plenty of large cray fiſh and fine carp of an extraordinary ſize, both which are ſold at ſuch low prices, that the common people eat them as the cheapeſt food   There are no Chriſtians in the town except a few Armenians, and two or three Greeks

who

who come with their goods, and lodge in the kanes. I faw here fome fragments of pillars of Cipollino marble, being of a moft beautiful pale green with a variety of fhades · I had feen of the fame fort at Alexandria in Ægypt, and it is probable the quarry is in this country.

Soley Bey was fo abfolute a mafter of Ifhecleh that he put an aga into it I thought it proper to make a fmall prefent to the governor, and the people were very civil · An effendi of the law came and fat with me, and was very inquifitive about the age of thefe antiquities. Another Turk came and informed me where all the antiquities were, and one of them fent to me to copy an infcription that was in his houfe, and I made this obfervation in general, that the Turks are commonly a better people where they are at a diftance from the fea, being much exafperated on the fea coafts by the treatment of the Corfairs.

The plain between Ifhecleh and the rife of the Mæander is bounded to the north and fouth by high hills, in this plain there is a river that falls into the Mæander, called Bouarbafha, which probably is the river Orgas, that is faid to have fallen into the Mæander above the Marfias, and Apollonias Metropolis might be about that place, as Sanaos probably was towards the fouth end of the great plain we came through, where I faw many ftones of antient buildings in the Mahometan burial places I make this conjecture from the order in which Strabo mentions the places to the fouth of the Mæander going from weft to eaft Ifhecleh is about fifty miles from Satalia in Pamphilia, the old Attalia

To the eaft of the rife of the Mæander is that part of great Phrygia, called Phrygia Parorius from the mountains of that name, which run acrofs it from eaft to weft. On the north fide of them was Philomelium, which I take to have been at Sparta; on the fouth was Antioch of Pifidia, which probably was at Bourdour, where there are great ruins, it is twelve miles from Sparta in the way to Satalia, thefe being about eighteen miles apart, thefe places are on the borders of Lycaonia and Ifauria.

On the twentieth we fet out with the caravan from Ifhecleh, croffed over the mountains to the north, and came into a large plain, towards the north eaft corner of it is Sandacleh, this plain opens into another to the fouth eaft, which feems to extend a great way, and which I take to be the north part of Phrygia Parorius I conjecture that Synnada might be fituated in this plain of Sandacleh, though it is rather too large for that which Strabo defcribes, as only fixty ftadia, or eight miles probably in length There are not the leaft marks of any antiquities at Sandacleh, except on a hill to the weft of the town, where there are ruins of an old caftle, on which there is a Turkifh infcription, and probably it is a building of the middle ages. A league before we came to this town we paffed by fprings of hot waters, and three baths built at them, there are here fome little ruins of buildings, but I think not confiderable enough for fuch a city as Synnada muft have been, where the Roman conventus was held The hot waters beforementioned have a ftrong chalybeat tafte, feem to be very good, and are greedily drunk by the people of the caravan who pafs by Synnada was famous for a quarry of alabafter, and I faw in thefe parts fome few pieces of the whiteft kind We ftayed that night at Sandacleh, and on the twenty-firft croffed over the mountains into a fmall plain that would better agree with the defcription of that, in which Synnada ftood, but I could not be informed of any antiquities about it. It was very cold frofty weather, and we afcended with great difficulty fome low mountains covered with fnow, being obliged to walk great part of the day; and not having water with us, I was fo exceedingly thirfty that I drank of the fnow water wherever I could find it, which, without any other effect, in about three days, as I imagined, caufed my arms to break out in blifters in feveral parts, fomething in the manner of St Anthony's fire. We came much fatigued to a village where they very officioufly fupplied us with fewel, and provided a plentiful fupper, without expecting any return. On the twenty-fecond we defcended the hills for two hours into a large plain, extending beyond view to the eaft, and at the foot of them came to Carahiffar towards the fouth weft corner of the plain.

CHAP. XX.

Of Carahissar the antient Prymnesia, and fome other places in Great Phrygia.

CArahiffar is diftinguifhed among the Turks by the name of Aphioum Carahiffar, on account of the great quantities of aphioum or opium which is made here. I had great fatisfaction in finding by an infcription that Carahiffar is the antient Prymnefia of Ptolemy, becaufe it is of great ufe in making conjectures as to the fituation of other places mentioned by that author. This city is commonly faid to be half way between Smyrna and Angora, being feven days journey from each, though it is computed to be a hundred and forty miles from Smyrna, and only a hundred and four from Angora, it is fituated at the foot of the mountains round a very high rock, about half a mile in circumference, on the top of which they have built a fortrefs, the rock is a fort of baftard brown granite, it is of a black hue, from which the town is called Carahiffar [The black caftle]; it is fo very fteep that it would be impregnable if fupplied with provifions and water, and it feems to be half a quarter of a mile in perpendicular height. The town is near three miles in circumference, and it is a great thoroughfare, has much trade, and good fhops provided with all forts of things, being in a plentiful country, and many caravans pafs through it. It is the refidence of a pafha. There are in the city ten mofques, one of them is a noble building, with a portico before it, the whole being covered with domes. There are neither Greeks nor Jews in the city, but about fifty Armenian families, befides feveral merchants and tradefmen, who ftay here part of the year, as they do in other towns, living in kanes, they have two churches, and of late they have had a bifhop, whom they call metropolitan. In the country between this and Smyrna, they make moft of the Turkey carpets, particularly the largeft at Oufhak, three days journey from Carahiffar, and at Goula two days journey further, and about a place called Gourds twenty miles to the fouth weft of Goula, and towards Akiffar, the old Thyatira, but further eaft they make moftly that

fort,

fort, which are called Turkomen carpets, without nap, and in broad ſtripes and figures

At this place they came to demand of me the tax which is impoſed on Chriſtians, and my firman or paſſport was carried to the judge, who had the high title of mulla, in order to convince him that I was a Frank. He told them that they could take no harach or tax of me, but very coolly laid my firman by him, and ſaid, I muſt pay him a certain ſum, and then he would return it me. I refuſed to preſent what he requeſted, and ſent him word, that if he would not return my firman I would complain to the paſha. To which he replied, I muſt make the paſha a preſent of a greater value than what he demanded I accordingly diſpatched the janizary to the paſha, who ſent one of his ſervants to deſire the mulla to let him ſee the firman, and the paſha gave it to my janizary I afterwards out of gratitude preſented his caia with coffee, and the paſha with ſome ſweetmeats I happened to have by me for ſuch an occaſion. Whilſt I was at Carahiſſar, a young Bohemian made a ſlave at Belgrade came to me, who had turned Mahometan on his maſter's promiſing him a wife

Achſhaher or Oxſhaher, is ſituated about thirty miles eaſt north eaſt of Carahiſſar, there are ſome ruins at that place, which I take to have been Eumenia, and that this plain is the country of Eumenia mentioned in Great Phrygia [a].

We

[a] As the road from Aleppo to Conſtantinople paſſes through this country, I ſhall give ſome account of that road, which I received from a friend who travelled twice that way, as it will give an opportunity of explaining many things relating to the geography of Aſia Minor He went from Aleppo twenty miles to a hamlet called Caffine, where there are ſeveral Greek inſcriptions, thirteen miles further is Teſeen, from thirty three miles beyond that is Antioch, from which it is twenty ſeven miles to Baylane, and twenty four further to Baas, though the laſt computation ſeems to be rather too great, it is ſeven miles to Curteulu, and thirty three further to Adana, moſt of which places have been mentioned before From Adana there is a pleaſant road over ſmall hills, and through fine valleys on the banks of a river, which, I ſuppoſe, is the Cydnus Twenty two miles from Adana there is a ruined kane called Chockel, from this place the road begins to aſcend mount Taurus, called by the Turks Hagem Dagh The way is very rocky, and there are ſeveral narrow paſſages in it, over one of them there is a fortreſs called Dulick or Davercnt, conjectured to be Fort Davara mentioned by Tacitus, it is about a mile from Ramadan Ogli, which is twenty-ſeven miles from Chockel The air of Adana being very bad, the people of that city remove to this place, and live here in the months of June, July, and Auguſt They dwell in huts built of mud and ſtone, covered with boughs The road continues thro' the narrow vales between mount Taurus, and leads to a river called Carſu [The black water], ſuppoſed to be the Cydnus Here it is conjectured Cyrus had his camp mentioned by Xenophon The road croſſes the river, and leads to a large village called Oluſia, twenty four

miles from Ramadan Ogli This place is remarkable for nothing but a breed of large maſtiff dogs, which the people take out with them to deſtroy the boars and other wild beaſts The road is moſtly over hills, almoſt as far as Eraglia, which is in a large fruitful plain, and ſeems to be part of Lycaonia, this town is on a river, which I ſuppoſe falls into the Halys, being to the north of mount Taurus, it is twenty four miles from Oluſia The ſoil of the plain is ſalt, and there is a very ſalt lake towards Carabonar [The black river], which is thirty-three miles further It is a barren ſandy plain, in which the road continues twenty four miles to Iſmit, and thirty three to Cognia, the antient Iconium, which is about three miles from a part of mount Taurus, called Gaur Dagh Cognia is ſituated on the ſmall river Marram, which is loſt in the gardens, and does not extend as far as Curchum baſhi, ſuppoſed to be Palus Trogilius, it is about eight miles to the north eaſt of the city, and is dry in ſummer This city is large and ill built, there are a great number of Greek and Latin inſcriptions in the walls From Cognia, the road is through the ſame kind of country ten miles to a ruined place, where there is an imperfect Greek inſcription, and twelve miles further to another ruined place called Curlunum, where there are ſome Greek inſcriptions, and the head of a coloſſal ſtatue of a black ſtone about two feet in length A mile further is Latine, conjectured to be Laodicea Combuſta, where there are a great number of Greek inſcriptions paſſing by a town called Arcut, thirty three miles further, there is a huge town called Ulpun, beyond it is a conſiderable ſtream, which pours down from the mountain, and ſoon afterwards makes a lake twenty miles in circumference, called the lake

We set out on the twenty-fifth with the caravan, which was going from Smyrna to Angora, and had frost and snow, and a very severe wind. We crossed the plain about two leagues to the north east, passing over a large stream, which possibly may fall into the Halys, and so into the Euxine sea. We went over some low hills, and among them came to a ruined village, where there are many sepulchral grots, and some signs of antient buildings, among them I saw a fine capital of the Ionic order. We lay at a village in a large kane built like a barn, about eighteen miles from Carahissar. On the twenty-sixth we came into a small plain, and going between other hills to the north east, we crossed another plain about a league over, in the middle of which there is a tower, well built of brick and stone, there being one tier of hewn stone, and five of brick alternately, it seems to be a building of the time of the first eastern emperors, there are in it two or three imperfect sepulchral inscriptions on stones wrought like folding-doors; and I saw many of the same kind at Carahissar. These stones probably stopped the entrance of their vaults or grots. Near it there are very large Mahometan burial places, in which there are many stones with reliefs in the same manner, a great number of broken pillars, and other pieces of marble. This place is called Eski-Jeldutch [Old Jeldutch] from a village of that name, which is to the east. I could not conjecture what place this was. Going over a hill, we came into a large plain, that hill ends about three leagues further to the east, where both the plains join. This

Chiaur-Ghiol, and was conjectured to be the lake Carabtis of the antients. The road afterwards is through plains, and over small eminences for thirty three miles to Oxshahar or Achishahar, which, I suppose, may be Eumenia in Great Phrygia. A river runs through the middle of it, which is probably that which I passed to the north of Carahissar, and supposed to fall into the Sagaris, there are many Greek and Latin inscriptions here, some ruins, and a relief of a Roman eagle in marble, I passing besides in this place. The road is very pleasant for sixteen miles to Seleuchtier under the mountains, which was conjectured to be Seleucia or Sigilassus, there being some ruins there, the country abounds in apples, pears, and other fruit more than any other part of Turkey. Here the road to Smyrna continues on directly with near the foot of the mountains, the way to Constantinople being to the north west, from this place the road to Constantinople crosses a plain, and over a river on a bridge made of some ruined buildings, this, I suppose, to be the river which I passed two leagues to the north of Carahissar, and about these parts a castle was seen to the south on a high rock, which I conjecture might be Carahissar. After sixteen miles the road to Constantinople passes through Belawoden or Bilezugain, a large town, and three miles beyond it, comes to the mountain called Emir Dagh, Anadon Dagh, and Ketchier Dagh, in which there are several grottos that seemed to be catacombs. The road was pleasant for thirty three miles to Shiroff Pushukure, where there is a large village, the way is good through a barren country for twenty four miles, to Sadd Gizell, where there is a large convent of Dervishes, from this

place the country is uneven for twenty four miles to Eski-shahar, about half way there are some ruins, and Greek inscriptions at a place called Angura, which was conjectured to be Ancyra of Phrygia. Eski Shahar is a large city at the foot of a stony mountain, probably Sipylus, a river runs near it, which was conjectured to be the river Hermus, and if so, this must be the beginning of the plain Hyrcanus. There is a delightful road to twenty-four miles through a pleasant wood called Summnes, and by many springs to a small town of the name of Seguta, the road is then through a country partly woody, and partly improved with mulberry gardens for the silk, there being great plenty of water, we went afterwards for five miles down rocky mountains to Vizier Han, on a river called Sochei Yenderefi, which runs between rocky hills. The road is mountainous, but affords a great variety of beautiful views, and at the end of eleven miles is Leftkey, situated on the river Garipo, the antient Gallus which falls into the Sagaris, there is a large bridge over it. From this place the road is bad for three miles, but afterwards it passes for nine miles through a most agreeable country, full of delightful scenes in the valley of Itnic, till it comes to Itnic the antient Nicæa. From this place to the bay of Nicomedia the road is pleasant for nineteen miles, and the passage by sea to the north west is about eight miles, six miles beyond it is Gaerze or Gebsi, which was supposed to be the antient Libyssa where Hannibal ended his day, and was buried, from this place, it was computed to be thirty five miles to Scutari, from which town they ferry over to Constantinople.

2

great plain in some parts is at least twenty miles broad, and extends beyond view to the north west and south east, it is an uneven down, of a very barren white clay, which produces little herbage, not being improved, except where it is watered by streams, on which the villages are situated, it is all an open country without trees, and so are all the plains after we left Konous Having travelled about eight miles in this plain, and thirty-six from Carahissar, we came to a village called Alekiam, where we lay · Here are some ruins, and a few inscriptions, one of them in Latin is of the time of Constantine [b] Going on about four miles we passed a bridge over a large stream, on which, and in a burial place near, are some fragments of sepulchial inscriptions Travelling six miles further on the twenty-seventh, we came to an ill built town called Sevrihissar, situated at the north east side of the plain, at the foot Sevrihissar of a long rocky hill of a bastard grey granite There are ruins of a fortress on the hill over the town, and in the Armenian burial place are several antient sepulchral stones, many having two setts of folding-doors cut on them in relief, and on some there are Greek inscriptions of no importance, there are also here three or four statues of lions, and I saw four or five in the town, on one I found a sepulchral inscription This I conjecture, from Ptolemy, might be Abrostola This town is governed by a mosolem sent by the kisler-aga, or black eunuch, to whom the town and a territory about it belong There are here about five hundred Armenians, who have a large church under the archbishop of Angora. It is probable from the ruins that are seen, and which the people give an account of, that there were many considerable antient villages and some towns in this plain, one of which might be at a place called Balahazar, four miles to the south east, where I heard there were several remains

---

[1] In this inscription I found the word Amori anorum, so that probably Amorium was in these parts, and this plain might be the country of Amorium mentioned by Strabo I conjecture that an antient monastery might have been at this place, that the stones were brought to it, and that the town of Amorium was probably at a place called Herpan, about six miles to the

south east of Jelduch, where I was informed there are antiquities According to the Tables Abrostole was eleven miles east of Amurio, which agrees with the order in Ptolemy, who goes from the north west to the south east, and then begins again at the north west, for his longitudes and latitudes are not to be regarded as to these places

CHAP. XVI.

Of GALATIA in general; and of ANGORA, the antient ANCYRA, in Galatia.

WE set out on the thirtieth, and went only four miles, where we first saw the fine Angora goats   On the thirty-first we had snow all the morning, and went only eight miles to the river Sacari, having travelled east north east from Sevrihissar   The river Sacari is the old Sagaris or Sangarius, which at this place is very small, not being far from its rise.

Galatia   We here entered into Galatia from great Phrygia, this river being the bounds between them as well as between Galatia and Phrygia Minor, or Epictetus, and also between Bithynia and the Mariandyni   We came into the south part of Galatia, which was inhabited by the Tectosages, the eastern part, being the seat of the Trocmi, and the western, of the Tolistobogii, all originally Gauls, the first being so called from a people of Celtic Gaul, the two others had their names from their leaders, who, after they had for a long time ravaged Bithynia, and the neighbouring parts, they had this country allotted to them, which was called from them Gallo-Græcia, and afterwards Galatia, every one of these three people were divided into four parts called tetrarchies, each governed by its tetrarch, judge, general, and two lieutenant generals   The council of these twelve tetrarchs consisted of three hundred persons, as may be supposed a hundred of each tribe, who met at Drynæmeton, and had the sole power of judging in all cases of murder   About the time of Augustus this country was subject to three governors, then to two, and immediately afterwards it was put under the government of Deiotarus, and afterwards made part of the kingdom of Amyntas, and after his death it became a Roman province

We were obliged to stop at the river Sacari, because the waters were high, they have great plenty of very large carp in this river, which the Turks skin, and throw away the head before they dress them   They are very much distressed in these parts for fuel, and commonly make use of dried cow-dung   On the first of April we crossed the river on floats of timber, the horses swimming over, the rest of the way was mostly over uneven downs to the east north east   On the second we travelled sixteen miles to a village which is twelve miles from Angora, where we were met by the broker janizary and servant of the English gentleman of that city, to whom I was recommended, and we lay at the house of the aga, who was a relation of Mahomet   On the third we proceeded on our journey, and about a mile from Angora I was met by all the English, and most of the French, and after having taken a collation that was prepared in a house near the road, I was mounted on a fine horse, and went to the house of my friend in Angora

Angora   Angora is called Anguri by the Turks, and by the common people Engurieh, it is the antient Ancyra, which was the castle or fortress of

the

the Tectofages   It was made the Metropolis of Galatia under the reign of Nero, and fo it is called in the inſcriptions that are found here   The emperor Caracalla having been a great benefactor to the city, it was called Antoniniana.   The antient city feems to have been on the fame place as the prefent, except that in fome parts it appears to have extended fomewhat further to the weſt.   On the eaſt ſide of the plain near the mountains there are four or five hills, Angora is on the weſt and fouth fides of one of the largeſt of theſe hills, which is furtheſt to the fouth, on the fummit of which there is a large caſtle, the city alfo extends a little to the north weſt of the hill, and ſtretches on the north fide to another fmall hill, or rather rifing ground, on the top of which is the principal mofque called Hadjee-Biram, near which is the temple of Auguſtus, and the famous inſcription of Angora   The walls extend further north, and go up the middle of a fmall high hill called Orta Daug, from which they come down to the fmall river Tabahanah, which runs eaſt and north of the caſtle-hill, where they are joined to the caſtle-walls by a wall twenty feet thick, built acroſs the river with two or three holes in it, through which the water paſſes: This feems to be defigned to keep up the water, in order to fupply the caſtle in a time of diſtreſs, for there is a private paſſage down from the caſtle, by which they could take up the water that comes from the river   The walls of the town are about a mile and a half in length, and extend near half a mile up to the caſtle, which cannot be much leſs than a mile in circumference, it has a wall acroſs the middle of it, and a ſtrong tower at the fummit of the hill, which to the north and eaſt is a ſteep precipice   The caſtle itſelf is like a fmall town, and is well inhabited both by Chriſtians and Turks   The river which runs by the caſtle, together with another rivulet called the Infueh, which runs to the weſt of the town, falls into a larger ſtream called Chibouk-Sueh, which paſſes near the Armenian convent a mile to the north of the city, and runs into the Sacari, and though there are fo many rivulets near the city, yet it is ill fupplied with water, which for common ufe they carry from the river to the higher parts of the town on horfes, either in leather bags, as at Cairo, or in earthen jars, put into a box or frame on each fide of the beaſt, but they have water conveyed by an aqueduct to the lower parts of the town from the river, and all the people of any condition fend for their water half a mile to a fountain   The air of this place is eſteemed to be very dry, and good for aſthmatick conſtitutions, but pernicious to the ſinguine. There being no wood in the country about it, fuel is exceedingly dear, and the common people are obliged to make ufe of dried dung   The prefent walls of the city are very ill built, and confiſt chiefly of the ſtones of antient buildings put together only with mud, fo that a great part of them are fallen down, they were built about fixty years ago againſt the rebel Gadick, who ravaged the country with twelve thoufand men, and was afterwards made a paſha   Though many of the houfes of the city are very good within, yet the buildings on the outſide make a very mean appearance, being all of unburnt brick, the ſtreets are narrow, and the city irregularly laid out   They have however a handfome ſtone building covered with cupolas, which is a bezeſtin for rich goods, theſe are buildings only of one floor with ſhops in them, like the exchanges in London, they have about twelve large mosques with minorets, and several small ones, near a hundred in all

As to antient buildings there are very few remains of any   To the west of the walls there is a small ruin which is built of brick and stone, and seems to have been part of some antient temple, but it is so destroyed, that no judgment can be made what sort of a building it was   The most curious piece of antiquity is near a mosque called Hadjee-Biram, which belongs to a college for Mahometan sophtis · It is an oblong square building of white marble, about ninety feet long, and fifty broad, it stands north and south, the walls are three feet three inches thick, and the stones are channelled at the joints   It is built on a basement, and there is a cornish round at the top, both inside and out, adorned with sculpture   At the distance of twenty feet from the south end, which is open like a portico, there is a grand door, the frame of which is very richly carved, at the same distance from the north end there appears to have been another partition, and it is very probable that there was such another door, and that there were four lofty columns to each portico, so that the middle room is about forty-four feet long, and has a second beautiful entablature seven feet below the upper one, which is adorned with festoons, and on each side below it there are three windows with semicircular tops, about four feet wide, and five high, which have before them a grate of marble, it is supposed to have been a temple to Augustus.   On the inside of the portico to the south is that famous inscription, which is the second volume, that Augustus left with his will in the hands of the vestal virgins[c], and ordered to be cut in two brass plates in the front of his mausoleum in Rome. The inscription consists of six columns, three on each side of the portico, each having between fifty and sixty lines in it, and each line about sixty letters, on the outside of the eastern wall I saw part of it cut in Greek, and part might be on the west side, I have reason to believe that it was in about twenty columns, I copied part of it   The letters appear to have been gilt on a ground of vermilion: Some houses are built against the other parts of it.   The title of the Latin inscription is in three lines over the three first columns, as that in the Greek appears to have been in one line on the east side, which is a good reason to suppose that the whole Greek inscription was on that side, because the Latin begins on the west side   The greatest part of the antient buildings were of an ash-coloured marble with veins of white in it, which are brought from the mountains to the south east, where I saw also a great quantity of red marble streaked with white   Most of the capitals here are of the Corinthian order, and I took notice of the capitals of some pilasters, consisting of a cymatium, two lists, and flutes about a foot long, and under them a quarter round, adorned with eggs and darts   Towards the north west corner of the city there is a very extraordinary pillar, the pedestal of which is raised on a stone work about ten feet above the ground   That work probably was cased with marble, which might have an inscription on it, and be adorned with reliefs, the shaft is about

[c] De tribus voluminibus, uno, mandata de funere suo complexus est   altero, indicem rerum a se gestarum, quam vellet incidi in aeneis tabulis, quae ante mausoleum statuerentur Sueton Octavius 101

I

four

four feet in diameter, and is composed of fifteen stones, each being two feet deep; it is worked all round horizontally with convex and concave members, which are about an eighth of a circle, divided by lifts, all those members being three inches wide, the capital consists of four plain circles something like pateræ, with leaves on each side of them, the work above this somewhat resembling a Tuscan capital The style of the shaft has no bad effect, but the capital is rather in a Gothic taste It may be supposed that this pillar was erected to the honour of the emperor Julian, when he passed through Ancyra from Parthia, there being an inscription to his honour in the castle walls There are many stone pipes of aqueducts about the town, such as are described at Laodicea, by which the water ran along on the ground, as it does at present from the river, there being towers at certain distances, in which the water ascends and descends in earthen pipes, to make it rise to the higher parts of the town, which is a method much practised in these countries

The city of Angora is governed by a pasha and cadi, some compute that there a hundred thousand souls in it, ninety thousand of which are Turks, and about a thousand of those janizaries The Christians are thought to be about ten thousand, of which three hundred families or about fifteen hundred souls are Greeks, the rest Armenians, two thirds of the latter are of the Roman communion, and have four churches, the other Armenians have three In rebuilding one of their churches not long ago, they found the bodies of seven children uncorrupted, I saw the head and hand of one them, they were like the bodies at Bremen, and at Venzoni in Friuli, but rather more fair and entire They suppose that these are of the twelve children, who were martyred when saint Clemens Ancyranus suffered. The Armenians have a large convent a small mile to the north of the city, here their archbishop of Ancyra resides, with his suffragan; they are not of the Roman church The Greeks also have an archbishop here, who is one of the twelve great metropolitans under the patriarch of Constantinople, is the fourth in rank, and has the title of Primate of all Galatia, [Ἔξαρχος πάσης Γαλατίας] he has now no bishop under him, nor have any of the archbishops of Asia Minor In a Greek church in the castle there is a transparent piece of alabaster of a yellowish colour, many authors make mention of it, and the Greeks imagine it has some miraculous effects, though there is a much finer piece of the same sort in the church of the convent There are in Angora about forty poor families of Jews The city was formerly very fruitful in hereticks, among whom was Photinus In the year three hundred and fourteen a council of eighteen prelates was held here under Vitalis patriarch of Antioch, and they made twenty-four canons relating to the penance of apostates, and some other points of discipline.

They have a trade here of the hair of common goats, which grows short under the long hair, it is taken off from the skin after they are dead, and is sent to England, and other parts, to make hats, the French also of late buy up yarn of sheep's wool, in order to send it to France, but the great staple commodity of the place is the yarn of the fine Angora goats wool, and the manufactures of it. These goats are peculiar to the country for about thirty miles round Angora, info-much that if they are carried to another place they degenerate, as to the east of the Halys, and on the other fide of a river that runs from the north into the Sagari, and alfo to the fouth of Sevrihiffar. They are very beautiful goats, moftly white, but fome are of an afh colour, and very few black; the hair or wool grows in long curled ringlets, fome of it is even a foot in length, the fineft is that of kids of a year or two old, and when they are about fixteen years old, it grows coarfe, and in a manner turns to hair, it is fo exceedingly fine that the moft experienced perfons could not know it from filk, but by the touch, they are fhorn without wafhing about the month of May, and the wool fells for two dollars an oke, the common fale of yarn is from two and a half to fix dollars, though they make it even to the value of thirty dollars. They here weave of it fine camlets of three or four threds, which they fometimes water, and they make a ftuff they call fhawl of two threds, which is like our fineft ferges, it is either plain or ftriped, and both are worn by the Turks for fummer garments, they make alfo camlets even to thirteen threds for European cloathes. The export of the wool out of the country is ftrictly prohibited, becaufe the inhabitants live by the fpinning of it, every thing that we call mohair, camlets, and prunellas are made of it, and alfo the beft plufhes, of which great quantities of the flowered fort are made in Holland. The export was pretty near equal to England, France, and Holland, amounting to about five or fix hundred camel loads to each, yearly, every load being one hundred and fifty okes, but I have been informed, that the trade to England is funk, and that the greateft export now is to France, and next to Holland, what is exported being from three to fix dollars an oke. This country produces a very good red wine, and they have excellent rice on fome rivers not a great way from Angora [d]

CHAP.

[d] At Angora I made the beft enquiry I could about thofe places, to which I did not find it convenient to go. Cogni, about four days journey, or feventy miles to the fouth fouth eaft is the antient Iconium in Lycionia. There are in it about fifty Greek families who have a church, in which, they fay, St Paul preached, near the town there is a Greek convent called Xyh, in which there are only four or five ca Joyers. About twelve miles nearer Angora is the falt lake, now called Cadoun Touftr, which is the antient lake Tatti, mentioned by Strabo, they fay now that a body, or any other thing thrown into it, turns falt, that is, I fuppofe, is incrufted over with falt. All thefe countries are fupplied with falt from this lake, it is brought in fmall white pieces, which are hard, and confequently muft incruft into a folid cake. The country about Cogni is called upper Hamma, and that to the north north weft is called lower Hamma, where there is a great fcarcity of water, and it anfwers to the defcription which Strabo gave of that part of Lycionia, but thefe are poweffed by two lords, and did belong to the fame another.

Cabira in Cappadocia is about a hundred and eleven miles to the weft fouth weft of Angora. The road goes over mountains called Almadaug for eight miles to Petzeh, then paffing Curekdaug [The fpade mountain], which may be mount Magabi, in fixteen miles it brings to Caragikilich, two miles from which there is a ruined convent or church called Petzeh, and at the door of it there are two ftatues of lyons. Half an hour further is a bridge over the Kiflermack, the antient Halys, which is built with feven arches. The road, I fuppofe, after this continues on near the Halys. Fourteen miles further is a village called Caman, and at the end of eight more, is the city Kirfaer, fituated in a valley. Sixteen miles further is a large village called Ha jee-Bertas, where there is a kan with a charitable foundation to give food to all perfons and their beafts who travel that way. Twenty four miles further is Baum Higilech, where there are no houfes, but fome grottos inhabited by about two hundred families. Ten miles further is Achmes Kahff, which is a caftle on a high hill over the river, oppofite to it is a high mountain, from which there falls a great cafcade of water. Here is a bridge of one arch over the Halys, the bridge is called Frenes Koue [The fring carch]. This bridge is five paces broad, and about a hundred and fifteen feet high from the water to the top of the battlement, and a hundred and fixty paces over. I was informed that at there was a Greek infeription

2

C H A P. XVII.

Of some places in GALATIA, and PAPHLAGONIA, in the road to Constantinople.

AS I found that there was nothing very remarkable in the direct roads to Constantinople or Boursa, I determined to go three days journey to the north of Angora into the great road from Persia, which is by the way of Tocat, Amasia, and Tocia to Constantinople.

We

inscription on it The Christians call it St Helen's bridge, being, as they say, built by her Twelve miles further, over the plain, is Cæsarea in Cappadocia, called by the Turks Kaisar This town is divided into a hundred and eighty Mahometan parishes called Mahalleh, to each of which there is a mosque with a minoret called Jamme, or a sort of chapel without a minoret, in which they cannot pray on Fridays at noon, and to these they give the name of Machif There are in the city one Greek and three Armenian churches, and the Greeks have lately founded a convent near the town They have a manufacture here of striped calimancoes, used by the common people for garments, and they have also a trade in that sort of goats hair, which is used to make hats. About an hour to the north of the city is the mountain of St Basil, called by the Turks Ali-Daug; it is an ascent of five hours Half way up there is a magnificent cistern, to which there are four entrances, it has fish in it, some of which, they say, weigh thirty okes, which is above a hundred weight On the top of the hill there is a church in two parts, one dedicated to the virgin Mary, and the other to St Basil, who was archbishop of Cæsarea An hour and a half, or a league to the west of the city is the cemetery of St Gregory Near the city also is mount Argias, the antient Argeus, which is always covered with snow, it is of a soft stone, and full of grottos, which are said by some to have been the habitations of hermits but it is more probable that they were the places in which the inhabitants of Cæsarea deposited their dead Towards the foot of it there are several monuments, which consist of a cupola, built on four pillars, there are inscriptions on them in a character not known, which they say, is Persian, and they call them the monuments of the Persians Three days journey from Cæsarea Adena, the antient Adam near Tarsus

It is about a hundred and seventy two miles to the west north west of Angora, and Changri is about thirty eight miles from Angora in that road, which, I suppose, is the antient Gangra and I was informed that there are remains there of an old building, it having been the place of residence of four of the kings of Paphlagonia Twenty four miles further is Tosia, which I imagine might be Pompeiopolis in Paphlagonia, because they place it in the way from Gangra to Sinope, though the distance of thirty five miles seems to be too great

Here also, they say, there are some antiquities Thirty miles further is Osmanjieck, which, if I mistake not, is at the passage of the Halys Twenty four miles further is Masouan, which must be in Galatian Pontus Here also, they say, there are some signs of antiquity, but what place it was I cannot conjecture, unless it might be Virasia of the Tables Sixteen miles further is Amasia, which retains its old name, and is on the river Coderlick, the antient Iris, this is the birth place of Strabo, here are likewise some ruins Tocat is forty miles further, which I should take to be Neocæsarea, it is situated on a hill, and has seven Armenian churches in it, and one Greek church, there are some Jews in the city About four days to the east of Tocat there is a great convent called Psulema, in which there are about forty monks, the convent has great privileges, and pays no harach or poll tax; this and three more I have mentioned being all the monasteries that I could hear of in Asia Minor This town has a traffic in copper vessels Eight miles east of this place is Gumenack, where, they say, there are some ruins Twenty-four miles from it is Siwas, the seat of a pasha, which might be Sebastiopolis, there being some remains of antiquity about it, it is only four or five days journey from Malatia on the Euphrates Tocat is twenty days journey from Aleppo, and forty from Jerusalem, and the road to it from Constantinople is one of the great roads into Persia From Angora to Sinope, where Diogenes the Cynic was born, it is near four days journey, about sixty four miles; no caravans go to those parts, the Euxine sea being dangerous, and the ports of it are bad, which is the reason why there is little trade that way; and if the black sea was much navigated, it would hurt both Constantinople and Smyrna, though the danger of it must be the principal reason why goods are carried such a long journey by land from Constantinople to Tocat, which cannot be above four or five days journey from the sea

Angora is computed to be about a hundred and seventy miles from Constantinople In that road eighteen miles from Angora, near a place called Aias, there is a very hot bath, which people can bear but a short time, and it is chiefly used for ulcers and scrophulous disorders Sixteen miles further is a town called Beybazar, situated on some small hill, and, is well I could learn, is not above seven or eight miles to the north of the Sagaris; if it was not a place

It it

We left Angora on the twenty-ninth of April, and, according to the custom of these countries, almost all the Europeans did me the honour to accompany me a mile or two out of the town. We made a caval-cade of between thirty and forty horse, and taking a collation on the side of a stream, two of the English gentlemen went on with me to the northward, and we lay at a place about twelve miles from Angora On the thirtieth we went about twenty miles through an uneven coun-try, and came into a narrow vale between the mountains, which much resemble Savoy At the first entrance into it I saw a bath called Kisdje-Hamam, they are chalybeat waters, not very strong but tepid, and are used both for drinking and bathing, chiefly the latter, but they are not much frequented, because there are other waters near which are more esteem-ed We lay at a village in which the houses are made of entire fir-trees; I saw gooseberry-trees grow wild in this country On the first of May we went about four miles to some waters which are stronger and hotter than the others, insomuch that the first entrance gives some pain, they are called Sha-Hamam, among many other virtues, they have performed wonderful cures in the dropsy, and it being a cool retirement the Eu-ropeans sometimes go there from Angora during the hot season A league further there is a village called Clesicui [Church Village] from a ruined church which is there: From this place my friends returned to Angora

Paphlagonia   Four miles further we crossed the mountains to the west into a fine country, which, I suppose, must be the antient Paphlagonia, and that these mountains were the bounds between it and Galatia. We lay here in a wooden village, where the people were very civil, and came and drank coffee with us. Paphlagonia was between the rivers Halys and Parthenius, having Pontus to the east, and Bithynia to the west, and was antiently governed by its own kings On the twenty-second we proceeded on our journey, and I saw a town called Cherkes to the north, which is in the Tocat road, and is about sixty miles to the west of Tocat beforementioned, this may be Anadynata of the Tables, and is the residence of the pasha of this country Eight miles from the mountain we passed over the small river Cherkes, which runs near the

that is very destitute of water, or, if there were any antiquities there, I should have thought it was Pessinus, concerning the situation of which once I could get no information, though it was so famous a city near the Sagaris, but as it was in the road of the Tables from Nicæa to Amu-rio, which was in Great Phrygia, it ought to be looked for farther to the south, it may be about the place where we passed that river to Angora It was a city of great trade, and fa-mous for the worship of the mother of the gods, called here Angdestis, who is the same as Cybele, it was adorned with a temple, and porticos by the kings of the race of Attalus There was a statue here of the great goddess, which they pre-tend fell down from heaven, and that this gave occasion to the name of the place the sta-tue was brought to Rome in the time of the se-cond Punic war on account of a prophecy of the Sibyline oracle, in order to facilitate the conquest of the Carthaginians The prophecy of the Sibyline oracle is thus related by Livy

"Quandoque hostis terræ Italiæ bellum intu-"lisset, eum pelli Italia vincique posse, si ma-"ter Idæa a Pessinunte Romam advectæ foret" Liv xxix 10 Juliopolis, the old Gordium, is situated forth to the north on the river Sagaris, this place was famous for the Gordian knot cut by Alexander the Great, but the city was de-stroyed before Strabo's time Twelve miles be-yond Bayboyzar is Sualar, a river runs by it, and to the west of this river the Angora goats degenerate About sixty six miles further, it is villa, called Gaivey, is the passage over the Sa-garis, which runs a great way to the west near to this place, and then turning north, falls into the Euxine sea This river would be navigable a considerable way up, if there were no some rock that run across it and methods might be found to make it navigable Thirty miles fur-ther is Ismit, the antient Nicomedia, which is thirty six miles from Sucatt Bonifacio is about the same distance from Angora as Constantinople

town, and came into the great road to Conſtantinople, and about ſix further to a larger ſtream called Gerede-Su, which runs eaſt, and, I ſuppoſe, it is the antient Parthenius; on the other ſide of it, about ſix miles further, is a large village called Bainder, which is fourteen miles from Cherkes, and may be the antient Flaviopolis This country is called Varanchahere [The ruined city]. I ſaw the ruins of an antient bridge below this, where I firſt came to the river, near Bainder the river Cherkes falls into the Geredy-Su. The river Parthenius is ſaid to have its name from a fable that the virgin Diana uſed to hunt about it, and the city Amaſtris was at the mouth of it From the name of this country of Varanchahere, I had hopes given me that I ſhould find ſome antiquities there, and had a letter to the waiwode, who is the governor of it under the ſultaneſs mother, to whom it belonged, but I found nothing except a ſmall encloſure near the waiwode's houſe, about thirty feet long, and twenty wide, in the middle of the further ſide there is a ſtone ſet up an end like the top of an antient ſtone coffin, and one on each ſide of it, as if it had been deſigned as a place for a ſtatue, the encloſure round conſiſts of ſtones ſet up an end about three feet high, as deſcribed near Konous the ſuppoſed Coloſſe I conjectured that there might be a ſepulchral vault under it, unleſs the place, which ſeemed deſigned to receive a ſtatue, might incline to conjecture that it was an open temple, in the manner of that near Tortoſa in Syria, there runs a ſmall river near it to the north eaſt, which may be the Billaus, near the mouth of which was Tios on the Euxine ſea, Philetærus was of that city, from whom the kings of Pergamus deſcended When I went to the houſe of the waiwode, I was conducted to the apartments allotted for ſtrangers, and ſent my letter and a ſmall preſent to him He was very civil, but I could not find that there were any antiquities to be ſeen Having gone out of the great road to this place, I returned to it on the third. In this country of Varanchahere is a famous water at a place called Sugergick, for, as they tell the ſtory, when a country is infeſted with locuſts, if this water is carried to the place by an unpolluted perſon, when they obſerve the locuſts have laid eggs, it always brings after it a great number of ſpeckled birds as big as ſterlings, who laying and hatching their eggs, they and their young deſtroy the locuſts which are produced by the eggs laid the year before, a ſtory that ſeems very improbable, but it is firmly believed in theſe parts, and is related with all its circumſtances by many travellers, but it is to be queſtioned whether theſe birds would not come and deſtroy them, though the water was not brought

Having gone out of the great road to this place, we returned to it again on the third to Geredy, which is fifty ſix miles from Angora, it is ſituated on a high ground on each ſide of the river Geredy I did not ſee the leaſt remains of antiquity here The houſes of this town, as well as all the others which I ſaw, after I came to the baths, are built of fir-trees ſquared out, laid one on another, and joined at the corners, the roofs are covered with boards They have in this town a manufacture of ordinary red leather, and the Angora goats are kept ſo far to the north and weſt, and the wool of them is bought at this town, and ſent to Angora, for they do not ſpin it in theſe parts This place is about fifty four miles from the Euxine ſea, the neareſt place on it being Eliry, which may be Heraclea; this river paffes by two places, Mangeri and Dourleck: Ciniata is mentioned in Paphlagonia under mount Olgaftrys, it was ufed as a fortrefs by Mithridates Ctiftes, and may be Anadynata of the Tables; it is not known where any of thefe antient places were

---

C H A P. XVIII.

Of BORLA, NICOMEDIA, and fome other places in Bithynia; and of the PRINCES ISLANDS.

THAT part of Bithynia inhabited by the Mariandyni and Cau- cones was between the rivers Parthenius and Hippius   On the fourth we travelled fixteen miles through a very pleafant coun- try, and came into a village in a beautiful vale, where I went to the houfe of the man of whom I had hired horfes, and had my carpet fpread in a grove by a ftream.   I obferved that they make ropes here of hemp without beating it, but only pick off the rind with their hands. On the fifth we went four miles further to Borla through a pleafant woody country, and near a lake, which is about four miles in circum- ference, called Chagah-Guel; this lake abounds in a fort of fifh that are looked on as unwholefom

Borla is towards the weft end of a fine vale, which is about a league broad, and four leagues long, it is a moft beautiful fpot, much re- fembling the country about Padoua, and the low mountains on each fide are well improved, having villages on them, and are like the Euganean hills   This place is fituated in the plain, and on the fouth and weft fide of a hill, on which there are fome little remains of the walls of the antient town, which was fituated much like Old Sarum   There are alfo about the town, and in the road to it, feveral fepulcral infcriptions cut on ftones, which are like round pedeftals, about two feet in diameter, and four feet high   It is probable this was the antient Bithynium, after- wards called Claudianopolis, which was the birth place of Antinous, and might receive a third name from him, and be Antiniopolis of the Tables   A pretty large ftream runs through the vale to the north eaft, which, I fuppofe, is the old Elatas, near the mouth of which was the city Heraclea   On the fixth we went eighteen miles further, thro' pleafant woods, moftly of hornbeam and beach   The country being al- moft entirely uninhabited, we came to a river, running in a deep bed, which is called Tinfu, and I take it to be the river Hippius, when we had croffed it, we paffed thro' a village called Tayah, with many houfes and canes in it, built chiefly for the convenience of travellers   I faw here a great deal of hewn ftone, and a round altar adorned with fe- ftoons, and conjecture that Prufa on the Hippius was fituated here, fup- pofed by fome to be the antient city Hippia, and that it received a new name from being rebuilt or enlarged by Prufias king of Bithynia   Near

this

this place they turn all forts of wooden vafes, and thofe Turkifh oval tables with one foot like a falver, which are made of one piece of wood The fituation of it agrees with the diftance of Cepota in the Tables, from Antiniopolis or Borla We went on and lay in a meadow near the banks of the river ; I obferved this day a great variety of trees of almoft all forts, (except birch and elm) and particularly apple, pear, medlar, acanthus, what I took to be the Roman laurel, and a dwarf fhrub with a pale green flower like the lelac It is probable the Mariandyni inhabited on the fea as far as the mouth of the Sagaris, and that Bithynia Proper being to the fouth of that country, was divided from the Mariandyni by the Sagaris, both to the eaft and to the north, being bounded in other parts to the eaft by Phrygia Minor, to the fouth eaft by the river Æfepus from Myfia, to the weft by the Propontis, and to the north by the Euxine fea, this part of Bithynia was inhabited by the Chalcedonii On the feventeenth we went fourteen miles, the latter half of the way being through delightful woods of tall oaks On the eighth we came to a fmall town called Handakè at the weft end of the wood, which may be Manoris of the Tables, it is chiefly fupported by the caravans that pafs through it We then came into the moft beautiful plain enclofed country I ever beheld, it is about three leagues broad There are large horn beam and walnut-trees all over the fields, without any regularity, low hills to the north, and higher to the fouth, covered with woods, between which the Sagaris runs through this plain, and we paffed that river on a large wooden bridge a hundred paces long Dufeprofolimpum of the Tables, might be about this place We lay at a village a little beyond it, having gone about five leagues in this country We foon came to fome low hills covered with wood and corn, which divide the plain into two parts, and render this country ftill more delightful, infomuch that it is the moft beautiful fpot that can be imagined To the fouth of thefe hills I faw a large arch built againft the hill, and at a little diftance a piece of a high wall remaining, but as we were with a caravan, I could not fatisfy my curiofity in going to fee it This may be Demetrium of the Tables, though the diftances don't well agree, they call it now the bridge of the old Sacari, as if the channel of the old Sacari had formerly run there There is one thing I obferved in all this country, almoft all the people who cultivate the land are janizaries, for being near Conftantinople, many of that body have, without doubt, fettled here, all whofe defcendants are janizaries, they diftinguifh themfelves by an unbleached coarfe linnen fafh, which they wear about their turbants We proceeded in our journey on the ninth, the large lake of Sabanjah is on the fouth fide of thofe hills which divide the plain, it extends about half a league in breadth from thefe hills, to thofe on the north, and it is above two leagues long, there are fifh in it, efpecially a large carp, which they fifh for in boats, hollowed out of one piece of wood, there is a little town called Sabanjah on this lake, where all the roads meet that go to Conftantinople, and this great concourfe is the chief fupport of the place, this may be Late is of the Tables, which is but twenty-fix miles from Nicomedia, though this place is but fixteen, I faw here fome ftones that were of antient work We went on near the lake through this delightful country, which exceeds

ceeds any that I have feen, the foil is very rich, and there are no ftones in it We ftopped in a beautiful meadow, where I made balm tea of the herb which grew on each fide of my carpet: We went fix miles further, and on the tenth travelled fix miles to Ifmit, which is the antient Nico-

Nicomedia media, faid to be firft built by Olbia, and had its firft name from him ; it was afterwards rebuilt by Nicomedes king of Bithynia, tho' Olbia feems rather to have been near it, and that the inhabitants of it were tranf-planted to this place That range of hills which divide the plain, as be-fore mentioned, extend along to the north of the bay on which Nico-media ftood The prefent town is fituated at the foot of two of thefe hills, and all up the fouth fide of the weftern one, which is very high, and on part of the other, it is near the north eaft corner of the bay. All the houfes have fmall gardens or courts to them, efpecially thofe on the hills, the gardens are planted with trees, and the vines being carried along on frames built like roofs, make the city appear exceedingly beau-tiful, and indeed the fituation of it is very fine, the country is well im-proved all round it, the little hills on each fide are covered with gar-dens and vineyards, and the country on the other fide of the bay has a beautiful appearance · The fhops are in four or five ftreets next to the fea, built round many large kanes. Their houfes are moftly up the fide of the hills, and the Chriftians live towards the top, as it does not fuit fo well with the Turkifh indolence to take the pains to afcend fo high. They have no quay to the town, but a fort of wooden piers like bridges built out into the water, and the great boats come up to them, it being a place of great concourfe, in order to embark for Conftantinople ; though, they fay, it is a hundred miles by fea, yet I think it cannot exceed fifty, meafuring round by the coaft, as it is but thirty-fix miles to Scutari by land, but here the caravans end their journey, and no people go to Scutari by land, except thofe who travel on their own beafts They have alfo a trade in building large boats, and a great commerce in timber brought in boards and rafters from the woods, in which the country abounds They have alfo an export of falt, there being falterns at the eaft end of the bay · The refidence of the pafha of the country is in this place There are about two hundred Armenian families with their archbifhop, who has a monaftery five or fix miles to the north eaft, where he fometimes refides, they have one church in the city, to which there belongs only one prieft There are about a hundred Greek families here, who have likewife an archbifhop, and a church out of the town called St Pantaleon, in which there is the tomb of that martyr, but I could not be informed any thing concerning S S Barba and Adrian, who were martyred here, as well as St Gorgon, whofe body is faid to be in France There are very few remains of the antient Nicomedia On the top of the higheft hill is the principal piece of antiquity that is to be feen, which are remains of very ftrong walls, with femicircular towers at equal diftances, for about a third part up it is built with hewn ftone, every ftone being encompaffed with brick, which feems to be a proof that the walls are not of very great antiquity, but pro-bably after Conftantine, the upper part of the walls is built with brick, there are alfo fome remains of them at the bottom of the hill which extend to the fouth weft, from which it is probable they were continued down to the

fe t,

sea, turning, as I suppose, to the east, at the bottom of that part of the hill, where I saw remains of thick walls built against the hill so as to keep up the earth, and on the east side they seem to have come down along the side of the high hill: To the east of this there is another hill, where the Jews have their burial place: There are remains here of a very magnificent cistern built of brick, which seemed to have had in it four rows of pillars, six in a row, about fifteen feet apart; and there are arches turned from them every way; the arches which cover the cistern are very flat and made of bricks set round in an oval figure· The bricks in the walls are an inch thick, and the mortar between them is three inches thick It is probable that there was antiently some great building over this cistern, and that it was made before the water was brought in a great stream along the side of the hills by a channel, as it is at present: There are a few Greek inscriptions about the town: It is thirty-two miles from Ismit to Isnick, the antient Nicæa, by way of Sabanjah before mentioned, which is twelve miles from the former, and twenty from the latter, and, I suppose, it is Lateas of the Tables, probably the same as Libo in the Itinerary, which is in the road from Nicomedia to Nicæa The gulph of Ismit was antiently called Astacenus and Olbianus, and the head of land to the south of it was called the promontory of Neptune. The bay of Ismit is about thirty miles long. Pronectus is mentioned on it as a place of great trade opposite to Nicomedia, which might be where Boisis Scale now is, directly opposite to Ismit. Drepane also is mentioned on this bay, which Constantine called Helenopolis in honour of his mother; but I had no grounds to conjecture where it was, nor could I learn any thing about Acuron, where it is said Constantine died when he was going to the river Jordan to be baptized, only that there is a place of that name about fourteen miles to the north east of Ismit. Arrianus the historian was of Nicomedia, and near this bay lived the famous prince Tekely or Thokoly at a country-house, which he called, The Field of flowers: He was buried in the Armenian cemitery at Ismit, and there is a Latin epitaph on his tomb.

We left Ismit on the eleventh, and went out of the road three miles to the north to an allum water, which is called Chaiesu; on the hill over it are the foundations of a church dedicated to the Virgin Mary, to which the Christians resort at a certain season of the year: This water has no particular taste, but has allum in it, and is sent in great quantities to Constantinople, it has been thought to be good for the stone, and, they say, that it is an approved remedy for a dysentery.

Ten miles from Ismit in the road to Constantinople there is a very small village on the sea, called Corsau, to the west of it is a hill, on which there are ruins of walls on the north and west sides, which coming down to the plain make an enclosure above half a mile in circumference, it seems to have been an antient town, and probably was Astacus, from which the bay had its name On the twelfth we went six miles to a little port called Mahollom, where the caravans of Boursa land from Dill on the other side of the bay. Eight miles further we came to a country town called Gebseh, situated on a height about a league from the sea It is thought that the antient Libyssa was about this place, but as I saw no marks of antiquity, I concluded it was nearer the sea

At that place, or near it, Hannibal lived after he had fled to Nicomedes king of Bithynia, and here he poifoned himfelf when he found he was betrayed: It is faid that he built a tower, with entrances on the four fides, by which he might efcape, in cafe he fhould be furprized; this build-ing was probably on fome advantageous ground, where he might always fee at a diftance any perfons that were coming, as we find they defcried the Romans, who were fent to take him. About a league to the fouth eaft of Gebfeh, on the higheft ground in thofe parts, there is a fmall mount, which commands a view of the whole country, and there are fome cyprefs-trees near it; it is poffible that the tower in which that great general lived might be on this fpot, and that this barrow might be the heap of fand under which it is faid he was buried. Eight miles further is Pantik, a fmall town on the fea, which muft be Pantichio of Antonine's Itinerary, fifteen miles from Chalcedon, and twenty-four from Libyffa, which latter diftance is much too great. I faw near the town a large round bafon built of brick, and a fmaller arched place near it, both of which feem to have been cifterns for water, the latter ferving for that ufe at prefent. We lay in the fields beyond this place; and on the thirteenth we found the country much improved in gardens and vineyards for the ufe of Conftantinople. We faw the Princes Iflands, which are at the entrance of the gulph of Ifmit, and are inhabited by the Greeks.

Princes
Iflands.

I failed from Conftantinople to thefe iflands, in company with fome Englifh gentlemen. We went firft to the largeft and moft eaftern ifland, fituated oppofite to Cortal, towards the mouth of the bay of Ifmit, and about a league from the continent, it is called by the Turks Boiuk Addah, [The Great Ifland] and by the Greeks Principe, it is about a mile long from north to fouth, and half a mile broad, and confifts of two hills and a plain fpot to the north, on which the town ftands by the fea-fide, it was tolerably well built, and is about a quarter of a mile in length, but is now in a ruinous condition. The ifland be-longs to the archbifhop of Chalcedon, and is inhabited by Greeks, who all live in the town, and in two monafteries that are in the ifland, there are four churches in the town; according to their tradi-tion, it antiently ftood at the northern foot of the hill which is to the fouth about the convent of faint Nicholas, where there are remains of a round cifterns built of ftone and brick fixty feet in diameter and fifteen deep, and there are fome ruined arches to the eaft near the water. There is a third convent in the ifland, which is ruined. The French ufed formerly to have country-houfes on this ifland, and retire to them, as the Greeks do at prefent, but they have now left them on account of the inconveniences of the water, and the danger of being detained by contrary winds. The chief fubfiftence of the inhabitants is fifhing and felling wine (brought from the continent, and the ifland Alonia) to the people of Conftantinople, who frequently come to thefe iflands for their pleafure. This ifland produces fome corn on the north and eaft fides, there are olive and fir trees on the hills, and it feems naturally to run into wood, efpecially the juniper. There is a fort of ftone in it, which looks like iron ore, and they have a tradi-tion, that there were antiently iron mines in the ifland, there is a well

z   near

near the town, the water of which has no particular tafte, but is purging, and efteemed good in venereal cafes. About half a mile to the eaft, there is an uninhabited ifland called Anderovetho, which is near a mile in circumference, and ferves for pafturage. We failed half a mile to the ifland of Halki, [Χάλκη] called by the Turks Eibeli, it is directly fouth of a village on the continent called Maltebe or Maltape. This ifland is about four miles in circumference, and confifts of two hills; at the eaftern foot of the northern hill is the fmall town, confifting moftly of taverns and fhops, it has only one church in it, on the top of the hill there is a convent of the Holy Trinity, with great conveniencies for receiving ftrangers, and there is a remarkable Latin infcription at the well. We went fouthward to the delightful convent called Panaiea, which is fituated between the two fummits of the fouthern hill, where I faw Pailfius, the depofed patriarch of Conftantinople, whom I had met at Famagufta in Cyprus, for he had been recalled, though not reftored. We went to the north north eaft to faint George's convent, on the eaftern foot of the northern fummit of the hill, where they have large buildings for ftrangers, who come to thefe iflands in great numbers when the plague rages at Conftantinople. The town belongs to this convent, which is the property of the archbifhop of Chalcedon, the other two convents belong to the patriarch of Conftantinople. This ifland produces a fmall quantity of good ftrong white wine, and fome corn.

To return to the continent, about a league beyond Pantek we came to another fmall town called Cortal, two leagues from it is Cadicui, a fmall town or village on the weft fide of the promontory, on which the antient Chalcedon ftood.

CHAP. XIX.

Of CHALCEDON, SCUTARI, the EUXINE SEA, and fome places on it.

THE promontory on which the antient Chalcedon ftood is a very fine fituation, being a gentle rifing ground from the fea, with which it is almoft bounded on three fides, that is in part on the eaft fide, as well as on the fouth and weft, further on the eaft fide of it is a fmall river which falls into the little bay to the fouth, that feems to have been their port, and I find is called by a certain geographer Portus Eutropii, as the point oppofite to the eaft, where there is a light houfe, was called the promontory Heræum, fo that Chalcedon would be efteemed a moft delightful fituation, if Conftantinople was not fo near it, which is indeed more advantagioufly fituated, for this place muft be much expofed to the wind in winter, and has not a good port. The cape is about half a mile broad, and a mile long, commanding a full view of the Propontis, of the Thracian Bofphorus, and of Conftantinople. There are no remains of this antient city, all being deftroyed, and

and the ground improved with gardens and vineyards: The Greeks have a small church here, which carries no great face of antiquity, and yet they pretend to say, that the council of Chalcedon was held in it · The church is in a low situation near the sea, tho' it is more probable that the cathedral church of Chalcedon was on a more advanced ground; and I find some travellers have placed it at a distance from this, though I could get no account of the ruins of any church on the height.

This part of Bithynia is hilly to the east, and the hills approaching near the Bosphorus to the north east of Scutari, the foot of them extends away to the south towards Chalcedon, and ending at the sea, makes a little bay, with the point of Chalcedon, opposite to Constantinople, where probably the arsenal was, which is said to have been at Chryfofopolis Over the north part of this bay is the seraglio of Scutari, where the grand signor commonly passes some days in the beginning of summer, it is a delightful place, and commands a fine view of the city. To the north east of it there are beautiful open fields for pasturage, and beyond them the burial places of Scutari, which being planted with cyprefs and other trees, are very pleafant; and from both thefe places there are some of the finest views that can be imagined, from one part particularly the land appears as locked in, in such a manner that the sea opposite to Scutari looks like a lake, and that city, together with Tophana and some villages to the north, appear like a beautiful city built round the lake, which has the finest effect that can be imagined.

Scutari Scutari is called by the Turks Scudar, and is suppofed to be the antient Chryfopolis, the south part of it is opposite to the point of the feraglio, and the north part to Tophana and Funduclı. The situation of Scutari is very beautiful, of which I should not have been fenfible, if I had not feen it from a minaret in the town. The hill is fhaped in a femicircle like a theatre, a little hill on each fide of the entrance to it adds to the beauty of it. The city is built all round up the fides of the hills, and in the area between, it is planted with trees rather thicker than Constantinople, and though I had feen it from feveral places before, yet the view from the minaret was one of the moft furprizing and beautiful fights I ever beheld · The town cannot be lefs than four miles in circumference, being the great refort for travellers from the eaft   The waladea mofque here, though not large, is very fine, and built in a good tafle, and beautifully adorned   The Perfian ambaffador refides at the fkirts of the town in a well fituated palace; he did not care to fee any Franks, the port being very fufpicious, and the minifter very wifely voided giving umbrage without any reafon, though the Perfians have a much greater regard for the Franks than the Turks, and accofted us in the ftreets with much civility   There is a hill over Scutari to the north eaft, which has two fummits, from which there are very extenfive and delightful views of Constantinople, and the adjacent places, the beauty of which indeed cannot be conceived without being on the place

Thracian
Bofphorus There are near twenty villages on each fide of the Thracian Bofphorus, or the canal, as it is called by the Europeans. The hills coming very near the fea on the Afia fide, for this, as well as for other reafons, the villages are fmall, but on the Europe fide they are fo large that it appears
pears

pears almost like one continued city for about three parts of the way towards the Euxine sea, as far as a village called Boyucderry, where the
French and Venetians ambassadors have country-houses. On both sides,
the grand signor has a great number of seraglios and kiosks, or summer houses, many of them built by viziers, and other great persons, all
whose estates are seized on by the monarch, whenever they are disgraced
or die. The canal is very pleasant, the villages all along, and the hills
over them covered with wood, make the view very delightful. The
Bosphorus, now called, The canal, is, according to the antients, fifteen
miles long, they computed it to be seven stadia in width from Chalcedon to Byzantium, but in other parts only four or five stadia broad.
The narrowest part is thought to be between Rumelli Hissari [The castle
of Romelia], and Anatole Hissari [The Eastern or Asiatic castle] and
consequently it must have been there, at the temple of Mercury on the
Europe side, that Darius built a bridge, in order to lead his army
against the Scythians. The castle on the Asia side was built by Bajazet
the first, when he besieged Constantinople about three hundred and
fifty years ago. That on the Europe side was the work of Mahomet the
second, before he laid siege to Constantinople. Here, all ships that go to
the Black sea are examined, and mutinous janizaries are often imprisoned, strangled, and thrown into the sea. Opposite to Scutari there
is a small rock or island, on which there is a tower called Kisculi, or
the virgin tower, and by the Franks the tower of Leander, there is a
little turret disjoined from it, on which there is a lanthorn for a lamp,
which they keep burning in it by night for the direction of shipping.
Under the tower there is a cistern of rain water. This tower was built
by the emperor Emanuel, and it is said that there was a wall from it to
the Asia side. Towards the mouth of the black sea there are two other
fortifications called Anatole Kala [The Asiatic fort], and Rumeli Kala
[The Romeli fort], and by the Franks they are called the new castles,
as those before mentioned are distinguished by the name of the old castles. These near the black sea were built in one thousand six hundred
twenty-eight by Amurath the fourth, in order to hinder the incursions
of the Colsicks, who had come into the canal, and burnt many of the
villages. Near the castle on the Asia side, which they look on is the
entrance into the Bosphorus from the black sea, there was a temple to
Jupiter Urius, which was five miles from the port of Daphne, probably
the bay at Boyucderry on the European side, which was ten miles from
Byzantium. Some think that the name of a place called Amur Ieri,
which is near the castle, was derived from this temple, opposite to it
there was a temple of Serapis. It is said that Jason returning from
Colchos sacrificed here to the twelve gods, and probably in particular to
Jupiter Urius, or Jupiter that gives favourable winds. In the temple of
Jupiter Urius there was a bronze statue, and the inscription, supposed
to have been on the pedestal of it, was found at Chalcedon, is explained by the learned Chishul, and the original inscription has been since
brought to England, and is now in Dr Mead's most curious collection of
antiquities. Opposite to Boyucderry there is a hill on the Asia side, where
they pretend to shew the tomb of Nimrod, it is a spot railed in, and
a piece of ground is laid out like a garden bed, four feet broad, and

forty-four feet long ; and the Turks have fome devotion for this place : To the fouth of it, in a very pleafant vale, there is a fummer houfe of the grand fignor's, which is known by the name of Tocat, it is about a mile from the canal Five miles further at the entrance into the Bofphorus were the Cyanean rocks or iflands, called alfo the Symplegades, one, on the Europe fide, the other, in Afia. That on the Afia fide lies further out of the canal to the eaft On both fides, at the entrance of the canal from the Euxine fea, there is a tower for a light houfe The Euxine fea is called by the Turks Caradenize [The black fea] It is looked on as a very dangerous fea, by reafon that it is fubject to violent winds, efpecially from the north, and has very few good ports ; it is navigated moftly by fmall veffels, which import provifions to Conftantino-ple, and fome larger that are employed in bringing timber and wood It is probable now the Mufcovites have Afoph, fome other trade may open from thofe parts, efpecially that of furs, which, during the war, had in part been carried on from Sweden by fhips of that nation. This fea is faid to be three hundred and fifty miles broad from north to fouth, and nine hundred long from eaft to weft, it is fuppofed to have fome fubterra-neous paffages, as fo many great rivers fall into it, and yet it has only the fmall outlet of the Thracian Bofphorus The northerly winds which blow from it moft part of the year bring clouds with them, and thefe cool refrefhing winds make the climate of Conftantinople very temperate and cool in fummer, whilft other places in the fame latitude fuffer much from the heat.

CHAP. XXI.

Of the DARDANELS, ILIUM, and OLD TROY.

WHEN I left Conftantinople, I went to Adrianople, Rodofto, Gallipoli, and fome other places in Thrace ; and on the twenty fourth of July embarked at Gallipoli, and failed to the Dar-danels on the Afia fide , it is called twelve leagues, but is no more than twelve miles, being fo far by land from Lamfac near oppofite to Gallipoli The Hellefpont was fo called by the antients, becaufe Helle attempting to fwim over here on the ram with the golden fleece, was drowned The Europeans call it the Dardanels, as well as the caftles about the middle of it, the Turks give it the name of Bogas [The mouth or en trance] The entrance to the Dardanels is now to be computed from the Afia light-houfe, about a league without Lamfac, and from the Europe light-houfe, half a league to the north of Gallipoli , the whole length is about twenty-fix miles, the broadeft part is not computed to be above four miles over, though at Gallipoli it was judged by the an-tients to be five miles, and from Seftus to Abydus only feven ftadia , they alfo computed it a hundred and feventy ftadia from Lampfcum to Abydus, feventy from that place to Dardanus, the diftance from which to Rhæteum is not mentioned, which may be twenty, but from

Rhæteum to Sigeum was sixty, in all thirty miles and a half, excepting the distance between Dardanus and Rhæteum ; so that it is probable they measured round by the bays on the sea. The land on each side the Hellespont is mostly hilly, especially to the west. About three leagues from Gallipoli the passage is wide, and the land locking into the south, it appears like a large bason, then follows the narrow streight, which is about a league in length; at the south end of it are the Dardanel castles, near the middle of the Dardanel passage ; they have been thought by many to be on the site of Sestus and Abydus, though some have conjectured that these places were at the north entrance of this narrow passage, where, on the Asia side, there is a long mound or rampart, with a barrow at each end, like the remains of a castle. On the Europe side there is a hill, and to the north of it is a ruined castle called Acbash, which at present is the habitation of a Dervishe, and may be some remains of Sestus, though the passage over the streight might be to the south east at some little distance from it   What induces me to think that those towns were here, is the distance mentioned between Abydus and Dardanus, which is eight miles and three quarters, for the promontory Dardanium, and the city Dardanus, must have been the cape called by the Franks cape Berbiere or Berbieri, only a league from the present castle, which some suppose to have been Abydus, the river Rhodius also is said to have been between Abydus and Dardanus, which seems to be the river called Chaie, that falls into the sea at the castle, washing the walls of it when it overflows, so that if Abydus had been there, it would have been said that the river, though south of the town, fell into the sea at Abydus, and not between that place and Dardanus   Strabo also says, that Abydus is at the mouth of the Hellespont and Propontis, from which one may argue, that it was rather at the north end of this streight towards the Propontis   Wherever it was, it is remarkable on account of the bridge which Xerxes made there from Asia into Europe. The Rhodius therefore falling in at the old castle of the Dardanels on the Asia side, we are to conclude that Cynosema, the tomb of Hecuba, was at the opposite castle, being described to be over-against the mouth of the Rhodius.   Abydus was built by the Milesians with the permission of Gyges king of Lydia, to whom it was then subject   The people of this place made a stout resistance against Philip the first of Macedon, and destroyed themselves when they could hold out no longer

The castles are sometimes called by the Turks Bogas Hissar [The castles of the entrance], but that to the east is called Natoli Eskihissar [The old Asia castle], it is a high square building, encompassed with an outer wall and turrets, there are fourteen large brass cannon without carriages on the sea shoal, they are always loaded with stone ball, ready to sink any ship that would offer to pass without coming to anchor, in order to be searched : They fire likewise with ball, in answer to any ship that salutes the castles: As this does much damage where they fall, so the lands directly opposite commonly pay no rent, there are eight other cannon towards the south ·

I saw among them two very fine ones, one is twenty five feet long, and adorned with flower de luce, which, they say, was a decoration anciently used by the emperors of the east before the French took those arms,

and

and I have seen them in many parts, the other cannon is of brass twenty feet long, but in two parts, after the old way of making cannon of iron of several pieces, the bore of this is about two feet, so that a man may very well sit in it, two quintals and a half of powder are required to load it, and it carries a ball of stone of fourteen quintals [a]. The town on the north side of the castle is a mile and a half in circumference, and has in it twelve hundred houses, two hundred of which are Greeks, a hundred Armenian, and fifty of Jews They have a great manufacture both here and on the other side, of cotton and sail-cloth, and they make here a sort of ware like that of Delft, which is exported to the value of fifteen thousand dollars a year. They also send out some wax, oil, wool, cotton, and cotton yarn; and build small ships The town is situated in a plain, which begins about two miles to the north, and extends to the promontory Dardanium, being about a league broad, I crossed it going near to the east by the river, and went in between the hills to Jaur-Kala, situated on a high hill, it is said to have been built in haste, and did not appear to be of any great antiquity A French consul resides at the castle of the Dardanels, and a droggerman for the English and Dutch, who is a Jew The other castle, called Rumeh Eskihissar [The old castle of Romelia] has in it twenty large brass cannon, one of which is of a great size, but not so large as that on the other side The town is near a mile round in compass, stands on the side of the hill, and is inhabited only by Turks, who carry on a great manufacture of sail cloth

At the castle I was with the English droggerman, who set out with me to the south on the twenty-seventh, in order to see the situation of old and new Troy We went by the sea-side, and in an hour came to the cape, called by the Turks Kepos-bornou, and by Europeans Cape Berbier or Berbreri, which I take to be the promontory Dardanium of the antients, and I observed on it a rising ground, which seemed to have been improved by art, and might be the spot where old Dardanus stood, which was but a small town Here Sylla and Mithridates met, and made a treaty of peace, some say, that Ganymede was taken from this cape, others from Harpagia, on the confines of Cyzicus and Priapus, there was here also a cape called Gyges, probably some small head of land that might be a part of this promontory To the north of the supposed Dardanus there is a vale, extending some way to the east, where probably was Ophrynium, and the grove of Hector, mentioned near Dardanus, as well as the lake Pteleus, for I observed that way some water, which makes it a sort of a morass ground Further to the south the high white hills, which run along to the north of the plain of Troy, end at the sea, on some of these eminences near the sea Rhæteum must have been, which was situated on a hill I concluded that it was near a Christian village called Telmesh, and more commonly Janicui, which is six miles from the old castle, and about three from the supposed Dardanus When I had passed these hills, I saw from the south a high pointed hill over the sea, which looked as if it had been fortified, and I judged that it was near west of Telmesh The Aianteum, where the sepulchre and statue of Ajax were, is mentioned as near Rhæteum on the shoar, and I observed it the descent to the plain

of

---

[a] A quintal is one hundred and ten rotoli of one hundred and forty four drams

of Troy a little hillock, on which a barrow was raifed, and there were
fome broken pieces of marble about it, but whether this was the tomb
of Ajax, would be difficult to determine We at length came into that
famous plain, juft within the mouth of the Hellefpont, it is about two
miles broad and four long, from the conflux of the Simois and Scamander, to the fea To the eaft of this plain is that hill, which, as
Strabo obferves, runs along to the eaft between the Simois and
Scamander, two chains of hills end on the north fide of the plain, one
between the Simois and the river Thymbrius, the other between the
Thymbrius and the fea, where the plain ends to the weft at the fea;
within the entrance to the Hellefpont there are falterns, and in the
plain near the fea, one paffes over ftanding waters on two or three
bridges, which are the marfhes that Strabo mentions, as the others are
the fea lakes, all which, he fays, were made by the Scamander, he obferves that this river brings much mud along with it, and has a blind
mouth or outlet, which is very true, for the fea fills the mouth of the
Scamander with fand, fo that, as in many rivers in thefe parts, there is no
vifible outlet, but a bank of fand, being at the mouth of the river, the
water paffes through it, unlefs when they are overflowed by great winter
torrents which rife above it, and this is what feems to be meant by a
blind mouth, for the Scamander is a very fmall rivulet in the fummer,
tho' the bed of it is wide, and is filled with the winter floods To the
fouth weft, a ridge of low hills runs near the fea from the Sigean
promontory, now called cape Ienechahere, which is at the entrance of
the Hellefpont · The antient Sigeum was on this cape, which was de- Sigeum
ftroyed by the Trojans, on account of fome jealoufies they had conceived
of the inhabitants There is now a village on the fpot called Ienechahere [The new city] or more commonly Jaurcui, and there are two Greek
churches in it, at one of them I faw the famous Sigean infcription.
There is a piece of a Sarcophagus of white marble near it, on which
are fome reliefs of fine workmanfhip, there is alfo here a mezzo relievo, as big as life, broke off at the hands, and is very finely executed,
it is a young man who holds in his hand fome inftrument, which being broke off, appears only as the end of a ftick, which might be the
handle of a fpear, on which he is reprefented as looking with a melan-
choly afpect This poffibly might be defigned to reprefent Achilles (who
was had in great veneration here) looking on that fpear with which he
had been mortally wounded To the north weft of this place, a little
lower on the hill, is a large barrow, and eaft of it a lefs, and to the
fouth of that another fmall one, and though it is certain that the fultans and their viziers, have fuch barrows made by their foldiers in many
parts where they pafs, the larger fort for the fultan, and the lefs for the
viziers, yet notwithftanding I cannot but remark, if I may not be
thought to give too much into conjectures, that thefe poffibly may be
very extraordinary pieces of antiquity, and the great one might be
raifed over the fepulchre of Achilles, as the other two might be on
thofe of Patroclus and Antilochus, who were buried here, and to whom
the Trojans paid a fort of divine honours To the north weft of thefe,
under the hill, is the new caftle in Afia, on the fouth fide of the mouth
of the Scamander, with a fmall village about it, and a little town in

it, being about a quarter of a mile in compass, in time of peace it is open and neglected, and any one may enter, it has about it some very fine large brass cannon, the bores of which are not less than a foot in diameter, there are twenty-one of them to the south west, and twenty-nine to the north, but in time of war with the Venetians a pasha resides in each of the four castles, there are a hundred and thirty men belonging to this, who follow their trades and employs

I hired two janizaries to go with me the next morning on the twenty-eighth towards old Troy, and to the mines, the road being very dangerous   The low hill which runs to the south east from the Sigean promontory, has three summits, or heights, divided by small vales, or rather hollow grounds; on that next the cape, was Sigeum, about a mile in compass, on the second there is no village, but to the south east of it there is a barrow, and in the hollow between it, and the third, are two small rising grounds; on the third hill is Ienecui [The new village] inhabited by Christians   To the south east of this there is a fourth, which extends to the north east towards the conflux of the two rivers   Ascending this height towards the north east end of it, I came to a village called Bujek, where there are great heaps of ruins, many broken pillars and pieces of marble; and at the burial place of Boscui, about three quarters of an hour further, there are a great number of hewn stones, columns, and pieces of entablature, and this I take to have been Ilium, which was once a village, and famous for an antient temple of Minerva; it was afterwards made a city by Alexander when he came to it upon his victory at the Granicus; and after his death it was improved by Lysimachus   The Scamander and Simois are said to meet under this place; and old Troy is supposed to have been at the Ilian village on the height directly over the meeting of these rivers   On the north east end of this rising ground, or hill, on which Ilium stood, there is a barrow, which might be the tomb of Aisyetes, said to be five stadia from old Ilium in the way to the modern city   In this plain of Troy most of the battles mentioned by Homer were fought   It is probable this whole chain of low hills from Sigeum were formerly called Sigia, for Strabo says, that was the name of the place where Ilium was built, by order of Alexander, after he had gained that signal victory on the Granicus   Achæum was adjoining to it, that is, its territory bounded on that of Ilium, and the town might be where Jenicui is now situated, and its port, towards Sigeum, was twelve stadia from Ilium   Adjoining to this was Larissa, which might be between Ilium and the sea, and also Colonæ, which probably was in the valley towards Esistambole, which is supposed to have been Alexandria, or Troas   On my return, going further east, I travelled by the Scamander, some miles before it joins with the Simois, where it is called Gosdah-su, as it afterwards has the name of Mandras-su.   I crossed from it to the south west over that high ground which is between the two rivers, descending a little above the confluence of the waters   I thought it would be in vain to search on this height for the ruins of old Troy, where it is supposed to have been, all this part being now covered with wood, and the site of it was not known seventeen hundred years ago. I then crossed over the river Thymbrius called Gimbrick-Chaie, the vale through which it passes must be the Thymbrian plains, mentioned as

Ilium

near Troy, in which the Lycians were encamped: This river fell into the Scamander at the temple of Thymbrian Apollo, mentioned as fifty stadia from Ilium. Under the height of the supposed antient Troy, the country abounds much in a low shrub wood, which probably is that rough spot mentioned by Homer under old Troy, and called Erineus.

From the supposed ruins of Ilium, I went about six miles eastward to a village called Eskiupjee at the foot of mount Ida, where I was recommended to the aga. There are mines here of silver, lead, copper, iron, and allum, of which very little profit is made, though any one may have leave to work them, paying only a fifth of the produce to the governor. Those who undertake this work are mostly Greeks, who have been obliged to fly from the islands, or other parts. The mines are dug like rabbit holes, so as that there is no need of ropes or ladders in order to descend. The allum stone as chalk is dug in pits, and being burnt, and afterwards boiled in water, which is drawn off at a proper time, the allum becomes solid, much after the same manner as they make salt-petre.

Ida is not a single mount, but a chain of hills, that extend from Mount Ida cape Lectus to the north north east, as far as the country that was called Zelia, bounding on the territory of Cyzicus. All the country to the west of it being the kingdom of Troy. The highest summit of this mountain seems to be that part which is directly east of the place where the Simois and Scamander meet; this probably is that part of it called Cotylus, which is computed to be about thirteen or fourteen miles from the supposed Scepsis. The antients say, that it was a hundred and twenty stadia, or fifteen miles from that place: The rivers Scamander, the Granicus, and Æsepus rise out of mount Cotylus, their sources not being above three or four miles apart; the Scamander is said to rise at Biramitch about six hours, or twelve miles from the mines. Another summit of mount Ida is Gargarum, probably more to the south; there was on it an Æolian city called Gargara. To the south of the mines there is a long rocky mountain called Chigut; on the top of it are ruins of an antient city, particularly of the walls, which are ten feet thick, and built of large grey stone without cement; they are about three miles in circumference, and there are eight gates to the city. I take this place to be Scepsis, and Eskiupjee, the name of the village near, seems to bear some resemblance to it. Old Scepsis was in another place, near the highest part of mount Ida, probably towards mount Cotylus; it was at the distance of sixty stadia from new Scepsis, to which the inhabitants removing, the old place afterwards had the name of Palæscepsis. Demetrius the grammarian was of this place, who is so often quoted by Strabo in relation to these parts, an author who wrote thirty books, only on sixty lines of Homer's catalogue of the Trojans and their allies, and a very remarkable account is given how Aristotle's library and manuscripts were preserved in this place for many years.

I went to the mines with a design to go to Troas, or Alexandria, opposite to Tenedus, but the aga would not advise me by any means to go to that place, which is now called Eskistambole, or to any of the places in the neighbourhood, because the pasha being in search of rogues, they were skulking about the country, and we should have a great chance of falling into their hands, so I determined to return to

the

the caftles by another way : We however ventured to go about two miles to the weft, to a high rocky hill, like a fugar loaf, called Kis-Ka-leh [The virgin caftle], there is a winding way up to it, and on the fummit of this hill is a ruined caftle, defended by round towers at the corners; it feems to have been built in hafte   To the weft there is a part of it which is lower than the reft, and fortified; and there are a great number of cifterns cut into the hill in that part   We went on to the tents of the Urukes, who are a poor fort of Turcomen that live among the hills, and are chiefly fubfifted by the fheep and goats which they breed.

We fet out from the mines on the thirtieth, and after travelling about five miles to the north weft, we came to a town called Enai, a little below which the rivulet Enaichaie falls into the Scamander; this feems to be the river Andrius which rofe in the country called Carafena, and fell into the Scamander: The pafha was here with his people, in order to clear the country of rogues, and I faw on the outfide of the town two of them on ftakes who had been lately impaled.   From this place I travelled by the Scamander, and croffed the hills, on which probably old Troy ftood, to the Simois and Thymbrius, and returned in a road more to the eaft, than that in which I came, to the Dardanels, or old caftle of Afia   It is to be obferved, that to the eaft of the territory of the city of old Troy (which without doubt was itfelf a little principality or king-dom) was the diftrict or principality of Cebrenia to the north of the Scamander, probably extending to the great height of mount Ida before-mentioned.

CHAP. XXI.

Of TROAS.

AFTER I had been at Bourfa and Nice, I returned to the Darda-nells, and went by Tenedus to Efkiftambole, fuppofed to be Alexandria or Troas, built by Antigonus, and called Antigonia; and afterwards improved by Lyfimachus, and called by him Alexandria, in honour of his mafter Alexander the great. It is thought to have been made a Roman colony by Auguftus   This place is fituated on a rifing ground, which ends in high clifts at the fea oppofite to Tenedus, the walls appear to have been about four miles in circumference, a plan of it may be feen in the fifty-feventh plate   At the north weft corner of the walls are the ruins of a tower A , under this to the weft, there is a plain fpot between the height and the fea, where there are remains of an old port or bafon, near half a mile in circumference, and about a furlong from the fea, with which it communicates by a canal Going along by the remains of the old walls towards the fouth caft, fomething more than a quarter of a mile, I came to the remains of the hippodrome or circus C, which is funk into the ground, a plan of it is feen below it D, at the caft end of it there are ruins of fome confiderable building, and further to the fouth is a fort of a deep

2

bed

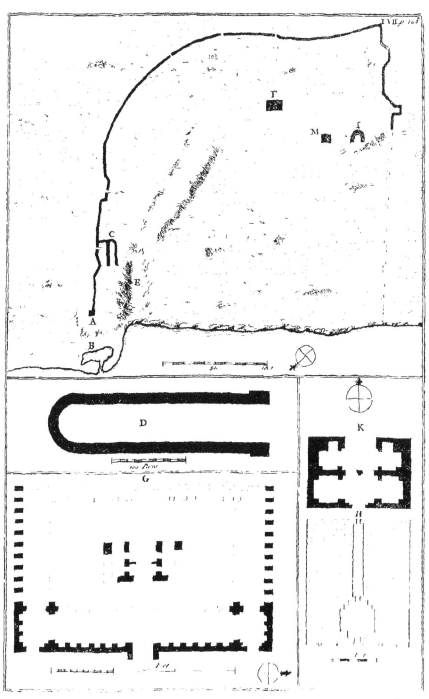

Γ

M   I

C

E

A

B

D

G

K

H

A PLAN of TROAS and of some BUILDINGS in It

bed as of a canal to the sea at E, which might serve as a port in order to lay up their gallies in the winter; to the east there is a winding valley, and beyond it is the high ground, on which a large temple F is situated, there was a wall carried from the town wall to the Hippodrome, and probably this might be the bounds of the old city before it was enlarged, and I observed that to this place the walls were built in the old manner, one tier of stone set up an end, and the other laid flat, the walls further east not being built in that style. I came to the east side, where there had been three or four gates, one about the middle, and opposite to the large temple F, near a quarter of a mile from it, of which there are great remains, it was very much after the manner of that building at Ephesus, which was either a temple or the gymnasium. The nature of this building will appear by the plan at G, it is a large enclosure built with arches on three sides, which are enclosed except on the north side, where they are open, as they were probably on the south, there seem also to have been considerable buildings to the north and south on the outside of this enclosure, the temple itself was in the middle, and was finished in a very magnificent manner, though it is so small that it seems to have been designed only to receive some great statue, which might be the object of their worship, and though there is a very grand entrance into the enclosure at the east end, yet, by what I could judge, the grand front of the temple was to the west, where there are three very large and beautiful arches remaining which made the front of it, the cornishes at the springs of them are very richly adorned with sculpture, and it is probable that the whole was cased with white marble. The peasants call this Baluke Serai [The palace of honey], because, they say, many bees and hornets make their combs in the holes of the walls, but it is more probable that it is derived from Baal, the eastern name of Apollo. On the south side of the city, a little way within the walls, are the remains of a theatre, which is beautifully situated on the west side of the high ground, commanding a glorious view of the sea, of Tenedus, and the islands about it, all the seats and front are destroyed, and there appears to have been only one arch at each end, on the ground to the east of the theatre are remains of a very thick high wall, where there might be a reservoir of water. On the low ground, at a small distance to the north of the theatre, are remains of a temple, or some other building, of a singular structure at M, they call it Kisla Serai [The Virgin's palace] which probably might be a temple of Diana, it seems to be a building of very great antiquity, a plan of the lower part of it may be seen at H, and of the upper at K, the principal front is to the south, which was adorned with pilasters, it appears as a large square building, and every tier of stone sets in on the other three sides at least half a foot, entring at the south front, there is a room which is not large, it is something in the shape of a cross, the part to the north is a passage thro' the building, as I suppose, though it is now closed up, over this passage, and on each side above, are the apartments to the entrance, which is from the north at K, and probably there was a flight of steps to it, though the ground is higher there than on the south side. The middle part at H, opens to the room below, exactly over the entrance to the long passage that leads to the north   This whole building is arched over, but flat at top on the outside, and it is very probable, that the grand temple was a room over all these of the size of the whole, and that there were some rooms under this upper story, to which there are now no entrance,   The walls of the city seem to be above a mile in length from east to west, and near a mile from north to south. Both the walls and these buildings, especially the first great temple, have been much destroyed by the command of the present grand signor, on his first accession to the throne,   in order to carry the best stones and marbles to Constantinople, to be employed in publick buildings, and, they say, he was led to it by a renegado, who perfuaded them that they should find great treasures in this place

About half a mile to the east of the city walls, there is a vale, in which there runs a salt stream called Aryeh-fu, on the west side of this stream there are many hot sulphurous salt springs, which seemed to have also something of chalybeat in them, there are two baths built over them on the side of the hills, and ruins of many buildings near it, some of which are very antient, and several arches of them remain, with the walls built of black and white stone set in lozenge wise, some have thought this to be Larissa   At one of the baths I saw a colossal statue of a woman of white marble; the head was broke off, but the drapery is very fine, and one of her hands appears to have been covered by the vest   Returning to the port directly from the baths, and leaving the old city to the south, I passed by some small square piers, which might be part of a portico to walk in

I took the two Greek boatmen to accompany me, but either out of fear or laziness, both of them soon left me, and I examined every thing without any one to accompany me but my own servant, which they pretended was very dangerous   Going from this place to Tenedus by sea, I observed the barrow, mentioned between the second and third hills from the Sigean promontory, was very much exposed to view from the sea, and so might more probably be the tomb of Achilles, that also on the fourth hill, supposed to be the burial place of Ayetes, appeared likewise to great advantage   All the country about this city, and the space within the walls also are under wood, being chiefly a particular sort of oak, with the large acorns, which are gathered by the country people, in order to be exported to Italy for tanning.

CHAP.

CHAP. XXII.

Of LAMPSACUS, and the iflands of the PROPONTIS.

AFTER I returned to the Dardanells, I fet out northwards by land, on the thirty-firft of July, towards Lampfacus. Between that city and Abydus fome places are named by Homer which were not known by the antient geographers, one of them is Arifba, the refidence of Afius, which was on the river Selleus About two hours, or four miles to the north of the caftle, there is a river called Muffacui Chaie, which may be the old Selleus, and the village of Muftacui, which is a little higher on it, the antient Arifba. Near four miles further is a larger river called Borgas-Chaie, which may be the river Pactius mentioned by the poet On the fide of the hills, over the plain thro' which it runs, there is a very pleafant village called Borgas, in one part of which there rife a great number of fine fprings, infomuch that it is called the thoufand fountains

Lampfacus firft called Pityufa on the Afia fhoai, near oppofite to Galhpoh, is about a mile further to the fouth than that city, this place was given to Themiftocles to furnifh him with wine Several great men among the antients were natives of Lampfacus, and Epicurus lived here for fome time, and enjoyed the company of the learned men of this city There is a little current on the fouth fide of the prefent fmall town, which is fituated on a height, and on the plain near the fea, the antient city feems to have extended up the rifing ground further to the eaft, I faw no ruins, except of an old thick wall in the town, it has two ports, very well defended by heads of land which extend out into the fea The little hills all about it are finely cultivated, being covered with vines and other fruit trees, I could not go fo freely about this place, as the plague was there at that time About a mile to the north of the town there is a pleafant village called Shardick, from which there is a great export of all forts of melons, and other fruits to Conftantinople, and this being directly oppofite to Galhpoh, it is the place from which they crofs over, a boat going every morning early, and returning before noon Mount Rhea was five miles from Lampfacus, where there was a temple to the mother of the gods, and in the territory of this city was a place called Gergethium famous for its vineyards

On the firft of Auguft in the evening I embarked to go to the ifland of Marmora Between Lampfacus and Parium was a city called Pefus, and a river of the fame name, when this city was deftroyed the people went to Lampfacus Fourteen miles eaft north eaft is a village called Kimere, and a fmall river in a bay on the weft fide of that cape, on which, I fuppofe, Parium and Priapus were fituated Kimere is near the north weft angle, which the cape makes with the bottom of the bay Here I found medals were to be met with, and I conjecture that it might be the antient Pefus, with the river of the fame name Returning

out

out of this bay, and continuing along the cape to the north for about two leagues, we saw a small bay in the side of the cape towards the north west corner of it, and to the north of it there are two small rocks, it is probable that Parium was here, which is placed in the Tables twenty-two miles from Lampsacus That city was built by the Milesians, Erithræans, and the people of the isle of Paros It flourished much under the kings of Pergamus, of the race of Attalus, on account of the services the city did to that house [a] On the confines of the territories of Priapus and Cizicus was a place called Harpagia, where, some say, Ganymede was taken, though others fix that story to cape Dardanium Between Priapus and the Æsepus was the river Granicus, so famous for the battle, in which Alexander routed the Persians, and for the rout of the army of Mithridates by Lucullus after he had raised the siege of Cyzicus And I was informed that between this cape and that of Cyzicus, there are two rivers, the largest discharges itself to the west of a small point opposite to the island Alonia, which, I think, is called Roia, and must be the Æsepus, which was the bounds of the kingdom of Troy, and seven or eight miles to the west is another river, which, if I mistake not, is called Teker Chaie, and must be the Granicus This river ran thro' the country of Adraste, and had on it a city, long ago destroyed, called Sidena, and a territory of the same name The Æsepus after having run about seventy miles falls here into the sea Strabo mentions that towards its rise, on the left side of it, was Polichna a walled city, Palæscepsis, and Alazonium, and on the right between Polichna and Palæscepsis, Neacome, where there were silver mines The river Carefus falls into the Æsepus, rising at Maluns between Palæscepsis and Achæum, which is opposite to Tenedus From this river the country was called Carasena, to which the country of Dardania extended The Æsepus run through the country of Zelia, which was ten miles from the mouth of it, extending to the foot of mount Ida, where it ends that way A little above the mouth of the river was the sepulchre of Memnon son of Tithonus, and a village called Memnon, concerning all which places nothing is known, by reason that the country is frequented by a bad set of people, and no caravans pass that way

Island's
Aphsia

On the third at noon, we arrived at an island to the south of Marmora, which is called in Turkish Ampedes, and by the Greeks Aphsia, it is about a league to the west of the island of Alonia, this island is about ten miles in circumference We went to a village on the west side of it near a small lake, it is inhabited both by Christians and

There was a place called Pityea in that part of the Priand Ilied, which went under the name of Pityais over it was mount Pityodes, so called from being covered with pines, it was between Parium and Priapus, near a place called Linus on the sea which was common to most of cockle it called Linus in cockle Between Parium and Priapus there was a city and country called Adrastea, from king Adrastus, who first built a temple to Nemesis there, the ruins of which, when it was said they did, were carried to Priium, and there was only an urn made, in the place of it, to the honour of the deity Here how an oracle of Apollo, Venus, and Diana, but where any of

these places are, is unknown, it not being secure to travel in that part The Tables place Priapus ten miles from Parium, which was also on the sea, and I think must have been about the angle which the cape makes with the land to the north east, it has its name from that infamous worship, which was in vogue in all these parts, it is sure Priapus the deity, the son of Bacchus and Nympha, according to others Adonis, being born in Lampsacus This city had a port, and some say that it was built by the Milesians at the same time as Abydus, others that it was founded by the people of Cyzicus

Turks,

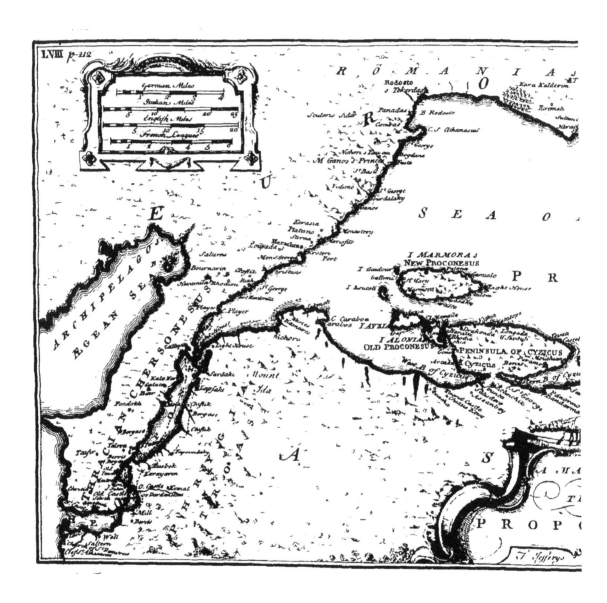

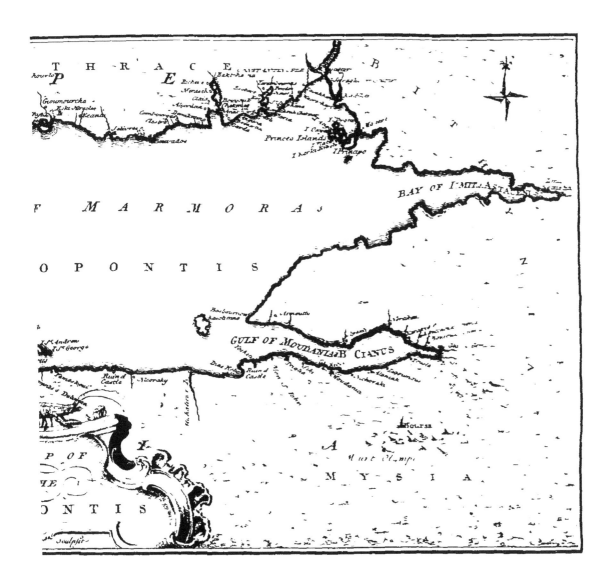

Turks, and there is a Turkish village on the east side of it, and also a small convent to the south This whole island is let for six hundred dollars a year they make some wine in it We crossed about two miles to the north west to the island of Cutalli, which is not so large, Cutalli. and has only one village of Christians of about seventy houses It is a fine spot of ground, and was formerly all covered with vineyards, but now the inhabitants apply more to the fishing trade This island pays also four or five hundred dollars a year, and these two little islands, with regard to the Christians in them, are governed by two or three of the chiefs, Proto-Ieraı [Πρωτόγεραι], as are most of the small islands, both in the Propontis and Archipelago, and it is these persons, or one of them, that commonly rent the island, in case it is not taken by a Turk, who comes and resides in them These islands and Alonia, are covered to the north by the island of Marmora, so that, when the winds are northerly, the boats that go to Constantinople sail between them, in order to be under the shelter of that island

On the fourth we sailed two leagues to the island of Marmora The Marmora antients mentioned the old and new Proconnesus on the sea going from Priapus to Parium The new Proconnesus I take to be Marmora, because a quarry of fine marble is mentioned to be in it, for which it is at present famous, being a beautiful sort of white alabaster I observed also here a rock of grey granite, which they have used in building, and is not much inferior to the Ægyptian This is the most northern of these islands, it is high and rocky, about four leagues long and one broad There are six little towns in it on the sea, mostly inhabited by Christians, there are also six convents in the island, two of which are in ruins, and the others inhabited only by two or three Caloyers This island is let for five purses a year, which is about three hundred and fifty pounds, by a person who has the title of waiwode. In this island, as well as the others, justice is administered by a cadi who resides here There is an uninhabited island, three leagues to the north west of Marmora

We sailed about three leagues southward to the island Alonia, which Alonia. is a very fine spot of ground about eighteen miles round, it is covered with vineyards, and is famous for an excellent dry white wine, which is commonly drank at Constantinople, and a great quantity is imported from the neighbouring continent under the same name, especially from the parts about Cyzicus, and is indeed a wine much of the same nature There is a semicircular bay to the north west of this island, opposite to which is a small island, and the harbour being covered by Marmora to the north, and by the island Aphisa to the west, it is an excellent port, and appears like a lake from the town This island has five villages on it; the greater part of the inhabitants are Christians, and it pays nine purses a year I take it to be the old Proconnesus, the other two islands being very inconsiderable The bishop of the four islands resides in the town called Alonia, where I was very civilly entertained by him at his house, he has his cathedral in this place, and is immediately subject to the patriarch of Constantinople He is commonly called the bishop of Alonia, but his true title is bishop of Proconnesus ['Ο Προκοννησου],

Vol II Part II.   F f   and

and I found he thought that no other ifland went by the name of Proconnefus but Marmora.

CHAP. XXIII.

Of Artacui and Cyzicus

Artacui

FROM Alonia we failed on the fifth to the weftward of that land, which was formerly the ifland Cyzicus, and afterwards fhaping our courfe for about two leagues along the fouth fide of it, we arrived at a town called Artacui, the fituation of which may be feen in the fifty-ninth plate. To the eaft of the town there is a fmall cape A, which was antiently fortified, between this and the land to the fouth there is a narrow paffage B, into one of the ports of the antient Cyzicus, which is a large bafin, about a league in length, and at the eaft end of it is the Ifthmus or neck of land that leads to the town of Cyzicus. Artacui is on the peninfula, which was formerly the ifland Cyzicus, the town is a mile and a half in circumference, having in it about fifteen hundred Greek families, and not above four hundred Turkifh houfes. It is the proper place of refidence of the archbifhop of Cyzicus, but as he is one of the twelve firft archbifhops, he ufually lives at Conftantinople, coming to this place only once in two or three years, there are no lefs than twelve churches in the town, and one in a fmall ifland oppofite to it. That ifland is a rock of marble, and there is a heap of ruins on it, and fome pieces of marble finely worked, which fhew that there was fome antient building on it, which probably was a temple. The fupport of this place is a great export of white wine, which is very good, and paffes for Alonia wine at Conftantinople, to which city they carry it.

The hill on the cape to the eaft was ftrongly fortified by a very antient wall acrofs the north fide of it, about half way up the hill, and it feems to have been built for a defence to the entrance of the port, there being many large hewn ftones about a church at the top of it called faint Simon, which gives name to the hill, and thefe are probably the remains of a ftrong tower or caftle. The wall is twenty feet thick, cafed with tiers of black and white marble alternately, the white being fet up an end, about eighteen inches deep, and the black laid flat, is nine inches thick, after the antient manner of building. Towards the eaft end there is a gateway with a tower on each fide, thirty feet fquare, and three more towers of the fame kind to the weft, a hundred paces apart.

On the feventh we went a league from Artacui by the weftern port to the eaft to the ruins of Cyzicus, a plan of which may be feen in the fifty-ninth plate, it is fituated to the north of the Ifthmus, or neck of land, where formerly there were two bridges, by which they paffed from the ifland of Cyzicus to the continent. The places where the two bridges

---

* This was doubtlefs the antient Artace, called so from Milteu. Strabo xn p c

were

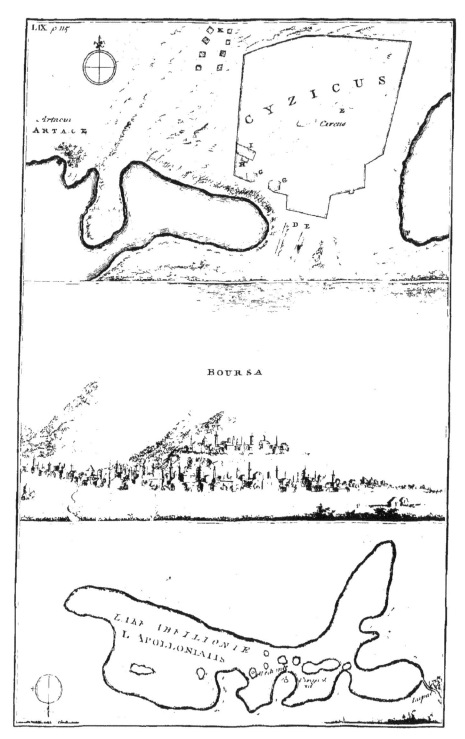

A MAP of CYZICUS and the *LAKE ABELLIONE*

And a VIEW of BOURSA

were are now to be feen, for there are two paffages or caufeways D, which are ufed at this time as roads, all the reft of the Ifthmus being a morafs, except two large fandy banks on each fide made by the fea   At the north eaft part of the eaftern bank E, there is a height, which feems to have been an ifland in the antient paffage, and oppofite to it the city walls are higher and ftronger than in any other parts   The ifland of Cyzicus was about fixty-two miles in circumference, and appears like a broad mountainous cape   The city had a great territory belonging to it, and was governed by its own wholefom laws, fuch as thofe of Rhodes, Marfeilles, and Carthage   This people was fo ftrong that they fuftained with great bravery the fiege of Mithridates, who had a hundred and fifty thoufand foot, befides horfe, and four hundred fhips, obliging him to leave the place   The hill on the oppofite continent was called Adraftea   The city was partly in the plain, and partly on the fide of mount Urfus, over which was mount Dindymon, with a temple on it built by the Argonauts to Dindymene the mother of the gods   There were two ports to the city which could be fhut with chains , the large one, I fuppofe, to the weft, and the other probably between the eaftern bridge, and the entrance to the port F , it had alfo above two hundred covered docks [νεώσοικοι] to lay up their fhips and gallies in.   There are ftill remains of the walls of the city ; thofe to the fouth, it is to be fuppofed, went clofe along by the Ifthmus, and extended for fome way to the weft near to the weftern port, though now the fea has retired in both parts. Toward the weftern port there are remains of two large octagon towers G, the one being near to the other, which I fuppofe might defend an entrance from the fea that way   To the north weft of thefe are ruins of a great building H, about a hundred paces fquare, of which very little remains but the fine arched paffages under-ground on which it was built, tho' many of them are deftroyed , they feem chiefly to run parallel from eaft to weft, and are from ten to fifteen feet wide, the walls between them being very thick, in which alfo there are fome narrower arches, the large arches are finely built of hewn ftone   To the north of this are figns of buildings, which I took to be an oblong fquare piazza, I , and that this building was about the middle of the fouth part of it   The piazza probably had a portico round it, becaufe in digging for ftones, they found at the weft end fixteen very large fquare pieces of marble, which probably were the foundations for fo many pillars , this piazza was about a hundred paces broad, and, as well as I could conjecture, four hundred long   The walls are almoft entirely deftroyed on the weft fide of the city, but feem to have run along to the eaft of a winter torrent, and to have afcended up the hill near the place where that torrent paffes a narrow ftreight between the hills, where there is a building on each fide K, it feems to have confifted of very high arches, which it firft made me fuppofe that it was an aqueduct, but the city walls being below thefe, I could not conjecture for what purpofe an aqueduct fhould be fo high, unlefs to convey water to the fummit of the hill without the city; the building on both fides feems to make part of an oval , it is indeed poffible that water might be conveyed from the weft fide, though I faw no arches any way joining to them, but it might pafs over the channel on arches, and be conveyed to the height of the eaftern hill, the

people

people call it the Princeſſes Palace, and ſay, that it was ſo high, that they ſaw both the eaſtern and weſtern bay from it · This building, as well as the town walls, are caſed with a baſtard grey granite, which probably was brought from Proconneſus, as well as the white marble, which they uſed about finer works . The walls go only about three quarters of the way up the hill, and turn down on the eaſt ſide at ſome diſtance from the clifts of the eaſtern bay A large theatre E, was built in the foot of the hill, the ſtones are all taken away, and that ſpot is now covered with trees; but I was informed by one well acquainted with the place, that there were formerly twenty-five ſeats, to the weſt of it there are ſome ſmall remains of a circus I ſaw the ſeats at the eaſt end a great way under ground, the people having dug down in order to take away the materials, which are of white marble, as well as I could meaſure it, I conjectured the area to be about thirteen paces wide, and two hundred and fifty long　There are ſtill many medals dug up in this place, and here the famous Peſcenius Niger was found, which is in the duke of Devonſhire's collection　The land of the peninſula of Cyzicus extending a conſiderable way to the eaſt as well as to the weſt, it makes another bay to the eaſt, which has a large opening oppoſite to the iſland Calolimno To the eaſt of this bay there is a ſmall town called Panormo , this place is about four miles from Cyzicus, in the way we ſaw a rock on the ſea called Monaſtere, there being a convent on it, inhabited by one Caloyer. We croſſed a ſmall river, and arrived at Panormo, which is a well ſituated town, and has a tolerable port for ſmall veſſels, but it is not ſufficiently ſecured from the north winds for larger ſhips, here they export corn and all ſorts of fruit, and wine to Conſtantinople.

CHAP. XXIV.

Of MEHULLITCH, BOURSA, and MOUNT OLYMPUS.

WE ſet out eaſtward on the eighth, and travelled over rich downs, and through a well inhabited country , I ſaw hills to the ſouth, which ſeemed to be the foot of mount Ida We paſſed Fenacui, called in Greek Deloke, and afterwards by Omarcui [The village of Omar], and ſaw at a good diſtance to the ſouth weſt the lake called Magnaas-Guel, which, for reaſons hereafter mentioned, I ſuppoſe to be the lake Daſcylis. After having travelled five hours from Panormo, I ſaw a village called Doulacui about a league to the ſouth, and a tower on a height near it , they informed me that there was a ruined town there, which I conjecture might be Miletopolis *, and

---

* At Panormo I met with a medal of Miletopolis in ſmall braſs, it had on it the head of the emprels Lucilla CI·BACTIΛΛOYΚIΛΛΛ, the reverſe is Pelas with a helmet, on the top of which is the head of an elderly man, and round it ΜΙΛΙΤΟΠΟΛΙ ΤΩΝ . Strabo writes it ΜΙ-ΛΗΤΟΠΟΛΙΤΙΣ, from which one may conclude that the antients pronounced the dipthong as the preſent Greeks, that is only the laſt vowel in the dipthong, and that Strabo writ it according to pronunciation

that a morafs to the eaft covered with water in the winter, was the lake
of that name   Having travelled about twelve miles to the eaft of Panormo, we came to a large town called Mehullitch, which is at leaft Mehullitch
two miles in circumference, though moft of it is built like a village ; it
is on a height, at fome little diftance to the eaft of a river of the fame
name, which is the antient river Ryndacus, that was the boundary between Myfia and Bithynia, it runs through a large plain, and is croffed
in the way from Bourfa to Smyrna. Four miles below Mehullitch is the
port to which the boats come up being four miles alfo from the fea   The
mouth of the river is faid to be oppofite to the ifland Befbicus, which
muft be Calolimno, though I thought that ifland was rather more to
the weft · There was a hill in it called Artace, which belonged to Cyzicus, and Strabo fays, that near it there was an ifland of that name,
and mentions cape Melanos, either the north eaft cape of the ifland of
Cyzicus, or that north of Panormo, they paffed by it in the voyage
from Cyzicus to Priapus · But as to the ifland Artace, I find on enquiry there is no ifland near Calolimno, except that of Monaftere which
is at too great a diftance, fo that probably Strabo is here corrupted

There are in Mehullitch about five hundred Greek, and two hundred
Armenian families, each having their church   They have a great trade
here in filk , the mulberry trees are planted thick like nurferies, and
are kept cut in fuch a manner as to be only about five feet high, as
they are alfo about Bourfa, and in all this filk country   The filk is
moftly exported to Conftantinople, as it is faid, to the amount of a hundred thoufand dollars a year , they alfo export much fruit and corn to that
city   The French buy up wool which is coarfe, as well at this place, as
at Panormo, and Caraboa, and carry one half to Conftantinople, and the
other half to Smyrna to be fent to Marfeilles. A very great aqueduct was almoft finifhed in order to bring water about four miles to the town ; it confifted of twenty-feven pillars, built like obelifks for the water to rife in to
keep it to its height, as defcribed before; but the perfon who was the benefactor dying, thefe indolent people had not the induftry to finifh it,
though they have only well water , I obferved feveral of their wells,
about three feet in diameter, which inftead of being built of ftone and
mortar within, have fort of hoops or tubes of earthen ware about two feet
deep, put one on another from the bottom to the top to keep the earth from
falling in   They have here a ftone or marble, which is a compofition of
red and blew pebbles with a cement of red, fome of this I faw very
finely polifhed at a mofque, and though the colours are not the brighteft,
yet it is a very beautiful and curious marble

The country between this place and Panormo is a very rich down,
well inhabited, and much improved about the villages   A league to
the eaft of the town, there is a ruined place enclofed with a wall called
Loupat, on the river Loupat, which a little way to the eaft comes
out of the lake Abelhonte, and falls into the Rhyndacus   This lake is
about twelve miles long from eaft to weft, and three or four miles broad
in fome parts, a large arm extends feven or eight miles to the fouth,
being about the fame breadth as the other part of the lake, a plan of it
may be feen in the fifty-ninth plate   On the north fide near the eaft
end there is a town on a little high ifland called Abelhonte, from which

they export filk and vinegar to Conftantinople. This ifland is fo near the land, that they can always pafs to it on horfeback, and in fummer it is almoft left dry, the lake extends fouthwards to the foot of mount Olympus, and to the eaft within eight miles of Bourfa, and as it is navigated by boats that go by the Loupat and Ryndacus to the Propontis and to Conftantinople, this makes the fituation of all the country about it very advantageous, and yet notwithftanding the country on the north fide of it is uninhabited, though a very rich foil, both becaufe it is a country often frequented by robbers, and on account of its being a day's journey from Bourfa, fo that any villages would be ruined by Turkifh travellers, who choofe to live on a village at no expence, rather than go to a town that is near. There is reafon to conjecture, that this is the lake Apolloniatis, and that the town in the ifland is the antient Apollonia, becaufe the Greeks at prefent call it Apollonia, but it being an ifland towards the eaft end of the lake, and the antient Apollonia, though mentioned with the lake, being called Apollonia on the Rhyndacus, I fhould rather take Mehullitch to be Apollonia mentioned by Strabo, though it is a league from the lake, indeed I found no antiquities there, except two or three fepulchral reliefs and infcriptions, but I heard that there were fome antiquities on the ifland, it is poffible, that both the one and the other were antient towns, and might be called by the fame name, and fo one diftinguifhed from the other by the name of the river it ftood on, of which Strabo might not be apprized.

It is faid, that the country between the Æfepus and Rhyndacus was inhabited by the Doliones, and from that river eaftward by the Mygdones, as far as the territory of Myrlea, that is, Apamea Myrlea, now called Montagna, which is twelve miles to the fouth of Bourfa. There are three lakes mentioned in thefe parts, Dafcylitis, Miletopolitis, and Apolloniatis. In the road from Panormo to Mehullitch, I faw a large lake called Migrais-Guel, which might be about ten miles north of Panormo; this I take to be the lake Dafcylitis, on which there was a town called Dafcylium, and the Doliones extending from the Æfepus to the Rhyndacus, and to this lake, it muft be underftood that their country was to the eaft of the river, and to the fouth of the lake. In the fame road nearer to Mehullitch, that is about five miles to the fouth weft of it, I faw a tower on a little height, which I was told was an antient ruin, and near it is a village called Dolou-Cui, I obferved fome water near, the country to the eaft is all a morafs, and I was told that in winter much water lays on it. This I take to be the lake Miletopolitis, and the ruin a remain of the antient Miletopolis, for Strabo fays, that above the lake Dafcylitis were two other lakes, Miletopolitis and Apolloniatis. He fays alfo, that the lake Dafcylitis belonged partly to Cyzicus, and partly to the Byzantines, and that the territory of the Cyzicenes extended to the lake Miletopolitis and Apolloniatis, from all which one may conclude that the lake Miletopolitis was between the two others, it is alfo to be obferved that Doulou-Cui bears fome refemblance to the name of the Doliones, the antient inhabitants of this country.

We fet out on the thirteenth with the caravan for Bourfa, and came to Luipat, a fmall ruined place encompaffed with walls, which are not well built, but feem to be of the middle ages. We travelled all day through a rich

ich unimproved country on the north side of the lake, till we came opposite to Abellionte on the island, and lay in the open fields. We went on a little after midnight six hours to Boursa, the antient Prusa, ^{Boursa} where the kings of Bithynia usually resided, which is about twenty-four ^{Prusa} miles from Mehullitch This city was built by that Prusias, king of Bithynia, who waged war with Crœsus and Cyrus. Boursa was taken by Seifeddulat of the race of Hamadan, in the three hundred and thirty-sixth year of the Hegira, but was retaken by the Greek emperor in nine hundred and forty seven after Christ· It was again taken in thirteen hundred fifty six by Orkan son of Ottoman, the second emperor of the Turks, who made it the capital of his empire [b], but when Constantinople was taken by Mahomet the second, in one thousand four hundred and fifty three, that city became the capital of the Turkish empire. Boursa is most pleasantly situated on the foot of mount Olympus over a plain, which is about four leagues long, and a league wide, having those hills to the north of it which run along by the bay of Montagna, a view of it may be seen in the fifty-ninth plate [c]. The city and suburbs are about six miles in circumference, the castle of Boursa is on the highest part; it is walled round, the rocky clifts below it being almost perpendicular, and beautifully adorned with the trees that grow on them, the rest of the town and suburbs are on heights on each side, but chiefly to the east, there being a very small part of the city on the plain to the north. The suburb where the Greeks live is to the west of the castle, there are about six hundred families of them with their metropolitan, and three churches The town is divided from the eastern suburb by a deep channel or vale A, over which there are several bridges, one of them with shops on each side, is ninety paces long and sixteen broad, the vale being planted with mulberry trees, makes the situation of the houses that are on it very delightful, a small stream runs through it, which swells to a torrent after rains· To the east of this is the suburb, where the Armenians live with their archbishop, of whom there are about eight hundred families, and they have one church It is said they have three hundred parishes and mosques in the city, and many little mosques arched over with one dome, and the great ones with several, as well as the kanes and bezestans, all which are covered with lead, these and the agreeable mixture of trees, together with the fine plain beneath, cultivated with mulberry-trees, altogether makes the prospect from the mountain most delightful The castle, as I observed, is walled round, which I take to be the antient city Prusa, it is near a mile in circumference, I saw one part of the wall remaining, built after the antient manner, with one tier of stone laid flat, and another set up an end, alternately, I saw also an inscription, which mentions that the emperor Theodorus Comenes Laskares built one of the towers of the wall Over the north brow of the hill are ruins of the grand signior's seraglio, which was burnt down some years ago, this being one of the royal cities which have been the residence of their monarchs. Orkan, who took this place, and his children, are buried in an old church in the castle, which is cased with fine marbles, and paved with Mosaic work,

[b] See Bibliotheque orientale D'Herbelot, at the word Burfah
[c] This is taken from Tournefort's view of it in order to fill up the plate

to

to the weſt of it there is a ſepulchre covered with a cupola, where, they ſay, ſultan Oſman is buried; and ſome ſpeak of Bajazet's children as interred near him, but I did not ſee their ſepulchres. This caſtle is governed by the janitzer aga, who reſides in it.

Trade

They make in the city a great variety of all ſorts of ſattins, moſtly ſtriped, which are uſed for the under ſhort garments of the Turkiſh habit; they make alſo a great quantity of meles, of flax and ſilk uſed chiefly for ſhirts, and a ſort of gauſe called brunjuke, which is much wore by the ladies for their undermoſt garments; they export alſo a great quantity of raw ſilk both to Conſtantinople and Smyrna.

Waters

The great number of ſprings that riſe all over the city make it a very pleaſant place, ſome flow in large ſtreams, and one in particular comes out of the mountain at the caſtle like a ſmall rivulet, where the Turks ſit in the ſhade, and where every thing is ſold which they delight in. There are ſeveral baths to the weſt of the town which are very famous, and have always been much frequented, in one called Cara-Muſtapha there is a ſpring of cold water, and another of hot, within the ſame room. That called Jeneh-Coplujah [The new ſpring] is the largeſt and moſt beautiful bath, it is a fine building, a large ſpring riſes in the middle of it, and two very hot ſtreams run through the room; near it there is a ſmall bagnio, called, The Jews bagnio. From this we went to a warm water, eſteemed holy by the Greeks, and is called Aie Theodory. Another bath is Culatlow-Coplujah [The ſulphur bath]. Half a mile further is a large bath, called Chekreeh-Cuplejah, which has not ſo much ſulphur in it as the other, and is more frequently drunk, tho' all the waters are taken inwardly, as well as uſed for bathing.

Mount Olimpus

I had a letter to the janitzer aga, which was delivered without a preſent, and I deſired him to ſend ſome janizaries with me up mount Olympus, but he ſaid, he could not anſwer for my ſafety, and added, that ſometimes they were even in danger of the rogues in the very ſkirts of the city, ſo I applied to an Armenian to whom I was recommended, who carried me to his houſe the day before I was to go up the mountain, and hired ſome horſemen well armed to go with me, and we ſet out very early in the morning. This part being probably inhabited by a colony from about mount Olympus in Theſſaly, may be the reaſon why the mountain had that name given it, the Turks call it Keſheſh Daug [The mountain of monks] from a monaſtery on the mountain which, as I was informed, was dedicated to the ſeven ſleepers; the firſt part of the aſcent is ſteep, covered with cheſnut, hazel, and beach, it leads to a plain ſpot on the ſide of the hill where the Urukes were decamping, the next part was alſo ſteep, and covered with ſeveral ſorts of fir, one of which is a very particular kind, the cones of it, like the cedar point upwards [a], a turpentine drops from the fruit of this ſort, which they call maſtic, and ſells dear, being uſed in ſurgery for wounds. Above this there is another plain, or rather two valleys, divided by a low hill, in each of which there runs a river, there is a very ſmall trout in them, which they call Allah Ballouk [The fiſh of God], being much eſteemed, though I could not perceive that they were different from our common trouts. There is another ſhort aſcent to a plain ſpot, which extends to the foot of the higheſt ſummit

[a] It is what the botaniſts call, Abies Taxifolia, fructu ſurſum ſpectante. Inſt. R. H.

of the hill; the afcent to which is to be looked on as the laft third of the way This upper part has always fnow in the hollow parts of the hill, which is carried every day to Bourfa· Above this plain there is no wood except fhrubs and the juniper, towards the upper part of the mountain I obferved that there was a baftard grey granite The profpect, they fay, from this hill is very fine when all is clear, it was indeed at that time clear all round and above us, but there were clouds below which intercepted the view Having fpent the whole day on this mountain, we returned in the evening to Bourfa

---

CHAP. XXV.

Of NICE, GEMBLICK, and MONTAGNA.

WE fet out with the caravan towards Nice on the eighteenth in the evening, and travelled along that fine vale to the north eaft, which is fo well improved with mulberry trees for the filk We went only four miles to a village called Suhgerly where we lay in the prieft's garden On the nineteenth we faw a town or village called Chioflec, there is a large old building on a hill to the right of it, and at the north eaft corner of the plain is a fmall lake called Oufhomah To the eaft is a fmall town, if I miftake not it is Chioflec, where they make velvet for cufhions ufed on the fophas all over Turkey, many of which are of a fort of beautiful flowered velvet, but moft of them are made with a ground of a hard yellow filk, they make them from fourteen dollars to eighty dollars a pair We croffed over the hills to the north, and came into the large plain of Ienichahere, in which there is a great lake extending from the town of Ienichahere at the north eaft of it, to the fouth weft end of the plain; in fummer the greater part of it appears like a morafs, being overgrown with reeds, the fituation of the town and lake may be feen in the fixtieth plate Ienichahere is a fmall town, where there are four or five mofques, and only one Armenian church, there being few inhabitants of that profeffion: I faw only one marble coffin here, with a defaced infcription on it I cannot conjecture what place this was, unlefs it might be Cæfarea, called alfo Smyrdiane, which in Ptolemy's order of places, is put between Nicæa and Prufa at mount Olympus From this place we croffed other hills to the north, and defcended to the lake of Nice, and going on the fouth fide of it about a mile, we turned to the north at the eaft end of it, and came to Nice This lake was called the lake of Afcanius, and now has the name of Ifnick, from the Turkifh name of Nice, it is about twelve miles long, a map of the lake may be feen in the fixtieth plate There are a great number of fifh in it, but it is navigated only by fmall boats which are cut out of one fingle piece of wood.

Nice

The city of Nice is situated at the east end of the lake of Afcanius, having a valley to the east of it finely improved with mulberry-trees, through which there run several small streams, which pass through the city, or near it. This city was first built by Antigonus, and called Antigonia, afterwards it had the name given it of Nicæa, from the wife of Lysimachus, a plan of it may be seen in the sixtieth plate; it is encompassed with very fine walls, which are almost entire, they are built of stone, with four tier of brick at the distance of every six feet, the walls being about fifteen feet thick and twenty high, they are made with battlements, a walk all round, and towers of brick at the distance of seventy paces, which are about fifteen feet higher than the wall, and are half an oval, on one side of the gate to the lake there is a large octagon tower A, and on the other side a round tower B, to the south of which are two or three other round towers. There are two gates, which seem to have been very fine triumphal arches, on one of them to the south, called the old gate D, are imperfect inscriptions to the honour of one of the emperors after Nero, whose name I found on it as an anceftor. Within this gate there are remains of another, on which there is an imperfect inscription, where I saw the name of the emperor Claudius. A plan and elevation of the north gate E may be seen at F; there are signs of an inscription on it which seems to have been made in copper. At this gate there are two large reliefs of Medusa's heads, with victories over them. On one side there is a fine mezzo relievo of three persons, as big as life, set against the wall, but it is much defaced, and on the other side there is a marble coffin, with a relief of a battle on it. I saw at a mosque two most beautiful pillars in in such large spots as are commonly seen in verd antique, some of a light brown, and of a grey, others of a whitish colour, being the only pillars I ever saw of that sort of marble, and would be of very great value to those who are curious. The Greek church, where they say the council was held, is built of brick, and though it is old, yet I take it to be a later building than the time of Conftantine, the cathedra or feat, and the semicircular steps at the end, are common in antient cathedral churches, and these are very ill built, there are some remains both of the mosaic cieling and pavement, a plan of the church may be seen at G. The Armenians have a small church in a sort of grot under the west end of it. To the north of the town there are two marble coffins, one is of red and white spotted marble, the other has a Medusa's head at each end, and in the middle of the front, is a relief of a man with a club as going away from a woman who is behind him, which is probably designed for Hercules refusing pleasure, and embracing a life of labour and industry, there is a woman on each side in different compartments, and an inscription over all. To the east of the town are the remains of an old channel of an aqueduct, out of which there now runs a large stream that is conveyed to the town by an ill built aqueduct. Over this, on the side of the hill, there is a very curious piece of antiquity now in ruins, tho' it seems to have been designed to have lasted for ever, but it has been destroyed by force, it is a room hewn out of one stone of grey marble, and seems to have been an antient sepulchre, it was probably moved to this place, and not cut out of the rock on that spot, unless

art

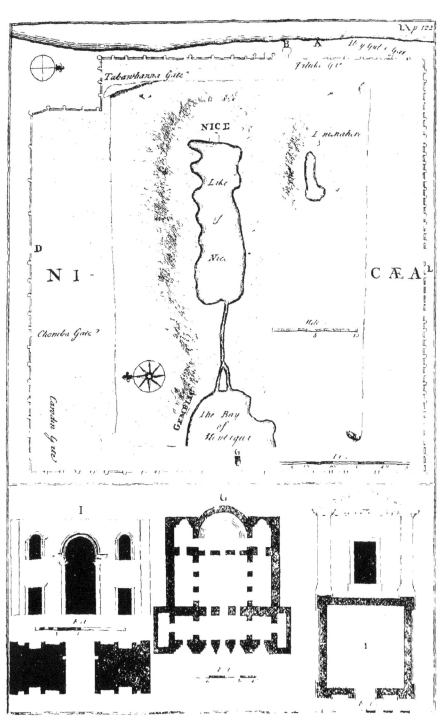

Tabawhanna Gate

NICE

Lake
of
Nice

I nenahere

D

NI- CÆA

Chomba Gate

Garden gate

GENBLE

The Bay
of
Hentigar

G

I

G

I

A PLAN of NICE and some BUILDINGS in it, and a HALF of the LAKE

A TRIANGULAR OBELISK near NICE

art has been ufed to deceive, for all round at the bottom it appears as if it was feparated from the rock, and there are other ftones under it on the outfide, as if defigned for the foundation , a plan and elevation of it may be feen at I , it is thirteen feet fix inches long, and twelve feet ten inches broad, it was cut archwife at top   On each fide there is a folid bench or bulk, I fuppofe to place the coffins on, and there feems to have been one coffin laid acrofs at the eaft end   On the outfide there is an infcription in Hebrew, very much defaced , but it does not feem to have any relation to the building, being in very fhort lines, and not in the middle of the eaft end   This room feems to be of the nature of that temple of Thebaic marble, or red granite, mentioned by Herodotus, which was cut out of the ifle of Elephantine, and carried down by water to Sais in Delta   Within the city walls there are fome very fine large arches now under ground, they feem to have belonged to a theatre, which muft have been very magnificent, the arches are turned with large hewn ftone , thofe which I take to be the inner ones are very wide, and in the front of each of them there are others, according to the plan at A, in the forty-feventh plate.

The walls of the city are at leaft four miles round, and yet the prefent town, which is much like a village, has not above three hundred houfes in it, and there are not more than twenty Chriftian families in the place, the greater part of which are Greeks. They have no trade but that of filk, which is bought up by the merchants, and fent either to Bourfa, or to Gemblik, to be embarked for Conftantinople   The air is very unhealthy here, occafioned probably by the rivulets not having a free courfe, and by turning them into their gardens within the walls , where the water ftagnates and corrupts the air   I was informed that Nice is about eighteen hours, or thirty fix miles from Nicomedia, and that it is near fixteen miles from Caramoufal, a port on the bay of Ifnit or Nicomedia, and twenty-four from another port in that bay further to the weft, called Debrendeh, where they commonly go to embark for Conftantinople

On the twenty-firft, we fet out and travelled on the north fide of the lake, and in about four hours came to an obelifk, about a mile to the north of it , the people call it Befh-Tafh [The five ftones] becaufe it confifts only of that number, a drawing of it may be feen in the fixty firft plate, it is of grey marble, and of a fingular kind, for it is triangular, and ftands on a bafe and pedeftal, fix feet nine inches fquare, and about eleven feet high   There is an infcription on the fouth fide of it, from which one may conclude, that it was erected as a fepulchral monument, probably to fome great citizen of Nice   The import of the infcription is, that C Caffius Philifcus, the fon of C Caffius Afclepiodotus lived eighty-three years

We travelled on between the hills and the lake, lay at a village called Ieranite, in the houfe of an Armenian, who endeavoured to intimidate me with regard to the fecurity of the road, which I found was only to put me on hiring him to go along with me   On the twenty-fecond we came to the weft end of the lake, and paffed through Bafirie, I obferved that the hills are finely improved along the fouth fide of the lake, we turned to the weft in that beautiful vale in which

the

the river Afcanius runs, it is finely improved with all forts of fruit-trees and vineyards, the hills on each fide being alfo under vines

Gemblic We came to Gemblic at the north weft corner of this plain, which is moft delightfully fituated on two little heights, and on the plain by the fea fide, it is the antient Cius, which was deftroyed by Philip king of Macedon, and rebuilt by Prufias, and from him called Prufias, there are fome infcriptions about the town   This place is twenty-four miles from Nice, the archbifhop of that city has his palace of refidence here, to which I went   As he is the fifth of the the twelve firft archbifhops, he lives moftly in Conftantinople, the Greeks, who are about fix hundred families, have feven or eight churches here, and likewife a nunnery, and two convents on the fide of the hill over the town, there are about fixty Turkifh families in the place, they have two mofques, and moftly inhabit the hill to the weft   They have a great export here of corn, of an ordinary white wine, and of all forts of fruits to Conftantinople   I find the rivers Cius and Hyli are mentioned here, probably they are the names of two mouths of the river Afcanius, and here the poets place the ftory of Hylas, the waiting boy of Hercules, in relation to his being conveyed away by the nymphs

On the twenty-third we had a moft pleafant ride for twelve miles along the fouth fide of the bay of Montagna, to the town of the fame name   To the north of this gulph is that head of land which was called the promontory Neptunium, and is between this bay and that of Montagna Nicomedia   Montagna is on the fea, about twelve miles to the north of Bourfa, and is fituated under the mountains, the town is about a mile long, confifting of one ftreet near the fhoar, there are about feven hundred Greek families in it, who have feven churches, and the archbifhop of Bourfa has a palace here, refiding in this town part of the year, the Turkifh families are not above three hundred   This is the port of Bourfa, and is computed to be a hundred miles from Conftantinople, it is a place of great refort for the export of filk, corn, and the manufactures of Bourfa, Tourcomen carpets, faltpetre, a poor white wine, and all forts of fruit to Conftantinople, from which they alfo import many commodities to fupply the city of Bourfa, and the country about Apamea Mylea it   The antient city Mylea was half a mile to the fouth eaft of the town, and on the eaft fide of the road to Bourfa, being fituated on a hill, which is ftrong by nature, it was deftroyed by king Philip, rebuilt by Prufias, and called Apamea from his wife, it was afterwards called Apamea Mylea, and Apamea of Bithynia   The firft city was built by Myrlus, who was of Colophon, and I fuppofe head of the colony from that place, it was afterwards made a Roman colony, and was doubtlefs a confiderable place, there are no remains on the hill, except heaps of ftones thrown out of the vineyards, it is probable that the city in length of time extended down to the fea, and as a proof of it I faw the remains of a fmall brick building about a mile to the eaft of the prefent town   I went to the kane, and then waited on the archbifhop of Bourfa, to whom I had a letter   He entertained me very civilly, tho he was in trouble on account of his brother, who was fent for to Conftantinople by the vizier, as it was thought, to fqueeze money out of him, when I returned to the kane, he fent me a prefent of wine and provifions   I

I   embarked

embarked on the twenty-feventh for Gallipoli, we were obliged by contrary winds to put into a port called Armocui, on the other fide of the bay near the point of the cape; there is a hot mineral water at this place, and another to the north weft, at a place called Joloway. I was informed alfo, that at the north weft point of the cape, at a place called Courai, there is a hot water, where there is a convent belonging to the monaftery of faint George of Halkè, which I have already mentioned, among the Princes Iflands. The Greeks go once a year to that place out of devotion, and to bath in the hot mud, it being efteemed a great remedy for many diforders, particularly the fciatica. We touched at Rodofto in the way to Gallipoli, where the plague had begun to rage, and I lodged there all night in a coffee-houfe, we went the next day to Gallipoli, where I immediately embarked for the Dardanels, when I was informed that the plague had alfo broke out in that city From the Dardanels we paffed by Tenedus, faw the ruins of Troas, embarked for Lemnos, and went from that ifland to mount Athos, of which I fhall give an account in the following book.

A

DESCRIPTION

OF

The *EAST, &c.*

BOOK the Third.
Of THRACE and GREECE.

CHAP. I.

Of THRACE in general ; and of CONSTANTINOPLE.

THRACE was bounded to the weſt by mount Hæmus, and the river Naſtus, and on the other ſides by the Propontis, Ægean, and Euxine ſeas It was a Roman dioceſe, and by the Greek church was divided into four provinces Europa, which was probably on the ſea to the caſt, Hamimontana, to the weſt at mount Hæmus, in which was Plotinopolis, Rhodope, about the mountains of that name, in which was Trajanople, and Thrace-Proper, probably in the middle between them, of which we may ſuppoſe Adrianople was the capital Thrace is very far from being a barren country, as ſome of the antients have deſcribed it, for the part I ſaw of it is naturally one of the fineſt countries I have ſeen, and the richeſt ſoil, and ſo they ſay it is to the weſt of Adrianople As mount Hæmus is to the weſt of it, ſo mount Rhodope runs along the middle of this country to the weſt of the river Hebrus, and I ſuppoſe extends away to the north

When I arrived at Scutari, they took my ſlave from me, as I had not the original writing by me to vouch the property of him, but on application I got him afterwards releaſed. I went from this place to the gentleman

ⅬＯ

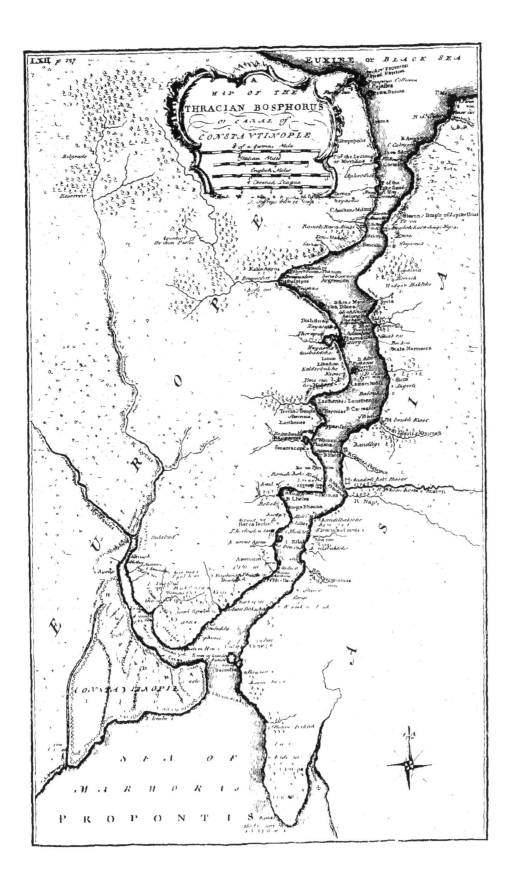

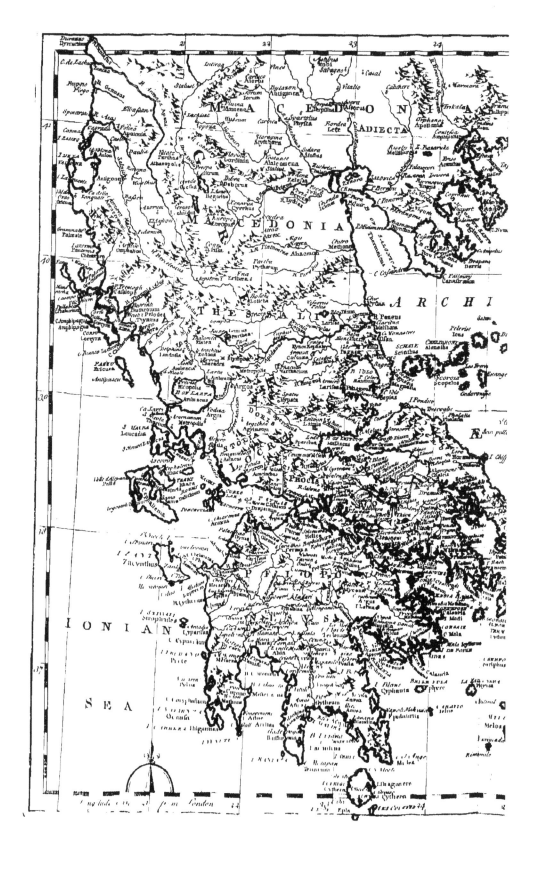

A MAP OF
THRACE
AND
GREECE

to whom I was recommended at Conftantinople, who did me the honour to come over and conduct me to his houfe, where I received all manner of civility during my ftay there, as indeed I did from all the gentlemen of the Englifh nation

As there have been particular defcriptions given of Conftantinople, it is unneceffary to fay much of it The beauties and advantages of its fituation have been much enlarged on, and no account can poffibly give a juft idea of it, as it furpaffes every thing that can be faid, infomuch that the fine views which it affords are alone a fufficient recompence to the traveller who goes to fee it This city is on a promontory at the entrance of the Bofphorus, having the Propontis to the eaft and fouth, and the port antiently called Ceras to the north, I found the fouth weft fide on the land to be feven thoufand feven hundred paces long, it has on that fide two walls built with fquare towers, and a foffee on the outfide of the outer wall, which is twenty paces broad, and faced with ftone on both fides Gyllius makes the fouth eaft fide equal to this, and the fide on the port a mile lefs, which would make it in all eleven miles in circumference, though he computes it to be near thirteen miles, it is from half a mile to a mile and a half broad The ground rifing from the port and from the fea round the end of the promontory, makes the fituation very beautiful, and it is not difficult to difcern the feven hills on which the city is built, the firft A, in the plan of Conftantinople, in the fixty-fecond plate, takes up the whole breadth of the promontory, on which the grand fignor's feraglio is built, five more are over the port, divided by valleys that defcend from the height, which joins fome of the hills, and goes near the whole length of the city, the Adrianople ftreet running all along on the top of it; on the fecond hill B is the burnt pillar; on the third hill C, is the magnificent mofque Solimanca, the valley D between it and the fourth hill is broad, the aqueduct of Valentinian croffed it, of which there remain about forty arches, the eaft end of it is deftroyed, and the water is now conveyed by channels on the ground, the mofque of fultan Mahomet is on the fourth hill E, and that of fultan Selim on the fifth F, the weftern walls of the city running along on the top of the fixth hill H Thefe hills rife fo one above another from the port, that they all appear from the mouth of the harbour, and moft of the houfes having a court or garden, in which they plant trees for the fhade and the refrefhing verdure, this adds a great beauty to the profpect The feventh hill I, is divided by a vale from the height that joins the three laft hills, which are to the north of it, this hill alone is computed to be one third part of the city, and is to the fouth of the fourth, fifth, and fixth hills, the others having the bay to the fouth of them, and that bay has to the fouth of it the north eaft point of the feventh hill and the three other hills to the north The pillar of Arcadius was on the feventh hill.

Great part of the houfes of Conftantinople are built with wooden frames, moftly filled up with unburnt brick, and a great number of houfes are made only of fuch frames covered with boards They have notwithftanding very good rooms in them, and the ftreets are tolerable, with a raifed footway on each fide The ftreet of Adrianople is broad, and adorned with many public buildings, to the fouth of it there is a vale, which

which is to the north of the seventh hill   The bazeſtans or ſhops of rich goods are ſuch as have been deſcribed in other places; and many of the ſhops for other trades are adorned with pillars, and the ſtreets in which they are, covered over in order to ſhelter from the ſun and rain   There are alſo ſeveral large kanes, where many merchants live, and moſt of theſe have apartments in them, where they ſpend the day, and retire at night to their families in their houſes. The bagnios alſo are to be reckoned another part of the magnificence of Conſtantinople, ſome of them being very finely adorned within   The fountains likewiſe are extremely

Fountain

magnificent, being buildings about twenty feet ſquare, with pipes of water on every ſide; and within at each corner there is an apartment, with an iron gate before it, where cups of water are always ready for the people to drink, a perſon attending to fill them, theſe buildings are of marble, the fronts are carved with bas reliefs of trees and flowers, and the eves projecting ſix or ſeven feet, the ſoffit of them is finely adorned with carved works of flowers, in alto relievo, gilt with gold in a very good taſte, ſo that theſe buildings make a very fine appearance

Moſques

It is ſaid that there are three hundred moſques in Conſtantinople, ſix of them are royal moſques, diſtinguiſhed by their number of minarets from two to ſix (others having but one), and are called after the name of their founders: I went into four of them, ſultan Achmed, Solimanea, or the moſque of ſultan Soliman, ſultan Mahomet; and ſultan Selim, they are all built, as moſt of the moſques are, with a court before them, that has a portico round it, which conſiſts of old pillars of the fineſt marbles   In that of Solimanea in particular there are four very large pillars of red granite between the ſtone piers which ſupport the dome, and the moſque is built in a very good taſte, there is a gallery round below, ſeparated by pillars from the iſle which goes round the part under the dome   There are two porphyry pillars in the portico of this moſque, of the ſame ſize as thoſe in ſaint Sophia, all theſe buildings are covered with cupolas, and ſome parts only with a quarter of a ſphere, the latter are moſtly built againſt the baſe of the great cupola, and all is covered with lead, abroad there are fountains to waſh on each ſide of the moſque, and the walls which encompaſs the great court before the moſque, are built with windows in a good taſte, with croſs iron bars in them   Near theſe moſques there are commonly places to prepare, and diſtribute proviſions to the poor on certain days, there are alſo generally near them ſhops and a bagnio for the ſupport of the moſques   The grand ſignor goes every Friday to one of theſe royal moſques, taking them commonly one after another, by reaſon that there is a benefaction given to the moſque he goes to, which I was informed, is five hundred dollars   The other two are the Walida moſque, and ſultan Bajazet, all of them having in them, and the courts belonging to them, many fine pillars, eſpecially of verd antique   There is alſo a royal moſque built by Mahomet the ſecond, to the weſt of the city at a place called Joupe, which has its name from Joupe a Turkiſh ſaint, to whom the moſque is dedicated   In this moſque the grand ſignor receives ſolemn poſſeſſion of his dominions, by having a ſword girded about him by the mufti   I was curious to ſee ſuch of the moſques as I could find had formerly been churches, and among them

2
particularly

particularly faint Sophia, there are in it eight porphyry pillars, and as many of verd antique, which, I believe, for their fize are not to be exceeded in the world, for the dome being fupported by four large piers, between them are four verd antique pillars on each fide, and a femicircle being formed as at each corner by thefe and four more piers, there are two porphyry pillars in each of them, and it appears plainly that there was a third, for there is an arch filled up next to each pier, which was doubtlefs done in order to ftrengthen thofe piers, the building having vifibly given way at the fouth weft corner, where the pillars of the gallery hang over very much, two of the porphyry pillars in the portico of Solimanea, might be taken from this mofque, and probably the other two might be found, if all the mofques and the feraglios were examined, thefe pillars are about two feet and a half in diameter, and of a proportionable height, there are pillars of verd antique in the galleries over them. Eight large porphyry pillars in faint Sophia are mentioned as taken out of a temple of the fun built by Valerian, and fent by Marfia, a Roman widow, to the emperor Juftinian[a], fo that if the others were of porphyry, they muft have been taken from fome other place   There are two porticos to the church, the inner one is wainfcotted with fine marbles   The mofque ftrikes the eye at the firft entrance, the dome being very large, but a great beauty is loft, as the mofaic is all deftroyed, except a very little at the eaft end, fo that all the top is whited over, but the fides are wainfcotted with porphyry, verd antique, and other rare oriental marbles, it is hung with a great number of glafs lamps, and the pavement is fpread with the richeft carpets, where the fophtis are always ftudying and repeating the alcoran, and the doctors preaching and explaining it, in particular parts of the mofque, to their feparate auditories   The top is covered with lead, and there is a gallery round on the infide of the cupola   This mofque makes a much meaner and heavier appearance on the outfide than the mofques that are built in imitation of it   On the fouth fide of it the grand fignor has erected a very fmall but neat library, which feemed to be about twenty feet wide and thirty long, there are preffes round it, and two in the middle for the manufcripts, the windows open to a court, round which the maufoleums of three fultans are finely built of marble, and in one of the windows of the library there is a fopha for the grand fignor, when he is pleafed to come and hear the law read to him in this place   The fineft mofque next after faint Sophia, which has been a church, is on the feventh hill, and near the feven towers, it is called by the Greeks Conftantine's church, but is the church of a monaftery called Studios, from a citizen of Conftantinople of that name who built it, there is a very handfome portico to it, with four pillars of white marble, which fupport a very rich entablature, there being another of the fame kind within   The nave is divided from the ifles by feven verd antique pillars, fix feet two inches in circumference, I took particular notice that they are of the compofite order   Over thefe there are as many more pillars of the Ionick order, and probably of the fame materials, but according to the Turkish taste they are whited over; there appears to have been a gallery on each side, which is not remaining There is a cistern under a court to the south of it, in which there are four rows of Corinthian pillars Another church converted into a mosque, is on the north brow of the fourth hill, it was dedicated to the Almighty, has two porticos, and is divided into three parts, the domes being supported with pillars of red granite, the whole is adorned with the figures of the apostles, and of the history of our Saviour in mosaic work, and the subject of each compartment is described in Greek; the Turks have disfigured the faces of all them On the outside of this church there is a very fine coffin of a single piece of verd antique of a very extraordinary size. There are crosses cut on it, and probably it is the only one of this sort of marble in the world. The magnificent church of the apostles, built by Constantine the great, was on this hill, where the mosque of sultan Mahomet is situated, there are now no remains of it, near it were the cisterns of Arcadius, where there is at present the largest bagnio in Constantinople, near which I saw the remains of some very thick walls, probably belonging to those cisterns There is also a mosque that was an old church on the fifth hill, and another at the foot of it, but there is nothing remarkable in either of them About the seventh hill I saw also two other mosques that were churches, they are not mentioned by any authors; and, if I mistake not, they are called the church mosques In this part also there are great remains of vaults and cisterns, one of them seems to be that which was near the church called Mocianus, built by Anastasius Dicorus; the cisterns were made by Justinian On the sixth hill there is a church to which they carry mad people, and lay them in a portico, thinking it a sovereign remedy to bring them to their senses: This I should take to be about the spot of the church of St John Baptist in that part which was formerly a suburb, called Hebdomum, it is said Theodosius brought to this place the head of St John Baptist from a village called Coslaum near Pantichium in the district of Chalcedon; for near this place there is a large hollow ground now turned into gardens, which seems to be the spot of the cisterns of Bonus, mentioned in this part. Another church spoken of by those who describe Constantinople is the church of the Virgin Mary in Blachernæ, at a place where there is now a holy water, which is had in great esteem among the Greeks, and there are some remains of very strong walls. To the east of this at the foot of the fifth hill is a part of the city called Phinni, where there is a wall built up the hill, they have a story, that it was erected in one night during a siege by candlelight; and that this gave name to that part of the city Here the patriarch of Constantinople resides, and also the patriarch of Jerusalem, the place being mostly inhabited by Greeks, and between this place and the fountain before mentioned, there are several Greek churches What they call the palace of Constantine, close to which the walls are built on the sixth hill, seems to have been only one room with the roof supported by pillars, though now it is divided, and made into two stories, it does not seem to be of great antiquity, and is probably a Genoese building, as there are coats of arms over the windows

There

I

There are very few remains of any other antiquities in Constantinople Of the several pillars and obelisks which were in the Hippodrome, there are now only three to be seen, one is the obelisk of red granite, thirty-five paces from which is the serpentine pillar, and forty paces from that an obelisk, which is built of hewn stone; all these have been very particularly described, the obelisk of granite appears to have been longer, the figures at bottom being imperfect: Both this and the other obelisks had two steps round them, which do not now appear, as they are continually raising the ground of the Hippodrome. The obelisk, which is built of hewn stone, was covered with plates of brass, and the holes to which they were fixed are seen in the stones. Part of the serpentine pillar is broke off, at the grand signor's seraglio of Sadabat, there is one made in imitation of it, but not so large: That in the Hippodrome is thought to be a very great piece of antiquity, being said to be the twisted serpents on which there stood a Tripos, supposed to be that which Pausanias and the cities of Greece consecrated to Apollo at Delphi. What they call the Burnt pillar is on the second hill, which, though not of one stone, yet when entire might be esteemed one of the finest pillars in the world, being singular in its kind, it is said to have been brought from Rome by Constantine the great, and that he placed on it that exquisite bronze statue of Trojan Apollo, which was a representation of himself, it is called the Burnt pillar, because the pedestal and pillar have been much damaged by fire, it is erected on a marble pedestal, about twenty feet high, which is much ruined; and probably there were some steps round it, the shaft seems to have consisted of ten pieces of porphyry, thirty-three French feet in circumference, each stone being nine feet four inches long, excepting a wreath of laurel half a foot deep at the top of every one, which had the effect to conceal the joining of the stones: Seven of these stones now remain, though an exact describer of Constantinople says there were eight, three of the stones, together with the statue, were thrown down by lightning, if I do not mistake, it was in the time of Alexius Comnenus, it was said to have been of the Doric order, and when entire must have been a most magnificent lofty pillar, it is not well represented even in its present condition by any cuts that I have seen of it, there are now twelve tiers of stone above the seven of porphyry, eleven of them seem to be about a foot deep, and the uppermost is something like a Tuscan capital, and about two feet deep. There is a Greek inscription on the fourth tier, which I had not an opportunity of copying, but it is said to import, that the emperor Emanuel Comnenus repaired it. Arius is said to have died near this pillar, as mentioned by the ecclesiastical historians. Near it is a cistern, the arches of it are supported by sixteen pillars in length, and fourteen in breadth, with as many more on them, it seems to have been a Christian work, there being a cross on some of them, and these letters K N. I saw what is called the pillars of Marcianus, which is mentioned by Gyllius, but he seems not to have seen it, he also mentions the virgin column, which probably is the same, though he might not know it; for it is now called by the Turks Kish-Tash ['The Virgin stone or pillar,] it is a very fine pillar of grey granite of the Corinthian order,

with

with a well proportioned pedeſtal which had ſteps round it, the ſhaft alone ſeems to be about twenty-five feet high, and this pillar, eſpecially the pedeſtal, is very ill repreſented by ſome travellers It is ſuppoſed that the inſcription was made in braſs, and they have been able to trace it out by the holes which were made in order to fix on the letters. A pillar like this was removed from ſome part of the town into the garden of the ſeraglio, which I ſaw from Pera between the trees. The hiſtorical pillar of Arcadius has been very exactly deſcribed, the ſhaft of it was taken down about thirty years ago, for ſome public Turkiſh building, ſo that the baſe and pedeſtals only remain, the baſe, and the column conſiſted of ſeveral tiers of ſingle ſtones of the ſame breadth as the baſe and column, and were laid one over the other, out of which the ſtairs were cut within, but the pedeſtal has two ſtones in each tier ſo nicely joined, that a very curious perſon has affirmed that there was but one in each tier.

Audience of the grand ſignor The ſeraglio and public audiences of the grand ſignor have been fully deſcribed, I ſaw part of the ceremony of an audience of the grand vizier, and was habited in the caftan, but I could not enter into the audience room to ſee the monarch, becauſe the number of perſons permitted to go in with the ambaſſador was full: A divan is always held before ſuch an audience, at which the ambaſſador is preſent, and the grand ſignor is at a lattice window over the ſeat of the grand vizier, but is not ſeen, though by ſome ſignal it is known that he is there, and when the buſineſs of the divan, as a court of juſtice, is done, (which is chiefly reading petitions of poor people, who are brought one by one into the preſence of the grand vizier), then ſtools are ſet before the vizier, the two cadiliskiers, the treaſurer and ſeal-keeper, who are always preſent; and about ſeven in the morning the dinner was brought on ſeveral ſmall plates placed on large diſhes, and put before them on the ſtools, without their moving from the place where they did the public buſineſs, the ſmall plates were very often changed, the ambaſſador eating with the grand vizier, and thoſe who go to audience with him, with the ſeal keeper, and treaſurer; the cadiliskiers being people of the law, are too holy to eat with infidels After this the grand ſignor's firman is read, which orders that the ambaſſador ſhould be introduced. The vizier holds the ordinary divans four times a week in the grand ſignor's ſeraglio, and on the other days he has a divan in his own houſe.

Two rivers fall into the bay of Conſtantinople, about a league to the weſt of the city, the northern river is the antient Lycus, the ſouthern one was called Hydralis There were many houſes of pleaſure and gardens of the great men near the banks of theſe rivers, and on the riſing ground, but in that rebellion, which ſet the preſent grand ſignor on the throne, the mob requeſted it of him, that they might be permitted to deſtroy thoſe houſes where the great people ſpent their time in luxury and idleneſs, neglecting the public affairs, and their petition not being refuſed, they levelled every thing to the ground, ſo that now they have their country-houſes along the canal in the way to the Black ſea On the northern river the grand ſignor has a pleaſant ſeraglio called Sudabat, the river is in ſuch a manner confined as to make a fine canal to it, which is about ſeventeen hundred paces long

ſ   It

It is is said, that every day there are consumed at Constantinople,
Scutari, and the adjacent villages thirty six thousand measures of wheat
These measures which are called a killo, are supposed to be sufficient for
a hundred persons, so that the number of souls may be computed at three
millions six hundred thousand; of these a hundred thousand are computed to be Jews, and sixty thousand Christians, though the former computation seems to exceed   They reckon that there are forty thousand
boats, like our wherries, which are uncovered, except those of the
grand signor, or grand vizier, the former being covered with red, and
the latter with green

There have been two Armenian presses in Constantinople for about *Printing*
forty years   The vizier Ibrahim Pasha having read an account of the
usefulness of printing, persuaded the late sultan Achmet to permit a
press to be set up under the direction of Ibrahim Efendi, an Hungarian
renagado, they printed twelve books, but about four years ago it was
dropped, but they have lately begun to print in Turkish the history of the Ottoman port for about sixty years past   I happened to see
Constantinople at a time when the Turks were in good humour, and
had no reason to be displeased with the Franks (except that the soldiery
would gladly have continued the war against the emperor) they had just
made a very honourable peace for themselves with that monarch, and
not a very disadvantageous one with the Muscovites whom they dreaded
as a power superior to them, so that I went freely all over Constantinople, and was so far from being affronted in the least, that I rather
met with civility in every place, entered publickly into such of the
mosques as I desired to see, and sometimes even on Fridays, just before
the sermon began, and when the women were come into the mosques
to hear their harangues   This is permitted by speaking to the keeper of
the mosque, and giving him a very small gratuity, and at other times
sending for him when the mosques were shut   And indeed to speak
justly of the Turks, they are a very tractable people when they are well
used, and when they have no prospect of getting any thing by ill treatment, and what makes them more troublesom and suspicious in places
on the sea is the rough usage they meet with from the Corsairs.

C H A P. II.

Of GALATA, PERA, the aqueducts, and some other places near CONSTANTINOPLE.

Galata.

GALATA is situated to the north of the port of Constantinople, it is encompassed with a wall near three miles in circumference, having the water to the south and east, and is built from the sea up the sides of the hill, it is very much inhabited by Christians, and by all the Europeans· Here they have their warehouses, custom house, and all European ships come to this port. The Greeks have three churches in Galata, and the Armenians two: The Jesuits, Dominicans, and Franciscans have each of them a convent in this place. During the time of the Venetian war a convent under the protection of Venice was seized on, and the church turned into a mosque, and such Franks as lived near it were ordered to remove, on which all the En-

Pera.

glish, and some others removed to Pera, which is on the top of the hill where all the ambassadors reside, and it is a much finer situation What they call the Quattro Strade are almost entirely inhabited by Franks and other Christians Pera is under the Topjee-bashaw of Tophana, and Galata is governed by a waiwode. Pera and Galata are the thirteenth region which was called Sicena The Trinitarians, two sort of Franciscans, and the Capuchins have each of them a convent in Pera. The ambassadors live here in greater state than in any other parts, because it is the custom of the country, and they keep open tables The king of the two Sicilies has lately obtained capitulations for trade, as well as the Swedes, and has a minister here This place and Galata having been much inhabited by Genoese who had obtained it of the Greek emperors, there are still some of those families remaining, many of whom are drogermen to the ambassadors, of which each nation has a certain number, one or two of them do most of the business of the nation, and the others are employed occasionally by the merchants There are also Gjovani de Lingue, as they call them, who are young men that have small salaries, take their turn in waiting at the palace, and attend on strangers or others, when there is occasion The French have twelve of these of their own nation, who are educated at the Capuchin convent at the expence of the king, are sent to different consuls abroad, and promoted as they deserve The Muscovites and Germans also have some of their own nation, but are obliged chiefly to make use of the natives of the place, who know best how to discharge the mysterious office of a drogerman The head drogerman of the port is always a Greek, and very often a prince of Moldavia; he is somewhat in the nature of a secretary of state, as well as interpreter, and has a great influence in relation to the affairs of the Europeans, and more particularly when treaties of peace are on foot. It is said the Venetian ambassador, who is called the Bailo, has an unlimited commission from the republic to draw for what sums he pleases,

5

and

and even that his accounts are not examined. So great an interest that state has to serve with the Port.

To the north of Pera is Tophana on another hill, and nothing can be imagined more beautiful than the prospect of the vale between them: On the brow of the hill, on Tophana side, there is a publick building called Galati Serai, (for this upper part of the hill is reckoned as a part of Galata or Pera); this building is finely situated round a large court; it is destined for the education of the itcheoglans for the seraglio of the grand signor, and contains in it about four hundred; they are mostly orphans or children of poor people who cannot educate their families; they are kept under great discipline, never stir out, nor can they so much as look out of their windows, and no persons are suffered to go in · They learn to read, write, ride, and draw the bow, and to chant their devotions, the grand signor goes there once in two years, and chuses out of them such as he pleases about twenty years old, who are made his itcheoglans; most of them are officers about him like pages, and attend him on horseback, or in the chamber, being something of the nature of chamberlains, and these, according to their merit, are often advanced to be pashas, and to the highest offices.

Tophana is so called from the foundery of Canon [Tope] It is go-*Tophana* verned by the Topejee-Bashaw [The captain of the artillery], as well as Pera, there are a great number of very fine brass cannon on the quay and other places about it, for now they make none of iron. One of their finest fountains is in this place To the north of it is Funduclee, and north of that two or three more places built up the side of the hills, which look like one continued town from Galata.

To the west of Galata, on the north side of the port, is the publick *Arsenal* arsenal or dock called Cassum-pasha, where there are covered buildings to lay up the galleys in winter, and here is what they call the bagnio for the grand signor's captive Christian slaves. I saw here eleven large men of war, and was informed that there are commonly about twenty, and that they have in other parts twenty more, the largest, called the Capitana, as I was informed, is twelve feet longer than the Royal Sovereign, being a hundred and eighty six feet long, and forty six feet eight inches broad, it is twenty-one feet deep in the hold, has three decks, besides the quarter deck, and a spare deck · The sheet anchor weighs ninety five quintals, and the cable is thirty-two inches in circum-ference, she carries a hundred and ten guns, and sixteen hundred men. The galleys go out every summer round the islands to collect the ha-rach or christian poll tax, and the captain pasha or high admiral sails with four or five men of war, and levies what money he can on the islands, and other places on the sea, which belong to him.

On the height, to the north west of the arsenal, is a down called the Okemeidan [The place of arrows] where they go to exercise with the bow and arrow, and there are many marble pillars set up to shew how far several grand signors have shot, some of which are at an incredible distance, it is a height which commands a fine view of the port, and Constantinople · There is an open Turkish namasgah, or praying place on it, where I was informed they circumcise the grand signor's children, in this place the grand fignor reviews the army before he goes out to war.

Water has been brought to Conftantinople at great expence, and is very neceffary in this country, where they drink it in fuch great quantities, and ufe fo much for wafhing and bathing; and the more care has been taken, becaufe a want of it would certainly caufe a rebellion in the city, for this purpofe they formerly made fo many large cifterns as refervoirs of the water of the aqueduct, in cafe it fhould fail; and the great ciftern under faint Sophia ferves for that purpofe at this time: The moft antient aqueduct was built by the emperors Valens and Valentinian, this aqueduct is feen in three places, it conveys water to the city at the diftance of ten miles, being brought for the moft part from places three or four miles to the fouth eaft of the village called Belgrade. Thefe three parts of the aqueduct are called the crooked aqueduct, the long aqueduct, and the high aqueduct, the laft is neareft to Conftantinople, and receives the water that comes from the other two which are different ftreams. The crooked aqueduct is fo called, becaufe it makes a turn before it croffes the valley from one hill to the other, this aqueduct is executed in a very fine tafte; it is a ruftick work, and confifts of three tiers of fine arches one over another. The water firft runs on a wall, and then on twelve arches, for two hundred and twenty one yards, it then turns and croffes the vale on the three tiers of arches; in the loweft there are four arches, in the middle ten, and there are paffages made through the piers in the length of the aqueduct, by which one paffes to the other fide of the valley, in the uppermoft tier there are twenty one arches, the feven or eight firft arches on each fide are built on the defcent of the hill, two or three on the folid wall, and ten over the middle arches, in the upper ftory alfo there are arches through fifteen of the piers, in order to pafs the whole length of the aqueduct, as it has been obferved there are through the piers of the middle arches; the aqueduct being in that part about fix hundred and feventy-two feet long, and a hundred and feven feet high. It is a very magnificent work, and the water is conveyed to it from a rivulet that paffes near Belgrade, and muft be the Hydraulis, the water of this river is ftopped in two different places by a wall built acrofs, fo as to make two large lakes, and runs in channels thro' the wall, which is built to keep them up, thefe feem to be Turkifh works, and defigned as refervoirs of water in cafe the rivulet fhould dry up in fummer, that they might be fupplied by two fuch great bodies of water to be let out by lower channels which are in the wall, and may be opened on occafion, from the laft of thefe the water paffes to a deep bafon, into which fome other ftreams are brought, and from that it runs partly in the channels made on the fide of the hills, and partly on arches over valleys, and hollows in the hills, to the crooked aqueduct already defcribed, from which it runs on the fides of the hills into another bafon, and fo does the water of the long aqueduct, and from that bafon it goes in one channel to the high aqueduct. The other, called the long aqueduct, feems to be a modern work, and, I fuppofe, was built by Soliman the magnificent, who is faid to have repaired the other aqueducts, and if it was, it is a work truly worthy of

him.

him ; and I saw on it a short Turkish inscription It was built as a further supply of water to be conveyed by the high aqueduct ; it is two thousand two hundred and twenty-nine feet long, eighty-five feet and a half high, and the wall is twelve feet thick , it consists of two stories of arches one over another , in the lower story there are forty-seven arches, and fifty in the upper : At the first descent, at each end of the hills, the water runs on a long wall Other streams are brought to this water by the side of the southern hill, which passes likewise on a small number of arches over the valleys that are in the way The water of this aqueduct, as observed, communicates with the crooked aqueduct, and both run to the high aqueduct, which is a vast massive rustic building, by which the water is conveyed over a valley , it is above eight hundred and forty feet long, and one hundred and twelve feet high , it consists of four large arches, is many over them, and three stories of small ones between them, there being nine arches in the upper and lower stories, and six in the middle one This irregularity, contrary to the manner of the antients, and the arches not being true, gives this aqueduct a very Gothic appearance, though it is a work of great expence and magnificence, for the walls are fifteen feet thick , and the great arches are above fifty feet wide Ascending by the hill to one of the small arches, there is an arched passage from it through the wall, consisting of forty-four steps, which leads up to the great arches above, where there is a passage thro' the piers, as in the crooked aqueduct, and a descent likewise by stairs at the other end · From this aqueduct the water runs along the side of the hills, in channels covered in with stone, there being arches built only in two or three places This water formerly run on those arches in the third valley between the third and fourth hill , but the east part of that aqueduct being destroyed, the water is conveyed in channels on the ground to the several parts of the city. About ten years ago a new aqueduct was built to supply Pera, Galata, and the neighbouring villages , the water comes from Bauchicui, between Belgrade and Bonjuederry, and runs across a valley there on an aqueduct which consists of a great number of arches that are very well built, from this valley it runs round the hills, and sometimes under ground, and crossing a low ground it rises in such square pillars as have been before described, in order to keep the water to its height As it passes, part of it is conveyed to the villages on the west side of the canal of the Thracian Bosphorus, and coming near Pera, it rises in the same sort of pillars, and runs into a reservoir, consisting of many little cells made to contain the water, and is conveyed from them to the several parts of Pera and Galata

The point of Galata opposite to the seraglio was called cape Metopon Beshicktash is said to have been formerly called Jason from his touching there , at that place there was a grove of cypress trees, and a temple of Apollo At Ortacui there was a port called Chidium, and lower there was a port in which the vessels of the Rhodians used to lie, which, I suppose, is the place where ships now ride at anchor near Beshicktash when they are ready to sail, because it is difficult to go out of the port with a strong north wind The cape at Cruchicsme was in the middle ages called Asomaton. The bay which had the name of Scala was at Arnautcui, below it is the cape of Esties , further there is a large bay, on which Bialesui is situated

The cape on which the caftle ftands, and where the bridge is fuppofed to have been was called cape Mercury. The beft port of the Bofphorus was at the river Ornoufdera, it is called Sarantacopa, and by Dionyfius Byzantinus, Leoftenion. Under Tharapia is the rock Catargo Here is a fmall river, and the port Pharmaias, which is faid to be fo called, becaufe Medea touching at this place opened her box of drugs there. The bay of Boiyucdery was called Sinus Saronicus from an altar there to Saron of Megara, the point of this bay to the north was called Amilton and Tripition by the Greeks The convent of Mavro-Molo higher up was deftroyed, becaufe it was a place of debauchery for failors and other inferior people As to the Cyanean rock on the Europe fide, at the foot of it there is a white marble pillar broken into three or four pieces, and a Corinthian capital near it, the fhaft is two feet in diameter, above on the rock is what has been thought by fome to have been its pedeftal, it is about three feet in diameter, and has round it four feftoons joined by bulls heads There are many names on it, which feem to have been cut by people that came there The name of Auguftus, mentioned by fome authors, I fuppofe, is SEBASTVS, which is cut on the ftone in Roman characters, much better than the other, and very near to the bafe of the pedeftal. This is more juftly thought to be an altar to Apollo, which the Romans placed on this rock, tho from the holes for irons both above and below, it feems as if fome other ftones were fixed to it, which would rather incline one to conclude that it was the pedeftal of a pillar On the continent near this ifland is the light houfe of Europe, which is a high tower Going along the coaft of the Euxine fea in Thrace towards the weft, the firft place mentioned is Phinopolis, which feems to be the court of Phineus, from which the Argonauts went (after they had been ftopped by contrary winds) to the Afia fide, and facrificed to the twelve gods It is poffible this place put in the Tables was on the weft fide of that broad cape, which is about two leagues to the weft of the cape at the entrance of the Bofphorus, where I faw a fquare tower on the height with fome antient ftones in it I obferved here in the fea clifts a layer of earth about three feet thick, which appears like planks of timber burnt to a coal About eighteen miles to the weft of this tower was Philea, or Phivgea on the Palus Phileatina, this place is about the fame diftance alfo from Pelgrade What is called the lake is a fort of gulph that runs into the land, and there are fome rivulets that run into it, is well as I could learn there is a bank of fand before the mouth of it, which is covered with water in winter, and when the wind blows ftrong from the north there is now a fmall port on the outfide of it The town was on a peninfula at the eaft end of the gulph, on very high ground to the weft and north, having a gentle defcent to the fouth: On the eaft fide it was defended with a wall, a great part of which is ftill remaining, and is called by the Turks Dourkous, town and lake If there had been a good entrance for fhipping, this town, which is not a mile in circumference, would have been very finely fituated for trade Halmedyflus or Salmedyflus is faid to have been forty miles further, they informed me of a port twenty miles off, which, if I miftake not, is called Arade, it is well frequented, and probably is the antient Halmedyflus, though there feems to be a miftake in the diftance I was informed

formed that there are some ruins there, especially of the wall that was built by the emperor Anastasius across the neck of the peninsula to Selivrè, the old Selymbria. I was informed that this place is about thirty-six miles from Selivrè, and as far from Constantinople. All the country this way is a very rich soil, and abounds with wood; and the village of Belgrade is situated in a wood, the English, Swedish, and Dutch Ambassadors reside there in summer, where they have cool shady walks in the woods by the two large basons of water which are to supply the aqueduct.

CHAP. III.

Of SELIVREE, and ADRIANOPLE.

I SET out with the caravan from Constantinople for Adrianople, on the seventh of July in the afternoon, the road is to the south west, thro' an open fertile country which is uneven as far as Selivree. It is to be observed that the present road to Adrianople goes out at the Selivree gate, and that the Adrianople gate is at a considerable distance from it to the west, through which, doubtless, the antient road to Adrianople went, though it is now disused, probably because it is a more uneven country. Near a league from Constantinople to the left of the road, there is a large building called Bayrcut Han [The powder house], where all the powder is made for the use of Constantinople, and the places on the Black Sea, and the ships take it in there. Five miles from Constantinople there is a small town called [The little bridge], from a bridge there near the sea, over the outlet of a lake, is well as I could learn, the lake receives a small river into it, which probably is the Bithenius of Ptolemy. We stopped here for about two hours, and then travelled almost three hours till midnight, and lay in a meadow near the road. On the eighth we went seven miles to a town called, The great bridge, where there is a large bridge over the mouth of another lake, into which probably the river Athyra of Ptolemy falls. Ten miles further is a village on the sea called Camourgit, and near a league beyond it there is a small town called Perridole, situated on a rocky eminence over the sea. Twelve miles beyond this we arrived at Selivree the Selymbria of Ptolemy, situated very near the sea to the west of the old city, the walls of which are entire, and stand on a small eminence, the old and new town together are about a mile in circumference, it is probable that the wall formerly mentioned, went across from the old town to the Black Sea. The Greeks and Armenians have each an old church adorned with Mosaic of the middle ages, about one of them I saw a relief of a man, with a pole or spear in one hand, and in the other a long shield that rested on the ground. The old town is thinly inhabited, the present city, which is a poor place, is to the west of it, and is chiefly subsisted by being a great thorough fare. I passed the day at Selivree in the kane, and in seeing the antiquitie, and set forward in the evening, p ing out of the town we faw a party of Tartars with their bows flung about their bodies   From Selivree the remainder of the way to Adrianople was near weft, and in ten miles we came to a fmall town called Keliclee, which might be Melantias of the Itinerary, faid to be at the river Athyras ` We lay in the fields about a mile further, and on the ninth travelled five miles to Chourley, which feems to be Izhrallon of the Itinerary, which is mentioned as eighteen miles from Heraclea in the way to Adrianople   Both the Greeks and Armenians have a church here, and I faw an infcription in the Armenian churchyard, which makes mention of a Perinthian, and probably this place was in the diftrict of Perinthus, called afterwards Heraclea, and at prefent Heraclee   I faw alfo about the town feveral marble covers of coffins, and ruins of a wall built of brick and ftone, which feem to be the remains of an antient enclofure   The fituation of Chourley is very beautiful on a rifing ground, commanding a view as far as the fea, and is computed to be five hours from Heraclee, and four from Rodofto, we ftaid here till the evening, and went about two hours further, and lay in the fields near a village called Bolavanna, on the tenth we went about two hours to a town called Borgas, which from the name, as well as fituation, feems to be the antient Berguhs   We travelled in the evening eight miles further to Biba, where there is a beautiful large Turkifh bridge over a fmall river, a fine mofque, and an old church entire, built of brick, this may be Burtudizum. We went eight miles further, and lay in the open air, on the eleventh we travelled four miles to Hapfa, which is eight from Adrianople, and feems to be Oftudizum.

Adrianople   Adrianople was firft called Oreftes, and had its prefent name from the improvements made in it by the emperor Adrian, the Turks call it Edrinch, the town is fituated on a rifing ground, and on the plain at the foot of it, the antient city feems to have been on the plain, where great part of the walls remain, though they feem to be of the middle ages, and there are many infcriptions which make mention of the later Greek emperors who repaired them   The river Meritchch, which below is the antient Heber, runs to the fouth of the town, and is joined by two other rivers a little lower, one of which called the Ardah is navigable from Philopopoli by floats, and muft be the Heber above the conflux, the other is called the Tounfah   The Meritchch is a fine river when it is joined by the other two, and is navigable down to Enos, a town at the mouth of the river which retains its old name, but as there are fome fhallows in the river, they do not navigate it in the fummer months   Adrianople is very delightfully fituated, in a beautiful plain, watered by three rivers   The fhops which are well built and furnifhed, and the kanes are within the city walls, but moft of the people live on the height over the old city, which is a more advantageous fituation, where moft of the houfes have their gardens, and enjoy a very fine profpect They have two or three beautiful mofques on the outfide of the city, the

---

* The port at the mouth of the river Athyras was called Navale Mulanticum This place was in the road to Conftantinople from Heraclea, and was twenty nine miles from the former probably by a fhort way acrofs the country Between it and Heraclea was Cccropanenfion,   which is faid to be between Selymbria and the river Athyris, but as Heraclea is but fourteen miles from Selivree, the diftances of thofe two places from Heraclea is much too great Cano-phanon ought to be corrected to fourteen, and Melantiada to thirteen

largeft may vye with the beft in Conftantinople, and is built in a good tafte. There are two mofques in the city which were churches, and there are two large verd antique pillars in the portico of one of them. This is one of the four royal cities in which the grand fignors have made their refidence : The feraglio is to the weft of the town, and of the river Meritcheh, which runs both on the weft and fouth fides of the city; it is built on a fine plain fpot, and there is a large meadow towards the river planted with trees, befides the principal building for the grand fignor, which did not feem to be large, there are many little houfes in the gardens for the ladies, and in other parts for the great officers, and as they are low, it has the appearance of a Carthufian cloyfter   No body is permitted to enter this feraglio without a particular order from Conftantinople.   The Boftangee-bafhaw refides in one part of it, to whom moft of the country belongs as far as Philippopoli, and a great territory round about it, of which he is the governor, and he is not fubject to the Boftangee-bafhaw at Conftantinople.   On the hill to the weft of the feraglio there is a large fummer-houfe which belongs to the grand fignor, from which there is a fine profpect of the city, and all the country round

The city is governed by the janitzer aga, it is a place of great trade, fupplying all the country with goods brought by land from Conftantinople, and from Smyrna, and other parts by fea, and up the river, they have a great plenty of all forts of provifions, they alfo make filk, which is chiefly ufed for their own manufactures   The wine of this place, which is moftly red, is very ftrong and well-flavoured, and they have all forts of fruits in great perfection · The Greeks have an archbifhop here.   There is a village called Demeilata, about a league to the fouth weft of the town, where Charles the twelfth, king of Sweden, refided fome years, till he was removed to Demotica, as it is imagined, by the inftigation of his enemies, who, it is faid, thought that this place was too near the great road   The French have two or three houfes here, and a conful   The English alfo have a perfon with confular power to act for them, though they have little bufinefs, but formerly when there was war with the emperor they had their factors here, and fold a confiderable quantity of cloth, tin, and lead   When I was at Adrianople I faw the entrance of an ambaffador extraordinary from the emperor on the conclufion of the peace.

CHAP. IV.

Of Demotica, Rodosto, and Gallipoli.

WE left Adrianople on the feventeenth, travelled fouthwards, and
paffed through a village called Ahercui, where there is a large
kane for the grand fignor's camels, which are bred in that
country. We went in between the hills, and arrived at Demotica on a
fmall river called Kefeldele-fu, which falls into the Meritcheh about a mile
to the north eaft, it is near twelve miles from Adrianople. The
prefent town is chiefly on the north and eaft fide of the hill, where the
antient town was likewife fituated, which is fuppofed to be Dyme,
there are remains of the walls of a caftle, and of feveral artificial grottos: The Chriftians live on the eaft fide of the hill, and have two
churches Charles the twelfth of Sweden lived at this place for fome
time. I was informed that he commonly rode out every afternoon, and
that fome few of his followers, who were given to gallantry, were
obliged to be very fecret in thofe affairs, the king having been always
very remarkable for the ftricteft chaftity, droggermen and people of great
confideration often came to him I fhould conjecture that Plotinopolis
was higher up the river on which Demotica ftands, as Trajanopolis
was twenty-two miles from it in the way to the city of Heraclea.
The hills that run along from the fouth weft to the north eaft near
Adrianople feem to be mount Rhodope Between Adrianople and
Plotinopolis, there was a place called Nicæa, where it is faid the Arians
drew up a confeffion of faith in order to impofe on the world, the place
being of the fame name as the city where the famous council was held.
On the eighteenth we went a mile to the north eaft to the river Meritcheh, which is here very rapid, we croffed it on a flat bottomed boat,
and travelled feven miles near caft through a very fine country to Ouzoun-Kupri [The long bridge], a town fo called from a bridge built
acrofs the plain, and over the fmall river Erganeh to the weft of the
town, which overflows the plain in winter, being near half a mile long,
and confifts of a hundred and feventy arches, it is built of hewn ftone,
and is a very great work If Dyme was between Plotinopolis and Trajanopolis, this would be the moft likely place for the latter At prefent
it is only a fmall town, having very few Chriftians in it, and no church
We went fixteen miles further to the eaft to another fmall town called
Jenbol, which feems to be a corruption from Hieripolis, this poffibly
might be Apris, where the roads from Trajanople to Heraclea and Gallipoli feem to have parted, we lay at this place, and on the nineteenth
went eight hours to Rodofto The whole country of Thrace I paffed
through from Conftantinople is an exceeding rich foil, which produces in
the downs the greateft plenty of herbage I ever faw in places entirely
unimproved, and a great quantity of excellent corn, and alfo fome flax
The country is moftly uneven, and has very little wood in it, fo that
the antients, who fay Thrace is a barren country, except near the fea,
were very much miftaken. Rodofto is the old Bifanthe, afterwards called

Rhedeftus,

Rhedeftus, and in the Itinerary Refifton, it is fituated in a very large bay on the fea, and up the fide of the hills, the town being near a mile in length, it is chiefly inhabited by Turks, though there are feveral Greek and Armenian families in the town, the latter have one church, and the Greeks five, and their archbifhop of Heraclea has a houfe here. They make exceeding good wine, and it is a place of great export of corn for Conftantinople. The late princes Ragotfki refided in this town, in a palace where feveral of their adherents now live, and receive their penfions from the port. To the north eaft is Heraclea the old Perinthus, about the point that makes this great bay to the north. When I arrived at this place I paid off my jinizary, and the next day he came and faid he was not fatisfied, that he expected to have been longer with me, and if I would not give him more he would oblige the conful at Adrianople to pay him, and at laft threatened me with the mequime, or court of juftice, but as he could not intimidate me, I heard no more of him, and on the twentieth embarked for Gallipoli, where I arrived upon on the twenty-firft. This is the antient Callipolis, finely fituated at the northern entrance of the Hellefpont on rifing grounds, and on the fouth fide of them, fo that it makes no appearance coming to it from the north. Lampfacus is on the other fide in Afia, about a league further to the fouth, a village called Shirdnck, being directly oppofite to Galli poli. This city, tho' it is three miles in circumference, is but a poor place, and has very little trade. The upper parts of the town, where the people chiefly live, are pleafant, and the houfes have gardens to them, the fhops are in the lower part of the town. There is a little rivulet to the weft of the city, and to the fouth a fmall enclofed port, and a fine bafon within the walls which is not now ufed, the old ruined caftle is above it to the north. To the eaft of the port there are about twenty ruined houfes which were built along the fhoar for the reception of gallies, probably during the time of the Greek emperors. Near a fmall bay to the north of the city, and on the Propontis, there is a fine powder houfe, where all the fhips of the grand fignor take in their powder that go out into the Mediterranean. There are about three hundred Greek families here, they have two churches, at one of which the archbifhop of Heraclea has a houfe, in which his fuffragan bifhop refides, there are fome families of Jews here. As paffengers often flop at this port in their way between Smyrna and Conftantinople, and other parts, fo the plague is frequently brought to this city. About two leagues to the north of Gallipoli is the narroweft part or neck of this peninfula, which was computed to be about five miles broad, there were three towns on it, one to the weft called Cardia on the bay Melanis, which makes the peninfula, one in the middle called Lyfimachia, which is thought to be a large village on the height called Boulaycre, it was built by Lyfimachus, who deftroyed Cardia, and was afterwards demolifhed by the Thracians, and rebuilt by Antiochus. The third town was Pactye to the eaft, which might be either in a fhallow bay rather to the fouth eaft and by eaft of Boulaycre, or on a little bay, fomething more to the north than that village, where a fmall rivulet falls into the fea. There was a wall acrofs this neck of land, and a town near it, which on this account was called in the Greek language

Macron-

Macrontychon [The long wall] Going to the south, a little north of the narrow passage, where, I suppose, Sestus and Abydus were situated, there is a ruin of an old castle or town on the height, about half a mile from the sea, it is called Acbash, and is the abode of a dervishe. This probably was Ægos, where the Athenians lost their liberty, being defeated by the Lacedæmonians, and that the rather, because, by the best information that I could get, there is a rivulet there as there was at Ægos, which went by the same name, and was to the south of the supposed Sestus, which I imagine was not where the castle now is, for reasons I have already mentioned, there is a deep bay here, at the bottom of which is a large village called Maydos, this probably is the port Cœlus [κοῖλος], which might have its name from the great hollow or bay, and it is described as south of Sestus. At this port the Athenians beat the Lacedæmonians by sea, and erected a trophy at Cynosema, or the tomb of Hecuba, which I suppose to have been the present European castle, commonly thought to be Sestus, being a high point of land to the south of that port, and so very proper for the erection of a trophy, on account of a victory gained in that harbour. Cynosema also is mentioned as opposite to the river Rodius, which seems to be the river at the castle over against it on the Asia side. Alopeconesus was at the western cape of the south end of the peninsula. The eastern cape was called Mastusia, where the outer castle of Europe is situated, in which a pasha always resides. To the north of it is a little bay, and a fine spot of ground, which probably was the site of Eleus, the tower or sepulchre of Protesilaus is mentioned near it, as well as a small temple to him.

CHAP. V.

Of Mount Athos.

WE embarked at Lemnos, and landed at Monte Santo, as it is called by the Europeans, on the eighth of September, it is the antient mount Athos in Macedonia, now called both by Greeks and Turks, Haion Horos [The Holy Mountain] by reason that there are so many convents on it, to which the whole mountain belongs. It is a promontory which extends almost directly from north to south, being joined to the continent by a neck of land about a mile wide, thro' which some historians say Xerxes cut a channel, in order to carry his army a short way by water, from one bay to the other, which seems very improbable, nor did I see any sign of such a work. The bay of Contessa to the north of this neck of land was called by the antients Strymonicus, to the south is the bay of Monte Santo, antiently called Singiticus, and by the Greeks at this day Amouliane, from an island of that name at the bottom of it, between which and the gulph of Salonica is the bay of Hagi-Mamma, called by the antients Toronaus. The northern cape of this promontory is called cape Laura, and is the promontory Nymphæum of the antients; and the cape of Monte Santo seems to be the promontory Acrathos. Over the former is the higheft fummit of mount Athos, all the other parts of it, though hilly, being low in comparifon of it, it is a very fteep rocky height covered with pine-trees, if we fuppofe the perpendicular height of it to be four miles from the fea, tho' I think it cannot be fo much, it may be eafily computed if its fhadow could reach to Lemnos, which, they fay, is eighty miles diftant, though I believe it is not above twenty leagues.

There are on Monte Santo twenty convents, ten on the north fide, and Convents. ten on the fouth, moft of them near the fea, there being only two on the eaft fide, and three on the weft, that are above a mile from the water, the cape itfelf not being above two leagues wide. Many of thefe convents are very poor; fome indeed have eftates abroad, and moft of them fend out priefts to collect charity, and the perfon who returns with the greateft fum of money is commonly made goumenos or abbot, till another brings in a greater. They pay a certain price for their lands, and a boftangi refides in their town to receive it, and to protect them againft injuries, every convent alfo pays a poll tax for a certain number. It is thought that they are obliged to give lodging and provifions to all comers; but where perfons are able they always expect charity, no female animal, except thofe that are wild, is permitted on this mount. Their manner of living is much the fame as that of mount Sinai; they never eat meat. The priefts and waiters, when in their refectory, wear the hood on their heads, and a long black cloak, and a perfon from a pulpit reads fome book in the vulgar Greek all the time they eat. In every convent they have many chapels adjoining to their rooms, probably fitted up by particular perfons, out of their devotion to fome faint, there are alfo houfes with chapels to them all over the lands of the convents, which they call Kellia, and might formerly be the cells of hermits, but are now inhabited only by a caloyer or two, who take care of the gardens or vineyards adjoining. Thofe houfes which are on their eftates at a diftance from the convents they call Metokia. Befides their lay caloyers, they have alfo hired fervants to labour, called Men of the world [Κοσμικοί]. They have no manner of learning among them, nor do they fo much as teach the antient Greek, though I was informed they did, fo that the priefts lead very idle unprofitable lives: And confidering them in a political view, any one would think that two or three thoufand perfons would be much better employed in the world in propagating the Chriftian race in a country where the number is daily diminifhing, fo that in this refpect it is the policy of the Turks to encourage this life. Some of their convents have been founded by princes of Bulgaria, Servia, and Walachia, and are filled with people of thofe countries, and thefe priefts are fo extreamly ignorant, that they can neither talk nor read the vulgar Greek. The convents are built round a court with a church in the middle, four of them on the eaft fide are the largeft and richeft, and of them Laura is the chief, and has the greateft intereft and command over the reft, and the monks of it are efteemed the moft polifhed, as well as the moft politick, Iverone and Vatopede are the moft beautiful both in their building and fituation on the water, the

fourth is Calandari. Four or five convents on the weft fide are very curi-
oufly fituated, being built on high rocks over the water.

When I landed I went firft to the convent of Laura, where Neophy-
tus, archbifhop of Naupactus and Larta refided ; he had refigned his
archbifhopric above twenty years   I was conducted to their refectory to
fee them dine, and to the archbifhop's apartment, at whofe table I always eat   The marble font in the church feemed to be an antient vafe.
On the ninth, I went to vifit the monafteries on the north fide of the
hill, and in four hours came to the poor convent of Caracallo, where we
took fome refrefhment, and in an hour more came to the convent Phi-
lotheo, which I viewed, and went on to the monaftery of Iveronè, which
is delightfully fituated on a flat fpot near the fea in the middle of beautiful meadows , it is a large convent, where I was very civilly entertained, prefied much to ftay, and faw an old bifhop of Lemnos who
had refigned, and an archimandrite of Mufcovy, who had travelled in
that country   I then went by water an hour to the north to the poor
convent Stavro Niketa, where I was very civilly entertained by the archbifhop of Philippi and Drame, who had refigned , he conducted me to
the orangery, and prefented me with a bough loaded with lemons.
Aged prelates often refign their bifhopricks, and come to thefe convents,
in order to end their days in a quiet retirement   I went by water an
hour further to the convent Pantocratori, where I lay, the abbot had
travelled in Spain, Italy and Germany, and talked Italian   This convent was founded by John prince of Walachia, who with fome of his
family are buried in it   I here faw a hermit at fome diftance in a wood;
he lived in a hut almoft inacceffible, by reafon of the briars , they faid, he
was a hundred years old, and had lived there forty years , he had no chapel, not being obliged either to attend the facrament, or to adminifter it,
or perform any offices of the church , he had nothing on but a coarfe coat
and trowfers, without a fhirt   On the tenth, we rowed to the large convent of Vatopede, where I received great civilities, and they fent to
my boat prefents of fruit and other things   We went two hours to the
north to the convent of faint Simenus, built by Pelfena daughter of
Arcadius   We here mounted on mules, and went half an hour through
pleafant fields to Kiliu Iari convent, which is one of the four great
ones, and was founded for Servians, by Stephen king of Servia , the
monks feemed to be very ignorant, and I was but very indifferently accommodated   On the eleventh, we went two hours up the hills to the
fouth to the convent Zographo , they fay, it was founded by a nephew
of Juftinian for Bulgarians , it is two miles both from the convents Ca-
flimoneto and Dokiario   We went to the fea on the fouth fide of the cape,
and arrived at Dokiario convent, we afterwards failed a mile to the poor
convent of St George Zenopho , and tafted a falt water in the way, which
is foft and purges   We then went by water to Simopetra convent, and afterwards to St. Gregorio and St John Dionyfius, where we lay   On the twelfth,
we went by water to the monaftery of St Paul, from which we rid two miles
round the hills over the fea to the hermitages of St Anne, near the
moft fouthern extremity of the cape, they confift of about forty houfes,
inhabited by near a hundred hermits , they are fituated in a femicircular

hollow

hollow of the hill, there are some hermits also near the convent of saint John Dionysius, and near Simopetra Two or three hermits live in each of the houses Some of them who retire in this manner have little fortunes of their own, and live on their gardens, and what bread or corn they can either get from the convents, or purchase, and when I was there, they were busy in gathering and drying their figs, raisins and nuts, they make also a small quantity of wine and brandy for their own use, some of them work and make wooden spoons, or carve images of devotions On Sundays and holidays they go to the church of St Anne, which is common to them all, where they shew the hand of that saint This place is four miles from Laura, and from the highest summit of the hill We returned to saint Paul's, and went by water to Simopetra, which is the most curious of all the convents, as to its situation, it is built on a rock which rises up out of the side of the hill towards the top of it, the whole hill being covered with trees, an aqueduct adds greatly to the beauty of the prospect, which consists of three stories of arches, it conveys the water to the convent from the neighbouring height On the thirteenth, we went to the convent of Zeropotamo, where, in the front of the church, there is a curious old relief of saint Demetrius in verd antique, and in the walls of the convent I saw two antient heads We went a mile and a half to the poor convent of Rusikon, which is to the east of Zenopho, we went an hour further to a large convent not half a mile from Cares, which is the only town on Monte Santo, and is about the middle of it, situated towards the top of the height on the north side, and is the most pleasant part of all the mountain The land of this place belongs to several convents, and most of them have houses and gardens here The town is inhabited by ca-loyers, who have their shops, and sell such things as there is a demand for; the only artists they have are those that make cutlery ware and beads, and carve reliefs very curiously in wood, either on crosses or in history pieces; and here they have a market every Saturday, when the people at the distance of three or four days journey bring in corn, and other provisions, all they send out from their mountain being those trinkets they make, and wallnuts, chesnuts, common nuts, and some black cattle which they buy, and sell when they are fit for the market, they are also supplied in part from abroad with wine, the cold, as it happened this year, very often destroying their grapes Many houses and gardens in Cares are purchased of the convents by two or three caloyers for their lives, who cultivate their gardens, make those images, and lead very agreeable independent lives.

Most of the monks on this mountain are what they call Stavrophori, from a cross they wear under their caps worked on a piece of cloth, which is called Stavromene, to which also they tie a very small cross made of wood, these have taken the vow on them, and then they can never eat meat, nor leave this life, whereas in other convents, there are very few of them As to those of the highest state in the monastic life called by them the monks of the Megaloskema, I believe there are very few of them, though I was told some old men in their infirmities, who were past the world, had taken this vow on them, which is an entire re-

nunciation

nunciation of the world, of property, and of all office, and employ, and an obligation to greater internal exercises of devotion: The hermit I saw in the wood, if I do not mistake, was of this sort.

CHAP. VI.

Of Thessalonica, and the places in the way to it.

FROM this country of men, into which none of the fair sex are permitted to enter, we set forward by land for Salonica on the fourteenth, with a little caravan, and went northwards to the gulph of Contessa, our journey afterwards being mostly to the west. We came to the isthmus, or neck of land, by which this land is joined to the country to the west, the whole length of Monte Santo being about thirty miles. At the north east extremity of it there is a small cape which extends into the gulph to the north, and, I suppose, is the promontory Acrathos. On the north side of the bay they shewed me a port called Esborus, which may be Contessa of the maps, and possibly the antient port of Amphipolis, the point to the north, which makes this bay, is not brought out far enough to the east in the common maps, for it appears to me that there was another bay to the north of this; the whole, according to the sea-cards, being the bay of Contessa. At the west end of this bay I was shewn another port called Eriso, where, they say, there are ruins of an old city called Paliocastro, which might be Acanthus, to which Xerxes led his army: To the north of this was Stagira, where Aristotle was born. The river Strymon, which was the bounds of Macedonia to the north, fell into the sea at this gulph, it is made to have two mouths, one of which might fall into this south part of the gulph, the other into the north part. To the north east of the Strymon was the country called Macedonia adjecta, inhabited by the Edones; it extended to the Nestus, and was a part of Thrace conquered by king Philip, and added to Macedonia. To the south of that coun-

Thasus try I saw Thasus, a large island, with four or five villages on it, being famous among the antients for excellent white marble, and for its mines of gold. I was well informed that in one part of the island are many graves and coffins cut out of the rock, it is forty miles from Lemnos, and opposite to Cavalla and the Nestus. The part of Macedonia from mount Athos to the peninsula of Pallene, or Phlegra, was called Chalcidice.

We soon came into an improved country inhabited by Christians, and lay at Palaiocori. On the sixteenth we proceeded on our journey, and having gone about half way, I saw at some distance to the north a long narrow lake called Bizaruke, where there is a lake in Dewitt's map, which, according to that, empties itself into the Singitic bay. We lay at Ravanah, and on the seventeenth, about ten miles from Salonica, we descended into a fine plain, in which runs a small stream that must be the river Chabrius, there is a salt pool near the sea, which, I sup-

pose,

pofe, is about the mouth of it. Four miles from Salonica in the fame
road are hot baths, the waters are only lukewarm, and I thought there
was a mixture of falt and fulphur in them, thefe are probably thofe baths
from which Theffalonica was firft called Therma, and gave the name of
of Thermaicus to this great bay, which is now called the bay of Salonica, the city being fituated about the north eaft corner of it, and has the
forementioned plain to the north eaft, fome hills to the north weft, and
a great plain to the fouth weft, extending beyond view to the fouth, I
fuppofe to the mountains Olympus and Pierus, and the other mountains
near Lariffa   In this plain, and near it were many places very famous
in antient hiftory   The country about Theffalonica was called Am-
phaxitis, the river Echedorus ran thro' it, which is faid to have been drunk
dry by the army of Xerxes, to the north on this river was the country called
Mygdonia   The rivers Axius and Lydias likewife run through this plain;
between them the country was called Bottiæa, in which Pella was
fituated, where the kings of Macedon refided, from Philip the father
of Alexander the great, down to Perfes, and where Alexander the great
was born   To the fouth of the river Axius in Emathia was Edeffa or
Ægæ, fifty-nine miles from Theffalonica, in the Roman road, Diocle-
tianopolis and Pella being between thefe places   In Ægæ the kings of
Macedon refided before they removed to Pella, and it continued to be
their burial place   Between the Lydias and the Aliacmon was the country called Pieria, in which was Methonè; at the fiege of this city king
Philip loft his eye, here alfo was Pydna, near which the Romans vanquifhed Perfes, and put an end to the kingdom of Macedon   To the
weft of thefe places was Berrhœa, fifty-one miles from Theffalonica; of
the people of this place faint Paul teftifies that they were more noble
than the Theffalonians, in that they received the word with all gladnefs:
Near mount Olympus was Dius, where Alexander fet up the bronze
ftatues made by Lyfippus of thofe brave men who died on the Granicus
in the battle againft the Perfians   It is to be obferved, that many places
both in Syria and Afia Minor, have the names of places in thefe parts,
which were doubtlefs given them by colonies that went out of Greece,
and by the kings of Syria, and the Greeks that followed them, after the
time of Alexander the great, who were doubtlefs fond of giving the
Greek names of their own native country, to thofe ftrange places they
went to inhabit, as of mount Olympus, Pieria, Magnefia, Heraclei,
Berrhœa, and many others

Theffalonica is faid to have its name from its foundrefs Theffalonica, Theffalo-
fifter of Alexander the great   The prefent walls, which feem moftly to mica
have been built under the Greek emperors, are five or fix miles in circumference, taking in the plain ground on which the city now
ftands, it goes up to the top of the hill, and joins to the caftle, the
prefent city not taking up above half the ground enclofed within the
walls, which were well repaired when the war broke out with the emperor   The walls come very near the fea, and the boats are drawn
up on the beach, there being no quay, the ftreets are not well laid out,
and the houfes are ill built of unburnt brick, having gardens to moft
of them   There are in the city fome few remains of antiquity, one of
the principal is a very grand triumphal arch much ruined, but

in the perfection of the sculpture, and costliness of the work, it seems to rival any arch that remains, it consisted of three arches built of brick and cased with marble, the plan and view of it may be seen in the sixty-fourth plate at B, as well as I could take it, amidst so many buildings which encompass it One member of the cornish under the spring of the arch is worked with one row of leaves like the Corinthian order: There were niches in the fronts between the arches, the piers all round were adorned with three compartments of reliefs one over another, as of some procession, the reliefs are four feet two inches deep, and are divided from one another by other reliefs which are a foot broad, and consist of running boughs and flowers, the reliefs are much defaced, but seem to have been cut in very great perfection, and the arch is said to be of the time of the Antonines It is probable, that the upper part was adorned in proportion to the rest, but whatever ornaments there were they are now destroyed, as the arch seems to be low in proportion, it may be conjectured that there was another compartment of reliefs also covered by the earth The shops and houses are built about it in such a manner, that it was difficult to take the measures, especially of the middle arch, which I have given by the best computation I could make Another piece of antiquity is the remains of a very fine Corinthian colonade, a view of which may be seen in the sixty-fourth plate at A, it consists of five pillars of Cipolino, the capitals are of exquisite workmanship, the pillars, two feet in diameter, are nine feet two inches apart, the frieze is fluted, and on the entablature is a sort of an Attic order of square pilasters with an architrave over it, the other parts of the entablature being taken away, if ever there were more, but the greatest beauty of this colonade are four alt-reliefs in both fronts, between the Attic pilasters, of a person as big as life, to the east is a Bacchus, Mercury, and two Victories, to the west Leda, a woman, a naked man, and a woman in profile, with something in her left hand held up, the sculpture of all of them is exceedingly fine By this disposition one would also imagine, that this was a triumphal monument in an extraordinary taste, it being otherwise difficult to conceive how two fronts of such a colonade could appear to advantage Within the south gate of the city, there is an antient gateway or triumphal arch remaining of hewn stone, on each side to the south there is a relief about three feet long, and two and a half wide There are several mosques in the city which were formerly churches, that which carries the greatest mark of antiquity, is the rotundo, and if it was not an antient temple, it was certainly built when Christianity was first publickly established, though I imagine it to have been a heathen temple, and probably a pantheon, the walls are very thick, and built of good brick, a plan of it may be seen in the sixty-fourth plate at C, the chapels round it are arched over with double arches of brick, excepting the two entrances to the west and south, there are in them oblong square niches which appear like windows, and are now filled up, above these the wall is not, I suppose, so thick by twelve feet, and over every one of these apartments there is an arched nich The cupola is adorned with mosaic work, appearing like eight frontispieces of very grand buildings, the perspective of which seemed to be very good, the apartment opposite to the en-

ARCHES and VIEW of A CHURCH at THESSALONICA

trance is lengthened out to twenty-seven paces, and ends in a semicircle, which, if it was a temple, I suppose must have been added by the Christians for the altar   They shew a sepulchre to the east of this mosque, in which, they say, Ortagi Effendi is buried, who took the city   The most beautiful mosque in the town, which was a church, is that which had the name of saint Demetrius, it is seventy one paces long, and forty-one broad, there are on each side a double colonade of white marble pillars, each supporting its gallery, with pillars over them, the gallery supported by the inner rows of pillars being under the gallery of the pillars that are on each side next to the middle nave, the whole church is cased within with marble, there is a church under it which is shut up, and no one can enter, it is said that St Paul preached in it.   Another mosque was the church of St Sophia, built something on the model of saint Sophia in Constantinople, having a cupola adorned with beautiful mosaic work, there are some fine verd antique pillars in the church and portico, and in the church there is a verd antique throne or pulpit, with two or three steps up to it, the whole being of one piece of marble   A fourth mosque was the church of saint Pantaleemon, which is but small, before it there is a sort of suggestum or pulpit, with winding steps up to it, all of one block of white marble, on the sides of it are cut three arches, supported by Corinthian pillars, under which are mezzo relievos of the Virgin Mary, and other saints. I saw such another at one of the mosques, these seem to have been made in the very earliest times of Christianity, before the art of sculpture was entirely lost   There are several Greek churches in this city; but I could not find out the tomb of Futyches, the adversary of Nestorius, they have an archbishop, and a small monastery on the hill within the walls   The number of Jews here is thought to exceed the number of Christians and Turks put together, insomuch that they have a great influence in the city.   The Turks drink much, and to that may be imputed their being very bad people in this place, the janizaries in particular are exceedingly insolent   They have a great manufacture of coarse woollen cloth in and about Salonica, which is exported to all parts of Turky for the wear of common people   The English, French, Dutch and Venetians, have their consuls here, the chief export being silk, wax, and cotton to Smyrna, in order to be embarked for Europe, and a great quantity of tobacco to Italy, as well as to most parts of Turky, as it is esteemed the best after that of Latichea   A pasha and janitzer aga resides in this city   Salonica is fifteen days journey with a caravan from Constantinople, being about a hundred and eighty miles from Rodosto, it is three days from Cavalla, Monte Santo and Larissa, sixteen miles from Veria, perhaps Berrhœa, and four days from Volo, the old Pagasa on the bay Pagasœus, now called the gulph of Volo.

C H A P

CHAP. VII.

Of the fields of TEMPE, of LARISSA, PHARSALIA, and the battle between CÆSAR and POMPEY.

THE road from Salonica to Lariſſa is dangerous and unfrequented; ſo that moſt perſons embark at Salonica for the port of Claritza in Theſſaly on the ſouth ſide of the bay of Salonica, being a voyage of about fifteen leagues We embarked for that place on the nineteenth in the afternoon, and arrived on the twentieth late at night, and lay in the open air at the foot of mount Oſſa in Theſſaly, in that part of it which was called Pelaſgiotis, the country of Magneſia, and mount Pelion being to the eaſt, and make that head of land which is to the north of the bay that was known to the antients by the name of Pagaſæus The next morning we went to the convent of St Demetrius on the ſide of the hill over Claritza This place is about two leagues from the river Peneus, which riſes in mount Pindus, the greateſt part of the way being a rich narrow plain not a mile broad, which may be the pleaſant fields of Tempe, that are deſcribed to be five miles long, and of the breadth of half an acre at the mouth of the Peneus On the weſt ſide of the Peneus is the famous mount Olympus, which the poets feigned to be the ſeat of the gods. We came to the Peneus where there is a bridge over it to the weſt ſide, here we were ſtopped at a cuſtom houſe where the officer made a demand, and talking high, he proceeded ſo far as to make mention of baſtinados, but a janizary I had with me anſwered very cooly, that the officer muſt exerciſe his ſeverity firſt over him, and ſhewing my firman, or paſſport, he began to be eaſy, and permitted us to go on We travelled on the eaſt ſide of the Peneus, where the road ſeems to have been levelled by cutting away the rock at the foot of mount Oſſa, the road leads to the ſouth weſt for about two leagues, the paſſage for the river being in ſome parts very narrow, with ſmall iſlands in the middle, ſo that the water of the Peneus might be confined on ſome great rains, and cauſe the flood in the time of Deucalion Some ſay the paſſage was enlarged by an earthquake, and the poets feigned that the giants put mount Oſſa on Pelion and Olympus, and made way for the river to paſs freely

We lay in a kane at Baba about four hours from the port, having travelled in all two leagues by the river On the twenty ſecond we came into a valley about two leagues long, and two miles broad, in which we went to the ſouth, the Peneus running along the north ſide of the plain towards the eaſt, we went ſouthwards between the hills which are to the weſt, and croſſed ſome low hills into that large plain, in which Lariſſa is ſituated about two leagues further on the river Peneus It is much to be doubted whether the firſt of theſe plains was not the fields of Tempe, as ſome authors mention that the Peneus paſſed thro' the fields of Tempe, and then between Olympus and Oſſa, though others ſpeak of them as at the mouth of the Peneus Xerxes failed with his army

z

from

from Theffalonica to this river, and it is to be obferved that Daphne was the daughter of Peneus, and that the fable of her and Apollo had its fcene here The Peneus is mentioned as a clear river by Homer. To the north eaft of Lariffa there is a defcent on every fide to a very level ground, which in fome parts is moraffy, and probably is the bafon of that lake which overflowing, together with the Peneus, caufed the Deucalion flood To the weft was Cynocephalæ, where T Quintius Flaminius vanquifhed king Philip in a very great battle Lariffa ftill retains its antient name, and is fituated on the Peneus, which runs on the weft and north fides of it, to the weft there is a large ftone bridge of ten arches over the river A fmall rivulet, which is dry in the fummer, runs into the Peneus near the bridge, and probably paffed through the weft part of the old city. Lariffa is faid to be thirty miles from the fea, but it is not more than eighteen It was for fome time the refidence of Philip king of Macedon Before the battle of Pharfalia, Scipio and his legion were quartered here, and after his defeat Pompey came to this city, and going to the fea, embarked on board a merchant fhip There are no fort of remains of antiquity in this place, not fo much as the walls, except fome pieces of marble about the Turkifh burial places The prefent town is three miles in circumference, and in the middle of it there is a wooden tower, with a large ftriking clock in it, which has been there ever fince the Chriftians had poffeffion of this country, and, I fuppofe, is the only one in all Turkey A pafha refides here, and they compute fifteen thoufand Turkifh houfes, fifteen hundred Greek, and about three hundred Jewifh families The people both Turks and Greeks have a bad character, and it is dangerous travelling near the city, except on the fide of the port of Claritza, it is a great road from Janina three days to the weft, from Albania the antient Fpirus, and from many other parts to go to the port, in order to embark for Conftantinople, Smyrna, and Salonica They have only one Greek church here, and their metropolitan Twenty-four miles to the fouth eaft of Lariffa is Volo, faid to be Pagafe, where the poets fay the fhip Argos was built, and near it is Aphitæ, from which place, they fay, the Argonauts failed The fouth eaft corner of this land is the old promontory Sepias, where five hundred fail of Xerxes's fleet were fhipwrecked in a ftorm

We fet out from Lariffa on the twenty-third on poft horfes, which are to be had in many parts of Turkey, and one travels on them with great fecurity, as the pafhas commonly difpatch their people this way, and fo it is fuppofed that thofe who travel in this manner belong to the great men, who would find out the rogues if they gave their people any difturbance When travellers have an order in their firman for horfes they pay only ten afpers an hour for each horfe, otherwife they agree as they can From Lariffa we went fouthwards over uneven downs, and defcended into a very fine plain about twenty miles long, from eaft to weft, and almoft a league broad at the eaft end, widening to the weft, which, without doubt, is the plain of Pharfalia, there is a fmall town to the fouth of the plain called Catadia, over it is a ruined place on a hill, which feems to be Pharfalus, being about thirty miles from Volo, the old Pagafa, as Pharfalus is faid to have been, a fmall river runs

Lariffa

Pharfalus

through the plain to the weſt, which muſt be the antient Enipeus that fell into the Apidanus, and ſo both ran together into the Peneus. To the north eaſt of the ſuppoſed Pharſalus the hills turn northward towards the river, and on theſe hills I ſuppoſe Pompey's army was encamped near the ſtream, as Cæſar's probably was on the hill to the eaſt of Pharſalus. Pompey had the Enipeus to the right wing of his army, for Cæſar ſays he had a rivulet to the right with high banks for his defence. Hiſtorians give an account that this battle was fought in the plains of Pharſalia near Pharſalus, and between that town and the Enipeus, which fixes the place, and yet it is very extraordinary that Cæſar ſhould not mention the name of Pharſalus and of the Pharſalian plains, he only ſays, that after taking Metropolis he choſe a place in the country for providing corn, which was near ripe, and there expected the arrival of Pompey. Perhaps he neglected all theſe circumſtances out of a ſort of vanity, as well imagining that every one muſt be well informed of the very ſpot where a battle was fought which determined the empire of the world. In the middle of the plain, about two leagues north weſt of the ſuppoſed Pharſalus, is a hill, on which probably Metropolis was ſituated, which Cæſar had taken, where I was informed there are ſome ruins, and about as much further are two hills in that part of the plain where it extends further northward, on one of which might be Gomphi, which he had taken before. The ſoldiers of Pompey had poſſeſſed themſelves of the higheſt hills near the camp, where being beſieged by Cæſar, and wanting water they fled towards Lariſſa, and Cæſar coming up with them at about ſix miles diſtance, and preparing to attack them, they poſſeſſed themſelves of a hill that was waſhed by the river, which I ſhould have thought to have been the firſt high hill to the ſouth ſouth weſt of Lariſſa, at the foot of which, I ſuppoſe, the Apidanus flows, if the diſtance was not rather too great.

We took ſome refreſhment at Catadia, and changed our poſt horſes; this town is ſeven hours from Lariſſa, that is, about twenty miles, and we ſet out the ſame day for Zeitoun, which is computed to be twenty-four miles from Catadia, it is ſituated near the bay, called by the antients Malliacus. The road is over rich hills, which extend to the eaſt, and make the head of land, that is between the bays Pagaſæus and Malliacus, and is the antient country of Theſſaly, called Phthiotis, from Phthia where Achilles was born. There was a town called Thebes in this part, and the Myrmidons were of this country, of whom the poets feign that of piſmires they were made men, but Strabo mentions their induſtry like that of a piſmire [μύρμηξ] in cultivating their land, as a more probable derivation of that name. Paſſing theſe hills I ſaw to the weſt a long narrow lake called Divelch, of which I can find no account, but poſſibly the river Apidanus may riſe out of it.

C H A P

CHAP. VIII.

Of ZEITOUN, THERMOPYLÆ, and other places in the
way to LIVADIA.

ZEITOUN is situated on the south side of a hill at the foot of
the high mountains, and on another hill to the south, inhabited
by Turks, on the top of the former there is a castle. It is
situated about four miles to the west of the north west corner of the bay
of Maliacus, and about as far north of the river Sperchius, consequently
this must be Lamia, famous for the Lamian war, which the Greeks
waged against Macedon after the death of Alexander. There may be
three or four hundred houses in Zeitoun, the greater part Christians,
who are said to be a good sort of people, but the air is unhealthy in
the summer.

When I came to Zeitoun I went to the kane, and chose for coolness,
and to be free from vermin, to lay in the gallery which leads to the rooms.
In my first sleep I was awakened by a terrible noise, and leaping up
found great part of the kane fallen down, and the horses running out
of the stable, I did not know what was the cause, but my servant immediately said it was an earthquake, so that we were in the utmost
consternation, the front and greatest part of the kane was destroyed,
and we got out with much difficulty. A Turk who lay on a bulk before the gate was covered with ruins, but was taken out alive, and not
much hurt. It was a moon shiny night, but so many houses had fallen
down, and such a dust was raised that we could not see the sky, the
women were skreaming for their children and relations who were buried in the ruins of the houses, some of them were taken out alive, but
several were killed. And going to the churches the next day I saw many
laid out in them in order to be buried, their houses being fallen down.
I got my things removed to a dunghill in a place most clear from buildings, and I felt near twenty shocks in about two hours time, some of
which were very great. The next day it rained, and I got into a shed,
but the people advised me to leave it, and every thing was attended
with the utmost face of distress, nothing was to be got, nor could I
have horses till the afternoon; and when I crossed the plain I was
shewn cracks in the earth about six inches wide, which they said were
made by the earthquake. This calamity chiefly affected the Christians,
whose houses were built only of stone and earth, but not one of the
houses of the Turks fell down, which were strongly built with mortar.
I observed as I travelled that the earthquake had thrown down many of
the houses in the neighbouring villages, but did no great damage on
the other side of the hills, which bound this plain to the south.

The valley in which Zeitoun stands is a fine spot of ground, it is about
five miles wide, and the river Sperchius runs along the south side of it.
This vale extends beyond view to the west. The Thummici are mentioned
as at the entrance to a great plain. Probably at the end of this plain there

may

may be a narrow pass between the mountains to another plain, which seems to have extended to Epirus, and to the bay Ambracius on the Adriatic sea, between which and the bay of Zeitoun seems to be the narroweſt part of Greece; and probably it may not be above a hundred miles from one sea to the other The country of Doris was at some diſtance to the weſt on the south side of the river, it was called Tetrapolis, by reason that it had four principal cities The firſt order among the Greeks called the Doric, was probably invented in this country, in the beginning it was a very simple order, as it appears even now in some places, the capital conſiſting only of a large liſt or square ſtone, and a large quarter round under that, and the entablature of a deep architrave of one face, a broad frieze, and a very simple corniſh The river Sperchius is a conſiderable ſtream Sperchia is mentioned in such a manner by Ptolemy as to ſhew that it was not at the mouth of the Spherchius, but to the north of it, probably where Leda now is at the north weſt corner of the bay, which is the port of Zeitoun, on the eaſt side of the bay, about the middle of it, is Achino, doubtleſs the antient Echinus

Thermopylæ

To the south of the Sperchius, and of the bay was the country of Locri Epichnemedii, the Opuntii being to the eaſt of it. Our road was between the sea and the high mountains, these mountains are called Coumaita, and are doubtleſs the old mount Oeta, so that I began to look for the famous paſſage called Thermopylæ, where the Spartans with a few men oppoſed the great army of the Perſians At the place where the road firſt turns to the eaſt, between the mountains and the sea, are hot waters which the Greeks called Thermæ, and gave the name to this ſtreight of Thermopylæ, that is, the gates or paſs of the baths It is certain, that this paſs is mentioned as ſixty paces wide, and in some parts only broad enough for a ſingle carriage, so that as the narrow paſſage is mentioned on the sea, in caſe it lead to the same road in which we went acroſs the mountains, the sea muſt have loſt, and left the paſſage wider, though poſſibly it was a way round the cape by the sea side, where there might be some narrow paſſes After going about ſix miles to the eaſt, our road was to the south between the mountains; I obſerved two ſources of the hot waters, which are ſalt, and impregnated with ſulphur, they incruſt the ground with a ſalt ſulphureous ſubſtance: The river Boagrius runs into the sea from between theſe hills, which is probably the ſtream that is so often paſſed in this road. The whole country of the Epichnemedii is full of high mountains

Negropont

Near the entrance of the bay of Maliacus is the north weſt corner of the iſland Negropont, the old Euboea, it is a very high point of land. The Greeks call this iſland Egripus, from the chief town the antient Chalcis, oppoſite to old Aulis, which now has that name, being on the Euripus paſſage, where the sea frequently flows and ebbs, and probably the preſent name is a corruption from this word, it is but twelve miles from Thebes in Baeotia, there is a paſſage to it by a draw bridge, and a paſha and janitzeraga reside there, the former commands the country to the weſt near as far as Salona This iſland is said to be three hundred and ſixty five miles round, in some parts forty miles broad, and a hundred and fifty miles long, though it cannot be so much, for from

Zeitoun to Athens, which is much about the length of it, is only a hundred and eight short miles, according to their computation. Eretria was the next city in it after Chalcis, which was destroyed by the Persians, rebuilt, and then taken by Lucius Quintius, here was the school of the Eretrian philosophers, and near it was Amarinthus, famous for the worship of Diana. At the promontory Artemisium the Greeks fought the first battle with Xerxes. I observed two points or heads of land on the south side of the bay, and saw the high rocky cape of Euboea to the north, which is now called Lebada, and is the promontory Cenaeum. I observed also a small island, which may be Myonnesus.

About ten miles from Zeitoun, we passed by Molo, and a little further had Andra to the left, we then went on southwards between the high hills, often crossing a stream, which, I suppose, is the antient Boagrius, at the mouth of which there was a port, probably near Andra, I saw a part of the mountain to the south, which has many summits, and is called Ihakora, we came to a poor hamlet called Ergiere, fourteen miles from Zeitoun, and lay in the open air, the earthquake having thrown down all their houses.

On the twenty-fifth we went on, and in an hour came to a guard house, where they keep watch in order to catch rogues, it is half way between Zeitoun and Livadia. I saw on the mountain to the west an old castle called Kidonietry, near which they say there are ruins of an old town called Paliocastro, which may be Thronium, the capital of this country, though the distance is rather too great from the mouth of the Boagrius, for it is mentioned only as three miles from it. Alope was situated to the south east of it, near which was Naryx, the native place of Ajax. We ascended the height of the mountains, and on the top of them passed by another guard, and descended into a vale about a league wide, and four leagues long, having that chain of mountains called Iapora to the south, which are said to be mount Parnassus, on the south side of which at a great distance was Delphi. From this part we saw Dathis, on the side of the hills to the north. This vale I judged to be part of Baeotia, in it is a village called Turcocori, inhabited chiefly by Turks. Here, or in some other part of the vale, might be Orchomenus, for near it I saw the fields covered with pieces of brick. I observed some dry beds of torrents in this vale, and towards the east end a river runs as from the north east, which we passed on a bridge, it is called Mavro Nero [Black water], it runs into another vale to the south, and must be the river Cephissus, which empties itself into the lake Copais, this second vale is about two miles wide, and winds round to the lake I shall mention, having mount Parnassus to the west. In this vale to the north of the Cephissus, I suppose was Cheronea, the country of Plutarch. We crossed over low hills, and came into the vale, about half a league wide, and two leagues long, extending eastward to the lake. On the south side of this vale on the foot of the mountains, is Livadia, the foot of mount Parnassus extends to the west of it, and the mountains south of it I take to be Zogara, which is mount Helicon, for both these are ranges of mountains, which extend some miles, though one part where Delphi was, might be the height of Parnassus, properly so called, which had two heads.

Livadia   Livadia is the antient Libadia, it is about twenty miles from Caftri the antient Delphi. This place was famous for the worfhip of Jupiter Trophonius, public games being performed to his honour here, and an opening of the earth is mentioned, where they worfhipped him, and there his oracle is faid to have been, it is mentioned alfo as a cave to which it was very difficult to defcend. The town of Livadia is divided by a rivulet which feparates the two parts of the hill on which it is built, this water has its fource from a very fine fpring without the town, the weft hill being a perpendicular rock, a room is cut into it about three feet above the ground, and twelve feet fquare, with a bench on each fide cut in the rock, it appears to have been painted, and this, without any enquiry, the Greek fchoolmafter told me was the place where they worfhipped Trophonius, there are feveral niches cut on the face of the rock to the fouth, and I obferved one round hole which went in a confiderable way, though it did not feem big enough for a man to get through it, but poffibly it might be the difficult entrance to the grot of Trophonius, and to the recefs where the oracle was uttered. There are fome imperfect infcriptions about the town which mention the name of the city. There are fix hundred and fifty houfes in the town, fifty of which are inhabited by Jews, and there are an equal number of Chriftians and Turks, the former have three churches, and there is a caftle on the fummit of the weftern hill.

CHAP IX.

Of the lake COPIAS, THEBES, PHYLE, and fome places in ATTICA.

Lake Topaia, Copas   FROM Livadia I fet out to the eaft for Thebes, which is in the road to Athens, and foon came near the antient lake Copias, now called the Valto of Topolia, that is, the marfh or fen of Topolia, which is a village on the north fide towards the north eaft corner of it, and is the lake took its name from Copa, which is faid alfo to be on the north fide of it, it feems probable that Topolia is the old Copa, tho' I at firft imagined it to have been under the hills, which we paffed over into the vale of Livadia, at the weft end of the lake, where there is a monaftery, and a village called, if I miftake not, Crupou, but as Coronea is faid to have been at the north weft corner of the lake, it is probable that it was there, and that the famous battle was fought near it, probably at the end of the plain in which the Cephiffus runs, in this battle Agefilaus beat the Athenians and Bœotians, and at Thebes I was told, that Granitzo, two hours to the fouth of Livadia, was the old Coronea. Mount Libethrius was near Coronea, on which were the ftatues of the Mufes, and this might be the hill between the two plains, or that to the north of the Cephiffus. At the north eaft corner of the lake was Medeon, and near it on the eaft fide Onchiftus,

and

and south of the lake towards the east end Haliartus, which might be at a ruined place in the middle way between Livadia and Thebes, which the common people say was old Thebes. Mount Cithæron is probably that mountain we had to the left, which extended to the mountains of Megara. The plain in which the lake of Topolia lies, seems to be about twelve miles long and six broad, that is, between thirty and forty miles in circumference, though Strabo makes it to be near fifty; the reason why it is called at present rather a marsh than a lake, is, that in summer the water does not appear, all being overgrown with reeds, though it has always water and fish in it. There are several pools about the plain, which probably have a communication one with another, and in winter the water rises very much, all over it there are dry spots, which are improved, and also some villages. Where the water remained it appeared green, the other parts looking white in the season of autumn, when we passed that way. This lake overflowed in such a manner, that it once destroyed two hundred towns and villages. It is very observable in this lake, that though the Cephissus, and many streams fall into it, yet there are only subterraneous passages out of it, which are said to be sixty, and are seen about Topolia. Strabo mentions a subterraneous passage from it to lake Hylica, and is a lake at some distance to the north of Thebes, and of the hills, which is now called the lake of Thebes, being about six miles over every way. It is probable that these lakes and morassy grounds had such influence on the air of Bœotia, as to affect the intellectual faculties of the inhabitants of this country, insomuch that a Bœotian genius for dullness became a proverb of reproach.

We arrived at Thebes about twenty-four miles from Livadia. This _Thebes._ city is said to have been first founded by Cadmus on the spot where the Arx-Cadmia was situated, and here Amphion is said to have made the stones dance into their places by the force of his music; but the city was so destroyed by Alexander the great that it never well recovered itself afterwards; it produced many great men, as Pindar, Epaminondas, Pelopidas, Hercules, and Bacchus; it is said to be situated on the river Ismenus, which, I suppose, is at some distance to the north. The city is in a plain about five leagues long and four miles broad; but the ground about Thebes is uneven, being divided into many little low hills by torrents which come from the mountains, and on one of these hills the present town is situated, which is about a mile in circumference, it is supposed to be the spot on which the antient city was founded by Cadmus, which was called Arx-Cadmia. To the east is another hill of greater extent, and rather lower, which plainly appears to have been built on, and upon these two hills, and the valley between them, the antient city seems to have been situated; there is nothing to be seen of the ruins of it, except some little remains of the city, or castle wall to the west, near a large square tower, by which it appears that the walls were cased with grey marble both inside and out, one tier set up an end remaining, so that probably they were built after that very antient Greek manner one tier set up an end, and the other laid flat. There is also an old gate standing ten feet wide, and arched over, all of large hewn stone, which, if I mistake not, was made for a portcullis, but without any ornament whatsoever. There is a fountain to the south of the town, and the water for the use of the city

city is conveyed in channels along the ground from the south east, paſ-
sing over the valley to the hill on some modern arches   They ſay there
were a hundred churches in and about the town, some of which are in
repair, fragments of inſcriptions have been found about them, and I
ſaw ſome Corinthian capitals of the fineſt workmanſhip   An archbiſhop
reſides here, and a waiwode and cadi, there being in the town about
two hundred Greek houſes, ſeventy of the Jews, and a thouſand of the
Turks   There are some hills to the north of Thebes at ſome diſtance,
which intercept the view of the lake   It is about eighteen miles from
this city to the paſſage to the Negropont, and Athens is about thirty-
ſix miles both from the antient Aulis and from Thebes

I went at Thebes to the kane, and the next day moved to the houſe
of a prieſt, and the archbiſhop of Thebes hearing of me, ſent and deſired to ſee me   I was very courteouſly entertained by him, and met the
archbiſhop of Ægina at his houſe, who was making a progreſs to collect
charity for his church   I ſaw two hills in the plain to the north weſt,
and they ſhewed me a hill to the north north weſt, which they ſaid
was Platæa, but that place was near the road from Athens to Megara

We ſet out for Athens on the twenty-ſeventh   The road leading to
that city goes to the eaſt for about ſix miles, it then turns to the ſouth
over ſome low hills, and at length croſſes the mountains called Ozia,
which are the antient mount Pentelicus, famous for its fine marble   Having
aſcended to the height of it, we came to Phyle on a high rock towards
the deſcent on the other ſide, to which Thraſibulus fled, when he was
expelled by the thirty tyrants, whom he afterwards drove out, the top of
the hill, not half a mile in circumference, is fortified with ſtrong walls,
which are almoſt entire, there is a view of Athens from it, though it is
at ten miles diſtance   Deſcending the hill we ſaw a road to the left,
leading to a convent between the mountains, which is called Panaiea,
and paſſing by Caſha we came into the plain of Attica, in which
Athens ſtands   This plain is about two leagues broad, and three in length,
from mount Hymettus on the eaſt, to the hills towards Eleuſis, but north
of mount Hymettus it extends to the eaſt to the ſea towards Porto Raſti,
which is near the promontory Sunium, and to the north towards Mara-
thon, where Miltiades defeated the Perſians.

CHAP. X.

Of ATHENS

TO the weſt of mount Hymettus, which was famous for its honey
and fine marble, there is a range of lower hills, that which is
neareſt to Athens is mount Anchelmus   Athens was about a
mile to the ſouth weſt of it, on a hill, which on every ſide, except to
the weſt, is almoſt a perpendicular rock, it is about three furlongs in
length,

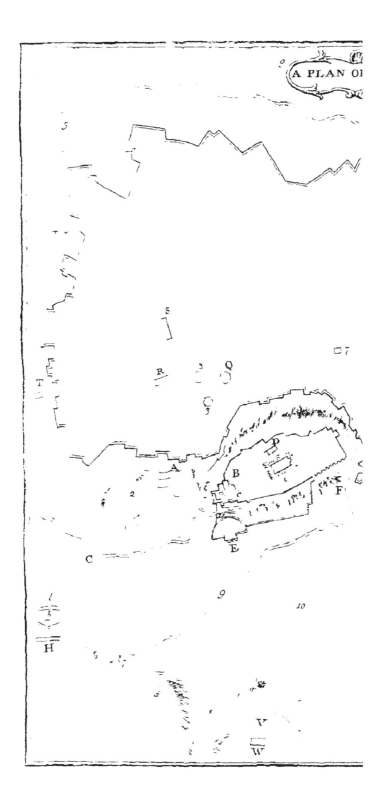

A PLAN OF

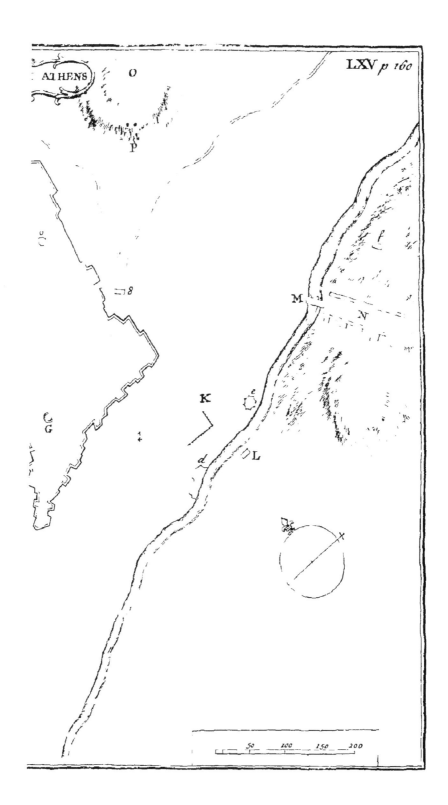

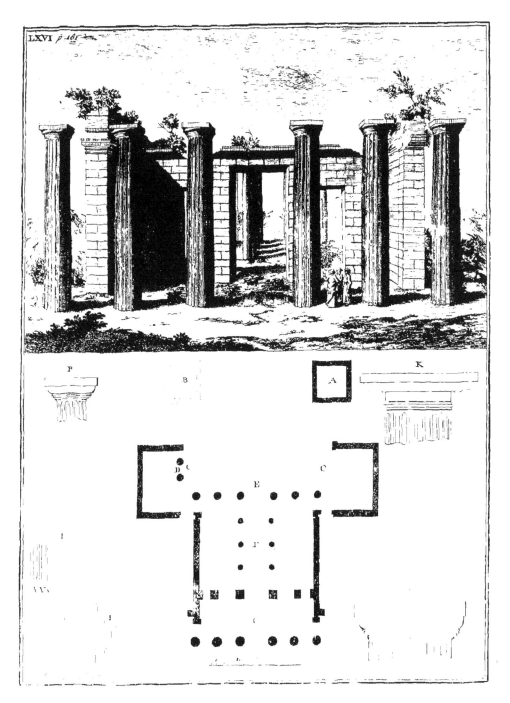

length, and one in breadth, this hill was the antient Acropolis, first called Cecropia, to the north of which the present city of Athens is built, a plan of it may be seen in the sixty-fifth plate ᵃ, as the antient city in length of time probably extended all round it, the walls, I suppose, being those modern ones with which it was defended when it was under the Venetians

Two rivers watered the plain, one the Ilissus, which run between mount Anchesmus and mount Hymettus, and so passed to the east of Athens. The Eridanus ran in the plain to the west of the city, and being divided into many parts to water their olive gardens, it becomes a very inconsiderable stream, as the other is quite lost, by diverting it into their fields.

Athens is situated about two miles from the sea, was built by its first king Cecrops, who was succeeded by several kings to Codrus, after him it was governed by Arcons, at first made during life, and afterwards for ten years, and last of all yearly: They were conquered successively by the Persians, Macedonians, and Romans, and for five or six ages past the city has undergone a great variety of fortune, and notwithstanding there are great remains of its antient grandeur, which are proofs in what a degree of perfection the noble arts of sculpture and architecture flourished in this city, which was the mother of arts and civil polity

The ascent A, to Acropolis is at the west end, there are three gates to be passed through in the way to the top of the hill, the propylæum was probably about the third gate, which was built at a great expence, there is a small square tower c, remaining a little way within it, which seems to be of great antiquity, as I observed by that antient manner of laying the stone so often mentioned, it has only a cornish round at top, and is not twenty feet square, it is said that it was adorned with fluted Ionic pillars, and a rich frieze covered with reliefs, and probably those reliefs which I saw on the wall within the gate were part of them, but this colonade does not remain, and the castle wall is built almost all round it, a plan of it may be seen in the sixty sixth plate at A. This might be the temple of victory without wings, built near the wall from which Ægeus the father of Theseus threw himself down, when expecting his son, and not seeing the signal agreed on, he apprehended he was dead, or it might be part of the propylæum, and have another answering to it at B, in the sixty sixth plate, and if so, the ascent probably was winding along the west side, and the grand entrance might

Its history.

Acropolis.

ᵃ It is taken from Lindsh' account of Athens, as it was under the Venetians in one thousand even hundred and seven The references to it in that plan, which are not in the following account, are here inserted, which shows the tradition of those times
1 The grot of Nineve, or Niobe
2 Burithion, from which they threw down condemned person
3 Mosques in the city
4 A column, on which was the statue of Socrates, not row feet
5 A church
6 A mosque, which served as a store house

7 A mosque, then the Lutheran church
8 Church Soteros
9 The way to the Piræum
10 The way to port Munychia
a The prison of Areopagus
b The temple of Mars
c Another way to the sea
d The fountain Enneacrunos according to Lindsh
e The temple of the Muse
f The temple of Diana
g The foot of the hill St George, falsly called Anchesmus

be from the fouth, probably by a magnificent flight of fteps, near to the fouth weft corner of the hill This tower is not above twenty feet to the fouth of the weft wing of, what is called, the arfenal of Lycurgus B, which might either be the temple of winds, or the citadel mentioned here by Paufanias, or a building he fpeaks of to the left of the temple of Victory, in which he defcribes feveral very famous paintings: It is a building of the antient Doric order, having a wing C, in the fixty fixth plate, on each fide to the fouth, in which there feems to have been two pillars D, the temple probably opened to the fouth at E, with fix pillars in front, and a colonade of three more on each fide at F, leading to a door, which has two fmaller doors on each fide of it Thefe inner pillars are higher than the others, as if they had fupported fome covering, and it is poffible there might be two other rows of pillars within There was alfo a portico with a colonade in the other front at G, and there are rooms under the whole, the capital of the pillars are reprefented at H, and the cornifh and triglyphs at I

Temple of
Minerva From this temple we went to the famous temple of Minerva called Parthenion C, it was built under Pericles by Ictinus the architect As it is of that plain Doric order before mentioned, it may be queftioned whether the other more beautiful orders were invented when it was built, as one would imagine they would have emblifhed this temple in the fineft manner of thofe times, when they beftowed fo much expence on it: It was miferably fhattered in the late Venetian wars; for the powder being kept in it, a bomb of the Venetians happened to fall in by the hole, which was in the middle of the arch, to give light within, which blew up the temple, fo that only the weft end remains entire, and the pillars and pediment of the eaft end, a plan and view of the weft end may be feen in the fixty-feventh plate The fluted pillars are very large in proportion to their height, and being without bafe or pedeftal, have not fo much as a fillet at bottom Two tier of columns are mentioned by fome modern writers as round the infide, and to have made a gallery, of which there is now no fign, and probably this was a Chriftian work, tho' in the plan of it, in the fixty fifth plate from Fanelli, there is no fuch thing, but the femicircle at the eaft end, which is almoft effential to a Greek church, as well as the pillars of the altar are fhown I faw the fign of the wall at A, which feparated the inner part of the temple from the pronaos, or ante-temple, and as there were two entrances to the temple, it is probable there was a pronaos at each end, as there was at the temple of Thefeus, only with this difference, that the pronaos there is open, having only two pillars in front, one of them remains entire, and there are figns within of the wall of the other. It appears notwithftanding that there were folding doors at the entrance from the portico to the weft, as by opening and fhutting them they had worn the marble pavement Probably they placed in the middle part of the temple, that famous ftatue of Minerva which was dedicated by all the Athenians, and was faid by the vulgar to have fallen down from heaven At each end of the temple of Minerva there is a double colonade, and from the floor on which the outer row ftands there are two fteps up to the fecond colonade, each a foot deep, fo that thofe pillars are near two feet fhorter than the outer row, and the pillars on each

5

fide

Pl. XVII. p.162.

The TEMPLE of MINERVA at ATHENS

The TEMPLE EREC'

ГHFION at ATHENS

fide are on a pavement about half a foot lower than the inner row
This made me imagine that possibly the outer pillars were an addition in
the time of Adrian, to erect on them those magnificent pediments, which
were doubtless the finest adorned of any in the world, and the ornaments
appear to have been made in Adrian's time, his statue and that of his
emprefs Sabina being among them, they are very fingular in their kind, not
being reliefs but entire figures of the finest statues, which appear as big
as life, being history pieces, that to the weft, Pausanias says, reprefented
the birth of Minerva I saw in the pediment one naked figure fitting,
two clothed, a woman as in a posture of walking, all without heads,
and two bodies in the middle ; one standing, and Adrian fitting with
his arms round a woman, and a naked figure fallen down, the history
on the eastern pediment was the difpute between Minerva and Neptune
about naming the city, where I saw remaining the head of a horfe, a
naked man which was fitting fallen down, two men fitting, their heads
being broke off, one like a woman as flying, the head likewise gone , the
middle part was all deftroyed, and on the other fide there remain only
three broken figures : There were in each of them at leaft a dozen
ftatues bigger than the life, befides a carriage and two horfes in one , fo
that if this ornament was not originally defigned, it is improbable that a
pediment fhould be made capable of receiving them, and by making
the pillars in front longer, they gave a lighter air to the building,
whereas if the double colonade had been at firft defigned, there would
have been the fame reafon for making all the pillars of one length, and it
muft rather have offended the fight to fee the pillars on each fide much
fhorter than thofe in the front All round between the triglyphs in the
freize, there are moft exquifite alt-reliefs of combats with centaurs, lions,
and many on horfes , and all round the temple on the outfide of the walls
there are moft beautiful bafs reliefs in the freize, which is three feet four
inches deep, being chiefly proceffions and facrifices, and was a work of
immenfe coft, but they are not feen to advantage, and if thefe and the
other reliefs are of the fame date as the temple, they are on the fuppofition I have made in relation to the hiftory of architecture, a proof that
fculpture was in the greateft perfection, when architecture was not arrived at its higheft improvements.

About fixty paces to the north of the temple of Minerva in the Acro- *Temple Erectheion*
polis of Athens, is a temple D, which is fuppofed to be the Erectheion ,
a plan and view of it may be feen in the fixty-eighth plate , Paufanias
fays it was a double temple , what now remains feems to be only one
part of it, the building is of a very beautiful Ionic order fluted within
eight inches of the capital, which fpace is carved with bafs reliefs of
flowers , the cufhion of the bafe is fluted horizontally, as defcribed in
Caria, the pilafters at the end of the wall appear as if they were Doric,
but in reality are only the cornifh between the pillars continued round
on the pilafters, and below it the relief of flowers is likewife continued
on them · The building extends in length from eaft to weft, the other
part feeming to have been to the eaft , at the weft end there is a fmall
door, not in the middle, and above, it is adorned with Ionic pilafters, which are about three quarters of a circle, at the eaft end
are fix pillars of a portico with fteps up to them , it appears that there

was

was a wall to the weſt of them, and it is to be ſuppoſed that the weſt end of the eaſt temple correſponded to this, at a proper diſtance to the eaſt, the room ſeems to have been divided into three parts; to the weſtern part on the ſouth ſide was a portico from which there was a door now almoſt buried under ground, this portico conſiſted of a colonade of cariatides four in front, and one more on each ſide, as it is to be ſuppoſed, though there is now only one on the weſt ſide; they are very fine ſtatues of women, with beautiful drapery, and their treſſes hanging down in a fine manner, they are ſeven feet long, each of them has over its head two quarter rounds adorned with eggs and darts; theſe members are round, over them there is a ſquare broad fillet which ſupports the entablature, and if there were ſix more ſuch ſtatues to the other temple, they might be the nine Muſes, and the three Graces, unleſs they might be the daughters of Erectheus, who were ſo renowned for their virtue: On the north ſide there is a portico of four pillars in front, and one more on each ſide The whole is built of marble, the walls being two feet thick, and the pillars of this beautiful building are all of hewn ſtone It is remarkable that there was a well of ſalt water in this temple, concerning which they had ſome fabulous ſtories.

Theatre

At the ſouth weſt foot of the hill are the remains of the theatre of Bacchus, E, it is built of large hewn ſtone, a plan and view of what remains A, B, may be ſeen in the ſixty-ninth plate, in the wall of the ſemicircle, oppoſite to the ſcene, are two arches A A, at an equal diſtance from the middle of the theatre There are thirty arches which extend to the eaſt from the theatre, they ſeem to have been an aqueduct, the ground is riſen to the ſpring of the arches: Some have taken this to be the portico of Eumenes, though they do not ſeem to have been arches of that kind. On the ſame ſide of the hill, towards the ſouth eaſt corner, there is a grot cut into the rock at F, about twenty feet wide, and twenty-ſix long, with a particular ſort of Doric frontiſpiece, a plan and view of it may be ſeen in the ſeventieth plate. The whole is crowned with a work, on which are two inſcriptions relating to two victories gained at the games by two tribes, and the archons mentioned in the inſcriptions ſhew it to be of great antiquity. There is a plinth over it as for a ſtatue, and on one ſide on the hill is a ſtone cut like a concave dial at A, to the weſt of the front of the grotto are two or three niches cut in the rock, probably for ſtatues, and a little higher on the hill are two Corinthian pillars, this has been thought to be the grotto, in which Apollo had his amours with Creuſa, daughter of Erectheus, but that is deſcribed as a little below the Propylæum, deſcending from the hill, and muſt have been either at the weſt end, or very near it, either on the north or ſouth ſides, and probably was that which in Fanelli's plan is called the grotto of Ninevch, or rather Niobe, as it is called in a Venetian plan of Acropolis, ſo that this building ſeems to have been erected on another occaſion to ſome deity by thoſe two tribes which had gained the victories, unleſs we can ſuppoſe that the way from Acropolis extended all down the ſide of the hill; and even then it is not probable that this ſhould be that temple, as it is mentioned under the Propylæum.

Further

The THEATRE at ATHENS and a VIEW of AREOPAGUS

A GROTTO at ATHENS

A TEMPLE at ATHENS

A SEPULCHRAL MONUMENT on the MUSÆUM at ATHENS

Further to the eaft, at the fouth eaft corner of the hill, is that curious Lantern of Den of he nes fmall building G, commonly called the lantern of Demofthenes, but it is faid to be a temple of Hercules, built in all probability on the occa-fion of the victory of the tribe Acamantis, when Euainetus was archon, which was in the hundred and eleventh Olympiad, that is, in the four hundred and eighteenth year of Rome, as appeared by an infcription on the architrave now defaced or hid, the convent of the Capuchins being built round the greater part of it, this circular building is of the Co-rinthian order fluted, having fix pillars round it, as in the feventy-firft plate, A, being the plan. There are two tripodes cut between the pil-lars in bas relief; from thefe to the folid bafement the wall between them confifts of one ftone, the architrave and frieze alfo all round are of one ftone in depth, the cornifh is compofed of feven ftones, and the whole is crowned with a fingle ftone hollowed within, as fhown in the fection B; it is adorned on the outfide with leaves, and on the top there is an orna-ment which is very much defaced, but is fomething like a Corinthian capital The reliefs of combats round the frieze, which are alfo defaced, are faid by fome to be the labours of Hercules.

To the fouth weft of Acropolis is the hill called Areopagus H, it is Areopagus directly fouth of the temple of Thefeus, and has its name from the trial of Mars there on account of the murder of Hallirrhothius, it is a rocky hill not very high. The place of judicature I, which was afterwards fixed to that very fpot where Mars was tried, feems to have been to the north of the height of the hill, as it is drawn at B, in the fixty-ninth plate; it makes a large femicircle to the north, and the fide of the hill that way is fupported by a wall E of very large ftones, and makes part of a circle, but does not rife above the ground of the area, to the fouth of it in the middle, there is a fort of tribunal C, cut in the rock as for a throne, with fteps up to it on each fide, and in the middle, and at fome diftance on each fide are four fteps D, cut in the rock to the higher part of the hill It was at this place that St Paul would have taught the Athenians the knowledge of that God whom they ignorantly wor-fhipped

To the eaft of the hill of Areopagus is the high hill called the Mu-Mufæum fæum V, from the poet Mufæus, who ufed to rehearfe his verfes there, and was buried on that fpot, it is directly fouth of the theatre of Bacchus, this place was well fortified by Demetrius There are fe-veral grottos, probably for fepulchres, cut in the rock round it, and on the top of the hill are remains of a very magnificent monument of white marble W, which is a proof both of the perfection of architecture and fculpture in Athens, a view of it may be feen in the feventy fe-cond plate, it is a fmall part of a circle, about fifteen feet wide on the outfide, to the fouth there is a bafement about ten feet above the ground, over which on four ftones feven feet nine inches deep, there are reliefs as big as life, beginning from the weft is the figure of a man, then one in a car drawn by four horfes abreaft led by one man, another fingle man, and further to the eaft five men ftand clofe one before another, if the building was perfect to the eaft, it appears plainly it is ruined to the weft, and that a third, and it may be a fourth pi-lafter is wanting on that fide, between the two pillars to the eaft there is an oblong fquare nich, in which there is a ftatue fitting, and under it this infcription ΒΑΣΙΛΕΥΣ ΑΝΤΙΟΧΟΣ ΒΑΣΙΛΕΩΣ Α[ΝΤΙΟΧΟΥ], fuppofed to be the anceftor of the perfon reprefented fitting in a larger nich to the weft with a femicircular top, under which ftatue is the name of the perfon to whom this monument is fuppofed to be erected ΦΙΛΟΠΑΠ-ΠΟΣ ΕΠΙΦΑΝΟΥΣ ΗΣ΄ΕΥ., it is alfo fuppofed, that to the weft there was another nich and ftatue of fome other anceftor of this perfon, the other fide of this building was adorned with Corinthian pilafters correfponding to thefe, two of them only remaining; on one fide of the pilafters between the ftatues is a Latin infcription to the honour of Antiochus Philopappus, and tho' this infcription is imperfect, yet it may be gathered from it that he was a conful, and preferred to the prætorian order by Trajan · Probably this monument is the fame as that mentioned by Paufanias only under the name of a Syrian, who might fome way or other derive his pedigree from the kings of Syria of the name of Antiochus

City of
Adrian

At fome little diftance to the eaft on the plain there is a fountain, which may be Enneacrunos, and further eaft are the remains of the city of Adrian K, as it is called on a magnificent gate to it, which is like a triumphal arch, it had alfo the name of new Athens, and I found an infcription to the honour of Adrian, put up, it may be, by the council and people of the citizens of both cities, though it is to be looked on as a part of Athens; it being only a compliment to give it the name of the emperor This gate, which fronts to the weft and eaft is of the Corinthian order, and very magnificent; a plan and view of it may be feen in the feventy-third plate, the capitals of the pilafters are very particular, as at A, the capital of a pilafter B, was found at Portici near Naples, and C is a round capital which I faw at Salamis in Cyprus. This little city of Adrian probably confifted only of a few public buildings erected by him, and was enclofed by a wall built with buttreffes, extending from the gate to the fouth at D, and it may be as far to the north, there are no other remains of this city, except fome very magnificent fluted Corinthian pillars to the number of feventeen, being fix feet in diameter, and confifting of fixteen ftones in the fhaft, each about three feet deep, as in the plan E, by meafuring their diftances, I could fee that there were fix rows, and about twenty pillars in each, which make in all a hundred and twenty, and Paufanias fays, there were a hundred and twenty pillars of Phrygian marble in that temple, which was built to Jupiter Panellenius, and Juno, and to all the gods. The grand gate at E, does not feem to have correfponded to this building, as it is not parallel with the pillars, fo that probably this gate led to the library and gymnafium adjoining to the temple, in which he fays there were a hundred pillars of Libyan marble. On two of the pillars there is a wall built with three paffages in it, one over another, and openings at the fides like windows and doors, which have made fome imagine, that the palace of Adrian was built on thofe high pillars, which would indeed have been a very bold work, but this wall appears to be modern, being built, as may be feen, after part of the entablature was broken down, and they pretend to fay, that fome hermit lived in that airy building.

The GATE of ADRIAN at ATHENS and A PLAN of
BUILDINGS near it

PLANS and VIEWS of the TEMPLE of CERES and of the
REMAINS of an AQUEDUCT at ATHENS

To the fouth of this part of the city, near the bed of the Ilissus, there is a standing water; and two ruined conduits, which they call the fountain Callirrhoe, and on the height, on the other side of the Ilissus, are remains of a beautiful small temple L, which is almost entire, and was the temple of Ceres Chloe; a plan and view of it may be seen in the feventy-fourth plate; it is built of very white marble, the walls being of one stone in thickness, the front is to the west, and had, I suppose, four pillars before the portico, the cushion of the base is fluted horizontally, and the work of the base ranges round the temple, and the inside of the portico, there were four steps all round on the outside, this temple was converted into a Greek church, but it is not now used by the Christians There is no water in the bed of the antient river Ilissus, except when the winter torrents run from the mountains, the waters being diverted above to their gardens and olive trees Continuing along to the north by the bed of this river, we came to a large bridge over it of hewn stone M, consisting of four arches, each twenty feet wide On the west end of it is the front of a building, which, they say, is the remains of a nunnery that was on the bridge before the Turks had possession of the country This bridge leads to the Circus N, on the foot of mount Hymettus above half a mile from the city, it was about two hundred and seventy paces long, and sixty two wide; the feats were built up the side of the hill, but nothing remains of it, except a small part of the wall on each side of the entrance. On one side towards the further end, is a passage up to the height over it, hollowed thro' the rock which feems to have been done for the sake of bringing the stone, though the common people say, that the conquered at the games went off that way, not to have the disgrace to return in the face of the people.

Near a mile to the north west is mount Anchesmus O, called St Georgio, from a church on it of that name, what is commonly taken for Anchesmus, is a small high rocky hill, about a mile to the north north east of Athens; though it is probable that the whole chain of low hills which runs to the north between the two rivers went by that name On the foot of this hill towards the town at P, are two Ionic pillars, supporting their entablature, as reprefented at B, in the feventy-fourth plate, each of them consists of two stones in the shaft, which rise about fourteen feet above the ground, and are two feet four inches in diameter On the eastern pillar are signs of the spring of an arch, so that it is to be supposed an arch was turned from it, and that there were two pillars on the other side, it is probable that on this arch was the remaining part of the inscription, which, if it were perfect, is supposed to signify that Antoninus Pius finished the aqueduct in new Athens, which was begun by Adrian, for this feems to have been a portico to a reservoir, of which I thought I saw some signs, there being an area cut to the north into the hill, with some little remains of the wall round it about forty feet wide, and a hundred long, the water was probably brought round the hill to this place, it may be from the Ilissus, and from this reservoir it might run on arches to the new city of Adrian.

Going from the house of the English consul, at the north west foot of Acropolis, I saw in a private yard remains of an antient wall of hewn

stones,

stone, one tier laid flat, and the other set up an end alternately, which
might be part of the old Prytaneum   To the north of Acropolis in the
city there are remains of a wall of hewn stone, which possibly might be the
temple of Venus Urania.   What is commonly called the temple of Winds,
is an octagon building, and remains entire, but the ground has risen within
a foot of the top of the door, which is next to the street; it was called by
the antients the octagon tower of winds, and was built by Andronicus
Cyrrhestes, there was a weather cock to it, which was a triton that
turning round, with a wand pointed to the wind that blew, a plan and
view of it may be seen in the seventy-fifth plate, and a section in the
seventy sixth, the top of it consists of a small round stone about three
feet in diameter, against which there rest a number of stone slabs
all round, which are about two feet wide at bottom, and diminish towards the top, the small pillars which support the cornish within are of
the same fluted Doric order which is seen in the other buildings here:
There is an entablature on the outside, and below the two faces of the
architrave are the figures of the winds larger than life in mezzo relievo;
the space they take up as they are in a flying posture, being about three
feet and a half in depth   The creator of Raphael moving over the
elements in his paintings in the Vatican gallery, are something in this
taste   Over every one, in the face of the architrave, is cut the name of
the wind in Greek, and each wind has some emblem relating to one of the
eight different seasons of the year, which seem to intimate that such
a wind commonly reigns at that time; so that dividing the year into
eight parts, allowing six weeks to each season, and beginning with KAI-
KIAΣ, or the north east, and with the month of October; this wind
has a plate of Olives in its hand, though I could not see it distinctly, by
reason that a tree grows before it, this is the season for Olives, which in
antient times, as well as now, were the great revenue of Athens · The
next is BOPEAΣ, or the north wind, which has a shell in its hand to shew
the power and dominion of the sea at that time: ΣKIPΩN, the north
west, is pouring water out of a vase, being a rainy wind. ZEΦYPOΣ,
the west, has a lap full of flowers, being a wind that reigns part of February and March   NOΓOΣ, the south, this and the following are hid
by the houses built against them, it probably may have later flowers, as
ΛIΨ, the south west may have early fruits   ΣYPOΣ, the south east,
hold its garment as if it were windy, and AΠHΛIΩIHΣ, the east, has in
the garment the latter fruits, apples, peaches, pomegranates, oranges and
lemons   Some of the antients called this the sun dial, there having been
on every side, below these figures, a dial, of which the lines are now
seen   The figures of the winds are a great instance of the boldness of
designing, and of the perfection of sculpture at the time this building
was erected
    Within the present town are the remains at R, of a portico of four
pillars supporting a pediment *, it is of that fluted Doric order already
described, a plan and view of it is in the seventy-seventh plate   this is
commonly called the temple of Augustus, and there is an inscription on
the architrave of the time of the Roman emperors, it is so defaced I could
not copy it, but it is said to be to the honour of Caius, tho' the building

* The town ought to have been the scene of this, and the seventy eighth plate

without

A *PLAN* and *VIEW* of the TOWER of ANDRONICUS
at ATHENS

A SECTION of the TOWER of ANDRONICUS at ATHENS

A PORTICO at ATHENS

The TEMPLE of JUPITER OLYMPUS at ATHENS

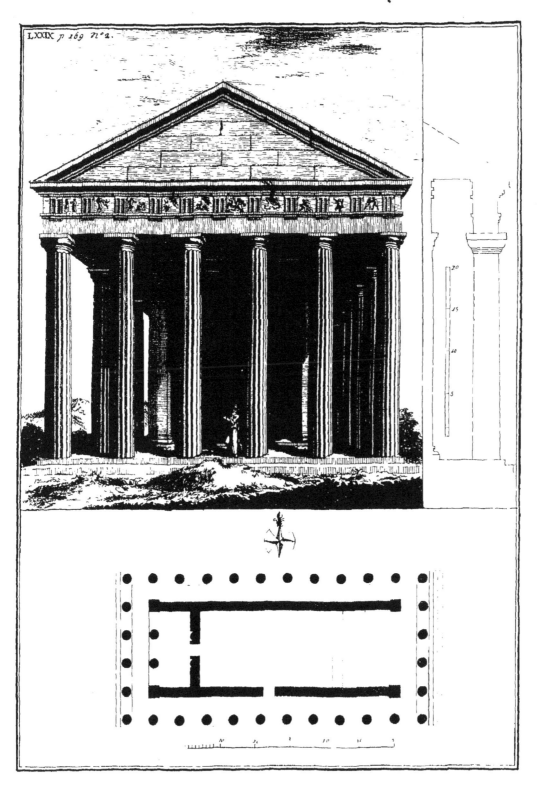

The TEMPLE of THESEUS at ATHENS

without doubt is of a much older date, on what occasion foever that infcription was put up · Near it on a long ftone, which might be the fide of the door-cafe, is that famous law of Adrian, concerning the cuftom to be paid on the oil of Athens

The moft magnificent and beautiful piece of architecture in this city is feen in the remains of a building, which is faid to be the temple of Jupiter Olympius; which was a very antient temple, faid by fome to have been built by Deucalion, but it was very much adorned and improved by Adrian, and what remains feems to be a building of that emperor's time, the ruins of a very large enclofure confirm that it is part of this temple, for it was four ftadia or five hundred geometrical paces in circumference, a plan and view of that magnificent part of it which remains, may be feen in the feventy-eighth plate, the three pillars which ftand together are fluted, and the lower part filled with cablins of reeds, is of one ftone, and the upper part of another, fo joined, that it is not eafily difcerned that they are of two ftones, the other pillars are plain, of one ftone, and have a very grand appearance, I faw a rough wall to the weft extending above a hundred yards to the north, and in one part there is a femicircular tower *Temple of Jupiter Olympius.*

The temple of Thefeus T, is on the outfide of the town to the weft, being to the north of Areopagus, and to the north weft of Acropolis, it is exactly the fame kind of architecture as the temple of Minerva, two fteps go all round the building, a plan and view of the front of it may be feen in the feventy-ninth plate The pillars in the portico or pronaos to the weft are four inches above the bottom of the others, and it had fuch a portico to the eaft, for at that diftance I faw there had been a wall; the Greeks having, I fuppofe, deftroyed the eaft end to make the femicircular place for the altar In the front between the triglyphs are mezzo relievos of fingle combats, being the actions of Thefeus, and from the corner on each fide are four fuch reliefs, and in the front within there are fine reliefs on the architrave, which is continued from the front of the portico or pronaos to the fide pillars, to the weft are the battles of the Lapithæ and the Centaurs, to the eaft are perfons fitting and others combating, all in a fine tafte, and of excellent workmanfhip *Temple of Thefeus*

Of the three ports of Athens, Phalereus and Munychia were to the eaft of a fmall promontory, and the Pyræum to the weft of it, the latter is much frequented, being a well enclofed port with a narrow entrance, and about a mile in circumference, it is called by the Greeks Porto Drago, and by the Italians Porto Leone, from a ftatue of a lion that was there, which is now before the arfenal at Venice. The foundations of a wall are feen from the Pyræum to Athens, which probably is that called Macrotychi, which was built in fo much hafte by Themiftocles *Ports of Athens*

At Athens I was recommended to the Englifh conful, who was a Greek, he accommodated me in his houfe, and introduced me to the waiwode, to whom I made a very handfom prefent, and on fhewing my firman, he faid, he was there to obey the grand fignor's commands, fo that I faw every thing in and about Athens with the utmoft freedom.

CHAP. XI.

Of ELEUSIS, MEGARA, and the ISTHMUS of CORINTH

WE set out on the fourth of September for Leſſina, and travelled in that road which was called the Sacred way, becauſe they went by it in proceſſion to the temple of Ceres and Proſerpine At the firſt entring in between the hills, above a league from Athens, we paſſed by a large convent, and afterwards near an oblong ſquare build-ing with buttreſſes round it, which ſeemed to be a ciſtern, and in half an hour came to a ruin on the right, which might be a ſmall temple, there being many niches cut in the perpendicular rock of the mountain which is near it, this may be ſome remains of the temple of Ceres, Proſerpine, Minerva and Apollo, which is mentioned in this part by Pau-ſanias Paſſing the hills we went cloſe by the ſea, in a road cut on the ſide of the hill, and came into the plain, having a ſalt lake to the right, which, without doubt, is ſome remains of the channels called Rheti, from which a ſalt water ran into the ſea, inſomuch that ſome were of opinion that the ſtream came from the Euripus of Euboea Theſe were the bounds between the territories of the Athenians and Eleuſinians. The Cephiſſus ran through the Eleuſinian territories, and is ſaid to have overflowed Eleuſis, ſo that it muſt be on this ſide of the hills, tho' I did not obſerve any river, and probably it is only a winter torrent which ſpreads itſelf over the plain There are many other fables of theſe parts relating to Ceres, Proſerpine, and Triptolemus, as Eleuſis is ſaid to be the ſcene of their ſtory To the north eaſt, in the way to Boeotia was Platea, where the army of Xerxes was routed by Pauſanias Having paſſed the lake, and coming towards the bay, I ſaw ſome broken pillars both towards the ſea and to the right, this might be the place called Erineon, from which, they ſay, Pluto carried Proſerpine to his infer-nal regions, for it is mentioned as near the Cephiſſus We turned to the ſouth into the plain of Eleuſis, which extends about a league every way, it is probably the plain called Rarion, where, they ſay, the firſt corn was ſowed There is a long hill which divides the plain, extending to the eaſt within a mile of the ſea, and on the ſouth ſide is not half a mile from it, at the eaſt end of this hill the antient Eleuſis was ſituated, about a mile before we came to it, I ſaw the ruins of a ſmall temple to the eaſt, which might be that which was built at the threſhing floor of Triptolemus In the plain near the north foot of the hill, are many pieces of ſtones and pillars, which probably are the remains of the tem-ple of Diana Propylea, which was before the gate of the city, and at the north foot of the hill, on an advanced ground, there are many imper-fect ruins, pieces of pillars and entablatures, and doubtleſs it is the ſpot of the temple of Ceres and Proſerpine There I ſaw the ſame ſort of Doric capitals as thoſe at Athens, except that they had only three liſts in the quarter round of the capital, and probably are very antient, a drawing of one of them may be ſeen at B, in the ſixty-ſixth plate I ſaw likewiſe ſome Ionic capital, and one of a pilaſter of the Corinthian order, which probably belonged to ſome later improvement of the temple All up the eaft end of the hill are ruins, and on the top of it are many cifterns cut down into the rock in the fhape of jars to receive the rain water; and to the weft on a higher part of the hill are remains of a tower, there is a ruin in the plain to the fouth, probably of the temple of Neptune, there are alfo two other ruins to the eaft, which are not far apart, one of them might be the temple of Triptolemus, and the other the well of Callichorus, where the women ufed to dance and fing in honour of the fupreme goddefs of the place. To the weft are the foundations of a gate of the city of grey marble, and a little further there is a fine trunk of a ftatue of a fheep with a curling fleece divided down the back, being the beaft which was facrificed to Ceres. At the temple of Ceres I faw the large buft or upper part of a ftatue, fuppofed to have been defigned for that goddefs; it is fo large that it meafured at the fhoulders five feet and a half broad, there is a circular fort of ornament on the head above two feet deep, the middle part of which is adorned with foliages of oak, as mentioned by travellers, but the face is much diffigured, I faw alfo what I took to be an altar of grey marble, cut like a bafon and funk into the ground, it is probably of the Taurobole kind for facrifices, in the fame manner, as feveral others I have feen, there is a drawing of it at L, in the forty-eighth plate The prefent poor village of Leffina is inhabited only by a few Greek families

Going on to Megara, which is fituated with regard to Eleufis as this is to Athens, and about the fame diftance, we went to the weft of the long hill that divides the plain, and on the fouth fide of it came to a fpring near the fea, the water of which is not good, it has been fuppofed to be the well Anthenon, at which Ceres fat down to repofe herfelf after the fatigue fhe had undergone in fearching after Proferpine. Paffing to the fouth over hills near the fea, we turned to the weft into the plain of Megara, which extends about three leagues to the weft, and may be a league wide, on the fouth fide it has for half way thofe hills which were called mount Nifus, at the eaft end of which Megara was fituated, the other part of the plain is bounded to the fouth by a chain of lower hills extending eaftward to the fea, being a little more to the north than mount Nifus · To the fouth of thefe laft hills is another plain, which is to the eaft of Megara, and extends about a league every way, at the eaft end of it is the port of Megara called Nifea, from the founder of it, Nifus, the fon of Pandion king of Megara Megara was partly on a Megara hill, and partly on the plain to the eaft, where there are remains of two towers of a gate of grey marble, on which is that curious infcription relating to the public games. The city walls appear to have been built from north to fouth up the hill, on which there was a famous temple of Ceres To the fouth of the city are remains of a fmall round building cafed with huge pieces of grey marble, on which there are feveral Greek infcriptions, that are much defaced, and tho' Paufanias gives an account of a great number of public buildings at Megara, yet there are no other remains of them They find here feveral medals, moft of which were ftruck in this city The whole bay between the Morea and Attica, had the name of Saronicus, and is now called the gulph of Engia, from the ifland of that name, the old Ægina The ifland Coloun, the antient Salamis, extends from the head of land towards the port of

Athens

Athens to the old promontory Minoa, which is south of Megara; Ajax was king of it, who sent his troops and twelve ships to the siege of Troy To the north of Megara about a league, are several old churches, the place being called Palaichoro, or the old village, and is supposed by some to be Rhus, mentioned by Pausanias; Euclid was of this place, and his school was kept here, his disciples being called Megarici.

We left Megara on the eighth, ascended the high hills to the south, and saw to the west under us the north east bay of the gulph of Lepanto, formerly called the bay of Corinth, and consequently we were on the Isthmus of Corinth, which is in Achaia. The little bay before-mentioned is made by a head of land, which extends to the west from the east end of the gulph, on the south side of which is the port of Argilio: Cromyon was on the other side of the Isthmus The rocks Scironides were about this place, where a famous robber Saron attacked people in the road, and threw them down the rocks, but Theseus took this robber, and served him in the same manner, throwing him into the sea, and the poets feign that his bones became rocks, it is probable there might be another road nearer the sea, for this we went in was at least a mile distant from it On the east side, on the top of the mountains, we came to a narrow pass, where Sciron might attack the travellers Adrian is said to have made this way broad enough for two chariots, to the east of this was cape Minoa We went on winding round the high hills, descended to a rivulet, and ascending again, came to a fine fountain on the hill, with three basons full of water, it is called Brisimiguisi We at last descended to that low ground, which is properly the Isthmus, the narrowest part of it seemed to be towards the north end between a bay on each side, and it is probable that with the help of machines they drew their vessels by land across that part to Schœnus. A ridge of very low rocks run across the Isthmus, near the first entrance of it, then at a little distance appear like ruins; and farther on is the canal, which was begun to be dug across it, where one sees the bank of earth that was thrown up on each side, it extends about half a mile from the west, and where they left off, I saw plainly the ground was very rocky, which doubtless made them desist from their enterprize, though it is said that the oracle at Delphi advised them against it The persons who at different times endeavoured to make this canal were Alexander, Pittas, Demetrius, Cæsar, Caligula, Nero, and Herodes of Athens Further to the north, about the middle of the Isthmus, runs a small stream from the east, and to the south of it is a very high steep bank, on which are remains of the wall that was built across the Isthmus by the Greek emperor Emanuel in one thousand four hundred and thirteen, and was demolished by Amurath the second in one thousand four hundred twenty-four, but rebuilt by the Venetians in one thousand four hundred and sixty-three, this wall might go to the port Cenchrea, but the present port of Corinth on the western gulph, which was called Lechæum, is at a great distance from it, and on the south side of the gulph This part was called Examilia, because it was six miles broad, and there is a village to the south east which now bears that name, notwithstanding the Isthmus is not above four English miles wide, but it is to be considered that the Greek miles were very short, at the end of this wall by the sea there are great remains of a large square

2 castle,

caftle, but I could fee nothing like a theatre, which feems to have been in another place. In the road to Corinth there was a temple of Neptune, and it is faid, that the theatre and the ftadium built of white ftone, were in the way to the temple, being on part of mount Oenius, called alfo the Mount of temples, from the great number there were on it, as the temples of Bacchus, Pluto, Diana, and many others. Here was alfo a foreft of pine trees, with which the victors at the games were crowned. I fuppofe thefe public buildings were on the foot of the hills to the fouth, fomewhere about the village Examile: It was here the famous Ifthmian games were held every luftrum or five years, inftituted by Thefeus in honour of Palæmon, or Portunus, to which all the people of Greece reforted, and thefe games, without doubt, anfwered fome end of trade; for which this place was fo well fituated on both feas; which made Corinth fo flourifhing a place.

CHAP. XII.

Of the MOREA in general; and of CORINTH.

THE Morea was firft called Argos, from the city of that name; Morea it was afterwards called Apia, from Apis the third king of the Argives, and then Peloponnefus from Pelops king of Phrygia, and laftly the Morea, becaufe, as it is faid, the figure of it refembles the leaf of a mulberry-tree. It is computed to be about a hundred and feventy miles long, a hundred broad, and fix hundred miles in circumference going round the bays: It is now governed by a pafha, and in the time of the Venetians was divided into four parts, Chiarenza, containing Achaia, Belvedere, in which was Elis and Meffenia, Zaconia or Maina, which was the old Laconia and Arcadia; and laftly, Sacania, which was the country of Argos. The Morea is mountainous, but the country on the fea and in the vales between the mountains is very rich, and produces a great quantity of corn, oil, and filk, the latter chiefly about Mifthra and the country of Calabrita, through which the Alpheus runs.

From the lower part of the Ifthmus there is an afcent up a fteep bank Corinth to a higher ground on which Corinth ftands near the fouth weft part of the Ifthmus, a fmall mile to the fouth of the gulph of Lepanto, and to the north of the high mountains, and rather to the north weft of that high hill called Acrocorinthus, on which the citadel was built. Corinth was firft called Ephyra, and was built by Sifyphus, fon of Æolus; it was deftroyed by the Romans in the Achaic war, but was rebuilt by Julius Cæfar, and made a Roman colony, the common people now call it Cortho. At prefent there are very little remains to be feen in this great city. There are fome ruins of walls towards the port which was called Lechæum, there having been walls on each fide of the road leading to it: This port is faid to have been two miles from the city, tho'

I fhould not have computed it to be above one. Cenchreæ alfo, now called Keerch, was computed as eight miles diftant The antient city feems to have been on the fpot of the prefent town, and to the weft of it in the plain Without the town to the north there are great ruins of a large building of very thick walls of brick, which might be antient baths, or the foundation of fome great building, for I obferved, that the rooms which are arched are very fmall: At the fouth weft corner of the town are twelve fluted Doric pillars about five feet in diameter, and very fhort in proportion, refting on a fquare bafe, as I obferved one of them, the bafes of the others being under ground; they feem to be much older than thofe of Athens, and differ from them in the capital; for inftead of a quarter round below the fquare member at top, there is a quarter of an oval, and five inches below the capital are three angular channels round the pillar, and below thefe the flutes begin; a drawing o it may be feen at K, in the fixty-fixth plate If I miftake not, they are all of one ftone, except that the upper part of the fhaft down to the flutes is of the fame ftone as the capital There are feven pillars to the fouth, and five to the weft, counting the corner pillars twice There is one pillar without a capital near them, which is as high as the architrave over the others The prefent town is very fmall, and more like a village: They have an export of corn, and fome oil. The caftle on Acrocorinthus is kept in repair, and fo ftrong that it ftood out a fiege of four months by all the Turkifh army In it is the fountain Pirene, facred to the Mufes, from which it is faid Bellerophon took Pegafus whilft he was drinking, which is doubtlefs the reafon why ufually the reverfe of their medals was Pegafus, and fometimes with Bellerophon on him It is faid that the city walls went to the top of this high hill, that is, probably the walls on both fides of the city were continued up to the caftle I faw no other ruins that I could make any thing of So little is now remaining of that city, which was formerly fo famous for its architecture, fculpture, and paintings.

CHAP. XIII.

Of the gulph of LEPANTO, and PATRAS.

THE gulph of Lepanto, formerly called the bay of Corinth, is about four leagues wide in the broadeft part, and, they fay, it is a hundred miles long, but the whole length from Corinth to the caftle of the Morea at the entrance of it, is computed but twenty-two hours travelling, it lefs than three miles an hour, fo that at the moft it cannot be above fixty miles On the north fide of this bay were the countries of Phocis, Locris, Ozolæ and Ætolia, Anfilio is the firft port to the eaft, which might be Pægæ of the territory of Megara, it is fituated to the fouth of a cape which extends to the weft from the Ifthmus In the length of Phocis there are three great mountains, which ftretch to the fea, the eaftern one is called Livadoftro, be-

ing

ing fouth fouth weft of Thebes; the next to the weft is Zogara, and is the old Helicon to the fouth of Livadia; and the third is Iapora, which is mount Parnaffus, and is to the north of Salone [a]. Corinth is eight hours, probably near twenty miles both from Argos and Napoli Romania, which was Naupolia the port of Argos, and it is about double the diftance from Leondari, the antient Megalopolis, which was the capital of Arcadia

We fet out from Corinth to Patras on the ninth, by a road which is on the fouth fide of the gulph of Patras: About four miles from Corinth there is a river, which may be the Afopus, and a mile further another, which probably is the Nemea, defcribed as near Sicyon, which was on a rifing ground to the fouth, a village called Vafilica is now on that fpot, Sicyonia was a diftinct territory from that of Corinth, but both of them were in Achaia Proper, about fix miles further there is a ruin on a high hill, which may be Ægira, faid to be a mile from the fea, and on a hill, many places are mentioned along this coaft, of which I could find no remains, only about feven miles further I faw a piece of a thick wall on the fea fhore, which appeared as if it had fallen down, where poffibly Helice might have been, faid to be overflowed by the fea, about ten miles to the eaft of the caftles, is a fmall town and port called Vortitza, which probably was Ægium, where the council of all Achaia was held; its country is faid to be watered by two rivers, the Phœnix, probably in a beautiful little plain a league to the fouth eaft of it, and the Me-

[a] Ten miles north weft of Argilio is Ifola bona, where there is a good port, and it has a convent on it Five miles from this is Ifola delli Afiri, which is uninhabited and woody, it is oppofite to Dibrena, the bay in this ifland is called D- port having two ports Five miles to the weft is the port called Livadioftro, which is the port of Thebes, being about twelve miles diftant from it acrofs the mountains, and fixty miles from that, according to their computation, is the great bay Prefpitia, which is the port of Livadia, being about twelve miles from that city This bay has three ports in it, Livadia to the north, Lafigiera to the weft, where there is a rivulet, and St Cedro to the eaft, it is probable that one of thefe was the antient Mychos Ten miles from this was the great bay of Salona, which has many ports in it, and is under mount Parnffus This bay was called Criffus Criffa was on the weftern promontory of it, and gave name to the cape, it might be at a ruined place called Pinara On the oppofite promontory was Anticyra famous for hellebore, to the north of which was Medeon Crifla was on this bay, I fuppofe it the bottom of it And about fix miles to the north is Salona, thought to be Amphifa in Locris Chileon alfo in Locris was north of Crifla, to the north of which was Delphi, now called Caftri, about eight miles weft of Salona To the weft of this was the country of the Locri Ozolæ, of fmall extent, and no places of note in it, but it is probable that the three following ports were in that country Vidi vir five miles weft of the bay of Salona, which might be Oreon, and five miles from that is Fifth, which may be Oeanthe, ten miles from this is St Nicola, oppofite to which is the ifland of Shifonu, which is about thirty miles from

Lepanto, the antient Naupactus in Ætolia, fituated on the fide of a hill at the firft entrance of the narrow paffage out of the gulph, which is not two leagues wide, this was in the hands of the Venetians when they had the Morea About three miles to the weft is a low point of land, the old promontory Antirrhium at the entrance of the gulph on which the caftle of Romeli is fituated, which was alfo in poffeffion of the Venetians, who near this place beat the Turks in a fea fight in one thoufand five hundred and feventy one There is a regular tide here, which at full moon rifes about three feet in the gulph Ætolia was bounded to the weft by the river Achelous, which probably is the river Afpero, and empties itfelf oppofite to the Curzolari iflands, to the weft of this was another river called Evenus, which may be the river Aphidare, near a cape of that name Between thefe two rivers was Ætolia proper; Ætolia adject being to the eaft of the Evenus, which was part of the country of the Locri, and is the reafon why Ptolemy places Naupactus, and fome other parts under the Locri The Achelous alfo was the bounds of Achaia the Roman province, which comprehended under it Doris, the Locri, and Opuntii, as well as Phocis, Bœotia, and Attica Between the two former named rivers was Pleuron near the fea, at the foot of mount Arakinthus, which may be the mountain called Gulata, at the eaftern root of which is the village Galata, and has been thought to be Calydon, which was the antient Ætolis, but as this was on the river Evenus, it ought to be looked for more to the weft Between this and Pleuron was Olenus About twenty miles from the caftle, there is a port much frequented called Meffalongi

ganitas, which may be the river that falls into the fea to the eaft of the town, and has a large bridge over it, at the weft end of the town I faw a ruin of a fmall antient building, and in the front of an old church a fine relief of a lion feizing a horfe Four miles to the weft was Rhypa, faid to be above the military way, and fo probably was at fome diftance from the fea towards the mountains · Further to the weft was port Erineus, probably the port of Lambirio four miles weft of Vortitza. The port Panormus was oppofite to Naupactus, and now there is a port called Tekeh over-againft Lepanto, it is three miles to the eaft of the caftles, which are built on the promontory called Rhyum, and alfo Drepanum, being a flat point, which is not a league from the oppofite caftle, this is called the caftle of the Morea and of Patras, being about four miles to the north of the town of Patras, in the middle between them is a port called Laia

Patras was firft called Aroe, then Patra, and being made a Roman colony by Auguftus, it had the name of Colonia Augufta Aroe Patrenfis, and fo it is ftyled on the coins of the city The reverfe being a man ploughing with a yoke of oxen. It had its fecond name from Pater, fon of Preugenes, who made great improvements in the city, and there are medals with his head and name, and the fame reverfe as the others Auguftus fent to Patra many of thofe who affifted him in gaining the victory of Actium. There were feveral temples in this city, and one near it to Diana Triclafia, with a grove, to whom a young man and virgin were yearly facrificed, in expiation of the crime of two young perfons, who, in the time of Diana, married againft the will of their parents The city is at the fouth weft foot of the hill of the caftle, on which it is fuppofed the firft antient city was built, it is about a quarter of a mile from the fea, and more than a mile in circumference There are fome fmall ruins, probably of a Circus, which on one fide feem to have had the advantage of a rifing ground for the feats, and acrofs a bed of a torrent to the eaft of the caftle are remains of two aqueducts, the fouthern one is built of very thick walls of brick, and is entirely deftroyed, the other is ftanding, confifting of two tier of arches one over another Near the fea there is a large uninhabited convent, where, they fay, they have the body of St Andrew in a ftone tomb, to which they pay great devotion, and fhew a little cell near the church, which is half under ground, where, they fay, the Apoftle lived, who converted thefe people to Chriftianity, and was martyred here at a place they pretend to fhew on a raifed ftone work about thirty feet fquare, which feems to be the crown of an arch that is under gound They have here an archbifhop and twelve parifh churches, to each of which there belong about eighty Chriftian families, and there are four other churches There are about two hundred and fifty Turkifh families, who are not the beft fort of people, and the others of that profeffion in the Morea may be ranked with them, there are about ten families of Jews The air of this place is exceedingly unhealthy in the fummer, as it is almoft all round the Morea, except that on the eaftern fide it is not fo bad, but Patras and Corinth are moft remarkable for bad air, infomuch that labourers will not live here in fummer, but come from abroad, and ftay during the winter months There is a fine plain to the fouth of the town covered with

olive

olive trees, the fruit of which produce only a thin oil fit for clothiers, and is sent to France They also export silk, and from the ports near, especially in the gulph, they carry a great quantity of corn to Christendom, though it is prohibited They have also tobacco for their own consumption, but about the gulph there is a strong sort used for snuff, and exported for that purpose They have here many gardens of oranges, lemons, and citrons, and the town and country are well supplied with all sorts of goods by the shops which are in this city The English consul-general of the Morea resides in this city, but the French consul lives in Modon, and has a vice-consul here The Venetians and Dutch also have their consuls, it being a road where many ships come to anchor, especially those which trade into the gulph, and to some ports near. Patras is reckoned twenty leagues from Cephalenia, thirty from Zanth, and forty from Corfu, from which island to Otranto in Italy it is near as many more, though from the nearest point it is computed only twenty leagues, which is the short passage they make from Patras and Corfu with their row boats

To the south of Patras, at a distance from the sea, was Pharæ, which might be at Saravalle about a league from Patras under the mountains, where there is an old castle. Further to the south was the river Pirus, which probably is the Lefca that waters the plain. To the south of this was Olenus, founded by Olenus, son of Vulcan, which is supposed to be Caminitza, about twelve miles from Patras; it is said to have been near the river Melas, which must be the river Caminitza. Beyond this there is a cape of low land, which extends a great way into the sea, making two heads, one stretching to the north west, and is called cape Baba, the other extends further to the west, and has the name of cape Chiarenza, where there is no town or village, only a custom house, this is supposed to be cape Araxus. On the south side of this cape towards the east, there is a ruined place, called by the Greeks old Achæa, this seems to be Dyme, a Roman colony, which was five miles to the north of the Larissus that must be the river Gastouneh, on which there is a town of that name: This river was the bounds between Achaia and Elis, as the Alpheus was between this and Messenia, the latter is supposed to be the Orpheo, about thirty miles south of the Gastouneh. The poets feign that Alpheus pursuing Arethusa, was turned into this river, Arethusa being metamorphosed into a fountain which ran under ground, and broke out near Syracuse in Sicily; and that the river Alpheus pursued her unmixed through the sea, and joined her at that stream, they also add that any thing put into the Alpheus, appeared at that fountain This is the river which Hercules is said to have turned, in order to clean the stables of Augeas, king of Elis, which held three thousand oxen, and had not been cleaned in thirty years

They have wolfs, jackalls, and some linxes on the mountains of the Morea It is computed that this country has in it about a hundred thousand Christians, seventy thousand having been sold when the Turks took it from the Venetians, who held it only twenty-five years, it then flourished more in people, being now thinly inhabited, tho' at present it has rather the advantage in a free trade, the Venetians not having permitted any thing to be exported but to Venice, whereas it would rather seem to have been more politic to have given a new conquered country all the advantages of a free trade.

The part of the Morea called Maina, from a town of that name, is divided into the upper and lower, from which the inhabitants have the name of Maniots, living among those inaccessible mountains, which are the antient mount Taygetus, where they have always preserved their liberty. To each part they have a captain or head, and these are generally at war with one another, and sometimes a pretender sets up, and causes a civil war. The upper Maina is to the west of the river Eurotas, the inhabitants of this part are the more savage people, and come little abroad, those of the lower Maina to the east, extending to the gulph of Coron, and near to Calamita are more civilized, go abroad to Calamita, and pay only a small poll tax when they are caught out, but the people dare not injure them. Their country produces nothing but wood, and all their export is of the large acron, with its cup, which is sent to Italy for tanning, so they go into the neighbouring parts, and labour the land for a proportion of the produce, and will pay nothing to the grand signor. It is said that any one recommended to their captain might travel in those parts very securely.

CHAP. XIV.

Of the island of CEPHALENIA.

AT Patras I embarked for Messina in Sicily on the twentieth of October, and we were obliged by contrary winds to put into the port of Argostoli on the south side of Cephalenia. This island is called by Homer Samos and Same, it is computed to be a hundred and seventy miles in circumference, and is about three or four leagues to the north of Zanth. C Antonius returning from exile came to this island, and began to build a city, but was recalled before it was finished Marcus Fulvius, after he had conquered the Ætolians, took this island, the city of Same sustaining a siege of four months. Cephalenia was given to the Venetians in one thousand two hundred and twenty-four, it was taken by the Turks in one thousand four hundred and seventy-nine, and retaken in one thousand four hundred and ninety-nine, it has in it about sixty villages. Same was to the east of the island, and was destroyed by the Romans, afterwards there was a town there called Cephalenia. To the north is the port Fiscardo, and to the south a very fine harbour called Argostoli. At the further end of it is a town of the same name, which is the capital of the island. The antient city Cranium was situated about this place, to the north of it is a castle on a high hill, and a village round about it. This hill, if I mistake not, is called mount Gargaflo, on which there were some remains of a temple

of

of Jupiter, it may be the old mount Ænus, where there was a temple built to Jupiter Ænefius. At the north weft end of the harbour is the town of Lixairi : There is another port to the weft called Valle de Aleffandro. This ifland is governed in the fame manner as Zant, by a provectitore, and two confihen, who fit with him, and have votes in hearing caufes, all three being noble Venetians, they have two or three Greek fyndics on the part of the people, to take care that the antient laws of the ifland are obferved In thefe iflands they keep the old ftyle In Argoftoli they have three Roman churches, and one at the caftle, and there are two Roman convents in the town The bifhop, who is a fuffragan of the archbifhop of Corfu, refides at Zant; they are Greeks in all the other parts of the ifland Cephalenia is well peopled and improved, confidering that it is a rocky and mountainous ifland This improvement confifts chiefly in vineyards and currant gardens, the currant trees are a fmall fort of vine, they export a great quantity, and the fruit grows like grapes, they make a fmall quantity of very rich wine of this fruit, which has its name from being the grape of Corinth, the beft, which are the fmalleft, are of Zanth, but they have them about Patras, and all up the gulph The ftate of this ifland is very miferable, for it is divided into two great parties under Count Metakfas, and the family of Anino, who judge in all affairs of their clients by force of arms, fo that often the whole ifland is under arms, it being the great aim of each party to deftroy the other. Another powerful family is the Coriphani, his anceftor was a fugitive from Naples, and with which foever fide he joins, that party is fure to be the ftronger, there are befides thefe other families of condition, which take part on one fide or other, and they are all defcended from fugitives, fo that the whole ifland is full of very bad people, and the Venetian governors find their account in thefe divifions A ftory they have invented will give fome idea of the character of thefe people, as well as fome others· They fay that the creator, when he made the earth, threw all the rubbifh here, and that there being three notorious rogues he fent one to this ifland, another to St. Maura, and the third to Maina We came into the port of Argoftoli on the twenty-fecond, and went to the town, I defired to be afhoar as one performing quarantain, and with a little money I might have obtained it, on the condition of being a prifoner with any one they fhould pleafe to name, to whom I fhould have been fure of being a prey, and in whofe houfe I muft have remained, and could never have gone out without him, and confequently fhould not have been in a very agreeable fituation, fo I chofe to remain on board the fhip, and we fet fail again on the feventh of November.

CHAP. XV.

A Voyage from LEGHORN to ALEXANDRIA in ÆGYPT.

HAVING made some observations in my voyage from Leghorn to Alexandria, I thought it might not be disagreeable to the reader to see them in this place. On the seventh of September, one thousand seven hundred thirty seven, we sailed out of the road of Leghorn on board an English ship bound to Alexandria in Ægypt. This sea is now called the Tuscan sea, lying between Corsica, Sardinia, Sicily, and part of Italy, to the south of the republic of Genoa, the antient Liguria.

Gorgona

We sailed about two leagues from the island of Gorgona, which is like a high rocky mountain, the clifts of which are almost perpendicular all round, except in one place to the east, where they have a small port called Gorgona, which is the only entrance to the island, being a shelter for small fishing boats. Over this port the grand duke has a fortress with about twenty soldiers in it, who, by their situation, are capable of hindering the landing of a considerable body of men; some fishermen live at this port, who chiefly are employed in catching anchovies.

Capraia

We afterwards sailed to the east of the island of Capraia, the Capraria of Pliny. This island is about two leagues long, and one broad, being mountainous and rocky. We had a plain view of the only town in it of the same name of the island, which is situated on the high ground over the sea to the east, to the south of it is a large castle on a rock, and the town extends to the north to a small bay, on which there is a fishing village, the chief support of this island being a trade in fish, which they carry to Leghorn. There is a Franciscan convent in the town, which belongs to the province of Corsica, this island being subject to the Genoese.

Elba

We afterwards passed by the island of Elba, the Ilva of the antients, it is about five leagues long, and three broad. Pliny says it was a hundred miles round in circumference, of which it may not fall much short, if measured round by the bays and creaks, of which there are a great number. The north part of this island, with the port of Ferraro, and a castle called Cosmopoli, belongs to the grand duke of Tuscany. The south part (except Porto Longone, which belongs to the king of Sicily, and all about it within cannon shot of the fortress) is subject to the duke of Piombino, in the territory of the latter, the iron ore is found, and they say, that having cleared the mines entirely of the ore, after leaving them about thirty years they find iron ore in them again, which perhaps give rise to what Virgil says of it.

Ilva

Insula inexhaustis Chalybum generosa metallis

And this also may be the reason of what Pliny affirms, that there had been more iron dug out of it in three thousand years than the whole island ifland would contain it is a very remarkable paffage, " Unde per tria " annorum milia plus effet ferri egeftum, quam tota contineret infula " They have a vulgar notion that the iron cannot be melted here, which poffibly may be owing to what Strabo fays of Æthalia, which fome have thought to be Elba, he affirms they could not melt the iron on the fpot, but carried the ore immediately to the continent; and therefore fome think there is a quality in the air which hinders the ore from melting or running, but it is more probable that they had not the conveniency of wood for their foundery in fo fmall an ifland.

Three leagues to the fouth weft of Elba we faw the flat ifland of Pla-^{Planofa} nofa, called by the Romans Planafia· The land of it is fo low, that it cannot be feen further than the diftance of four or five leagues I was informed that ruins of houfes and caftles are feen on it from the fea, when they fail near it, that fifhermen and others go there in the day-time, but that it is not inhabited for fear of the Corfairs, this ifland belongs to the duke of Piombino

Four leagues fouth of Elba we faw the ifland of Monte Chrifto, which^{Monte Chrifto} appears like one high mountain, it is now uninhabited, and I have many reafons to think that it is Æthalia of Strabo, which has fo much puzzled the geographers, many of them having conjectured that it was Elba, but as Strabo himfelf was at Populonium on the promontory of Piombino, and faw all the iflands of this fea from that place, we cannot fuppofe he could be miftaken, and in another part he mentions both Ilva and Æthalia, fo that it cannot be Elba, he alfo makes Æthalia equally diftant from Corfica and Populonium, that is, three hundred ftadia or thirty-feven miles and a half, and Monte Chrifto anfwers exactly, meafuring on the fea charts about twelve leagues or thirty-fix miles from each There is alfo no other ifland on that fide of Corfica and Sardinia, except Capraia, which can be feen from Populonium, and Monte Chrifto being fo near Elba, is moft likely to partake of the nature of the foil of it, producing iron ore in the fame manner, which might grow again in the pits, the knowledge of which may be loft by reafon that the ifland is now uninhabited Strabo mentions the port Argous in this ifland, which he obferves (according to fabulous hiftory) was faid to be fo called from Jafon's touching there with the fhip Argos, when he was in fearch of the habitation of Circe, Medea, as they fay, being defirous to fee that goddefs

Three leagues weft of Monte Argentato in Italy we faw the ifland of Giglio, called by the Romans, Idilium, Ægilium, and Iginium, we^{Giglio} could but juft fee the flat ifland of Gianuti, four miles fouth weft of Gi-^{Gianuti} glio, thought to be Dianium of Pliny, called by the Greeks Artemifia and Artemita We had for a confiderable time a fight of the ifland of Corfica, and a plain view of the town of Baftia, on the flat fhore on the eaft fide of it We were feveral days eaft of Sardinia, having often a fight of that ifland, as we were frequently becalmed, and fometimes had contrary winds, fo that we did not fee Sicily till the thirteenth day from the time we fet fail, though the voyage in other refpects was by no means unpleafant, as we had very fine weather

We did not fail a great way from the moft weftern of the Lipari iflands, called Uftica, which I take to be the ifland Euonymus of Strabo, to agree with whofe defcription of it, the old geographers in their maps have made an island south east of the others, and called it Euonymus, because Strabo says, that it is the fartheft to the left sailing from the isle of Lipara to Sicily, and that on this account it had its name But for reasons I shall mention, I apprehend that Strabo meant it was on the left, sailing from Sicily to the isle of Lipara, for, he says, this island is farther out in the sea than any of them, which could not be properly said of an island to the south east of the others, because that would be nearer to the land both of Italy and Sicily, and if it were not for this objection, it might be an island called Volcanello, to the south east of Volcano, at a very little diftance from it, which is a very small island, that has a smoaking Volcano, the other Volcano, breaking out in flames. I muft obferve, that all the maps, especially those of the old geographers, are very false with regard to these islands; and I find the sea charts are moft to be depended on for the number and situation of them, tho' I observed that De Lisle's map only is right in making two Volcano islands, one larger than the other, who, notwithftanding, if I am rightly informed, is mistaken in placing the little one to the north, which ought to be to the south east. I could not but pleafe my self with the imagination that I was near the place, where the Romans, at the Lipara islands, gained their firft sea victory, in a moft fignal engagement with the Carthaginians, under the conduct of the conful Duilius, who was not only honoured for it in a folemn manner, but had a fort of triumph decreed him during his whole life, and the famous Columna Roftrata was erected to his honour, which is now to be feen in Rome with a long infcription on it, and is one of the greateft and moft curious pieces of antiquity remaining, being about two thoufand years old

I faw cape Gallo, which is very near the port of Palermo, and falling in with the weft of Sicily, we failed between the iflands called by the antients Ægates, though in all the maps we fee particular names given them by the old geographers, yet I cannot find that the old names of these three islands are certainly known, that to the north eaft oppofite to Trapano, from which it is ten miles diftant, is now called Levanzo, fouth of it is the island Favagnana, which is ten miles in circumference It is a fine fertile fpot of ground, being moftly a flat, with a high hill towards the north fide, on which there are three caftles garrifoned by the king of Sicily, in one of which the governor refides This place was a great refuge for the Corfairs, and they frequently came out from it, and infefted the feas till Charles the fifth carried his arms into Africa The third island, thirty miles weft of Trapano, is called Maritimo, it appears like a high mountain, to the north eaft of it is a rocky promontory, which is a peninfula, and much lower than the reft of the island, on which there is a caftle built, where they keep a garrifon The islands called Ægates are famous for a fecond fignal victory by fea which the Romans obtained over the Carthaginians under the command of the conful Lutatius Catulus, concerning which the hiftorian fays, that after the battle the whole fea between Sicily and Sardinia was covered with the wreck and ruins of the enemies fleet, and this total defeat put an end to the firft Punic war

The mountain of Trapano is one of the firft things that ftrikes the eye to the weft of Sicily, on the top of it is a caftle, and at the foot of

this

Ægates

this hill to the weft is a flat point of land which ftretches into the fea, and the city of Trapano ftands there, on the fpot where the antient Drepanum was fituated This is called by Virgil Illætabilis ora, becaufe here Æneas loft his father Anchifes, and, after his return from Carthage, he celebrated divine honours to his memory in this place This city is remarkable for actions in the Punic wars, as well as the fmall ifland of Columbaria oppofite to it. The mountain of Trapano to the weft is mount Eryx, fo famous for the worfhip of Venus, who on this account was called Venus Erycina Virgil makes the temple of this goddefs to be built by Æneas and his followers, when he was about to leave behind him the women, and infirm people to fettle on the ifland .

> Tum vicina aftris Erycino in vertice fedes
> Fundatur Veneri Idaliæ

Strabo fays, that the town on the top of the hill was originally inhabited by women dedicated to the goddefs by foreign nations, as well as by the Sicilians, but that in his time, it was inhabited by men, and the temple was ferved by priefts, who lived in great poverty, the place not being then frequented He adds that the Romans built a temple to this goddefs at Rome without the Porta Collina, called the temple of Venus Erycina, fo that probably, the devotion was removed to that place

To the fouth of Trapano I had a plain view of the city of Marzala, built where Lilybaum ftood, which was the port where they ufually embarked for Carthage The promontory and town alfo are often mentioned in hiftory, efpecially that of the Punic wars It is faid the port was deftroyed by the Romans, in order to hinder the convenient paffage of the Carthaginians to and from the port, in cafe they fhould afterwards recover it, and it was entirely filled up again by Don John of Auftria in one thoufand five hundred and fixty-feven Auguftus brought a colony to this town The fea coaft being fhoaly, it anfwers in that refpect very well to the defcription of Virgil in this verfe,

> Et vada dura lego faxis Lilybeia cæcis

I faw between Sicily and Africa the ifland of Pantelera, which was called Cofyra by the Romans, and by Strabo Cofura, who fays it was equally diftant from Lilybaum, and the city of Afpis, or Clupea of the Carthaginian, it is confirmed to be that ifland from the name of Coffra which the inhabitants of Africa, now give it in the Arabic language . It belongs to Sicily, and is made ufe of as a place of banifhment To the fouth eaft of this is the ifland of Limofa, and a few leagues fouth of that, a larger ifland called Lampidofa, which did belong to a Chriftian hermit, and a Marabut or Turkifh hermit, and ferved as a place both for Chriftians and Turks to take in provifions, with an agreement that neither of them fhould fuffer from thofe of the different religion. The Marabut dying not long ago, the Mahometan Corfair feized on what was in the ifland, and carried the Chriftian away captive, of which great complaint was made by the French conful, who demanded the captive

Strabo in three places mentions the ifle Ægimurus, together with Cofura, in one particularly, fpeaking of feveral fmall iflands in general is

Pantelera

Lampedo

ne 1

near Coffura and Sicily, he only mentions Ægimurus in particular, and therefore probably it was the largeft of them The three iflands which are near Pantelera or Cofyra, are Semetto, Limofa, and Lampidofa, and the laft being much the largeft, probably it is Ægimurus On this ifland, in the firft Punic war, the Carthaginian fleet was fhipwrecked in the confulfhip of Fabius Buteo

We thought we faw cape Bona, which is the north eaft promontory of the great bay of Carthage The fea to the fouth of Sicily was called by the antients the Libyan or African fea, and comprehended that part of the Mediterranean, which is on the coaft of Africa, from the entrance into this fea at the pillars of Hercules, or the ftreights of Gibraltar, to the eaft bounds of Cyrenaica, where the Ægyptian fea begun This is now commonly called the fea of Barbary along the Afric coaft, and on the fide of Sicily the fea goes by the name of the channel of Malta.

When we approached Sicily I found we were failing along the fame coaft by which Æneas made his voyage, and as I had a view of the cities and places on the fhoar, I could not but obferve the juftice and poetical beauties of the defcriptions of the great mafter of the Latin Epic poetry

As foon as we had doubled the fouth weft point of Sicily we faw the city of Mazra, the antient Mazara, from which one third part of Sicily is now called Valle di Mazara . Some way to the eaft of it was the famous city of Selinus, which was deftroyed before Strabo's time The poet makes mention of it as abounding in palm trees :

Teque datis linquo ventis palmofa Selinus.

We afterwards had a very plain view of the city of Xiacca on the fide of a high ground Sailing on I faw the city of Girgenti on the fide of a hill, being built up to the top of it, this town is about four miles from the fea, and is the antient city of Agrigentum, where the tyrant Phalaris refided This city remained when moft of the other towns on the fouth of Sicily were deftroyed in the Carthaginian wars It was firft a colony of Ionians, and afterwards a colony was brought to it from the cities of Sicily by T. Manlius the prætor Under the Greek name Acragas Virgil defcribes its eminent fituation, as well as mentions its having been formerly famous for a fine breed of horfes .

Arduus inde Acragas oftentat maxima longe
Mœnia, magnanimûm quondam generator equorum

At the fame time I had a plain view of mount Ætna, which now among the vulgar goes by the name of mount Gibello, and is feen almoft all along the fouth and eaft coafts of Sicily I difcerned a very little fmoak afcending from the top of it This mountain, fo famous among the antients, is very beautifully defcribed by Virgil, as feen by Æneas from the coafts of the Cyclops about Catani, where Ulyffes had put in not long before, and where both thofe heroes, according to the fictions of the poet, met with fuch extraordinary adventures in relation to Polyphemus I foon afterwards faw cape Locate at the mouth of the river Salfo, the antient Himera, near which there was a caftle called Philinum, where

where it is said the brazen bull was kept. There is also a river called Rocella, which runs into the sea to the north of Sicily, the source of which is near the fountains of Salso, and the Rocella was formerly also called the Himera, which gave occasion to the antients to make a very extraordinary story, affirming, that these two rivers were one, and called Himera, and that part of the river run north, and the other part south, and that in some places the water was fresh, and in others salt; of which Vitruvius gives the true cause, that one part of this river, or rather one of these rivers passed through places where they dug salt, for in the middle of the island, about the source of the river Salso, there are mines of rock salt, which probably is the reason of the modern name of this river

Further to the east I saw a city called Terra Nova, near a river of the same name, this is supposed to be Gela, which had its name also from the river, as is mentioned by the poet :

> Apparet Camarina procul, campique Geloi,
> Immanisque Gela fluvii cognomine dicta.

There is but one city more mentioned by Virgil on the south side of Sicily, which was in ruins in Strabo's time : The place where it stood is now called Camarana, the old name of the city being Camarina, a colony of the Syracusans.

We had a sight of Malta at a great distance, and at length came up with cape Passaro, the old promontory Pachynum, as it is a peninsula, and the land very low to the west of it, so it appears at a distance like an island, with a castle built on it, in order to hinder ships from going into the port, to lay in wait for other vessels The ground off this cape is very foul, and ships cannot come to anchor there without danger of cutting their cables, so that it answers very well to the poet's description of it.

> Hinc altas cautes, projectaque saxa Pachyni
> Radimus.

Over this cape we saw the high lands about Syracuse.

To the east of Sicily is that sea which was called by the antients, first the Ausonian sea, and afterwards the Sicilian sea, it extended from the streights of Sicily, now called the Faro of Messina, to the promontory of Iapygia in Italy, to the mouth of the Adriatic sea, to the bay Ambracius in Greece, and as far as Crete, having the African sea to the south. I do not find any particular name for this sea at present, but the mariners call all these seas as far as the Adriatic, by the general name of the Mediterranean, as they call the seas farther to the east the Levant

We lost sight of Sicily on the twenty-first of September in the evening, and making a great run on the twenty-fourth in the morning we saw to the north of us the high mountains of Candia, the antient Crete, which is remarkable, as it was the scene of so many fables of the antients

From Crete eastward near to Cyprus it was called the Ægyptian sea, extending westward on the coast of Africa to Cyrenaica, where the African sea began.

On the twenty feventh of September we came in fight of the coaft of Africa about cape Solyman, in the kingdom of Barca, and juft on the confines of Ægypt, which was that part of Marmarica about little Catabathmus, where the famous temple of Jupiter Ammon was fituated, to which Alexander the great travelled with fo much difficulty to confult the oracle Near it there was a famous fountain of the fun, which, they fay, was cold at noon, began to grow warm at night, and was very hot about midnight The next day we came in fight of the tower of Arabia, and the day after faw Alexandria, as we approached it we had a very agreeable profpect of the famous column, of the walls of the old city, of the country covered with palm-trees, which grow to a great height, rifing up above the buildings of the city And on the twenty ninth we arrived in the port of Alexandria, after a very pleafant and agreeable voyage of twenty-three days.

CHAP. XVI.

Of fome ANTIQUITIES found in the Eaft.

THE bronze foot A, in the eightieth plate, was brought from the island of Mycone in the Archipelago by the Right honourable John earl of Sandwich, when his lordfhip made his fecond voyage into the eaft in 1739, and was returning from Ægypt It was found at the bottom of a well, and is of the natural fize of a very large foot of a ftatue, which muft have been about eight feet high, for the foot is twelve inches long, and five broad, the fandal is of a very fingular kind: The whole foot except the toes appear to have been covered with fomething which appears like linen, the hinder part, and thofe parts which the thongs of leather pafs feem to have been of fome metal, if ever fuch a fandal was really ufed, becaufe it does not yield to the thongs, which come againft the end of the toes, as it would be difficult to walk in that manner, fo it has been conjectured, that fuch a fandal could never be ufed, and that it might be no part of a ftatue, but hung up as a vow on fome deliverance I brought from Afia Minor the piece of a marble foot B; it muft have belonged to a Coloffal ftatue, as it is fix inches wide, the workmanfhip is very fine, but the great particularity of it is that it feems to reprefent the wooden fandal, the upper part of which is about an inch deep, and the lower part three quarters of an inch It appears as if the ligature had been fixed on each fide to the wood, that there was a covering of the foot under it from that part upwards, and that this covering was fixed to the fandal by a ftring which went between the toes I bought the earthen lamp D, it kept in upper Ægypt, which is the antient Coptus in the Thebaid, it feems to have the name of fome faint on it, the letter H being under the handle, confequently it is a Chriftian work I brought from Aleppo the bronze ftatue C, which, as well as the lamp, and the other drawings which follow, is of the fize in which it is reprefented, it feems to have been defigned as in

2

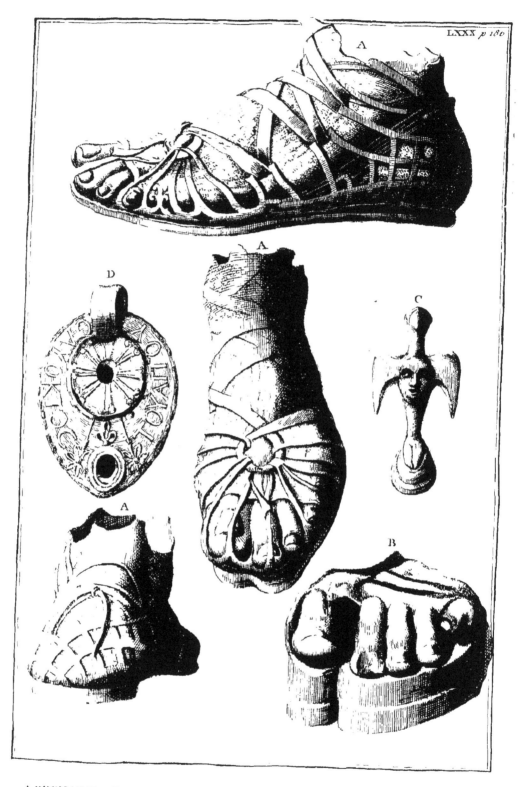

A BRONZE FOOT A A FOOT of MARBLE B A BRONZE STATUE C A LAMP D

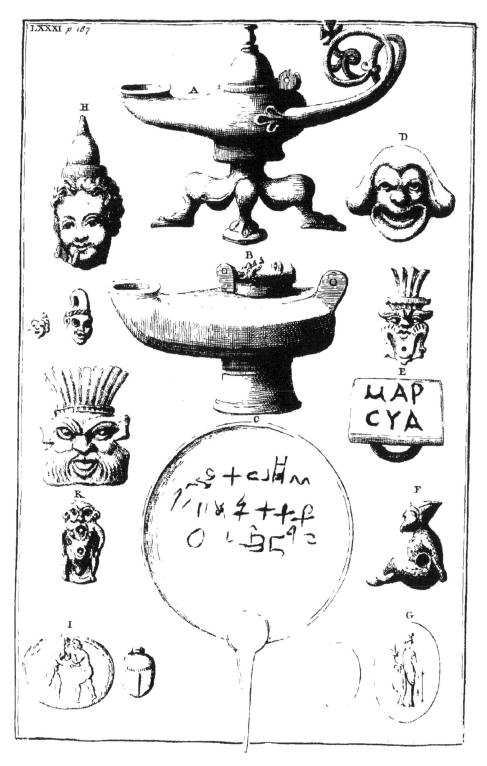

ANTIQUITIES from the EAST

ornament, is of a rough workmanſhip, and is left unfiniſhed behind, as if it was not to have been ſeen that way In the eighty-firſt plate, A is a braſs lamp brought from Salonica, it is of a good deſign, but from the croſs it appears to be a Chriſtian work. The braſs lamp B, I bought at Aleppo; both of them have a hole in the bottom, with a ſocket riſing up into the vaſe within, in order to fix them on ſome foot at a proper height C is of ſteel, and made for a wooden handle, the back part of it appears to have been ſo finely poliſhed, that probably it ſerved for a mirrour, the characters which are on the other ſide ſeem to be Phœnician The braſs figure D is a maſk from Aleppo, and appears to have been fixed to ſomething as an ornament, E likewiſe is from the ſame place, and of braſs, it ſeems to have been a weighty ring, as the letters are not reverſed for a ſeal, when ſo many buſhels of rings of the ſlain were found after a battle, they were probably of this ſize F is an extraordinary figure from Aleppo, with its hands tied behind, and there is a hole from the fundament to the poll, as well as through the body, as ſeen in the drawing, one would imagine that it repreſented ſome antient puniſhment like impaling. It is to be obſerved, that the cap is of the Phrygian kind G is an intaglio, or ſeal bought at Bayreut in Syria, and is of a mixed coloured yellow jaſper All the others were brought from upper Ægypt, and are all amulets, except H, which is the head of a very chearful Harpocrates, and is of earthen ware I, is a tortoiſe in cornelian, there is a bad deſign on it, which ſeems to repreſent two wreſtlers The others are all in earth, enamelled or glazed over. Such a figure as that at K, I ſaw in relief on an antient Ægyptian capital, repreſented in the firſt Volume.

CHAP. XVII.

Of PLANTS found in the Eaſt, and ſome other countries.

THE ſeven firſt plates are of plants found in the Holy Land, the eighth is of Cyprus, which I did not ſee in any other place.

In the eighty-ſecond plate the plant Alyſſon is particularly deſcribed

a Capſula ſeminalis

b Capſula longitudinaliter diſſecta.

c Semen

In the eighty-ſixth plate the plant Rhamnus orientalis of Plukenet in his Phytographia, ſeems to be what the Arabs call Zoccom, it is mentioned by Veſlingius in the Amſterdam edition of Proſper Alpinus's natural hiſtory of Ægypt, and ſeems to be deſcribed by Plukenet in the flower, I have already given an account of it at the river Jordan, it anſwers exactly to the Myrobalanum of Pliny My ſpecimen was loſt except the wood and the fruit For a further deſcription, ſee the plate.

a Rhamnus orientalis, Plukenet Phytographia

b An. fructus ejuſdem. Zoccom, Arabice.

c Fructus

c Fructus tranſverſaliter inciſum

d Semen

In the ſeventy-eighth plate a fine ſpecimen is engraved of a very curious plant Tragacantha orientalis, called in Arabic, Wolf's eggs. The flowers and ſeed are particularly ſhown.

a Flos cum calice

b Flos diſſectus

c Capſula ſeminalis

d Capſula tranſverſaliter diſſecta

e Capſula longitudinaliter diſſecta.

f Semina

Platanus orientalis, in the eighty-ninth plate is deſcribed under Cyprus, in that plate the ſeed is ſhown

a Capſulæ ſeminales

b Semina

I have added a catalogue of the plants I collected in the eaſt and other parts, by the ſame hand as that in the firſt Volume. Thoſe marked thus * being come up in the phyſic garden at Chelſea, from the ſeeds I brought to England.

Plants of PALÆSTINE.

1 Acer orientalis hederæ folio, Cor Inſt.

2 Alnus folio oblongo, C B P.

3 Alyſſon incanum ſerpili folio minus, C. B. P.

4 Alyſſon Græcum fruteſcens, ſerpili folio ampliſſimo, Cor. Inſt.

5 Anonis ſpinis carens lutea minor, Bot Monſp

6 Anonis viſcoſa ſpinis carens, lutea major, C B. P.

7 Aperine ſimia minor annua floribus, in capillamente abeuntibus, Cor. Inſt

8 Arbutus folio non ſcirato, C B P

9 Aſparagus orientalis foliis Galii, Cor Inſt

10 Aſparagus creticus fruticoſus, craſſioribus & brevioribus aculeis, magno fructu, Cor Inſt

Idem longioribus & tenuioribus aculeis, Cor Inſt

11 Aſter orientalis conyzæ folio, flore luteo maximo, Cor. Inſt.

12 Aſtragalus orientalis, foliis viciæ glabris & ramis tomentoſis, Cor. Inſt

13 Aſtragalus orientalis candidiſſimus & tomentoſus, Cor. Inſt.

14 Atriplex Græca fruticoſa humifuſa Halimi folio, Cor. Inſt

15 Atriplex orientalis fruteſcens, folio ampliſſimo argenteo, Cor Inſt.

16 Azedarach, Dod

17 Buxus orientalis oleæ folio, N D

18 Campanula pentagonia flore ampliſſimo Thracica, Inſt R H

19 Campanula orientalis maxima, floribus conglobatis in foliorum alis, Cor Inſt

20 Capparis non ſpinoſa, fructu majore, C B P

* 21 Carduus ſtellatus foliis integris flore purpureo, H R Par

22 Caryophyllus orientalis fruticoſus, tenuiſſimo folio flore laciniato, Cor Inſt

23 Cedrus folio cupreſſi major, fructu flaveſcente, C. B. P.

24 Ce-

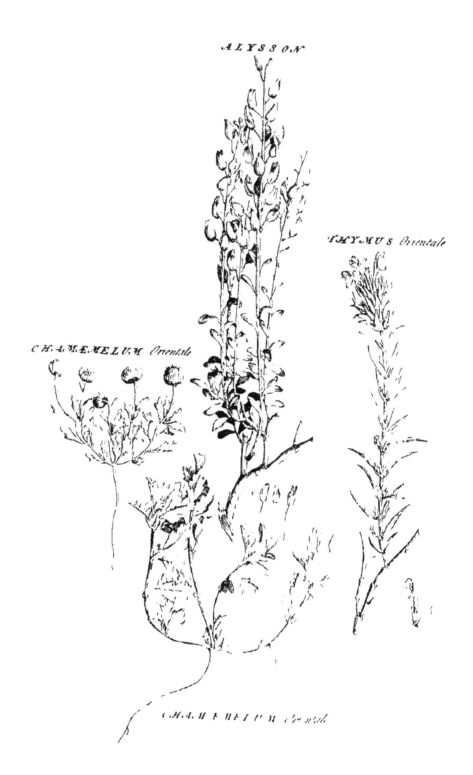

ALYSSON

THYMUS Orientale

CHAMÆMELUM Orientale

CHAMÆMELUM Orientale

AZADERACH

24 Cedrus orientalis fœtidiſſima, arbor excelſa, ſeu ſabina orientalis foliis aculeatis, Cor. Inſt.

25 Chamæmelum orientale abſinthii folio, Cor Inſt

26 Ciſtus ladanifera Cretica, flore purpureo, Cor. Inſt

27 Clematitis orientalis apii folio, flore e viridi flaveſcente poſterius reflexo, Cor Inſt.

28 Clematitis orientalis latifolia, ſemine breviſſimis pappis donato, Cor Inſt

29 Clymenum Græcum flore maximo ſingulari, Cor. Inſt.

30 Colutea veſicaria, C. B. P.

31 Cuminoides vulgare, Inſt R H.

32 Cytiſſus hirſutus, J B.

33 Dracunculus polyphyllus foliis lituris albicantibus obliquis notatis, Cor. Inſt.

34 Echium orientale verbaſci folio flore maximo campanulato, Cor. Inſt.

35 Elichryſum anguſtiſſimo folio, Inſt R. H.

36 Elichryſum orientale glutinoſum lavendulæ folio, Cor. Inſt

37 Elichryſum ſylveſtre anguſtifolium flore magno ſingulari, Inſt. R. H.

38 Elichryſum Germanicum calyce ſanguineo, Inſt. R. H.

39 Erica orientalis, coris folio, flore globoſo, Cor. Inſt.

40 Ficus humilis, C B.

41 Harmala, Dod.

42 Helleborus niger amplioribus foliis, Inſt R. H.

43 Hypericum tragum olens, Inſt. R. H.

44 Hypericum orientale ſaxatilis majoranæ folio, Cor. Inſt.

45 Jaſminides jaſmini nucleati foliis, Michel.

46 Ilex folio ſubrotundo ſubtus villoſo, marginibus nucleatis.

47 Iſatis orientalis maritima caneſcens, Cor. Inſt.

48 Iſatis orientalis Lepidii folio, Cor. Inſt.

49 Juniperus Cretica ligno odoratiſſimo, κέδρος Græcorum recentiorum, Cor. Inſt.

50 Lapathum orientale aſperum folio ſubrotundo, fructu magno purpureo, Ribes dictum.

51 Lepidium humile minus incanum Alepicum, Inſt. R. H.

52 Leviſticum vulgare, Dod.

53 Lotus hæmorrhoidalis humilior & candidior, Inſt R. H.

54 Lotus Græca maritima folio glauco & velut argenteo, Cor. Inſt.

55 Lunaria fruticoſa perennis incana leucoii folio, Cor Inſt

56 Lychnis Cretica anguſtifolia floribus longiſſimis pediculis inſidentibus capſulâ, pyramidatâ, Cor. Inſt.

57 Mandragora fructu rotundo, C B. P

58 Melilotus cretica humifuſa flore albo magno, Cor Inſt.

59 Meſpilus apii folio laciniato, C B P.

60 Meſpilus orientalis apii folio ſubtus hirſuto, fructu magno luteo, N D.

61 Nigella anguſtifolia, flore majore ſimplici albo, Inſt R. H.

62 Oſmunda foliis lunatis, Inſt R H

63 Pancratium maritimum floribus albis.

64 Polium erectum anguſtifolium.

65 Polium montanum album, C. B P.

66 Polium Smyrnæum fcordii folio, Cor. Inft

67 Polium montanum album non ferratum viride folio caule incano, Barrel Icon.

68 Polygonoides orientale Ephedræ facie, Cor Inft.

69 Quercus latifolia magno fructu, calyce tuberculis obfito, Cor Inft.

70 Quercus orientalis glande cylindriformi longo pediculo infididente, Cor. Inft

71 Quercus orientalis caftaneæ folio glande recondita in cupula craffa & fquamofa, Cor Inft.

72 Quercus orientalis anguftifolia glande minori cupula crinita, Cor Inft

73 Quercus orientalis latifolia foliis ad coftam pulchrè incifis, glande maxima, cupula crinita, Cor Inft

74 Rhamnus Creticus amygdali folio minori, Cor Inft

75 Rhus folio ulmi, C B P.

76 Rubeola Cretica faxatilis frutefcens, flore flavefcente, Cor. Inft.

77 Rubus Creticus triphyllus flore parvo, Cor. Inft.

78 Ruta fylveftris minor, C B P

79 Salvia Samia verbafci folio, Cor. Inft

80 Salvia Samia frutefcens, foliis longioribus incanis non crifpis, Cor. Inft

81 Salvia Cretica frutefcens pomifera, foliis longioribus incanis crifpis, Cor Inft.

82 Smilax orientalis farmentis aculeatis excelfas arbores fcandentibus, foliis non fpinofis, Cor Inft

83 Spartium tertium flore albo, C B P.

84 Stachys fpinofa Cretica, C. B P.

85 Symphytum Creticum echii folio anguftiori longiffimis villis horrido flore crocco, Cor Inft

86 Symphytum Conftantinopolitanum borraginis folio & facie, flore albo, Cor Inft.

87 Tamarifcus Narbonenfis, Lob Icon.

88 Tamarifcus orientalis foliis planis, flore purpureo, Cor. Inft.

89 Thymelea Cretica oleæ folio fubtus villofo, Cor. Inft.

90 Thymelea orientalis buxi folio fubtus villofo flore albo, Cor Inft

91 Thymus capitatus orientalis, capitulis & foliis longioribus, Cor Inft

92 Tithymalus orientalis, anacampferotis folio, flore magno criftato, Cor Inft

93 Tithymalus Creticus characias anguftifolius, villofus & incanus, Cor Inft

94 Tragacantha Cretica foliis minimis incanis flore majore albo, Cor Inft

95 Tragacantha orientalis, erectior foliis, vicia glabris & ramis tomentofis, T Cor

96 Trifolium bituminofum arboreum anguftifolium ic fempervirens, Hort Cath.

97 Vicia orientalis multiflora incana anguftiffimo folio, Cor Inft

98 Vifniga, J B

99 Xylon five Goffypium herbaceum, J B.

Other

N?hnt del. s fe

MESPILUS Orientalis

ACER b...

Other Plants of PALÆSTINE.

100 Abutilon althææ folio villofa, N. D.
101 Acacia vera, J. B.
102 Acetofa Canopica minor, Lippi
103 Anonis flore luteo parvo, C B. P.
104 Arum Byzantinum, J B.
105 Afterifcus annuus foliis ad florem rigidis, Inft. R. H.
106 Atriplex Græca fruticofa humifufa halimi folio, Cor. Inft.
107 Chryfanthemum Creticum, Cluf.
108 Ciftus mas major, folio rotundiore, J B.
109 Glaucium flore luteo, Inft. R. H.
* 110 Hyofcyamus Creticus, luteus, major, C. B. P.
111 Ilex folio agrifolii, Inft R H.
112 Lentifcus vulgaris, C. B P.
113 Limonium peregrinum, foliis afplenii, C. B. P.
* 114 Malva rofea ficus folio, C B. P.
115 Paronychia Hifpanica, nivea, polyanthos, Cluf
116 Platanus orientalis verus, Park. Theat.
117 Polium Gnaphalodes, Inft R. H.
118 Ptarmica orientalis Santolinæ folio, Cor. Inft.
119 Rhus folio ulmi, C. B. P.
120 Rofa lutea multiplex, C. B. P.
121 Siliqua edulis, J. B.
122 Siliquaftrum caft Durant.
123 Smilax orientalis farmentis aculeatis, excelfas arbores fcandentibus, foliis non fpinofis, Cor Inft.
124 Terebinthus vulgaris, C B P.
125 Vifcum baccis albis, C. B. P.
126 Vitex foliis anguftioribus cannabis modo difpofitis, C. B. P.

Plants of SYRIA.

127 Acei orientalis hederæ folio, Cor. Inft.
128 Alaternus 1 cluf Hifp
129 Alchimilla pubefcens minor, H R Par
130 Alkekengi fructu parvo verticillato, Inft R H.
131 Allium orientale latifolium flore magno lacteo, Cor Inft.
132 Anagyris fætida, C B P
133 Apocynum Africanum erectum falicis folio angufto glabro fructu villofo, P. Bat
134 Arifarium latifolium alterum maculis albis variegatum, Cor. Inft.
135 Ariftolochia clematitis, C B P.
136 Arum minus Nymphææ foliis efculentum, Sloan, Cat
137 Afcyron magno flore, C B. P.
138 Afphodelus albus, C B P
139 Campanula pratenfis flore conglomerato, C B P.
140 Capparis fpinofa fructu minor folio rotundo, C. B. P.
141 Capparis non fpinofa fructu majore, C B P.
142 Carpinus, Dod.

143 Cataria orientalis minima lamii folio, flore longissimo, Cor. Inst.

144 Cedrus magna five Libani, J. B.

145 Cistus ladanifera latiore folio flore albo, Cat. Hort.

146 Clematitis cærulea erecta, C B P.

147 Cuminoides vulgare, Inst R. H.

148 Cytissus orientalis latifolius subtus incanis, Cor. Inst.

149 Cytissus spinosus siliquâ villosâ incanâ, Cor Inst.

150 Cytissus orientalis flore magno ex purpuro flavescente.

151 Delphinium flore cæruleo, C. B. P.

152 Echium orientale verbasci folio, flore maximo campanulato, Cor Inst

153 Elæagnus orientalis angustifolius, fructu parvo olivæ formi subdulci, Cor. Inst.

* 154 Fabago Belgarum five Peplus Parisiensium, Lugd Hist.

155 Fagonia Cretica spinosa, Inst R. H.

156 Ficus sylvestris foliis magis dissectis.

157 Fœnum Græcum Siculum frutescens siliquis ornithopodii latioribus, Inst R H

158 Fraxinus florifera botryoides, Mor H R Blaf.

159 Glycyrrhiza orientalis siliquis hirsutissimus, Cor. Inst.

160 Harmala, Dod.

161 Helianthemum salicis folio, Inst R H

162 Hypericum orientale polygoni folio, Cor Inst.

163 Hypericum orientale fœtido simile, sed inodorum, Cor. Inst.

164 Jacea Epidaurica candidissima & tomentosa, Inst R H.

* 165 Jacea Cretica saxatilis glasti folio flore purpurascente, Cor. Inst.

166 Lychnis viscosa angustifolia rubra, C B. P.

167 Marrubium album candidissimum, Inst R. H.

168 Mespilus Cretica folio circinato & quasi cordiformi, Cor. Inst.

169 Molucca lævis, Dod

170 Molucca spinosa, Dod.

171 Myrtus communis Italica baccis albis, C. B. P.

172 Muscari uva ramosa majus, Inst R H.

173 Nerium floribus rubescentibus, C B. P.

174 Padus Theophrasti, J B

175 Pastinaca orientalis canescens tordylii folio, Cor. Inst

176 Phillyrea foliis minoribus subrotundis & serratis

177 Phlomis Samia herbacea Lunariæ folio, Cor Inst.

178 Pimpinella spinosa seu sempervirens, Mor. Umb.

179 Prunus Cretica montana humifusa flore suaverubente, Cor. Inst.

180 Quercus orientalis folio longo angusto & pulchrè sinuato.

181 Rhamnus orientalis alterni folio, Cor. Inst

181 Rhamnus orientalis spinis uncinatis atropurpureis olæ five ligustri folio, cujus ad imum petiolis umbilico inarticulatur, Plut Phyt tab 55 f 7 Arabicè Zoccum

182 Ruta chalepensis tenuifolia florum petalis villis scatentibus, Mor Hist

183 Salvia pomifera Cretica, Cluf Hist

184 Salvia Cretica frutescens pomifera foliis longioribus incanis crispis, Cor Inst.

185 Sclarea

QUERCUS Orientalis

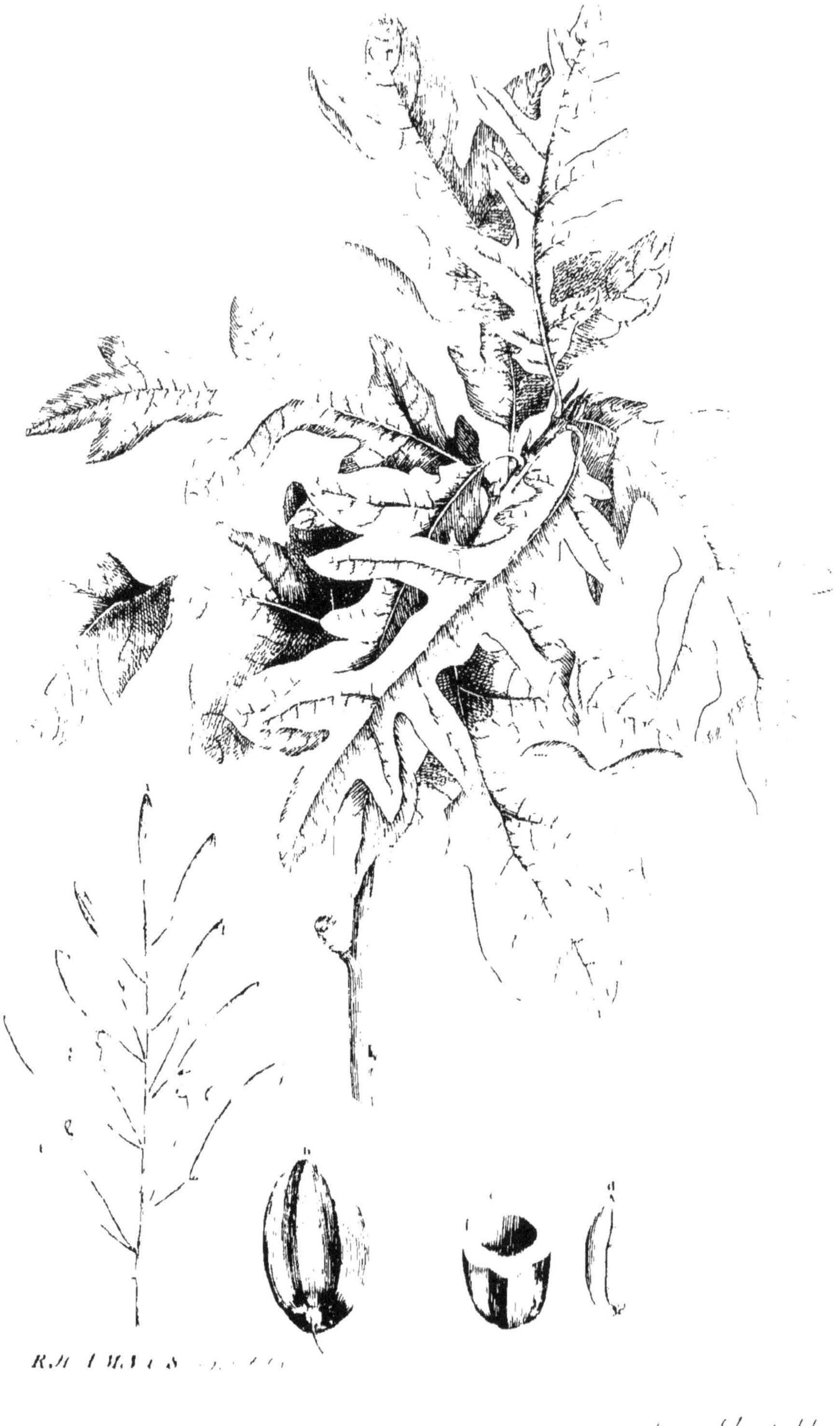

QUERCUS Orientales

185 Sclarea orientalis verbafci folio, flore partim albo, partim flavefcente, Cor Inft.
186 Sideritis orientalis phlomidis folio, Cor. Inft
187 Sideritis Cretica tomentofa candidiffima flore luteo, Cor. Inft.
188 Smyrnium Creticum paludapii folio, Cor. Inft.
189 Stœchas purpurea, C. B P.
190 Suber latifolium perpetuo virens, C B. P.
191 Tamarifcus Narbonenfis flore albo, C B P.
192 Terebinthus vulgaris, C. B P.
193 Teucrium frutefcens ftœchadis Arabicæ folio & facie, Cor. Inft
194 Tithymalus Græcus amygdali folio acutiffimo & glauco, caule
purpureo, Cor. Inft.
195 Tithymalus orientalis falicis folio minor, & glaber fructu verru-
cofo, Cor Inft
196 Trifolium Creticum bituminofo fimile plane inodorum flore purpureo, Cor Inft
197 Valeriana fylveftris major, C. B P
198 Veronica aquatica longifolia, Inft R. H.
199 Vifnaga, J. B.
200 Vitex foliis anguftioribus cannabis modo difpofitis, C. B. P.
201 Xylon five Goffypium herbaceum, J. B.
202 Ziziphus fylveftris, J. B.

Plants of ASIA MINOR.

203 Abies Taxifolia fructu furfum fpectante, Inft. R. H
204 Cedrus folio cupreffi major fructu flavefcente, C B P.
205 Colutea orientalis flore fanguineo luteâ maculâ notato, Cor. Inft.
206 Conyza Cretica fruticofa folio molli candidiffimo & tomentofo,
Cor Inft.
207 Cyclamen hederæ folio, C. B. P.
208 Lentifcus vulgaris, C. B. P
209 Lilac folio laciniato, Inft R. H.
210 Lupulus mas, C B. P.
211 Parietaria minor ocymi folio, C. B. P.
212 Siliqua edulis, C B P.
213 Solanum vulgare, C. B P.
214 Stœchas purpurea, C. B. P.
215 Tithymalus tuberofa pyriformi radice, C B P
216 Tithymalus Græcus heliofcopius maximus, foliis eleganter crena-
tis, Cor. Inft.

Plants of BITHYNIA.

217 Campanula pentagonia, flore ampliffimo Thracica, Inft. R. H.
218 Celtis orientalis folio ampliore fructu magno, Cor Inft.
219 Cytifus foliis argenteis, Wheel. H.
220 Euonymus latifolius, C. B P.

VOL. II. Part II. C c c 221 Heli-

221 Heliotropium majus villosum flore magno inodoro, Cor. Inst
222 Sideritis Cretica tomentosa candidissima flore luteo, Cor. Inst.

Plants of MESOPOTAMIA.

223 Asphodelus albus non ramosus, C B. P
224 Cucubalus Plinii, C. B. P.
225 Cumminoides vulgare, Inst. R. H.
226 Fagonia Cretica spinosa, Inst R. H.
227 Harmala, Dod
228 Helianthemum salicis folio, Inst R. H
229 Lepidium humile arvense incanum, Inst R H
230 Lunaria fruticosa perennis incana leucoii folio, Inst R. H.
231 Mandragora fructu rotundo, C B P
232 Polium erectum tenuifolium flore albo capitulo breviori, Inst.
R H
233 Tithymalus Creticus characias angustifolius villosus & incanus,
Cor Inst
234 Visnaga, J B

Plants of ISTRIA, CARINOLA, STIRIA, CARINTHIA, and CROATIA.

235 Anonis spinosa flore purpureo, C B P
236 Anonis montana præcox purpurea frutescens, Mor. Hist.
237 Astragalus sylvestris, C B P.
238 Astragalus purpureus perennis spicatus Pannonicus, Mor. H.
239 Balsamina lutea sive Noli me tangere, C. B P
240 Belladona minoribus foliis & floribus, Inst R H.
241 Campanula Alpina folio longiori lucido, Inst R. H.
242 Campanula maxima foliis latissimis flore cæruleo, C B. P.
243 Chamædrys major repens, C B. P.
244 Cistus mas folio breviore, C. B P
245 Cistus ladanifera Monspeliensium, C B P
246 Clematitis peregrina foliis pyri incisis, C B P.
247 Cnicus Atractylis lutea dictus, H. L
248 Colutea vesicaria, C B P
249 Cornus hortensis mas, C B P
250 Crithmum sive Fœniculum maritimum minus, C B P.
251 Cyclamen autumnale folio subrotundo, lucido, molliori & crenato, bası rubra, flore niveo maximo, Syriacum, Hugnetau dictum d'Chauveau, Joncq Hort
252 Helichrysum sylvestre angustifolium capitulis conglobatis, Inst
R H
253 Helichrysum sylvestre angustifolium, flore magno singulari, Inst
R H
254 Eryngium montanum amethystinum, C. B. P.
255 Euonymus latifolius, C B P

TRAGACANTHA Orientalis

PLATANUS Orientalis

256 Frangula rugofiore & ampliori folio, Inft. R H

257 Gallium luteum, C B P

258 Gallium nigro-purpureum montanum tenuifolium, Col Ec.

259 Genifta tinctoria maxima, Auftriaca Boerh

260 Herba Paris, C. B P.

261 Hypericum folio breviore, C B. P.

262 Jacea caliculis argenteis minor, Inft R H.

263 Juniperus maxima Illyrica, J B

264 Kali fpinofum foliis craffioribus & brevioribus, Inft R H.

265 Lentifcus vulgaris, C. B P.

266 Lentifcus anguftifolia Maffilienfis, H R. Par.

267 Lilium rubrum anguftifolium, C B. P

268 Limonium minus bellidis folio, C. B P.

269 Lithofpermum majus erectum, C. B P

270 Lupulus mas, C B P.

271 Lychnis orientalis longifolia, nervofa, purpurafcente flore, Inft. Cor

272 Lycopodium Sabinæ facie, Flor. Jen

273 Medica orbiculata, fructu fpinofo, Inft. R H.

*274 Molucca fpinofa, Inft R H.

275 Myrtus latifolia Romana, C B P.

276 Olea fativa, C. B P.

277 Paliurus, Dod

278 Polium erectum tenuifolium flore albo capitulo breviori, Inft. R. H.

279 Sambucus racemofa rubra, C B P

280 Scrophularia ruta canina dicta, C B P.

280 Sorbus fativa, C. B. P.

281 Staphylodendron Math.

282 Thalictrum pratenfe anguftifolium, C B P.

283 Tinus fecundus, Clufii Hift.

284 Trifolium montanum anguftiffimum fpicatum, C B P

285 Vitex foliis anguftioribus cannabis modo difpofitis, C B. P.

286 Zizyphus, Dod

287 Zizyphus fylveftris, C. B P

Plants of HUNGARY.

288 Apocynum majus Syriacum rectum caule viridi flore ex albido, Pit B.

289 Armeria prolifera, C B P.

290 Afclepias latifolia, flore flavefcente

291 Afphodelus albus non ramofus, C B P.

292 After montanus Hirfutus, Lob. Icon.

293 Blattaria purpurea, C. B P

294 Campanula nemorofa anguftifolia magno flore, Major Inft R.

295 Cerinthe quorundam minus, flavo flore, C B P.

296 Clematitis five flammula furrecta alba, C. B. P.

297 Clematitis cærulea erecta, C. B P.
298 Cytisus hirsutus flore luteo purpurascente, C. B. P.
299 Echium vulgare, C B P.
300 Eryngium vulgare, C. B P.
301 Fraxinella, Cluf.
302 Fraxinus florifera botryoides, Mor Hort. Reg. Blaf.
303 Galeopsis procerior fœtida spicata, Inst. R. H.
304 Genista tinctoria, C B P.
305 Gramen murorum, spica longissima, Ger. Emac.
306 Juncus capitulis tomentosis, C. B P
307 Lilium convallium latifolium, C. B. P.
308 Linum sylvestre, C. B P
309 Mayz, C. B. P.
310 Melisa humilis latifolia, maximo flore purpurascente, Inst R. H.
311 Milium semine albo, C B P.
* 312 Milium Indicum arundinaceum Sorgo nominatum, C. B. P
313 Opulus Ruelii.
314 Orobanche major garyophyleum olens, C B P
315 Panicum Germanicum sive panicula minori, C. B. P.
316 Pseudoacacia vulgaris, Inst R. H.
317 Pulsatilla folio crassiore & majore flore, C B P
318 Staphylodendron, Math.
319 Tithymalus foliis pini, fortè Pityusa Dioscoridis, C. B. P.

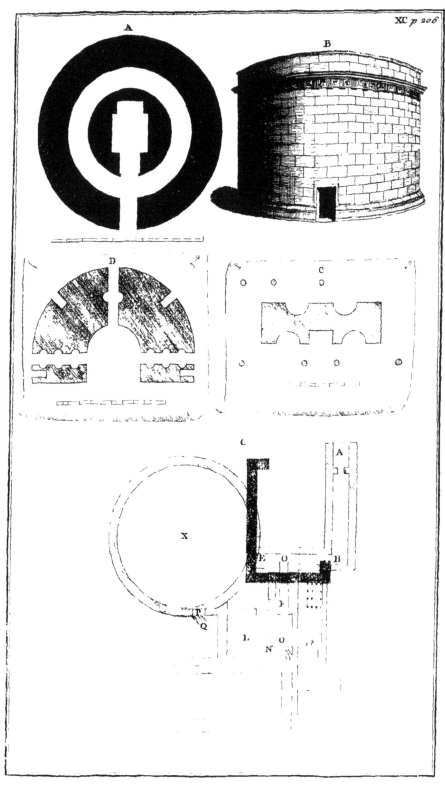

A PLAN and VIEW of a SEPULCHRAL MONUMENT at GAETA, PLANS of an
ANTIENT BAGNIO at ROME and of some RUINS at AUGST

A FRAGMENT of an OBELISK at ROME.

ΒΑΣΙΛΕΥΣ ΜΙΘΡΑΔΑΤΗΣ

ΕΥΠΑ ᵐ ᴺᴬ ΩΡΤRΙΕΝ·ΟΤΟΥ

ΥΜΛΛΣΙΟΥΕΥΠΑ ΤΟΡΙΣ ΤΑΙΣ

ΓΥΦΑ ΔΙΑꝫΩΖΕ

An ANTIENT VASE found at ANTIUM

A

DESCRIPTION

O F

The *EAST*, &c.

BOOK the Fourth

Obfervations on fome parts of EUROPE.

CHAP. I.

Of Messina.

FROM Cephalema I landed at Meffina, on the thirteenth of No-The Faro
vember, one thoufand feven hundred and forty, paffing part ofof Meffina.
that famous ftreight, which was called by the antients *Fretum Sicu-*
lum, and by the Italians at this day the Faro of Meffina, from the light-
houfe either at that city, or on the promontory *Pelorum*, and by the
mariners of thefe parts it is called the Vere. This ftreight was computed
to be fifteen miles long, and about a mile and a half broad in the narroweft part; the firft entrance from the eaft, into the current which
runs here, as the tide, according to the moon, is at Spartaventi, which is
the old promontory *Leucopetra*, however, this is not properly what the
antients underftood to be the ftreight, for it is computed to be thirty miles
from Meffina, but probably, according to them, the entrance of the
Sicilian ftreight was about the road which is called Fofla di St
Joanni, where it is wideft, being now computed about twelve
broad in the wideft part, the other entrance, which is from the
north, is between cape Peloro in Sicily, the old promontory *Pelorum*,
and a cape in Calabria, called Coda del Volpe [The Fox's Tail] which
feems to be the promontory *Cenis* of the antients, where the paffage is
computed only a mile and a half, which is the moft that it can be at

Vol. II Part II.   D d d   the

the ſouthern point, which makes the port of Meſſina Near the little cape,
called by the Italians Il bracio di S° Rinieri, the famous whirlpool is
ſeen, called by the antients Charybdis, which was, and is to this day, ſo
dangerous, that at certain times, when the tide runs ſtrong there is ſuch
an eddy current as will ſuck in ſmall veſſels, and is very dangerous
even to great ones On this head of land there is a high tower with a
light-houſe, and a ſmall ſquare fortification round it Whatever was
ſucked in by this pool was carried under water by the violence of the
current to the ſhoar of Tauromenium, now called Taormina, about thirty
miles to the ſouth, which for that reaſon had the name among the Greeks,
of the Dunghill ['Η κοπρία] ſo that every thing was carried by the current to
that part, where the land turns to make the old cape Argennum, now called
S Aleſſo, and, if I miſtake not, has the name of Santa Croce among
mariners, it was here the Spaniſh fleet, was ſeen by the Engliſh, who
were in Meſſina in one thouſand ſeven hundred and eighteen, and the
latter made towards the enemy, who moſt of them run aſhore about Ca-
tania Reggio is about a mile further to the ſouth than Meſſina, from which
place the ſhoar ſets out to the weſt to make the cape oppoſite to Pellorum,
and the ſtreight being narrow at cape ſaint Rinieri, and the Italian ſhoar
ſtill extending further weſt, is the reaſon of the danger obſerved by the
antients of running on the rock Scylla, when they endeavoured to avoid
Charybdis, for Scylla is the rock of that promontory which is oppoſite
to Pellorum, and is ſaid to be about four miles to the north of cape
Ceni, which, I ſuppoſe, is the ſouthern cape of the head of land, as
Scylla ſeems to be the northern one, in order to paſs this ſtreight, they
always take a pilot, though the people of Italy do not eſteem it ſo dangerous as our ſailors, who avoid paſſing this way as much as poſ-
ſible, and yet as well as I could judge, the rock of Scylla is not further
caſt than cape Saint Rinieri and if ſo, there muſt be much art to
ſteer a ſhip where the current is ſo ſtrong, and there are two dangerous
places which lie in a manner in a line from north to ſouth, one being
the whirlpool, and the other the rock Cape Saint Rinieri is computed
about a ſmall mile from the preſent city, being at the entrance into the
harbour It is ſaid that Orion, in the year one thouſand four hundred
and thirty five of the world built a city on it, and called it Zancle, probably from Zanclus, then king of Sicily There is a ſilver medal of this city, or rather ſtruck by the Meſſanians, in memory of their
mother city, with a fiſh on it, which, they ſay, is called Spacla, and
there is this inſcription on it DANKLE, and as it is in Latin characters,
was probably coined after the Romans came into Sicily, which may alſo
furniſh ſome obſervations with regard to the orthography. In the
twenty-ninth Olympiad, Anaxilus of Meſſena in Peloponneſus, and tyrant of Regium, having called over many of his countrymen, deſtroyed Zancle, and built the city of Meſſina, which he called from
their own city, there are medals of this place, with a head ſuppoſed to
be that of Anaxilus, who had been for a long time victor in the Olympic
games, the reverſe of it is a chariot and horſes Meſſina recovered its liberty,
and was governed as a republic The inhabitants received the Mamer-
tini into their city in the fourteenth Olympiad, which were either a people of Locri, or Samos, who inhoſpitably murdered all the old inhabi-

ſ   tants,

tants, and this new people called the city and every thing after their own name. This happened about the time of the Carthaginian wars, and there are medals with a head on one side, and a man holding a horse on the other, with their name on it, MAMLP-TINΩN. This city was remarkably faithful to the Romans, and as the reward of it, was made a confederate city with them, there being but one more of that kind in Sicily, which was Tauromenium, it afterwards recovered the antient name of Messina, and has ever since followed the fate of Sicily. The present city called Messina, is situated on the sea side, and a little way up the foot of the mountain, which is to the west of it, the port is entered from the east at the north east corner, the entrance being near a quarter of a mile broad, the port stretches about half a mile to the south between the town and that land, which was the spot of the antient Zancle. The beautiful quay extends on the west side, the whole length of this basin, and appears like a small segment of a circle, the houses are four stories high, all built in the same manner, with beautiful window cases of hewn stone, and there are several entrances to the street that lead from it, with gateways like triumphal arches, and inscriptions over them, which all together make it one of the most beautiful views in the world. On the north and south side of the entrance there are two modern fortifications, that to the south consists of four great bastions, and is called saint Salvadore, it was built by Charles the fifth, on the spot where there was a convent of monks of the order of saint Basil, which was made an abbey by Roger count of Sicily. To the south east of this there is a very convenient Lazaretto on an island now divided into three parts by artificial canals, the whole being built round a large court, which is separated from the other islands by these canals, there are warehouses here, and other great conveniences for performing quarantine. To the south of this is the strong citadel fortified with double ramparts; this, and the other forts before mentioned, so command the port, that it is almost impossible to take Messina by sea; and tho' there are forts on the sides of the hill which might be easily taken by land, yet they are in such a situation, that the houses of the city must be destroyed before they can arrive at the citadel, however, being within cannon shot from the hills, the citadel may easily be demolished from them. The prince Perlinga has a curious collection of antient Camœos, as they were procured by the way of Venice, they probably belonged to the empresses of the east, for they are made up in necklaces, and other ornaments for the ladies, like those I saw afterwards at Hesse Castle.

CHAP. II

Of the places between REGGIO and NAPLES.

Reggio   I Croſſed over from Meſſina to Reggio, the antient Rhegium in the
the country of the Bruttii, now called the Further Calabria Saint Paul
came to this town in his voyage from Cæſarea to Rome[1], and they
now ſhew a pillar at the church of his name, near which, they ſay, he
preached, and have ſome legend concerning it. About that place they
dig up many columns and antient ſtones, and at the north eaſt corner
of the walls there is a ruin which is ſaid to be remains of the temple
of Caſtor and Pollux I obſerved that ſome part of the walls of the
city were very antient, caſed with hewn ſtone, ſet up an end, and laid
flat alternately Calanna to the north eaſt of Reggio, ſeems to be the
antient Columna, the river Cenis to be the preſent Cratais, and the cape
which is near it, was probably the promontory Cenis

On the eighteenth of December, we ſailed from Meſſina ten miles to
the north eaſt to Scylla, which is a ſmall town with a caſtle, inhabited
by the prince of Scylla, it is ſituated on a ſmall rocky promontory,
which ends in a point, and there are ſome rocks extending from it
into the ſea, which are thoſe that were ſo much dreaded by the antients, and when they bore off from them, they were in danger of
falling into the whirlpool called Charybdis, which has been thought to
be near Scylla, though, upon a ſtrict examination, I could find no other
part that anſwered the deſcription but that which I have already mentioned near Meſſina, and is now taken for it by the people of the
country

From Scylla we ſet out by land for Naples, a journey which very
few ſtrangers have undertaken, we went through Bagnari, where the
duke of the place reſides, they have a great trade there in an export of
bouds and wood for hoops We arrived at Palma, which may be Mal-
lus of the Itinerary, and lay at a gentleman's houſe, where, after the
eaſtern manner, none of the family ſupped with us The trade of this
place conſiſts in oil of olives, and Seminara a place near it is famous for
the ſweeteſt ſort, probably the harbour of this place was the antient
port Medama The nineteenth we went on, paſſing through fine olive
yards, and a beautiful country to the plain, which, according to the maps,
is on the bay of Gioia, the river Murro or Metauro, runs through this
plain, which muſt be the antient Metaurus The town of Gioia is beautifully ſituated on a height Six miles further we came to Roſano, which
ſtands finely on a riſing ground We deſcended to the plain, croſſed the
river Meſuri or Metimno, paſſed by S. Petro di Mileto, and afterwards
a mile to the left of Mileto, which is a biſhop's ſee Niotere is
to the weſt of it on the ſea, which retains its antient name, and is
placed by the Itinerary eighteen miles from Vibo, which is thought to
be Monte Leone Paſſing through the uneven country which extends to

[1] Acts XXII 13

2   the

the weſt, and makes the large cape Vaticano on which Tropeia is ſituated   We arrived at Monte Leone, which is a town very advantagiouſly ſituated on the weſt ſide of a round hill, it is thought to be the antient inland town of Hippo, afterwards called Vibo Valentia, which was made a Roman colony; and this conjecture is the more probable, as the port which belongs to it at the diſtance of three miles is called Bivona, which muſt be the port of Hercules, as the gulph of St Euphemia is the antient bay of Vibo   I ſaw at Monte Leone ſome antient inſcriptions, and begun to be ſenſible that we were got into a very bad country for travelling, as in this large town we could only be accommodated with a miſerable inn.

The road being very bad from this place to Cozenza I was adviſed to hire a litter, and on the twentieth we went over a large plain, extending to the bay of St Euphemia   Under Monte Leone we croſſed a rivulet called Langeto, which, I ſuppoſe, is the ſame as Angitola   We went in all twelve miles to Oſteria Fondaclero, the firſt poſt from Monte Leone, and travelled four miles further to the large river Delamata, probably the antient Lametus, which, with another river to the eaſt, is the bounds between the further and nether Calabria.   We left St Biagio to the right, which might be the antient town Lametia or Clampetia, we came to the north ſide of the bay near cape Cartajoue, and going by the ſea ſide arrived at Caſtiglione, which is a village conſiſting of many ſcattered houſes, it is called thirty miles from Monte Leone, and may be Ad Turres of the Itinerary, in which it is computed to be twenty one miles from Vibo.   On the twenty firſt, going by the ſea ſide we came in four miles to the river Savuto, which muſt be the river Sabbatum of the Itinerary, it is a deep rapid ſtream, ſo that we were obliged to hire a man to conduct us over on the horſe which carried our baggage   About a fortnight after, I had an account at Naples, that the poſtman paſſing this river ſoon after on a greater flood, was carried with his mule into the ſea, and both were loſt   In three miles we came to a rivulet, probably the Turbido, and a mile further to the great torrent Oliva, travelling five miles along the vale, we croſſed it very often, this may be the river Ocinarus   Coming in between the Apennine mountains, which run the whole length of Italy, we paſſed under Aiello, ſituated with its caſtle on a great height to the right, and aſcending up the mountains, we ſaw La Terrata to the left on the high mountains, which may be the antient Terina   We deſcended to the village of Lago in a bottom between the hills, where I was civilly received in a good private houſe, and ſent out for every thing I wanted, there being no inn   On the twenty-ſecond we aſcended about four miles, and afterwards deſcended for eight to Coſenza, ſituated on the Crati, the antient Criſhus, ſeventeen miles from the neareſt port to the weſt called Lucito, and forty by the road they go to the eaſtern ſea, moſtly winding by the river Crati   This town is the antient Coſentia, which was the capital of the country of the Bruttii   I hired horſes here to go towards Naples, and on the twenty-third travelled, according to their computation, forty miles along the plain, and aſcended the hills to a poor town called Caſtia Villari, where we had no accommodations but an old empty houſe This may be Caprasia, or Capraras of the Itinerary, twenty eight miles from Cofentia On the twenty-fourth we went on, came into the valley of St Martin, and travelled about thirty miles, having a difficult defcent to the Fiumera of Mercurio, and came to Lavria. We were now in the nether principality of the kingdom of Naples, and in the antient Lucania, the mountains are of a good foil, well peopled, and the villages all over them are built like little towns. On the twenty-fifth we paffed by a fmall lake not a mile in circumference, came to Rovelo Nero, and leaving the Appenine mountains, we defcended into the vale of Diana, and went about ten miles in it to Salavilla On the twenty-fixth we travelled twenty miles in an exceeding bad road to a good country inn, having paffed by a place where there is a toll paid, near which the river Negro, the old Silarus (the bounds between Lucania and the country of the Picentini) runs about half a mile under the hill, and comes out again, which is marked in the map near Polla On the twenty-feventh we paffed by Ducheffa, and arrived at Evoli, here I took poft horfes, paffed thro' Salerno, the antient Salernum, where I faw fome infcriptions, and coming into Campania felix had a glorious view of Naples, and arrived at that city Having undertaken this difficult inconvenient journey, of very little curiofity, to avoid the greater trouble of going by fea in a felucca

---

CHAP. III.

Of Sorrento, and the iflands of Capri, Procita and Ischia.

Sorrento

I Made a voyage from Naples to Sorrento, the antient Surrentum, which is finely fituated a confiderable way up the fide of the antient promontory of Minerva, to the fouth of the bay of Naples, at the diftance of about five miles from Amalfi on the other fide of the cape, where, they fay, they have the body of St Andrew The country abounds in lemon and orange gardens, and vineyards, having formerly been famous for wine To the eaft of the town there is a very deep foffee, or cleft in the rock, faid to be two hundred palms, of nine inches in depth. Near the archbifhop's houfe there are feveral infcriptions and fine reliefs, and two antient altars · Further to the weft I obferved remains of high brick arches over the foffee We went on to the point at the cape of Sorrento, where there is a little high peninfula, on which there are remains of cifterns, and there feems to have been a caftle on the fpot Up the hill further to the fouth there are fourteen arched cifterns about twenty feet wide, and fifty feet long, communicating with one another by arched door places, and there is an opening at the end of each of them, by which one may look into them Going to the other end of the town we faw feveral cifterns behind a palace, they fay there are four and thirty of them, that they are fifty palms wide, and two hundred and twenty long There are feveral grottos at the Dominicans, which we had not the opportunity of feeing

From

From this place we failed to the ifland of Capri, the antient Caprea, to which ^{Capri} Tiberius retired fo difhonourably from the care of the public, and conducted himfelf in fo fhameful a manner, that he began to be a burthen to himfelf, as well as to mankind The only town in the ifland is fituated a great way up between two rocky hills, of which, and of a little plain ground between them, a confiderable height from the fea, the ifland confifts We afcended to the top of the eaftern hill, where there are very fine lofty cifterns built of brick, which are divided into feveral parts ; and without doubt, there were other buildings over them . To the weft below thefe there are fome others. We returned down part of this hill, and afcended another fummit to the north, where there are other cifterns, and below them a long ruinous arch. We then went to the north weft part of the ifland to the place where, they fay, the palace of Tiberius ftood on a plain fpot on the north fide of the hill, at a confiderable height over the fea, there remain only a few arches, and fome walls of terraces, to the weft there are confiderable ruins, which are partly on the fea. It is a very fine fituation, from which there is a view of all the coaft of Naples, and of the iflands of Procita and Ifchia, to which I went from Baiæ The ifland of Procita, the old Prochyta, is _{Procita} about feven miles in circumference, it belongs to the king, and is, they fay, inhabited by ten thoufand people . It is one of the fineft fpots I ever faw, being almoft all improved with gardens and vineyards At the fouth weft part there is a wood called La Caccia, where the king's partriges are preferved, the town on the eaft fide rifes beautifully up the fide of the hill to the caftle, which is the king's houfe.

We failed to the town of Ifchia, in the ifland of that name, which is _{Ifchia.} the antient Inarime, or Ænaria, mentioned by Homer, there is a high rock to the fouth eaft of the town, they have built a caftle on it, to which there is a way by a bridge, and a curious paffage cut thro' the rock. About a mile to the north of the town are fome baths, which, if I miftake not, are a mixture of falt and fulphur, there are two fprings, one being ftronger than the other Moft part of the way to them is between black rocks, which appear as if there had been an earthquake there, and an eruption of fire We went on to the north, and came to the Stufe [Stoves], called Caftiglione, of which there are feveral in this ifland For where there is a hot air they convey it by earthen pipes into a little grot, in which the patient fits and fweats, and thefe grottos they call Stufe : Further on to the left are the Stufe Ciccata We went to a large village where there are a great number of baths which have different names, one called Dente, becaufe it is good for the teeth, Gurfitello is proper for diforders in the head, one is called Ferro, another Oro, and a third Argento, by reafon that they find thofe particular minerals prevail in them ; and there is one of them which is called Timore We went round towards the fouth weft part of the ifland to Teftacca, where there is a ftove for fweating At the Sollatara near Naples, thofe who are curious in natural hiftory will obferve a natural fal armoniac, which, if I miftake not, is made by the fteam of a hot water which incrufts the ftones laid over it with that falt, which it is faid by naturalifts cannot be made without animal falts that may be in the earth The grotto on the fouth fide of the lake of Averno, called the

grot

grot of the Sibyl, I imagine to have been a paffage under the hill, as well as the grotto of St Peter, which goes into the hill from Cumæ, and might have a paffage out to the lake; though I did not fee the latter, and any one who examines it may judge whether it is probable that it ferved for that purpofe. Arco Felice, on the top of the hill, feems to have been built to defend the pafs.

CHAP. IV.

Of mount VESUVIUS, PORTICI, BENAVENTO, and NOLA.

Mount Ve fu ius

I Went twice up to the top of mount Vefuvius, I alfo defcended the hole, which is at the top of that fummit, and may be near a mile in circumference, there being only a narrow path round, at the top of it This hole is full of fmoak, which is fo thick that it reflected my fhadow from the fetting fun, the wind blew in fuch a manner when I went up the fecond time, that I could fometimes fee down to the bottom of the hole, I conjectured that the defcent is about half a quarter of a mile At one place near the top there is a hot fand, and about three quarters of the way down a fulphureous eruption; and when I was hot in my return, I found it very difficult to breath as I paffed by it, there are large ftones at the bottom of this hole, and at the north weft part of it, is another hole about a hundred feet in diameter, the fides of it are almoft perpendicular, I could not fee the bottom, not by reafon of the fmoak, but becaufe it would have been dangerous to have approached near enough to it, and afking my conductors whether I could defcend into it, they told me, that if I would come another day, they would bring ropes and let me down, but I did not find that any one had ever defcended into it. I apprehend that this hole was made, or very much altered in the laft eruption. I took fome pains to obferve the feveral ftreams of melted matter which run from mount Vefuvius at feveral eruptions, they look black like melted metal and the cinders of a forge, fuch a current they call in Italian Lava, I firft obferved them as I went round the bay by water to Capri. The firft I faw comes into the fea a little to the weft of Portici, which run in one thoufand fix hundred and thirty one, as appears by an infcription in the road to that place, the fecond is to the weft of Torre dello Greco, which fome faid run thirty-five years ago, when I went by land I faw a third at Torre dello Greco, which it is faid run twenty-four years ago, the fourth it is Torre, is that which run at the great eruption on the fifth of May, one thoufand feven hundred and thirty feven, and continued to flow for four days, the current is forty paces broad, and fix feet deep, it came to the convent and church called Madonna delli Carmi, and broke down an arch which fupported a gallery, entering the church a little way, where it is now feen, they have hewn it away like a foffee

round

round the buildings, that the weight of it might not hurt the walls, for here it is fifteen feet deep, it is a speckled grey stone, which receives a fine polish, but the upper part is yellow, and softer, being mixed in veins with the other; it divided at the church into two streams; one stopped at the west end of the church; the other stream, which is less, run to the south west through a vineyard, and into the road that leads to the sea, where it stopped about a furlong from the sea, the people say it is still warm, but I thought it was only the heat of the sun. They say they can get some silver out of the stone, but that it does not answer the expence; at the time of this eruption a grotto in the garden of the convent was full of smoak, and a monk going into it some time afterwards dropped down dead, and, they say, his body being left there some days, did not corrupt. We returned to the boat, and saw a fifth stream to the east of La Torre, which run in one thousand six hundred and thirty-five, according to an inscription which is set up, it is a very broad stream, and is the only one of these five which runs from the north, the others running from the east to the south

When I went by land I saw a sixth to the east of the Camaldoli, and, if I do not mistake, it went to the sea. A seventh is half a mile further to the east, where two streams join, which ran at different times, but they told me did not go to the sea, the western one running further than the other. The eighth went to the sea, to the west of the church called La Parochi di Tre Cafe A ninth, a little way to the east, did not go to the sea The tenth divides into two parts, to the west of a large village called Bosco, and did not run to the sea These are the chief streams to the west and south, they say there are many others to the east and north, all of them have broke out, chiefly about the plain spot, which is half way up the hill, where I observed there was much smoak.

Some time ago in digging at Portici, they found ruins under ground, Portici and since that they have dug in search of antiquities, there are two entrances to the works, one by a well, and another from a hollow way to the west of it, by which I went into it, and saw some fresco paintings In a court of the king's palace here, which is kept locked, I saw several fragments of statues and inscriptions, some of which were Greek In the small theatre there are some statues of men, most of the heads of them are bald: In a room where they repair the antiquities, I saw some urns and beautiful feet of tables, some coarse mosaics and fresco paintings of boys. Many other things have been found here, which are not commonly shown, but they design to have them all drawn, engraved, and published This is thought to be the antient Herculanium, part of which was destroyed by an earthquake ' I saw here before the convent of the Augustinians a milliary with the number six on it

About seventeen miles from Naples in the way to Benevento, we came to the streight of Arpaia, which leads into a valley between the hills, this seems to be part of the country of the Samnites, to the north west there is another passage out of this valley, through which there is a road that leads to Capoua, which is not so narrow, this I take to be the famous Furca Caudina, to which the Romans were drawn by the Samnites, and were obliged shamefully to surrender themselves. As soon as we entered the vale, which is every way encompassed with hills, we saw Ariola on a hill to the north at the end of the vale, and another village on a height to the north east at the foot of mount Sarchio, under which we went up the hills into the territory of Benevento belonging to the Pope

Benevento   At the gate of the city of Benevento I saw a statue of a bull of red granite, six feet and a half long, and three feet high, which is set on a pedestal, and there is a modern inscription on it   At the archbishop's house there is a front of a marble coffin set in a wall, with a fine relief on it, in which is represented a woman sitting in a chair, and the hunting of a wild boar, there are other reliefs here, and at the cathedral there is a fine one of a boar dressed for the sacrifice, with a fillet over his body, and flowers hanging down from his ears, and below the cathedral is an obelisk of red granite, about a foot and a half square at bottom, there are hieroglyphics on it, among which are lions, a man sitting on some of them   At a Franciscan convent without the town there are several ruins, particularly an arch built of brick and stone, which from the ground seemed to be the remains of a circus, and at the mill there are ruins of a bridge, where there are some imperfect inscriptions   All travellers ought to go from Naples to Benevento to see the arch of Trajan, which for its architecture and sculpture is one of the finest remains of antiquity

In our return we left the road to Naples, and went eight miles to Nola, which is about six miles to the east of mount Vesuvius, here Marcellus was first able to make head against Hannibal, and in this city the emperor Augustus died   There are some inscriptions about the town, and they dig up many Hetruscan vases here of the finest sort, the more ordinary kind being commonly found at Capua   At the last eruption the ashes of mount Vesuvius covered the city, and when I was there I saw them on each side of the street   The whole country between this city and the mountain was covered with ashes, the trees were all blasted, a great number of them killed, and the vineyards were almost entirely destroyed

---

CHAP. V.

Observations from NAPLES to FLORENCE.

Gaeta   HAVING drawn and taken the dimensions of the sepulchral monument on the hill at Gaeta, a plan and view of it are engraved in the nineteenth plate at A, B   Those who go to Rome ought particularly to enquire for all the statues which have been lately dug up at Villa Hadriani, among which the principal are the two centaurs, and the mosaic work of two partriges, which are the finest that have been seen made of natural stones   They should well examine the collections placed by the late pope in the capitol, and greatly augmented by the present, Benedict the fourteenth, they ought to buy the engravings of all the

works

works done by the late pope, and view thofe things, of which there is no account in the writers of Rome. Among the antiquities of the capitol there is a bronze vafe, lately found in the port of Antium, which is engraved in the ninety-fecond plate, from a drawing fent by abbot Revillas. There is an infcription round the infide of the vafe, which was traced of, as it is engraved on it, and fhews exactly the circumference of the vafe, according to the obfervations of the learned profeffor Ward of Grefham college this vafe is fuppofed to have been the prefent of Mithridates Eupator, king of Pontus, to the Eupatoriſtæ of the Gymnafium of Delos, thofe officers are fuppofed to have been called fo in honour of this prince, and confequently the vafe was brought from Delos to Antium. The ninety-firft plate fhews the four fides of a fragment of red Ægyptian granite in the ifland of the Tiber at Rome, it is before the entrance to the convent of faint Bartolomeo; and is fuppofed to be part of an obelisk which was erected there before the temple of Æfculapius, the fifh, centaurs, and feveral other particulars, are remarkable in thefe hieroglyphics. The plan C, in the ninetieth plate, was exactly meafured by abbot Revillas, it is of a building found under the garden of the convent of faint Alexis in Rome, of which he was abbot, it is fuppofed to be the remains of fome baths A, B, E, is an aqueduct to it, F, O, the defcent to the aqueduct, the height of the aqueduct to the top of the arch is eleven palms, and from the bottom of the ftairs to the new apartments above fifteen palms. G, H, is the wall of the prefent library. The apartment I had in it a mofaic pavement of fmall pieces of marble. N, O, is a little aqueduct which comes out of the wall N, and goes under the pavement of the room L. P is an opening like a door, under which there is a fmall aqueduct Q. Q, X, is a round bagnio.

The prefent pope has begun to put up miliary ftones in the road from Rome, and I faw fome about Perugia which were fet up above a hundred years ago. Spello the antient Hifpellum, two miles *Spello* from Fuligno, in the way to Affife, is fituated on a fmall round hill at the foot of the Appennine mountain, I obferved remains of the old walls of fmall hewn ftones which appear very neat. There are fome antient infcriptions in the town, among them is a long one of the time of Conftantine. At the foot of the hill I faw remains of the antient amphitheatre. We came into one of the fineft plains in Italy, over which Affife is fituated to the eaft, and Perugia to the weft.

In the piazza at Affife, the antient Affifum, there is an antient por *Affife* tico before the church called La madonna della piazza di Minerva, it confifts of fix fluted Corinthian pillars, which fupport an angular pediment, they are ten feet five inches in circumference, and fix feet fix

* It would be an addition to the tour which is commonly taken in Italy, to hire horfes Civita Caftellana to go to Capriroli, Orti, Orvietto, Cortora, and then to take poft horfes to Arezzo, Eu gubio, Perugia, Affife, Todi, Narni, and fo to Oricto, and to make an excurfion from Euro to Urbin And thofe who would make a curious journey, and would not regard the want of accommodations, might make a tour, which I believe has not been done by any travellers, and that is to

go along the eaftern coaft to Jurento, from which city there is a fine road to Naples, and they might make excurfions to Cuma, and to feveral other places remarkable in hiftory I have been informed that the plain in which Rieti is fituated, where Velpafian was born, is one of the moft beautiful fpots in the world Volterra alfo a place of great antiquity, which would afford matter to gratify the curiofity of a traveller, and is but very few

inches

inches apart These pillars ftand on pedeftals, which are very particular, as the lower member of the cornifh is worked in dentils; there are figns of an infcription in the frieze, the letters of which feem to have been of fome metal There are fome infcriptions in the piazza. This place is famous for the birth of St Francis and St Clare, who are both buried here in different churches The tomb of Euculæa queen of Cyprus is in the church where St Francis was buried At the foot of the hill is the firft convent that was founded of the order of St Francis, it is called Madonna Degli Angeli, where St Francis lived and died.

Perugia Perugia is a fine city, and has feveral beautiful churches in it; the citadel was built by Paul the third to curb the city, which had been in a rebellion There are two large piazzas, in which are the brafs ftatues of Julius the third, and Sixtus the fifth, there is a fine old Gothic gate to the town, which is in a ruftic ftyle In the way to Cortona we paffed by the

Lake Thrafimene lake of Perugia, called Thrafimene by the antients, famous for the defeat of the Romans by Hannibal There is a narrow pafs at Pefignano, and on confidering the ground, and the account of this battle, the Roman army feems to have been at D, in the ninety-third plate, which is a fmall plain, Hannibal's troups to the eaft behind the hills at C, thofe to the weft behind the mountains at A, and a detachment might be fent from behind the hill B, to guard the pafs at Peffigniano. They have a notion that the battle was fought at Offaia, which is to the north weft of the lake.

Cortona At Cortona the collection of antiquities made by the academy ought to be feen I had a view from this city of the moraffy country called

Arezzo Chianapalude At Arezzo there is a fine piazza, and fome infcriptions in the portico, the windows of the cathedral church are beautifully painted, there are two pillars of porphyry at the entrance of it, and before it a ftatue

Florence in white marble of the grand duke Ferdinand. At Florence the room in the gallery is not commonly feen, in which there is a ftatue of the hermaphrodite fleeping, like that in the Villa Borghefi at Rome The fitting coloffal ftatue of mount Appennine at Pratolino, which is built of ftone, and is the work of John of Bologna, is a very curious thing · If it was ftanding it is computed that it would be feventy feet high. Near St Pietro à Sievo in the way to Bologna is one of the four convents of the ftrict order of La Trappe, where any one may fee the practice of the fevereft rules in the monaftic life, they are famous for making the beft fealing wax in Italy There are remains at Lucca of an amphitheatre, two views of which may be feen in the ninety-fourth and ninety-fifth plates, and in the town houfe there is a fine relief of a curule chair. At Maffaciucoli about eight miles eaft of Lucca are ruins of a temple of Hercules, a view of it may be feen in the ninety fixth plate Going from Florence to Leghorn we paffed over the river Elfa, into which a rivulet runs, called the Seni, the waters of which, they fay, incruft over wood with a fort of ftone Near the Elfa I faw caftle Fiorentino, which was the habitation of the anceftors of Boccace.

Cortona

Perugino

Ossaia

A *MAP* of the LAKE THRASIM

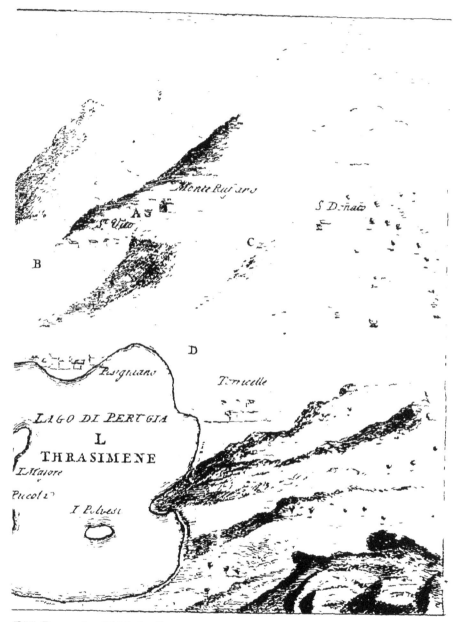

Monte Rufaro

S Donato

A

St Vito

B

C

D

Pasighiano

Torricelle

LAGO DI PERUGIA

L

THRASIMENE

L Maiore

Pucola

I Polvesi

ENE, and *THE COUNTRY* about It

A VIEW of an AMPHITHEATRE at LUCCA

A *VIEW* of the otherside of the AMPHITHEATRE
at
LUCCA

RUINS of a TEMPLE of HERCULES at

HASSA CICCOLI

CHAP. VI.

Obſervations from FLORENCE to the confines of GERMANY.

IN the way to Bologna we croſſed the river Sieve, to the ſouth eaſt of which, towards the Arno, is the country called Caſentino, which is thought to be a corruption from Cluſentinum, and it is ſuppoſed that this was the road Hannibal took from Cluſium Novum, and ſeems to be the way mentioned by Strabo, as the military way from Gaul into Etruria, the other more eaſy and common way was by Ariminum, and through Umbria, but Hannibal found that way was well guarded, and ſo he took this road, and met Flaminius at the lake Thraſimene. We paſſed through Scarperia, famous for cutlery ware, and by the valley of Muſello, noted for producing good wine and cheeſe. At Modena the Secchia Rapita ought to be ſeen on account of the hiſtory which relates to it. At Parma the theatre is eſteemed the fineſt in the world; and in Palazzo del Giardino are fine paintings by many great hands, there is a college here for the education of the children of nobility, with excellent regulations, they come to it from Germany and all parts of Italy. The cupola of the cathedral here is painted by Corregio. *(marginal notes: Modena; Parma)*

At Piacenza the ſtatues of Alexander the firſt, and Ranuſio the firſt, dukes of Parma, and the reliefs about them, are very beautiful. A little above the place where we croſſed the Po, the Trebia falls into it; oppoſite to which is a plain called Campo Santo, where they have a tradition that Hannibal firſt defeated the Romans. Pavia, the antient Ticinum, is famous for its univerſity, in the manner of living, and in the regularity of their habits, they are more like the univerſities of England than any I have ſeen, the different colleges are diſtinguiſhed by the different colours of their gowns, and they take only the doctors degree, in ſeven years, and then leave the univerſity, there are in all eight colleges. To the weſt of the Benedictine convent is a narrow valley or hollow ground, which may be the old bed of the Po, as Ticinum is mentioned on that river. The two famous lawyers Baldus and Alciatus are buried at the Franciſcans, and at the Auguſtinians, they ſay, they have the body of ſaint Auſtin, the great Boetius is alſo buried in their church, and Lionel, duke of Clarence, ſon of Edward the third of England, was interred in this church in one thouſand three hundred ſixty eight, and afterwards removed by order of the council of Trent. Richard de la Pole, duke of Suffolk, in Henry the eighth's time, was buried here. There are alſo many other monuments of perſons who were killed in the battle near the Carthuſian convent in the way to Milan, in which Francis the firſt of France was taken priſoner, and near this town Didier king of Lombardy fell into the hands of Charlemagne. The fine Carthuſian convent in the way to Milan is worthy of the curioſity of ſtrangers, who ſhould not fail to hear the echo at a country palace near that city. *(marginal notes: Piacenza; Pavia)*

I ſaw an execution at Milan, which was remarkable for the decency and ſolemnity of it, three were hanged, and two were broke on the wheel, as they call it In the procession first a cross was carried, then came the community of the dead, consisting of cavaliers or nobles dressed in a short muslin surplice, tied round with a girdle which had white tostles to it, over this was a white short cloak which hung behind the right arm, a large crucifix being worked on the left side of it; and they wore white hats· Then came the priests, and the criminals, who, if I do not mistake, were drawn on sledges A stage was erected, and to the west of it a gallery, those to be hanged were brought singly on the sledges, one of the nobles holding a crucifix before the face of the criminal; whilst the offices were performing, a noble held his cloak over him, and, I suppose, that part of it which had a crucifix embroidered on it, when all was finished, he was sprinkled with holy water, and conducted up the ladder, one of the nobles first putting a cover of muslin on his face with holes in it for the eyes and mouth, the nobleman going up on another ladder, and holding the crucifix before his eyes, this being over, another was brought, and the large crucifix was placed before the person who was hanged to hide him from the eyes of the person who was to be executed, the third, who had killed a priest, had his right hand cut off, and the stump was tied up in a cloth, that it might not sprinkle the people, when they were turned off the hangman put his feet on their shoulders to press them down, and others laid hold on their legs · They then proceeded to the execution of the two youths, who would have ravished a woman with child, and murdered her, a boy about eighteen was brought first on the stage, small ropes were fixed to it, and the person to be executed was laid on his back, his legs, hands, and neck were tied down to the stage, and a cavalier held the crucifix before his eyes, till the man struck his breast with the axle of a small wheel, and immediately another cut the throat, he then turned the wheel, and with the edge struck again on the breast, then on the thighs, legs and arms, and the man cut the throat a second time, by which the head was half cut off, then the other was executed, the nobles all the time making use of some short ejaculations, when this was done they untied them, and put them on a large wheel set up on the stage on a short pole ; one leg being put in between the spokes

Lago Majore
From Milan I went to Lago Majore, and to the Boromean islands, on the west side of the lake is Arona, where S Charles Boromeo was born, they have erected a colossal bronze statue of him, it is made of several pieces joined together, and, they say, that it is sixty braccia high, each of three palms or twenty-seven inches, but, I suppose, the pedestal is included, which is ten feet square, and seems to be about thirty feet high The two Boromean islands must be very delightful in summer, one is called Isola Bella, and is about half a mile in circumference, it has on it a fine palace and hanging gardens adorned with statues and water works Two miles to the south south east is Isola Madre, rather larger than the other, the house is very indifferent, there are hanging gardens on one side, and on another an aviary and grove The post for Geneva goes to Marguzzo on the lake, and from that place to Geneva in forty-eight hours, a journey which takes up four days at the ordinary rate of travelling.

At

At Como, on the lake of the same name, they have inscriptions to Como the honour of the two Plinies, who were of that city, and in the cathedral is the tomb of Jovius the famous historian Returning to Milan we passed through Barcasina, where they say St Peter the martyr was murdered by the hereticks The canal of Martesana, brought from the Adda to Milan, as it is said, by that great genius Lionardo da Vinci, deserves to be taken notice of as a very curious work, as it is carried in many parts much above the natural level of the ground Going to Lodi, we saw Lodi vecchio to the north, which is the antient Laus Lodi Pompeia Lodi is famous for its fine earthen ware like that of Delft, and for the best Parmesan cheese There is nothing very remarkable at Crema We went by Pizzighitone to Cremona, at the former place Francis the first was kept prisoner by Charles the fifth till he ordered him to Genoa, to be embarked for Spain Campi being a famous painter and architect of Cremona, has left several monuments of his genius in and about that city, and wrote also a description and history of Cremona Sixteen miles further north is a place called Labina, where it is thought Otho's army was vanquished by Vitellius I saw the convent of Benedetto, to the south of Mantoua, to great disadvantage, having been the head quarters of the king of Sardinia in the late wars, but it is a very magnificent building, the church, and especially the chapel and tomb of the countess Matilda, the great benefactress to the see of Rome, is very fine, it was founded by her grandfather on the spot where his palace stood In the parish church is the statue of Venerable Bede, with this inscription under it,

VEN. BEDA GALLIS ET ANGLIS PSALT MAR AUTHOR SEC. XIII

This country is famous for the defeat of the French and Sardinians by marshal Konigsegg, which in two or three days was followed by a defeat on the other side in the battle of Luzare, or Guastalla, occasioned, as it is said, by an engagement of one of the generals, contrary to express orders.

The inside of the old cathedral of Mantoua is of the architecture of Mantoua Julio Romano, and very fine, there are good paintings in it by Andrea Zan, and at the church of St Andrew there is an extraordinary bell In the church of St Sebastian there is a vase two feet square, and eighteen inches deep, it is used for the holy water, and seems to be very antient, on one side is a relief of a mountain cut with trees, over it FIDES, and below OAYMHOS There is also another antient vase, which serves for the same purpose in the church of saint Catharine, where there are some paintings of Julio Romano There are several valuable pictures in the ducal palace, and the palace Favourita without the town is much admired for its architecture There are in the court three or four broken statues, one is a trunk of a man in a coat of mail, finely adorned with reliefs At the palace De Te likewise there are some antient statues, but what it is most famous for is the fresco painting of Julio Romano, and it is said there are some of the school of Raphael, though others affirm, that they were done by Julio Romano when he was young Near the island of Te is the place where, they say, Virgil was born, and it is called Virgiliana. Mantoua, and the country about it, is governed by a council of two presidents, as many vice presidents, and four nobles,

under

under the governor of all the countries in Lombardy, which are subject to the house of Austria, who resides at Milan, there having been a governor here till the last peace was made.

At Villa Franca there is a wall built a considerable way from the castle to the east and south west, which seems to have been a military work. This country between Hostiglia and Verona is famous for many great actions. Some are of opinion that Marius gave the decisive battle here to the Germans and Cimbri, tho' historians are not agreed about it: There is also a tradition, that Sabinus Julianus, who would have usurped the empire, was overcome and slain here by the emperor Carinus: And Odoacer king of the Heruli Tucelingi who usurped the power in Italy, and vanquished Orestes and Augustulus, was himself beat by Theodoric king of the Ostrogoths, near the river Sontius, or Lysonzo, and rallying his forces here, was entirely defeated by Theodoric, after a battle that lasted for three days. And here Arnold duke of Bavaria, who had in a manner made himself king of Italy, and was proclaimed so by the people of Verona, was entirely defeated by Hugo Borgounone. Here also Lambert, son of Guido, king of Spoleto, was killed by Berengarius, with fourteen hundred Hungarians. And here the second Berengarius was killed and deprived of his kingdom by Rodoltus the Burgundian; so that this was the spot where they often contended for the liberty, or mastery of Italy to prevent the passage of the Po, which was always looked on as the great barrier and defence of that country.

Eight miles beyond Villa Franca is Buossolongo, or Gussolengo, most delightfully situated over that fine valley in which Verona stands. There is a beautiful altar at the church of St Valentine, adorned with festoons, held by cupids; those who travel this way may go to see some springs near Negarino, concerning which they have several extraordinary stories. We passed not far from Lago di Garda, said to have its name from a castle near it, in which Adeleida the wife of the emperor Lotharius was kept prisoner. The antient name of the lake was Benacus. Some say that cape Sirmione, at the south end of it, was the estate of the poet Catullus. At Venice, in the palace Grimani Spago, is a statue of Agrippa, which, if I mistake not, is the only one of him. I cannot find that it has been engraved before, and may be seen in the ninety-seventh plate, together with a medal of him in middle brass, which shews the resemblance, and the two arms and feet that have been added to the antient statue are marked by the lines, which shew where they join. In the same palace is that beautiful model of an antient temple in white marble, the plan, front, side, and soffit of which are engraved in the ninety-eighth plate, and the inscription on it has been published by Spon.

                                                            C H A P

I had the following observations in a letter to Venice, from some gentlemen who made a considerable stay in that city.

The manuscripts left by cardinal Bessarion to the public library of saint Mark, are now in good order, and recourse may be had to them, there being a catalogue of them published in two volumes in folio, with many curious observations. And on comparing it with a catalogue annexed to the cardinal's will, it appeared that very few books were wanting. At the entrance to the library there are several antient statues, relievos, and inscriptions, most of which were given by cardinal Grimani, and have been lately engraved in two volumes in folio by Zanetti, a relation of the librarian's

                                                            The

A STATUE OF AGRIPPA

XCVIII p 212 Nº 2

An EX VOTO in the form of a PORTICO of a TEMPLE in which it is supposed that a
STATUE of CYBELE was placed

CHAP. VII.

Obfervations from TRENT to SWISSERLAND.

IN the bifhoprick of Brixen, at a place called Mauls, to the fouth of Stertzingen, I faw an antient infcription and a curious relief of Mithras acrofs a bull as killing him, there being a man before him with a club lifted up, and another behind refting on a club, and fome other figures At Iefen beyond that town, there is an infcription and relief in copper, relating to the meeting between Ferdinand king of Hungary, and Charles the fifth, when he returned from Africa in one thoufand five hundred and twenty

The collection of antiquities and of curiofities both natural and artificial **Caftle of** at the caftle of Amras near Infpruck, is very large, efpecially for the time **Amras** when it was made, but, I think, it excels all others I have feen in the curious collection of armour of coats of mail, many of them having belonged to great men There is alfo a great collection of gold medals, they fay they have fixteen pound weight, and three thoufand cameos and intaglios, though I faw but few that were very fine, many of the antiquities were fent to this place by Charles the fifth Infpruck has been thought to be Ænipons, though the fituation of Oeting on the Inn is judged to agree better with it. They have on the mountains white hares and partridges, and one fort of the latter of the colour of wood-cocks, they have alfo a fort of black pheafant called Spilhound or Pirg-hound. We faw the falt fprings and falt works at Hall near Infpruck, and in the way to Saltzburg came to Raiephel in Bavaria, where there are mines of filver, lead, and copper, and about Reichenthal there are falt fprings of which they make a great quantity of falt

The cathedral at Saltzburg is built on the model of faint Peter's at **Saltzburg** Rome There are fome good pictures of Guido Reni, and others, in

---

The Pifani library is open for the publick three times a week. Within the great room is a fecond where there is a great collection of prohibited books, a licenfe from Alexander the eighth, being hung up for reading them in this place, and the heads of Luther and Calvin in relief are in that apartment In this place the famous collection of inf riptions is kept which belonged to the Corini family, they were publifhed without any explanation of them, and it is faid, that father Alberto Mazzolem, a learned Benedictine of Bergamo, has lately publifhed obfervations upon them

The library of fignor Sorenzo, a noble Veronian, is a curious collection books, among them the manufcripts of monfieur Trevefani, late bifhop of Verona, who is daily increafing his collection, and when his library is in order, he delights to let the learned world have the ufe of it

In the palace Giuftiniani Spigo there are many noble antiquities, thofe in faint Mark's library were brought from a room in this palace, where there are fome ftill remaining, particularly al-tars, bufts, and very fine marble vafes

The collection of medals of the Theopoli family are well known to the learned world, by the catalogue which has been lately publifhed of them

In collection of ftatues and bufts of Monfieur Trevifan, late bifhop of Verona, belong to his nephew fignor Suare, and were offered to be fold for 6000 fequin, many of them are very curious, and the bifhop had about fifty of them engraved, very few copies of which are got abroad

The collection belonging to the family of Capello is worth feeing, and it is faid that the perfon who poffeffed them about ten years ago was ready to oblige the curious with any of them, he had a great collection of the Roman filver medals, well preferved, with many rare ones among them

The library and drawings belonging to Mr Smith, the Englifh conful, and the cameos and medals of fignor Zanetti, ought to be feen by all ftrangers

the archbishop's palace, and a very fine antient bronze statue, the right hand of which is in a pointing posture. The castle here is very strongly built on a rocky hill, and is not commonly seen by strangers. At the archbishop's country palace of Helbrun the gardens are famous for the canals, grottos, and water works. Kleisham is another country palace belonging to him. The salt mines at Hall are very curious, and ought to be seen by all strangers. This country of Saltzburg is famous for fine marbles.

Munich is a place visited by most of the strangers who go into Germany; the elector's palace in the town was finely furnished; there are many curious antiquities, and several good modern busts in the gallery. The small chapel is lined with a composition, which is an imitation of the pietre comesse of Florence, it is perfectly singular, and very beautiful. The palaces of Schleisham and Nimfeberg are very fine, the gardens of the latter, and the buildings about them exceed any in Germany. There is a very particular charity in Munich, which is a nunnery that is open for teaching poor girls, and serves also for boarders, it was founded by Mary Ward of Yorkshire about a hundred and thirty years ago, and they have flourished so much that there are seven more houses of them in different towns. Freising, a sovereign bishopric, may be the antient Fruximum. At Augsburg there are some antient inscriptions at the Benedictine abby of saint Ulric. This place is remarkable for its fountains, for a secret gate, for workers in silver, and in several other arts.

In the way from Ulm to Anspach we passed through Schawningen, where the margrave has a fine palace of Italian architecture, and very beautiful improvements about it. We went to Anspach in a pleasant road, planted like an avenue, with four rows of trees. This city is in a valley between hills which are beautifully improved. The palace of the margrave is a grand new building of very good architecture. In these parts some rivers rise very near one another, which fall into the Danube and the Mayn, and it was proposed by opening a communication between them to unite the navigation of the Rhine and the Danube. The arsenal for the artillery at Nurenberg is esteemed the largest in Germany. They have also a fine fountain which was never set up, it consists of a colossal statue of Neptune in bronze, adorned with several other figures. In the house of a patrician here of the name of Piller there is a very fine collection of paintings, all capital pieces of Palma, Titian, Bassano, and Vandike. They are here great artists, especially in works of silver, and there is a custom in this city and at Augsburg of fixing a looking glass, in such a manner over the door, on the outside of the window of the upper room, is to see in it the persons who come to the door, and so to admit them, or deny themselves as they think proper.

At Christian Erling there is a fine palace of the margrave of Bareith, who sometimes resides there. This town consists chiefly of French refugees, who have established several manufactures in the town. We went by Pommersfelden where there is a most magnificent new palace of the Shoabrun family. The emperor Henry the second founded the bishopric and cathedral of Bamberg, he and his empress he buried there, and her statue is on the right hand, because, as the vulgar say, the

dead

[marginal notes, left column: Munich; Augsburg; Anspach; Nurenberg; Erling; Bamberg]

died a virgin He founded also the Benedictine abbey In the treasury of the cathedral they shew their crowns, which are very particular, they have also many other things which belonged to these princes It is commonly said if an emperor is chosen who has no dominions, that the bishop of Bamberg is obliged to give up his palace to him We passed through Kala in the principality of Altenberg, which belongs to the duke of Sax Gotha, opposite to it is a fort of that prince called Leichtenberg, situated on the high hills, and must be a pleasant place in summer

Iena is a famous Lutheran university, there are two thousand four hundred students in it, three parts of which study divinity, one the law, and the other two physic Many of them come from Livonia, Poland, Silesia, and Hungary, it being a cheaper university than Hall or Leipfic Many of them retain here the old custom of going in boots, they live in private houses; but there are a hundred and fifty who eat gratis at the college, and, I suppose, are the poor students. I went to see the house of the great astronomer Vogelius Erfurt belongs to the elector of Mentz, the inhabitants are half Roman and half Lutheran, with equal privileges, so are the professors of the university, tho' the greater part of the eight hundred students are Lutherans, there is a Scotish priory here dependant on the abbey of that nation at Ratisbon.

The whole principality of Gotha is an open corn country and well improved, there are many villages all over it. The city of Gotha is on the river Leina, on the north and south sides of an eminence, on which the duke's palace is most delightfully situated The library, the great collection of natural and artificial curiosities, and the medals are well worthy of the curiosity of a stranger, and no one can go away without being charmed with the great politeness of the ducal family. This great collection is the more extraordinary, as it was begun, and almost all got together by the late duke Frederic the second · Some of the medals are published in one volume in folio The country palace and gardens called Fredericstatt just without the city, and the grotesque room at the end of the latter, are very beautiful At Creutzburg, in the territory of Idenach, there are both salt springs and salt works.

At Hesse Cassel the models of the last prince are very curious, being not only of houses but of towns, and all in a good taste. A small part of his designs are finished here, that is, a very fine green house and a bath, which within is most exquisitely adorned with very fine reliefs in white marble Among the collection of curiosities there are several fine cameos which belonged to the Palaeologi, the Greek empresses of the east, the chief of them are set in a gold enamelled pectoral like a stomacher, and there are others which make a necklace, they were bought, by the late prince, of a noble Venetian We went four miles westward to Waterein to view part of a grand design which I had seen in the model, and is probably the finest artificial cascade in the world On the top of the hill there is a very grand open building on arches, in a rustic style, on which there is a pyramid, and on the top of that a bronze colossal statue of Hercules, thirty feet high, the head and trunk of it consist of about five pieces, each of which were cast finely, they say it weighs a hundred and eighty centners, each consisting of a hundred

2   and

and eight pounds, it was made by a common worker in copper who was then alive From this building there is an artificial cafcade down the hill, from the bottom of which up to the ftatue there are eight hundred and forty-four fteps, on two or three terraces below the building there are ftatues, water works, jett-d'eaus, and bafons of water, then there is a fteep piece of rock work, thro' which the water runs down in three ftreams, and there is a fheet of water on each fide, which has four breaks, below this is the grand cafcade, which confifts of a fall in the middle about twenty feet wide, with one on each fide fix feet broad, and fteps down, on each fide of the whole, eight feet wide, it is divided into four parts by three oval bafons, there being about ten breaks of the water made by deep fteps between each of them, and there is a larger bafon at bottom, with a gallery round, adorned with ftatues; it was defigned to be carried down much further to the palace, which was to be built at the foot of the hill, and it is a very fine fight to fee the waters play

Wurtzburg At Wurtzburg the bifhop, who is of the Shonburn family, is building a moft magnificent palace, in which there is a chapel exquifitely fine, there is a Scotch benedictine abbey in this city We embarked on the Main, and went by boat belonging to Mentz, near it there is a manufacture of crown glafs, which they make eight feet long, and five wide, and, if I miftake not, to the value of fourteen hundred florins each piece

Wertheim We came to the Lutheran town, and ftate of Wertheim, which is governed by its counts, I faw in their vault the bodies of two of the counts, and a child, the fkin of which is uncorrupted, as at Bremen The country both above and below produces not only what is called Francken wine, but alfo Rhenifh, and likewife fome that is fold for Mofelle We

Shaffenburg ftopped at Shaffenburg on the north fide of the river, belonging to the elector of Mentz, it is very pleafantly fituated on a height, there is a palace here built round a court by an elector of Mentz in one thoufand

Dettingen fix hundred and fix We afterwards paffed by Dettingen, remarkable for the battle fought there in one thoufand feven hundred and forty three Hainau is a neat Calvinift town belonging to Hefle, and is much inhabited by French refugees, the prince's palace of Hefleftat is very pleafantly fituated on the river Hochft is near Mentz, about which the beft Hock wine is produced

Mentz What they call the tower of Drufus in the caftle of Mentz, feems to be a Roman work, the walls of it are very thick, the bafement is about fifteen paces fquare, and fifteen feet high, the building above is round, the whole appears to have been cafed with hewn ftone, which is now taken away, fo that what is left is of rough ftone, except that at certain diftances there are large hewn ftones in order to bind the building The palace at Heidelberg has been in ruins ever fince it was deftroyed by the French, and the great tun is empty, which is exceeded by that at Koningftein, near Drefden, there are fome antient reliefs and infcriptions here The front of the cathedral at Strafburg, and efpecially the fpire, are ftupendous mafter pieces of Gothic architecture

C H A P.

CHAP VIII.

Obſervations on SWISSERLAND, SAVOY, FRANCHE COMTI, ALSACE, and LORRAIN

AT Baſil many things are ſhewn in the library in relation to _{Baſil} Eraſmus, and his tomb is in the church, as well as thoſe of the learned Buxtorfs The outſide of ſome houſes here are painted by Holbein, and his famous dance of death is ſtill to be ſeen, which has been often repaired They have a cuſtom of hanging up in the arſenal the inſtruments with which perſons have killed themſelves, with an inſcription on them, as a perpetual mark of infamy The famous council was held in the library, in which there was a pope choſen The family of Feche in this city have a collection of medals and other curioſities

At the church of St Urſus, in Solothurn, there are two pillars with Solothurn an inſcription, which makes mention of their antiquity, and in a charnel-houſe near Morat, are the bones of the Burgundians who died in the famous battle in one thouſand four hundred and ſeventy-ſix At Wiſleſberg, or Avanche, there are ſome ruins of the antient Avan- Avanche, ticum, which was a colony ſent by Veſpaſian, I ſaw part of a circular wall, probably the ruins of an amphitheatre, there are alſo ſome remains of the old walls of the city and of a gateway. Milden, or Moudon, has Moudon. been thought to be the antient Minnodunum, and I found it confirmed by an inſcription lately dug up. At Lauſanne there was a great crack Lauſanne made in the church by an earthquake, and twenty years afterwards another earthquake cloſed it again

There are mineral waters at St Prex, as well as at Prangen, and there are mines at the latter. Nyon is thought by ſome to have been Colonia Nyon Colonia Equeſtris, though others place it at Geneva, and ſome it Lauſanne, I Equeſtris ſaw ruins here, and a high ſquare tower, which ſeemed to be antient From Geneva I went to the Glacieres in Savoy, an account of which has been lately publiſhed Travelling to the ſouth of the like of Geneva, we went to the Carthuſian convent of Ripaille, where the anti-pope Ripaille. Felix, of the houſe of Savoy, retired, after he was depoſed We croſſed the Rhine from Savoy into the country of Viax At Bevveux near Aigle in that country, there are very curious ſalt ſprings, and ſalt works, Salt works. one of the paſſages to the ſprings is four thouſand five hundred and ſixty feet long, there is alſo a ſulphureous ſpring, and the air ſometimes is very unwholſome, to remedy which, a great wheel blows two pair of large bellows, in order to purify the air. Vevay is moſt delight- Vevay fully ſituated on the lake, Ludlow, one of the judges of king Charles the firſt, and Broughton, are buried in the church, it ſeems to be intimated in the epitaph of the latter, that he read the king's ſentence We went to the baths of Waterſwyl, near Zug, which are of an allom Waterſwyl water At Zurich I waited on the profeſſor Bodmer, who had ſtudied Zurich the Engliſh language on purpoſe to tranſlate Milton into High Dutch,

which he was then employed about. At the fmall town of Winterthur
they have a library, a good collection of medals, and fome other curiofities; and they have a bath of mineral waters. Altn-Winterthur is the
antient Vitodurum, it was a Roman ftation, and it is faid that there
are fome ruins at it, among which they find medals, and there is an old
road from it which leads to Frawenfield   Pfin, beyond this place, is faid
to be Ad Fines, which was fortified by the Romans againft the Germans, and
had its name from being on the bounds between the Rhœtii and Helvetii. In the ifland of Reichenau, near Conftance, they fay there was a ftatue of Aleman, the idol of the antient Alemanni, which the emperor
Maximilian carried to Infpruck in one thoufand five hundred and ten,
and, if I do not miftake, is in the caftle of Amras · The emperor
Charles le Gros is buried in the abbey there. At Shaffhoufe the bed of
the Rhine is rocky, infomuch that at the town there are fome fmall falls
of three or four feet, but the famous fall of the Rhine is about two
miles lower, at Lauffen, there are two falls of four or five feet, which
are above the great one, at this there are two rocks covered with fhrubs and
trees, which divide the river into three parts, it falls with a great noife,
and dafhing againft the rocks below, the fprey rifes like a cloud as high
as the rocks above, the fall of water makes great waves in the river,
which roll to the fhoar, and the water is covered with froth for a confiderable way, the fall is faid to be a hundred or a hundred and twenty
feet, but I did not think that it was half fo high   We embarked
below it, and found the river at firft very rapid, infomuch that we came
to Rhynaw in twenty minutes, which is computed to be a league; we
landed at Kaifarftool, fuppofed to be Forum Tiberii. Several of the
counts of Hapfberg are buried at the Bernandine convent of Wettingen
near Baden   Wyndich, the old Vindoniffa, on the high ground at the
confluence of the Har and Reufs, is one of the fineft fituations I have
feen. Many antiquities have been found here, and there are fome at the
church. A little to the fouth of Wyndich is Kunigsfeld, where there was
a convent of Francifcans, and a nunnery of Clares, founded on the fpot
where Albert king of the Romans was affaffinated, it was a charity of
his wife and daughter, the latter being queen of Hungary   Seventeen
princes and princeffes of that family were afterwards buried in a vault
there : In the chancel are the portraits of the archduke Leopold, and of the
twenty feven nobles, who were all flain in the battle of Sempack, in
one thoufand three hundred and eighty, to the fouth of the church are
the apartments where the queen lived   On a hill not far from this place,
and near Bruck, is the caftle of Hapfberg, belonging to the counts of
that name, from whom the prefent houfe of Auftria is defcended   They
fay Altenberg, which is on the river and nearer Bruck, is the place where
the family originally lived, but there are very little marks of the antient
buildings, it is probable that Hapfberg was their caftle to which they
retired in time of danger, and it is a very fine fummer fituation, commanding a glorious view of a moft beautiful country   At the foot of
this hill are the baths of Shinzenach, with good accommodations for
ftrangers, they are a warm fulphureous water, which is bitter to the
tafte, are purging when drunk, and they heat them for bathing   Returning to the Rhine at Zurlack, we came to the fall of Coblentz,
where

where the water is so rapid, that it is very disagreeable to go down in a boat, and when the waters are low, a ridge of rocks appear across, there being only room in the middle for two small boats, and they can cross over on a board Some say, that this is Coblentz, or Confluentia, which was the quarters of the Roman cohorts. There are some iron mines below Waldshut At Lauffenberg there is a gentle fall for about a quarter Lauffenberg. of a mile, but large boats can descend. At Augst, the old Augusta August Rauracorum, are some ruins, the Rhine being shallow there, the Germans used to endeavour to make incursions this way, it is said that there was a bridge made over it afterwards, and that some ruins of it have been seen This place is supposed to have been built by the Romans, to hinder their incursions I saw here the remains of a building C, in the ninetieth plate, which seems to have been only a portico round a solid wall that has niches in it for statues. The building called the nine towers, D, in the same plate, was doubtless a theatre, it was cased with small hewn stone, to the east of it is a building, which is called the city wall, but I take it to have been part of the citadel.

At Chatenoy beyond Belfort are iron mines, and the ore being in Chatenoy round pebbles, it is called Kidney-ore; there is of the same sort about Montbeliard, which, with its territory, belongs to the duke of Wirten- Montebe- burg, this place had a citadel, which was destroyed by the French harft They are Lutherans here, and a good sort of people; and have a set of very laborious and learned clergy, who keep a press employed in printing books for the use of the people. We went about four miles to the south of Montbeliard to Mandeurre on the river Doux, where there Mandeurre. are great ruins of some antient place, which seems to have been a Roman town, and may be Equestris mentioned by Ptolemy, as a city of the Sequani, on a supposition that it was a different place from that which belonged to the Helvetii, which was near Geneva, according to the Itinerary and Tables; for Ptolemy places it to the north of Avanticum, whereas the other was much to the south; this was probably destroyed in the middle ages: There is a raised road near the river, which went from this place to Besançon In the way to that city near Baume, I saw in the month of June an extraordinary grotto called Glaciere, Grotto of by reason that it always has ice in it, this grotto is in a wood, and ice the mouth of it opens to the north After descending about two hundred feet we came to the mouth of the grotto, and still descending, arrived at the bottom which is covered with ice, and may be about fifty paces long, and thirty-five broad, and at least sixty feet high, there are several cones of ice which rise up in it, and are made by the droppings of the water, and two great icicles hang from the top I could not find that the water was salt. At Besançon, the antient Vesontio of Besançon the Sequani, there is an entire triumphal arch, very highly ornamented, but not in the best taste, it is said to have been erected to the emperor Aurelian, though I could not think it to be a building of so late a date; a full account of it may be seen in Dr Chiflet's Vesontio, it consists of two stories of the Composite order, in the lower one the capitals are composed of three rows of leaves, the highest being like those of the palm tree. The situation of Dole agrees with Didattium of Ptolemy. Dole

Going

Going towards Colmar from Montbeliard I saw iron mines near Rott of the same kind of kidney ore as I have mentioned before. At Cernay they brought me to drink the mineral waters of Sultzbach two leagues off; they seemed to be of the nature of those of Piermont, and to be very good, and that place is much frequented on account of them The sovereign council, or court of judicature of all Alsace, resides at Colmar, which is in a very fine country, abounding in wine, with which they supply Strasburg and part of Swisserland. I went a mile to the east to Horburg, said to be the antient Argentuaria, where there was a famous inscription to Apollo, which has been taken away, and a modern one is left in the place of it, on one side Ensishem seems to be Stabula, and Kems Cambetesa, and on the other side Benfeld, or Erstun, might be Elcebum.

At Myleho in Lorrain there are silver mines which produce also lead and copper Beyond Neufville I saw a village called Baccarach, which is finely situated on a low hill, being within the walls of some old town, probably of the middle ages, and further on I observed at a distance the salt houses of Lore, where, I suppose, they have salt springs I saw king Stanislaus at Luneville, he delights in building and gardens, and has erected a pavilion for himself in his gardens, and little houses near it for his first great officers, with little gardens to them. The church at the town of St Nicholas is to be esteemed among the finest Gothic buildings Nancy has falsely been thought to be the antient Nasium: A grand palace has been begun there by the dukes of Lorrain, and was never finished Half a league from the town king Stanislaus has made a calvary with stations to it, and some gardens; and built a very plain house near the site of the grand palace of the dukes, which has been pulled down. We passed over the Moselle on a fine bridge at Pontamousson, which may be the antient Scarpona, it is in the dutchy of Bar. At Jouï I saw the remains of the famous aqueduct of Metz, which was built across the river, and is of stone cased with brick, the cornish from which the arches spring are of white marble. Metz is the Divodurum of the Mediomatrici The cathedral is a beautiful Gothic building; and there is a very curious piece of antiquity in it which serves for a font, it is an antient coffin of one piece of porphyry, which is about twelve feet long, five wide, and three deep; there are on each side two rings in relief, and towards the bottom a head, which seemed to have had long ears In the church of the Benedictines of St. Arnau is the tomb of the emperor Lewis, son of Charlemagne, it is of the Doric order, and there is a relief of a battle and procession, on a coffin of white marble, the sculpture is but indifferent, and probably was of those times, the following inscription is on it

D. LVDOVICO PIO D CAROLI MAGNI FIL GALLIAR. RIGI IMPERATORIQVL ROM.

St. Clement of the Benedictines, the casterns or barracs for the soldiers, and the hospital for the sick and invalids among them, are worth seeing, they are supplied here with sea coal, brought by water from the country about Sar Louis.

CHAP.

A SEPULCHRAL MONUMENT at *IGEL* near *TREVES*

CHAP. IX.

Of some parts of GERMANY and FLANDERS.

AT the village of Igel, which is on the Moselle, about two leagues above Treves, there is a very curious and magnificent piece of antiquity, which was probably a sepulchral monument, a plan and view of it to the north may be seen in the ninety-ninth plate [*]. From the drawing any one may judge that this building is ornamented in the richest manner, and the whole work is all very well executed. I could see no entrance to this monument, but the people say there is one, which, I suppose, is under ground, and that it is lined with copper, adorned with figures.

The city of Treves, the old Augusta Trevirorum, has been miserably Treves destroyed by wars, and is but thinly inhabited. To the north west of it is Apollo's hill, and that of Mars to the west, and on a hill to the north north west there is a small building, which they call the house of St Hieronymus.

Going down the Rhine from Mentz we passed by Bingen, the an-Binge tient Bingium, a Roman fortress, and afterwards by Erlach, where I Erlach have been since informed are the tombs of the counts of Nassau, and that there is a magnificent monument over them. Beyond Baccarach, opposite to Caub, is a castle on an island called Pfaltz-Graff, which, they say, is the antient house of the elector Palatine's family. We passed by Boppart, thought without any reason to be Baudobrica, which I should rather think to have been at Berncastle on the Moselle, and that they went to it from Treves, it may be by water, and then by land to Salhsso, which might be Acgerthal, and so to Bingium, and Magontiacum, or Mentz. In the country of Wied, opposite to Andernach, they make that blue and white stone ware, which is sent all over Europe. The elector of Cologn has a palace at Bonne the antient Bonna, Bonne in which he usually resides, and an unfinished palace near the town,

---

[*] It is raised on a pedestal or basement, which is on two plinths; the corner ones being two feet deep, and the upper three, both setting in six niches: the die of the pedestal consists of two tier of stone, and is about five feet deep, it was adorned with reads, those to the east and north are defaced; on the west side there is a loud dance carried on by two more, with a man on the further side of each horse, they seem to have a rhythm in their hands. To the north a man with a bow in his hand, the other being another behind him, and on one side of him two feet a table, and two stand to the east of it, this also is much defaced. In the die of the pedestal at to the east and west, the relief are all entirely defaced, and much more to the south, but I could discern a person sitting, with one standing on each side, that to the east holding the person who sits by the hand. In the freeze, to the west, in a light

persons in procession to the east is a person sitting, and a boy standing at a round table, another likewise at a table, and two persons standing, the freeze to the south is divided into two parts by three pilasters, in the middle compartment one sits at a table, and two at each end, to the west there is a table, and other utensils, and two persons standing, to the east one is at a stove, and two as walking off towards the middle. At the east, a woman sits in a bed, on which there is a man, a person standing at the feet of the bed, to the west there is a man in a car drawn by beasts, which seem to have horns, to the south two persons, and there was a third in the middle, probably sitting. In the pediment, the reliefs are all defaced, except to the south, in which there are three figures, the middle one, which is naked, seemed to resemble Hercules.

in the former there is a fine piece of shell work, in which birds and other animals are represented in a curious manner; it is the work of Monf. Poitrich, who adorned a chapel in the same manner at Falcoufe, two leagues from Bonne, which is said to be a most beautiful performance.

Cologn At Cologn, the antient Colonia Agrippina, there are some capitals of a modern invention in the Jesuit's church, which succeed better than any I have seen that differ from the antients. St Gereon is said to be built by the empress Helena, and it something resembles the Greek architecture of that age   At the town house I saw several arrows and old bows, such as I had seen at Beer on the Euphrates, there are some Roman inscriptions in the arsenal, and a fine stone coffin: There is also a mummy in a coffin hewn out of wood, in shape of a mummy, all being very much after the Ægyptian manner, except that there is no mask on the face, and it is wrapped up in garments, very much like those of the priests, it was found at St. Gereon

Juliers In the duchy of Juliers they have a stone coal, and a manufacture, both of fine woollen, and also of linen, which has the name of Julic linen from this country   In the way to Juliers we passed thro' Bergen, thought to be Tiberiacum, as Juliers is the antient Juliacum.

Aix la Chapelle Aix la Chapelle, the antient Aquisgranum, had its present name from an old chapel in the middle of the town, which is ruined.   The octagon church, in which Charlemagne was buried, is somewhat in the Greek style of the middle ages; a choir, and other additions, having been made to it of Gothic workmanship   The body of Charlemagne was deposited in a vault directly under the middle of the dome, it was set in his imperial robes in a chair, which we saw; it is of pieces of white marble joined together, and was covered with gold, they say the royal mantle he sat in is that in which the emperors are now crowned, the crown is now kept at Nurenberg; he had in his hand the gospel, which they now shew in the sacristy, his figure, as he was thus placed in his tomb, is represented in alt-relief on the side of this gospel in silver gilt; the crown divides into two parts at top, as the imperial crown is represented, they say the leaves of the gospel are of papyrus, but they seemed to me to be of very fine vellum, it is the Latin gospel wrote in a square letter. They shew the cutlass that was hung to his side, on the scabbard of which are ornaments of silver gilt, they have likewise what they call his horn, which is of an elephant's tooth, and, if I mistake not, was likewise about him   The body of the emperor is now under the high altar   The gold that was on the chair was made use of to adorn the pulpit and high altar, the former is in a semicircular form, and covered with gold, inlaid with steel, the ornaments of it are beautiful, and there are about it several precious stones, cameos, and intaglios, and particularly a large oval sardonyx, which is five or six inches long, and three broad, and, as I conjectured, near two in thickness   The part over the altar is covered with massive gold, adorned with reliefs in twenty-four compartments of sacred history, but not of the best workmanship We were then shewn the fine coffin of white marble, on which there is an alt relief of the rape of Proserpine, it is kept locked in a nich, in which there is a bust to the middle of Charlemagne   This relief is executed in the highest taste.   Charon's long-boat seems to be the scene of the

4   whole,

whole, who fits rowing in it Towards the head of the boat is a chariot drawn by four horſes, repreſented with great force and fire; there is a cupid behind Pluto, a perſon in armour is behind Proferpine, both as to hinder her from going away, and from looking back, he alſo has a cupid behind him, laſt of all there is a chariot of Furies, drawn by two dragons with wings, as driving over the women of Proſerpine, with their baſkets of fruits and flowers In the ſacriſty they have ſeveral very curious cameos, one is of cornelian, with the heads of an emperor and empreſs; he has a large beard, the empreſs has a diadem placed round her hair in a very particular manner, I thought it might be Severus Alexander, another conſiſts of near half the body, being an oval Sardonyx three inches and a half long, and three inches broad, the face is young, with a crown of lawrel, the Roman eagle cut in it, which, if I do not miſtake, is held by the emperor, I conjectured it might be Auguſtus, or ſome of his family Before the door of the church on one ſide, is what ſeems to be the pine-apple in bronze, and on the other a curious ſtatue of an animal in bronze. Otho the third is ſaid to be buried in this church, probably under a tomb of black marble which is in the middle of the choir. The baſin in the emperor's bath is kept locked, a cake of ſulphur ſettles round it, which is eſteemed the beſt in the world for medicine, is ſtronger than that of the Solſatara near Naples, and ſells very dear

There are ſome mines between Aix la Chapelle and Limburg, particularly of lapis calaminaris, and I was informed that there is a lead-mine near Aix la Chapelle of a red ore, and that there are ſome ſulphur works near Chaud-Fountain, between Liege and Spaa. The quarry at Maeſtricht is, I believe, the fineſt in the world They have good ſtone coal about Namur, and a black fat earth, which they make up into cakes, it is called Terrehoule, and they uſe it chiefly for making lime. King Dagobert is buried in the abbey of ſaint Amand, between Condé and Tournay Caſtel is ſituated on a hill from which there is one of the moſt extenſive proſpects over Flanders, and it is ſaid that they can ſee ſixty cities or towns, they have a view of the ocean, and in a clear day can ſee England

A DE-

A
DESCRIPTION
OF
The *EAST*, &c.

BOOK the Fifth.

Obfervations on GERMANY, BOHEMIA, HUNGARY, ISTRIA, and fome parts of ITALY.

CHAP. I.

Of the circle of WESTPHALIA.

WE left England in May one thoufand feven hundred thirty-fix, and travelled thro' Flanders, the United Provinces, and the Duchy of Cleves, and entering into the Circle of Weftphalia, came to Benthem, where a very large improvement has been made in the wood, in which there is a mineral water. In the road towards Ofnaburg, in the county of Lingen, which belongs to the king of Pruffia, there is a falt fpring, and great falt works; they told me they obferve that the fpring fails when the fouth wind blows, and flows moft plentifully when the wind is eafterly, there are alfo coal mines in this country.

At Ofnaburg there is a grand palace built by Erneft Auguftus, duke of Brunfwick and Lunenburg, who married the princefs Sophia, the prince their fon, the late duke of York, and bifhop of Ofnaburg, died here, and his memory is adored by all the people, as he was a prince of great humanity and courtefy, lived like a father among his fubjects, and was

4   entirely

entirely beloved by them   In this town house they shew the room where
the famous treaty of Westphalia was held   In the way to Munster we
passed through Lingen, at the foot of the hill on which Tecklenberg
stands, thought to be the antient Tecelia   Ferdinand, bishop of Pader- Paderborn
born, writ an account of his diocese, and endeavoured to fix to certain
places many remarkable things in relation to antient history, where he
has set up inscriptions, which are printed in that account   The river
rises at Paderborn in a very extraordinary manner, coming out in a great
stream of water · I was informed that there are four rivers about two
leagues to the east of the town, which go under ground and are lost,
possibly some of them may rise again at this place   The mineral waters of Melbrun are very famous in this country, one of them, they Melbrun
say, kills any birds that drink of it, they die in convulsions, and their
lungs are found much contracted, but if they give them salt in time,
they recover, and a little vinegar perfects the cure

There are two or three places we did not see in these parts, one is
Hervorden, a protestant nunnery, of which the princess Elizabeth was Hervorde
abbess, who was esteemed as a miracle of her sex, some of her Latin
letters are seen among Descartes's epistles   She was daughter of the
king of Bohemia, and sister to the princess Sophia, duchess of Brunswick   To the west of this place is Engern, the antient Angaria, capital Engern
of the Angari, or Angrivarii, where the tomb of Witikind is seen, who
was king of the Saxons, he was born and resided about Minden, and
from him the Saxon family is descended

A little before the entrance of Piermont there is a salt spring and salt Piermont.
works   We put a duck into the Piermont spring, which immediately
began to shake its head, and then it dropped into the water, and being
drawn out dead, the blood appeared very black, flies, which approach
too near, fall into it, and I saw many of them dead on the water, and
a young man bathing here some years ago, was so affected, that they had
great difficulty to recover him   Digging down in a quarry near the town
about twenty years ago, they perceived a noxious vapour, which became so
strong, that they turned an arch over it, and made several steps down to it,
the vapour is sometimes so strong, that if people hold their heads over this
descent, which may be about fifteen feet down, they are obliged immediately to retire, we snapped a pistol four feet from the ground, and it
would not go off, but fired when it was held higher, a candle went out
before we could bring it opposite to the door, a fowl appeared as dead in
less than half a minute, but recovered, we tried it even to a minute
and a half, and carrying it away for dead, notwithstanding it recovered
I observed that the vapour had turned the sides of the door case yellow
for about three feet in height, after we had fired into it two or three
times the vapour was not offensive, it is strongest in the morning and
evening, and the poor people sit in it about noon in a chair, in order to
sweat, but some have been almost overcome with it   The town of Ha- Hameln
melen is on the Weser, and belongs to the elector of Hanover, it is well
fortified, and famous for the locks which were made by king George the
second, on which account there was a medal struck   By this great work,
which was done by cutting away the rock in many places, the Weser is
made navigable up from Minden to this place

C H A P. II.

Of the circle of L O W E R S A X O N Y.

Hanover

HANOVER is thought to be the antient Lephana of Ptolemy In a saloon of the palace there are pictures of all the great men of the ducal family, of which four have been emperors; there are also some apartments richly adorned with antient silver furniture of chased work. Many relicks are preserved in the chapel of the palace, which were brought from Jerusalem by Charles the Lyon, duke of Brunswick, and in the treasury is a very extraordinary piece of silver ore, which is two feet long, about a foot and a half broad, and weighs ninety pounds; it cost the king sixteen hundred and thirty-five crowns, and twenty grofs; it was dug out of the mine of Andersberg in Hartz-forest, and great part of it is pure silver In the chancellary or secretary's office, there is a large library filled with a very good collection of books and several valuable manuscripts The king's stables are grand, and there are in them the finest sets of coach horses of different colours that I ever saw. Almost every thing is on the same footing here as if the king was present, the same officers, public tables, and diversions, being kept up for the benefit of the subjects The gardens of Herenhausen are deservedly admired, the jet d'eau is the finest in the world, the waters being forced to it by machines which are well known, and are the invention of Mr. Holland, the water is brought from a river which is lower than the basin; it commonly rises eighty feet, and by playing another pipe, it throws the water a hundred and twenty feet high, the pipe in the basin seems to be eleven inches in diameter, round which the water rises in a circle an inch and a half in thickness, and appears like a solid body of water of eleven inches diameter The sylvan theatre is very beautiful, which, and the walks near it, have on some occasions, been illuminated with five thousand lamps It was one of the most beautiful sights in the world to see a ball here at night, and a grand entertainment in the drawing-room at the palace, which is two hundred and fifty feet long and fifty broad, and is adorned in a beautiful manner with paintings and busts

Hildesheim

In the cathedral at Hildesheim the statue of the Virgin Mary is on a very particular pillar brought from Westphalia, they say the Germans used to put the statue of their god Iomergal on it At Saltzderfurt beyond Hildesheim there are salt springs, which by boiling the water produce a great quantity of salt We omitted at Marieburg in the road to Lampsling to enquire for a mountain near it, which, they say, abounds in pieces of marble, that smells like burnt horn when it is broken, and has a mixture of black earth in it To the south east of Hildesheim is the English Benedictine abbey of Lampsling, governed by a mitred abbot, who is building a new monastery

Hartz forest

We went to Hartz-forest, thought to be part of the antient Hercynian wood At Wildeman there are copper, lead, and silver mines, which belong to the elector of Hanover, and the duke of Wolfenbuttle,

as well as thofe of Cellerfield ; and at the latter they have likewife a mint in common   A little further there is a fmall town called Clau- Clausthal fthal, about which there are a great number of filver mines belonging to the electorof Hanover. I went down fix hundred feet into fome of them ; thirteen of the mines produce great profit ; and in Hartz-forreft the mines bring in thirty thoufand pounds to the king clear of all expences.   At Claufthal they commonly coin nine or ten thoufand crowns, or dollars, a week , and they coin yearly about thirty-fix pound weight of gold into ducats, which is produced by the mine at Ramelsberg.   The miners before they go down to their work have prayers every morning read by one of them at a houfe near the mine   The bufinefs they are employed about foon waftes the flefh, and when they are turned of thirty they begin to look thin, and are much fubject to plurifies and palfies , the former frequently carry them off, and the latter difable them   From Claufthal we went to Andersberg where there are great number of mines, fome of which are very rich   We paffed in fight of Altenaw, at which place there are five mines and a foundery ; and went by a mineral water, which feemed to be impregnated with iron   There are mines in feveral other places, fome of which are of iron and copper ·
But the moft curious of all is that of Ramelsberg near Goflar, of which Ramelsberg the king and the duke of Wolfenbuttle have equal fhares   The emperor Otho the firft opened this mine in nine hundred fixty eight , it is one rock of ore, every piece of which has in it fulphur, lead, copper, filver, and gold , the mine is a thoufand feet deep, the firft defcent being by wells, then there is a gentle defcent by narrow paffages to large grottos, or vaults, out of which they have taken the ore for feveral hundred years, and the extent of them is between three and four thoufand feet   When they go out of the mine they make fires againft the rock in order to loofen it , and when the grottos are high they build folid walls almoft to the top, and make fires on them   When they go out they light the fires, where they have worked away all the ore that was loofened, and ftay out eight hours, always remaining in the mines fixteen hours, and work thirteen of them , fometimes it happens that pieces of the rock fall down and kill the workmen   The fire has two other effects, it keeps the water from coming in any great quantity into the mine, and drying up the vitriol water as it hangs on the rock, it makes the vitriol, which is of feveral colours   At the firft going in one perceives the moft ftifling and difagreeable heat, occafioned by the fmoak of the fulphur and vitriol, which muft be very noxious, and we could not ftay in fome places above three or four minutes, the labourers work almoft naked   There is one thing fo extraordinary in this mine, that if it was not well known by naturalifts, and if there were not the fame in Hungary, and, as I have been lately informed, in the fouth of France, I fhould not venture to relate it   That is, there is a vitriolwater, under the droppings of which they put old iron, and in about thirteen weeks the vitriol wifhes off the particles of iron in a fort of mud into a trough , the vitriol water leaves behind it the particles of copper, and a hundred and ten pound weight of iron make, near the fame weight of mud, which produces about ninety pound weight of copper , but what is more extraordinary, in one place the form of the

iron is preserved, and the copper particles of the vitriol are left behind, so as to make it a solid piece of copper, and in the cabinets in Germany it is a common thing to shew a copper horse shoe, which has been made in this manner from iron, and I have pieces by me, in which this change is almost perfected

Wolfenbuttel The library at Wolfenbuttel is a fine oval room, with galleries round it one over another In the arsenal there is a large pillar of black granite or porphyry, much resembling that at Wilton At the country palace, called Saltzdall, which is near, there are several curious things to be seen

Brunswick There are many great princes of the Brunswick family buried in the cathedral at Brunswick They have here the largest bronze mortar in Europe, which weighs eighteen thousand pound, is ten feet six inches long, two feet seven inches in the bore, and five inches thick, that is, three feet five inches in diameter, it throws a ball of seven hundred and thirty pound and a half, with fifty pounds of powder; and it carries three thousand three hundred paces

The country between Zell and Ferden consists of barren heaths, they cut down the heath and strew it every day over the places where they keep their cattle, in order to manure the land, they have also a great number of hives on shelves in little enclosures, the bees live on the heath flower, and the people make a great profit of the honey and wax

Bremen Bremen is thought to be the antient Fabiranum In the vault of the great church, there are eight bodies in coffins, which in part remain uncorrupted, they were opened accidentally about forty years ago, and found in that manner, the skin seems to be hard, and the flesh under is dryed to powder, which is thought to be the effect of the air of this vault Near Butchude we saw an antient monument called Willensfwein, consisting of a stone eight feet long, three broad and thick, lying about three feet above the ground on three stones, and there are several barrows near it

Lunenburg Lunenburg is thought to be the antient Marionis of Ptolemy In the church there was an altar piece of gold, embossed in several compartments of history pieces, and adorned with precious stones, but the greatest part of it has been stolen away There are great salt works here at the salt springs in the town, which are very strong They have a tradition in the country, that the first Saxons who settled in England came from Ultzen above Lunenburg on the river Ilmenau In the way from Lunenburg to Hamburg, near a village called Himwar, I observed on little heights several antient monuments made of stone set up an end, one particularly, had five or six round it at some distance, it was thirty feet long, and nine feet wide, there being nine stones on each side between two and three feet high, about eighteen inches broad, and so far apart, at each end the stones are about six feet apart, and a stone lies crofswife between them at the south end, on this stone, and on the stone on each side of it, there is a large convex stone eight feet long, six broad, and very thick, towards the other end there is a stone not quite so large laid across, and there is one stone on each side between that and the end of the enclosure, there is another at a little distance to the south which is ten feet broad, and between fifty and sixty long, it has two stones across at each end on the ground, but there is no stone

lnd

laid on them, the ſtones are moſtly a grey ſort of granite, and they carry them to North Holland in order to defend the piles of their dykes againſt the force of the ſea

In the duchy of Holſtein, towards Keil, we ſaw ſeveral monuments of Holſtein this kind, and trees were planted round ſome of them, they are in a valley between two hills, which made me conjecture, that it had been the ſpot of ſome battle, and that they erected theſe monuments over the great men who fell in it. Thoſe who come this way ought to ſee the delightful ſituation of Ploen, on a riſing ground between the lakes Ploen. Lubeck is thought to be Treva of Ptolemy, which ſeems the more pro-Lubeck, bable, as the preſent name of the river on which it ſtands is Travè, the old name of it was Chalurus, and it is ſuppoſed to be the bounds between the Saxons to the north, and the Angli to the ſouth. In a church here there are ſome verſes relating to a ſtag, which had a collar put on his neck by Charlemagne, and, as they ſay, was taken four hundred years after his time

The duchy of Mecklenburg is a very pleaſant open corn country, it Mecklenis diverſified by ſeveral riſing grounds, with large timber trees and firs burg ſcattered all over the country, and ſeveral ſmall groves, and there are little lakes between the heights, which ſupply ſuch a quantity of fiſh, that the people in a manner live on it, and cultivate all their ground for corn to be ſent to Sweden. We went near Gadeſbuche to ſee the field Gadesbuche of battle between the Danes, and the Swedes headed by Charles the twelfth and Steinbock in one thouſand ſeven hundred and twelve, in which the Danes were defeated. The water of the bay of Roſtock is not ſalt, and there is ſo little ſalt in the ſea water at Wiſmar, that I could not perceive it, tho' they ſay at the latter it is not fit for uſe, the freſhneſs of the water is occaſioned by the great number of rivers which fall into the Baltick in theſe parts.

CHAP. III.

Of the circle of UPPER SAXONY.

THE publick buildings of Stralſund were miſerably deſtroyed by S Stralſund. the ſiege, we were curious to be informed of every thing relating to that ſiege, and to Charles the twelfth, and went into the iſle Iſle of Ruof Rugen, to ſee the field of battle between the Swedes, and the Danes gen and Pruſſians, in which the Swedes were entirely routed. I was informed that at the north point of the iſland are ruins of the ſtrong town of Arcona, where Stechenbecher the famous pirate reſided, the town Arcona having been deſtroyed in eleven hundred and ſixty eight, by Woldemar king of Denmark

The packet goes from Stralſund to Sweden, a voyage of about twenty-eight leagues, but in the winter ſeaſon, when thoſe ſeas are frozen, croſſes by the Sound. Monſieur Weſtphal, librarian and profeſſor

Gripswald — in the univerſity of Gripſwald, which is to the ſouth of Stralſund, ſhewed us ſeveral urns of different ſizes, made like earthen jars, they were full of burnt bones, they found alſo in them ſwords bent in ſuch a manner, as to be put into the urns, alſo heads of pikes, whetſtones for their arms, and round ſtones, ſuppoſed to be uſed for ſlinging, there were no letters found on any thing, and he ſaid, that he had near three hundred of them dug up, they were firſt diſcovered in ploughing the land at Levenhagen about a league to the ſouth of Gripſwald, and were not found in a vault, but in the earth cloſe to one another, a large monument of ſtones being near, where they dug and found but one urn; he was of opinion that they were the tombs of the Vandals   In an iſland of

Wolgaſt — the Oder oppoſite to Wolgaſt there are remains of one of the moſt magnificent old caſtles I ever ſaw, in which the dukes of Wolgaſt reſided, they talk much of a ſtatue being found in a vault of a young woman with ſcythes inſtead of arms, with which criminals, who were let down, were cut in two

Penemunder — We croſſed to the iſland of Uſedom to ſee the fort of Penemunder, which was ſo bravely defended by Col Dylep, who died fighting after it was taken, in obedience to that extraordinary letter of Charles the twelfth, which is ſaid to have been found in his pocket

Poland — Going a little way into Poland, we made enquiries concerning the Plica Polonica, which is not frequent in this part of Poland, the common people only are ſubject to it   In this diſorder the hair twiſts and mats together, and it cannot be combed; it is attended with a ſmarting pain, and ſometimes with a ſwelling of the head, but there is no danger if they let it alone, and it goes off in time: If they cut the hair, it generally makes them blind, or mad, or they die; and they very rarely recover   The vulgar have a notion that it is cauſed by witchcraft, and they informed me that there were ten old women had been lately burnt together for witchcraft in this part of the country

Marquiſate of Brandenburg — In Brandenburg we paſſed by ſome eſtates of the knights of St. John of Jeruſalem of the Lutheran religion, who at the reformation withdrew with ſix commanderies from the grand maſter, and choſe one of their own, who at this time was prince Charles, nephew of the firſt

Franfort — king of Pruſſia   I enquired at Franckfort on Oder about a petrifying water, and the Oſteacolla, and was informed, that there is only ſome quality in the water which does harden wood in ſome degree, but a phyſician of Berlin aſſured me, that no Oſteacolla is found here, and that the waters do not petrify

Berlin — The new city of Berlin, the palaces, the immenſe treaſures of plate, the library, the chamber of ſciences, the arſenal, and ſeveral other things, are worthy of the curioſity of a ſtranger, and all travellers are well acquainted with them   The famous Puffendorff is buried in the church of St Nicholas, and has this epitaph over him.

Dno SAMVELIS LIB BARON DE PVFFNDORFF, CONSIL INTIMI SERENISS ELECT BRAND OSSA HFIC RECVBANT ANIMA COELO RECEPTA, FAMA PER TOTVM ORBEM VOLITAT NATVS IS b Jan 16, MORTVVS 6 Oct 1694

They had here a particular manner of recruiting the army, a certain number

number of parifhes were named to fupply fuch a company, and the officers could engage particular perfons at any time, even from the cradle; and if they did not anfwer in fize, they might follow any other employment: The king alfo commanded any of the fons of the nobility and gentry into the fervice whenever he pleafed, and when inferior officers have deferted, which fometimes has happened, they had a cuftom to hang them in effigie in the public fquares, fome of which we faw. The glafs manufacture which was at Potfdam is removed to Rifpen, for the conveniency of fuel, the glafs is the beft in the world, they cut it very finely, and make curious devices on it, infomuch that large drinking glaffes have been made, which have fold for a hundred, and even a hundred and fifty pounds, and what is for common ufe fells very dear; they alfo make it very well in imitation of garnate   We faw at Potfdam Potfdam one of the king's grenadiers, Kirkland, of the county of Longford in Ireland, he was twenty-feven years old, was feven feet three inches high, and the calf of his leg was one foot eight inches in circumference; he was well fet and ftrong, and every way in proportion. The Longobardi, who invaded Italy, and gave the name of Lombardy to the north part of it, are thought to have been the antient inhabitants of the country about the marquifate of Brandenburg

Luther and Melancthon are buried at Wittenberg, and they fhew Wittenburg many things there in relation to the former, and the houfe of doctor Fauftus near the town, concerning whom they have a great number of ftories.   There are copper mines near Mansfeldt and Eifleben, the ore is Mansfeldt. a black flate, which often has the figures of fifh in it, and they get fome filver out of the copper   The palace of the counts is built with a dendrite ftone, full of the figures of trees   Luther was born at Eifleben, Eifleben and many things are fhewn there in relation to him   There is a falt ftream runs from the mines into the lake of Eifleben, the waters of which are alfo falt, and there are feveral vegetables in it like fea weeds; but it abounds in carp and other frefh water fifh

At Hall there are fome of the falteft fprings in Germany, of the water Hall of which they make a great quantity of falt   This is a famous univerfity, and the orphanotroph here is a very particular foundation for grammar learning and philofophy, it was begun by profeffor Frank in one thoufand fix hundred and ninety-feven for orphans, but by degrees enlarged itfelf   There are a hundred and eleven poor children entirely maintained and inftructed in it, and befides thefe there dine every day in the refectory a hundred ftudents in divinity, two hundred and forty-eight other ftudents, who muft give in their names in the morning, and twenty four fervants of the houfe, forty orphan girls are alfo maintained here   They have two hundred and eighty boarders, children of little fortune, who pay a very fmall fum for their diet and lodging, and have their dining room by themfelves   Another part is what they call the pedagogue, which is for noblemen and gentlemen, there are fix youths in each room, with a mafter over them, of thefe there are two tables, and two prices for their diet   The whole fociety rifes at five, prayers are faid in their rooms till fix, they have an hour, from nine for breakfaft, and from eleven, from one, from fix, and from eight for exercife or amufement, from twelve for dinner, from feven for fupper, and from nine

for

for prayers, and at ten they go to repofe, three times a week they walk
out into the country with their mafters for two hours.   They are taught
Latin, Greek and Hebrew, and attend the public fchools for philofophy   The orphans and the fecond fociety exercife themfelves at leifure
hours in fawing wood, thofe of the pedagogue have feveral fine amufe-
men's, as gardening, turning, drawing, painting, anatomy, and botany,
experimental philofophy, the practical parts of aftronomy, grinding
glaffes, and making telefcopes, and other inftruments for the improvement of natural knowledge, and alfo mufic, making up a concert twice a
week, every diverfion being directed to fome end, they entertain themfelves
within their bounds, but cannot go any where abroad   They fpend
their Sundays altogether in reading and devotion, and the laft year
they are invited to attend lectures on the Scripture, and to perfect themfelves in the Greek and Hebrew languages, and when they have gone
through their philofophy entirely, they go out into the univerfity, take
lodgings, and attend the fchool of the profeffion they are to ftudy. In
a word, this is one of the fineft eftablifhed focieties for education I ever
faw   In this place, and in the univerfity, they compute two thoufand
ftudents   We here had the pleafure to converfe with Mr John-Philip
Barratiere, and as he was a prodigy of a youth, I thought it would not
be difagreeable to give a full account of him, as I took it down at that
time   He was born at Swoback, four leagues to the weft of Nuren-
burg, on the nineteenth of January, one thoufand feven hundred and
twenty-one, his father was born at Romans in Dauphine, and was at that
time minifter of the French reformed church at Hall, his mother was a
native of Chillons-fur Marne in Champagne. French was his mother
tongue, and as foon as he could fpeak his father taught him Latin, and foon
afterwards Greek, in which he made great progrefs, always delighting in
reading even at that age, at fix he began to learn Hebrew, and afterwards
the Rabbinical language, Chaldee, Syriac and Arabic, and having ma-
ftered thefe, he undertook the ftudy of hiftory, efpecially that of the
church, and among other hiftorians he read Jofephus, Tillemont, moft of
the Greek and Roman hiftorians, and all the Claffics, and afterwards feveral of the fathers of the church, he ftudied philofophy, criticifm, divinity,
and at eleven years old was a great mafter in all the abovementioned languages and parts of learning, and it is remarkable that he never read
any one grammar, he had no mafter but his father, and read fo faft
that he had gone through a huge folio in twelve days, and had fuch a
memory, that it all came to his mind as any thing occurred to recall it,
infomuch that he hardly ever read any hiftory twice, and took no pleafure in it, nothing that he had read feeming new to him, but if at any
time accidentally he looked into a hiftory a fecond time, all came to his
mind as he went along   He had always flept much, going to bed at eight,
and rifing at nine, but all his other time was employed in reading,
fometimes for his health he took a walk alone with a book in his hand,
taking no great pleafure in going abroad, or in any fort of diverfion Ma-
thematicks was his favourite ftudy, in which and aftronomy he had made
great progrefs when he was in his eleventh year, and he was much pleafed
with the ftudy of hiftory and philofophy At eleven years old he began to
tranflate out of Hebrew into French Rabbi Benjamin's travels, which he
                                                                     publifhed

published in eighteen sheets in duodecimo, to which he added about eight dissertations historical and philological of about twenty four sheets; he was only a month in translating it, though he did not allow above two hours a day for it; in another month he made most of the notes; in a third the eight dissertations; all which was done in the two last months of his eleventh year, and the first of his twelfth, tho' the book was not published till one thousand seven hundred and thirty-four, and the dissertations are esteemed to be very well wrote. At thirteen years old he begun to answer in Latin what Crellius the Socinian had writ on the beginning of the first chapter of St. John's gospel, under this title, " Initium Evangelii Sancti Johannis apostoli ex antiquitate ecclesiastica " restitutum, indidemque nova ratione illustratum;" it is thirty-four sheets in duodecimo, in Latin, shewing a great judgment, a knowledge of the Hebrew tongue, of the Scriptures, and of the Fathers, and is writ with much spirit and religious zeal, and the Latin in which it is writ was as familiar to him as his mother tongue; the title of this book is, Anti-Artemonius, printed at Nuremburg in one thousand seven hundred and thirty-five, he writ the preface to it the last day of his fourteenth year. About the spring of one thousand seven hundred and thirty-five his father being called to be minister of the French church at Stetin, and passing through Hall with his son, the child conversing with the professors of that university, they were surprized at his learning and knowledge, and took care to have the king informed of it, who ordered him to be brought to that university, and made his father minister of the French church in the town. Here he began to study philosophy, read Wolf's system, Malebranch, Cartesius, and Sir Isaac Newton, having gone thro' that of Antony Le Grand, in Swoback, he studied also algebra, mathematics, and astronomy, but he seemed to look upon algebra as a dry study, astronomy and antient history being the studies he most delighted in. When he came to Hall he was not entirely master of High Dutch; but when we saw him he was very perfect in it, and had studied English a little, having read part of Milton and some of Pope's works, with which he was much pleased, as well as with English plays. He understood Italian likewise, but had not applied much to it. After he came to Hall he studied the history of all the Roman emperors, and had read about a hundred books after he came to this place. The king had directed him to the study of the law, which, tho' not very agreeable to him, yet he had made a great proficiency in it, and sent a treatise of the law of nature three quarters of a year before to be revised by the fellows of the royal society at Berlin, of which he was a member. Most of these things we had from his own mouth, and heard him turn the oriental languages into Latin very readily, and were charmed with his conversation, which was full of knowledge and learning. After this, in the eighteenth year of his age, he published in Latin a chronological enquiry concerning the succession of the bishops of Rome, with four dissertations, two of which related to the apostolical constitutions, another concerning the writings of Dionysius, falsly called the Areopagite, and the fourth, of the years of Agrippa the younger, king of Judaea, all looked on to be works of great learning. He was of a moderate stature for his age, had a comely sensible countenance, good eyes, was very genteel, modeft, well behaved, and manly, anfwering all queftions readily, talked very fluently, and was mafter of philofophy, or arts at Hall He feemed to be rather of a puny conftitution, tho' his countenance was fomething on the florid, and he was troubled with the head-ach after much reading, and fometime ago had a fort of humour, either of a fcrophulous or cancerous nature, in the fore-finger of his left-hand, which came to that height that half his finger had been cut off; it was not then healed, and the humour feemed to continue: And having fuffered much from the furgeons, he did not care that they fhould meddle with it any more, fo that the confequence of it was much feared, and accordingly he died October the fifth one thoufand feven hundred and forty, in the twentieth year of his age.

Mersburg The emperor Rodolph is buried in the cathedral of Mersburg, where we faw his hand which was cut off, and occafioned his death, it is very remarkable that he took it up juft before he died, and made fome reflections on lifting up that hand againft his leige lord and fovereign the emperor Henry the fourth, which had brought him to that end.

Leipfick In the univerfity library at Leipfick there is a black wooden ftatue of the German god Puftei, called alfo Beuftard and Beuftrie, found at Rattenberg, it is about two feet high, and is like a fat Bacchus, the head is held out looking a little up, with the right hand on it, his left leg is fet forward, and his left hand is on the knee, a copy of it is feen in bronze at Sunderfhaufen in the palace of the prince of Swartzburg, and there is a pamphlet wrote concerning it We went to Altramftad where Charles the twelfth of Sweden had his head quarters for a whole year, and there, two famous treaties were concluded: Between this place and Lutzen, we faw the field of battle, in which Guftavus Adolphus received his mortal wound, and they fay there is a ftone fet up in the fpot, which has no infcription on it

Meiffen The only manufacture of Drefden Porcelane is at Meiffen, I faw as much of the nature of it as is fhewn to ftrangers, and got the following account of the invention of this manufacture. A boy, of the name of Bedker, apprentice to an apothecary in Berlin, had a powder or tincture given him by a Jew, which, as they fay, turned all forts of metals into gold, he was fent for by the king of Pruffia, but afterwards efcaped to Wittenberg, to which place the king of Poland fent for him, and kept him at the caftle of Konigftein, and it is faid he could tranfmute metals to gold as long as his tincture lafted. He afterwards made feveral experiments on earths in Saxony, and at laft found out the art of making porcelane, and was fixed at this place, was created a baron, and had a ftipend fettled on him The manufacture was begun near forty years ago, and the inventor has been dead above twenty. It belongs to the king, and is fold only in one place in Drefden and Leipfick, and the cheapeft of it is dearer than China-ware of the fame quality in England. At firft it was only made of red earth which was not glazed, but they polifhed it at a great expence as fine as marble, they afterwards left off making that fort. Organ-pipes have been made of it, and ftatues of men about three feet high, and alfo of feveral forts of birds and beafts painted in their natural colours, and many of them large pieces.

5

I faw

I faw vineyards on the hills towards Drefden, but the wine of the country which they fell, feems to be mixed with fpirits A fmall days journey to the fouth weft of Drefden, about Fridberg, there are feveral mines of filver, lead, copper, antimony, and arfenic, which belong to the elector of Saxony, and they have a particular way of managing the ores Fridberg is the burial place of the electoral family at this time, as Meiffen was formerly. I was informed that at Sneeberg they have a manufacture of the powder blue called fmalt, made of cobalth They have feveral fine marbles in Saxony, and a fort of foft green marble, which they call ferpentine, of which they make a great number of fmall vafes and toys; they have alfo very fine jafpers, agates, and the asbeftus, and a great quantity of precious ftones are found in the mines, particularly, amethyfts, topazes, opals, chalcedony, and in fome of the rivers of Voightland they find gold duft

Drefden is a place well known by all thofe who travel in Germany, and it would take up a volume to give a particular account of it, and of the extraordinary collections made in every way by the late king, who was the greateft encourager of arts and fciences, and of every thing that is curious. In the Zwinger Garten, there is a great collection of natural and artificial curiofities, of mathematical inftruments, and all forts of prints. In the king's treafury there is fomething of every thing of art which is moft curious, and in the moft coftly materials, there being a great variety of precious ftones, moft of them contrived to adorn the royal family. In another place is a collection of trappings for horfes, and of all forts of armour. The palace of Holland, called alfo the Indian palace, contains every thing curious from China and Japan, being a very extraordinary collection, and they have placed in it a great variety of the Drefden porcelane, and the whole furniture is Indian The fmall Turkey palace is all furnifhed after the Turkifh manner, and with pictures relating to thofe countries. The palace of the great garden without the town is filled with antiquities; and ftands in the middle of a garden adorned with a great number of modern ftatues Part of the palace of Pilenitz, three leagues from the town, is built after the Chinefe manner. The bridge over the Elb, which was widened by the late king, is one of the moft beautiful in Europe, it is five hundred and forty feet long, and thirty-fix broad; it confifts of nineteen arches, and is built of hewn ftone, there is a foot way on each fide, all the people that go out of the town keep on one fide, and thofe that come in on the other, for which purpofe there is a gate at each end of half the breadth of the bridge, which is opened only for thofe who are to go on that fide, the other part being always open

The fort of Koningftein, which is a little out of the road to Bohemia, is on a rock which is perpendicular every way, and is from a hundred to three hundred feet high, and about half a mile in circumference No ftranger can fee it without an order from the governor of Drefden, the afcent is very curious and difficult; there is a well in it cut through the rock, which, they fay, is fixteen hundred and fifty feet deep. It is famous alfo for the tun which was built by the order of the late king; the ftaves are near a foot thick, it is thirty feet long, and finely adorned, this tun is always full of Rhenifh wine, and holds four hundred

and

and feventy hogfheads, which, they fay, is above eighty hogfheads more than the tun of Heidelberg.

CHAP. IV.

Of BOHEMIA.

WHEN we came on the other fide of the hills in Bohemia we had a very fine and extraordinary profpect of that country. We could not go to Teplitz by reafon of the badnefs of the road, and the fnow, that place is famous for its warm baths, and for the quarries of chalck, in which they find a great quantity of mundike. Bohemia was antiently inhabited by the Boii, and afterwards by the Marcomanni. The fituation of Prague, thought to be the antient Marobuduum, is deferved/efteemed as one of the fineft in the world: The antient town was probably where the old city is, and it may be was firft of all on the height at Viffehrad, where the firft dukes of Bohemia had their caftle, on which a church was built in one thoufand and eighty-eight by king Wratiflaus   The cathedral is famous not only for being the burial place of the kings of Bohemia, but of the two patrons of the country Wenceflaus, and St. John Neopomucenus   The chapel of the former is lined within with all forts of Bohemian jafpers of fine colours, in many of which there is a mixture of amethyfts and agates, but they are put together in a very irregular manner: The fhrine of the latter is very much adorned with ftatues, and other decorations of filver.   The kings of Bohemia are crowned in this church by the archbifhop, and the queens by the abbefs of St George.   John of Hufs was the parifh prieft of the church of St. Gallus; and here they fhew his chalices and pulpit, and have feveral manufcripts of his people, and of thofe of Wickcliffe. The Jefuits college is one of the largeft in Europe, and the Irifh Francifcans have a monaftery, in which there are about feventy members. The famous Tycho Brahe is buried in the church of Teyna, he attended the court of Rodolph the fecond, and was a great favourite of that emperor   On a ftone againft a pillar of the church there is a relief of him in a coat of mail, his left hand on his fword, and his right on a globe, there is a chain about his neck, with a medal on it, and round the ftone is this infcription

ANNO DOMINI 1603 DIE 24 OCTOBRIS OBIIT ILLVSTRIS ET GENE-
ROSVS TYCHO BRAHE Dns IN KNVDSTRVP SACRAE CAESAREAE
MAJESTATIS CONSILIARIVS CVJVS OSSA HIC REQVILSCVNT

Over this there is another monument of marble, with a long epitaph on it. There is a famous univerfity at Prague, they fay it confifts of fix thoufand ftudents, and that formerly there have been no lefs than thirty thoufand.   In the court of the royal palace there is an excellent equeftrian ftatue of St George in bronze, which was made in one thoufand three hundred and thirty-three.   The mathematical houfe in the garden,

den, though it is not without faults, yet altogether it may be looked on
as a fine piece of architecture · If I do not mistake, it was either built
for Tycho Bache, or applied to his use   Count Lobkowitz has a beautiful palace here of very good architecture, as are those of the counts
Webna and Colowrat, of the archbishops, and Norbertins, but most of
the others are in a bad taste   The counts Gallash and Straka have very
grand palaces; but that which exceeds them all as to its magnificence is
the palace of prince Tschemen, the stair case and a suite of rooms in it
are very grand, one bed-chamber is entirely hung and furnished with
cloth of gold, adorned with silk Indian work

The bridge of Prague over the Mulda is one of the finest in Europe, *Bridge*
it was begun by the emperor Charles the fourth in one thousand three
hundred and fifty seven, and was not finished till one thousand five
hundred and two, it is fifteen hundred and eighty feet long, and thirty
feet four inches broad, there are seventeen arches, and the whole is
built of hewn stone   Over every pier they have put the statue of a
saint on each side

Near the city they have begun to build a magnificent hospital for in- *Hospital*
valids on a private benefaction, and have near finished two courts of
thirteen, which they say are designed   A league to the north of Prague
there is a palace of good architecture called Troya, belonging to the
counts of Pelting   At Weffenberg, or the white mountain, we saw the
spot where the Imperialists under Ferdinand the second obtained a com-
pleat victory over Frederick the elector Palatine, who married the daughter
of James the first of England, by which he lost both the kingdom of
Bohemia and his palatinate, after he had been crowned in Prague, and
the conquerors built a church on the spot   Near this place is the park
of Eynstern, in which there is a very curious fabric, which from its
figure is called the star building, it consists of three stones, and of six
points, and there are six rooms in the shape of a lozenge, with a passage
between each of them, and a round apartment in the middle   The ceilings
of the rooms of the ground floor are adorned with compartments of history reliefs, exactly after the Roman taste, the middle story is without any
ornament, and there is only one room in the highest, in which the history of
this battle, and some others, is painted on the ceiling in several compartments.   It is thought that the city of Prague is exceeded by no other cities *Nobility of*
in Europe, but Rome, London, and Paris, both in the riches and gran- *Prague*
deur of the nobility, they all travel and live in every respect in a manner
becoming their rank, and so agreeably among themselves, that few of
the heads of families care to accept of any employment which will oblige
them to leave the city

At Carlsbad there are two springs, one rises in the bed of the river, *Carlsbad*
which is very hot, and where it runs, there is a sediment, which, near the
source, becomes a stone which polishes, and is as beautiful as the finest
jaspers, this probably is occasioned by the particles of stones and minerals which are brought by the waters   Digging lately for foundations of buildings, they found a rock of a soft kind of white stone, in
which there was a great quantity of round white stones cemented together, exactly like dried peafe, and some like cups, both consisting
of several fine coats one over another   In the baths they find a sediment

on the top of the water about as thick as a wafer, which, when it is dry, becomes a fine powder. This mineral water is said to be a composition of chalk, red bolus or mountain earth, nitre, allum, vitriol, iron, and a volatile spirit of sulphur The mill-spring at some distance from this is of the same nature, but not so hot, nor so strong of the minerals as the other; it is used for bathing on the spot, and both for bathing and drinking by persons of warm and weak constitutions ; the other waters being proper for the cold and robust ; these waters in general are good for all obstructions, particularly for the gravel and barrenness There is a spring half a mile from the town, which they call the sowr spring, it is a chalybeat water, and I thought it was near as strong as the Spaw, they drink it with wine, and it is laxative.   Two leagues from Slackenwald there is a spring of the same nature, which is more esteemed, and is brought to Carlsbad to be drunk with wine ; the prince of Baden has a palace and fine gardens at that place The course of drinking the waters, bathing and sweating, is very severe and disagreeable. The nobility of the neighbouring countries frequent this place much, especially those of Bohemia and Saxony, and the great Czar Peter was here three times to drink them   They have a manufacture of pins and cutlery ware, swords, and fire arms, and they are famous for making handles of knives of steel inlaid with gold and silver, they have also a great manufacture of pewter vessels of the ore of Slackenweld, which is much esteemed, the ore is of a crumbling kind, they have also tin mines at Shonfield and Lauterback, and at Crazlitz, six miles distant, they have a foundery for making brass

Five leagues from Carlsbad in the way to Egra, we saw a chalybeat spring, at a village called Hammersberg, which is not so strong as the spaw, and further on we met with another mineral water   At Shonbach, very near to the borders of Saxony, there are mines of cinnabar, out of which they extract cinnabar and quick-silver A league to the north of Egra there is a famous mineral water of the nature of Piermont, it is used both for drinking and bathing, and there is another near it of the same kind, but not being clear, it is used only for bathing Some think that Egra is the antient Usbium, though others place it at Befenbeug on the Danube opposite to Ips

Bohemia is governed by a burgrave (who is a sort of viceroy) in conjunction with the council at Prague   All the nobility keep their lands in their own hands, having stewards to take care of their estates, the boors are vassals, and go with the land, and, excepting their lives, seem to be entirely in the power of their lords ; they cannot marry or make a will without their consent, they have a great aversion to their masters, of which their sovereigns make a proper advantage, and they may upon any occasion be threatened that freedom will be given to their vassals   They are famous in Bohemia for making glass, which is thick and strong, and almost as good as the English , and, I suppose, they make some in great perfection, for the best of it is ground in figures at Breslow, and I saw a glass, the cutting of which alone cost twenty pounds The kingdom of Bohemia abounds in natural curiosities, besides those I have mentioned, there are mines of silver mixed with copper at Kutenberg to the west of Prague, in which there is a crystal that is thought to be Flores cupri, they find likewife both white and yellow mundic, and formerly they had antimony there. At Joachamfdale, fix leagues to the north of Carlsbad, there are filver mines, and at that place they have what they call Medulla faxi, a fort of earth which polifhes like marble; I omitted to inform myfelf whether it is not that foft marble of which vafes are made, and is commonly called Serpentine. Near this place are the mountains of Garnate, which contain in them fome filver, as well as iron, the garnates of Bohemia are efteemed among the beft that are found. This country abounds alfo in precious ftones, particularly the amethyft, opal, and topaz; they have likewife very fine cryftals, and thofe of a yellow caft, are frequently fold for topazes.

CHAP. V.

The circle of BAVARIA.

WE entered into the upper Palatinate of Bavaria near Egra, and faw a very beautiful Ciftercian abbey at Waldfaflen. We came into lower Bavaria, and to Ratisbon on the Danube, that river Danube. is called the Ifter by Appian, from the confluence of the Save, and by Strabo, from the cataract near Axiopolis. We here entered into the antient Vindelicia, fo called from the rivers Vinde and Lycus, which unite Vindelicia below Augsburg. When the Romans conquered this country and Rhœtia, they made it one province under the name of the latter, and called the people of the former Rhœti Vindelici.

Ratisbon was called Reginum, from the river of that name which Ratisbon falls into the Danube, near it was Caftra Regimenfia, it was the capital of the Boii who fettled in thefe countries, when they were drove out of Bohemia. It is thought alfo to have been called Augufta Tiberii, and that Tiberius planted a colony here. This place was the ftation of the third Italic legion, and was therefore called Quartanorum Colonia: There is a Scotch abbey in this city. The bridge of Ratisbon is efteemed the fineft on the Danube; it confifts of fifteen arches, is about three hundred and fifty yards long, and eight yards broad.

We embarked on the Danube for Vienna, that voyage may be performed in a very fhort time, for they go with two oars about a league and a half in an hour, they draw large boats up the Danube loaded with goods, which are near a month in their paffage.

Four leagues below Ratisbon there is a village called Auburg, which Auburg agrees with the fituation of Auguftana Caftra. Straubing is thought to Straubing be Serviodunum. The windows of the collegiate church are finely painted, and the drawings better than ufual in a work of that nature: We faw Ofterhoven, which is thought to be Petronfia Caftra, and at Kinzen they place Quintiana. Paffaw, the antient Batava Caftra, is on Paffaw the Inn, the Ænus of the antients, to the eaft of which is Noricum, a country formerly famous for iron, and the fwords made of it were much efteemed, Boiodurum was on the other fide of the Inn. Great devotion

z I 3

is paid to a Madonna at Paſſaw. There is in this city a coloſſal head of a ſtatue of ſtone ſet in a wall near the cathedral, which we were informed was the head of a ſtatue in the old cathedral, probably of St Chriſtopher, though they have many ſtories in relation to it. The river Iltz falls into the Danube oppoſite to Paſſaw, it is famous for pearl, which are found in large muſcles, and though many of them have a blackiſh caſt, yet the beſt ſort come very near the oriental pearls. The water of this river is thought to be very wholeſom, and good in ſcrophulous diſorders, it is of a blackiſh colour, the Inn is of a pale green, and the Danube yellow, ſo that one ſees the different colours for ſome time after they run in one channel

---

CHAP. VI.

Of upper and lower AUSTRIA.

Lintz

LINTZ is certainly Lentia, and it is ſaid that a Roman road has been found leading towards it from Saltzburg, and that a milhary was dug up in the road. Lintz is a beautiful town. The archduke of Auſtria has a palace here, and the knights of the Teutonic order a commandery or priory. They are famous in this city for making barrels of guns, and have a great publick manufacture of woollen ſtuffs and ſilk. Inis is Anaſus of the middle ages on the river of that name, now called alſo Inns. At Lorch, half a mile to the ſouth of the walls of this town, there are ſome remains of the antient Lauriacum, called alſo Aureliana Lauriacenſis, the ſecond legion was ſtationed here, and at Lentia. The Roman emperors when they came on this ſide the Alps, at firſt reſided in Sirmium, and afterwards removed to this place. The cohors prætoria was alſo certainly here, probably at the time, when it was the reſidence of the emperors. This city was deſtroyed by the Hunns in five hundred and ſeventy, and in ſeven hundred and thirty ſeven, it was entirely craſed, nothing being left but the cathedral. From the north weſt corner of the old city there are ſigns of a foſſee, which extends to the church of St. Laurence it Lorch, and takes in a large compaſs, this may be the remains of the antient walls, for they find many medals about theſe ruins, which are chiefly the Roman ſilver, and others of the lower empire, and we ſaw men looking for them in new ploughed ground. There is a relief at the church, and one in the town of Inns. We ſaw here the lines which were drawn from Inns againſt the Turks. Near Greyn there are

Inns
Lorch

Abbey near Lintz, is ſaid by ſome to be Joviacum. Lorch is thought to be Lentium Juvar, or called Locus Felicis, is conjectured to be Ober Wels, which I ſuppoſe is Nidu Will. See in Hoſman's map Ipſa Ad pontem Iſis, and ſeveral medals are found about Lorch, which ſuppoſed to be Arlape, and Mellch to be Namare. It is to be obſerved that Stau-

menum might be it Neykirken, between Alchaw and Paſſaw, as Lefterding may be Ovilahm. Lauriacum is conjectured to be Trigiſamum, Pix enfort Puromtorium, and the abbot of Kremſ-ward thought that Creizelmair was the moſt likely place to be Comagenis, which is two leagues from the Danube, and not on it, is ſome map's place it several rocks in the bed of the Danube, which make it very rough, insomuch that it is a sort of a cataract, and below it are several whirlpools. On the hill above Melck there is one of the most magnificent abbies in Europe, belonging to the Benedictines, and the church, with regard to the statues, carving, and gilding, makes a most rich and splendid appearance. They have found four bass reliefs in and about the abbey, which are set into the walls of the church, one is of Romulus and Remus sucking the wolf, and another is sepulchral, they find also some medals here, and more at Pecklarn. We passed by the castle of Diernstain, where, they say, Richard of England was kept prisoner for about eighteen months. They find medals on the banks of the river about Stein. Two miles to the south east of Maubern is the rich Benedictine abbey of Gotweich, commonly called Ketwind. The present abbot Godfreid Beselius is a prelate of great humanity and extraordinary knowledge, especially in polite literature, he has published a chronicon of the abbey, with a map of Germany of the middle ages, and a specimen of the manner of writing manuscripts in different times. He has a great collection of medals, and of every thing that is curious, particularly figures of flowers and animals in stones, found near Wurtzburg, more curious than any I ever saw. Many medals have been found on this hill, and also three inscriptions, some are of opinion that it is part of Mount Commagenus. At Cloyster Newburg we came to those hills which divided Noricum from upper Panonia, on the east side of them is a place called Calenberg, and over it a ruined castle, which was the palace of residence of the antient dukes of Austria, when they removed from Melck. This place is thought by some to be Cetius, according to the Tables, or it might be at Cloyster Newburg, for it is suspected that the Itinerary is falsified in relation to the distance of this place.

I shall not attempt a description of Vienna, we made some excursions from it to several places. Baden is thought to be the antient Aquæ, famous for its waters, which are used only for bathing. The archdukes have a palace at Nieustat, to which the emperor Maximilian the first frequently retired, he had a hermitage there, and is buried in the church. The counts Senni, Frangipani, and Ragotzki were imprisoned here, the last escaped out of prison, the two others were beheaded, and their monument is seen here. Mansdorf to the south of Petronel is thought to be Mutenum of the Itinerary, others with very little reason have conjectured that it was at Musa. There is a spring here of warm water impregnated with sulphur, and used for bathing.

The antient Carnuntum, capital of upper Panonia, seems to have been on the site of Petronel, Altenburg, and Haymburg; it was a very antient city. The consul Licinius besieged it in vain in the first year of the war against Perses king of Macedon, which was a hundred and seventy-one years before Christ. In the tenth year of Christ, Tiberius brought it under the Roman yoke, the fourteenth double legion was stationed here, and the Roman fleet for the Danube, it was also the residence of the Roman præfect: A colony was brought to it, it was made a municipium, and the emperor Aurelius spent much of his time in this city. Altenburg and Petronel are two poor vil-

villages, not a league diftant, and about half way between them I faw marks of the old walls to the eaft, which feemed to have been about a mile in circumference, the fuburbs probably extending a great way on both fides, as may be concluded from the bricks and ruins which are feen over the fields, efpecially in the park, and near the river, where many medals are found, all thefe parts were probably fortified in the time of the Romans. Towards Steinabrun we faw an old road pointing to the fouth, which probably was the way in the Itinerary to Scarabantia, Sabaria, and Pætovio, between this road and Steinabrun there is a fpot which feems to have been a camp. It is thought by fome that Carnuntum, built by the Panonians, was about Haymburg, that of the Roman colony at Petronel, the palace and baths at Altenburg, and that all thefe were contiguous, and made one town. About a quarter of a league to the fouth of the ruins, which are to the weft of

Petronel Petronel, there are remains of an arch in the middle of the fields, two views of it may be feen in the hundredth plate, the lower part is built of rough ftone, the upper has a mixture of brick in it, the whole feems to have been cafed with hewn ftone, it is remarkable that there are many ftones in it which appear to have belonged to antient buildings, fo that probably it was erected in hafte, the arch is about twenty feet wide and ten deep, and the piers are twelve feet broad, the crown of the arch is about twenty-four feet from the ground, which has rifen confiderably, the building over the piers is about fixteen feet high, and it plainly appears that there was another arch joined to it, fo as to make four arches in all, like the forum of Janus at Rome, but as it is fo far from the river as not to be convenient for trade, and out of the town, it is more reafonable to think that it was a triumphal arch of the nature of that at Laodicea in Syria, in the twenty-eighth plate, and probably it was erected to the honour of Tiberius, as we are informed by Dion Caffius, that a triumph was decreed him, and two triumphal arches in Panonia. About half a mile to the fouth weft of this arch are remains of a building, which I thought might have been an amphitheatre. There are fome antient infcriptions at Petronel, one at count Traun's palace makes mention of a portico, there are two reliefs on the ftone, one is a Mercury with his emblems, the caduceus, purfe, and a cock, the other feemed to be Vertumnus, with a wheatfheaf in one hand, a hammer in the other, and a dog near him. Another infcription is feen at the

Altenburg archduke's palace at Altenburg, and two it a ftone-cutter's. There is a well here of mineral water ufed for bathing, in which fulphur feems to prevail. The moft curious infcription is that in the town-houfe at Haym-

Haymburg burg, by which it was difcovered that Carnuntum was a municipium, there are two reliefs on the ftone, one feems to be a perfon reprefenting the city with a turreted crown, a patera in the right hand, and a cornuco-pia in the left, as the other relief his likewife, and a rudder of a fhip on a globe in the right. To the eaft of Haymburg there is a hill, on which there feems to have been an encampment, and much barbarous filver coin has been found there, with a head on one fide and a horfe on the other. They have here a great manufacture of fnuff made of tobacco brought from about Debreckfin in Hungary, they make alfo fome cloth. In one thoufand fix hundred and eighty-three the Tartars

came

VIEWS of the ARCH at PETRONEL.

came here, and most inhumanly murdered most of the inhabitants, who had taken refuge in the castle

Returning to Vienna, we saw about twelve miles from Petronel, some signs of an old enclosure about a mile from Vishmund, this probably was Æquinoctium, as Mansworth seems to be Ala Nova, and may be the same place as Villigai, of the Tables. Sweckat is noted for a manu- Sweckat facture of printed cottons or callicoes, and for the meeting of the emperor Leopold and John king of Poland, after the latter had raised the siege of Vienna, and chased the Turks out of Germany, in memory of which an obelisk is erected with an inscription on it. The emperor has a palace at Ebersdorf, in which there is a picture of the Hauson fish Ebersdorf caught in the Danube, seventeen feet long, and weighed eight hundred and eighty seven pounds, they are commonly caught below Buda, and are very good

At New Gebaw, Rudolph the second enclosed the camp of Solyman New Ge- the Magnificent after the Turkish manner, with walls and turrets, and baw made a garden in the middle of it. To the west of it there are signs of an entrenchment, probably part of the Turkish camp; and to the north is a most magnificent banqueting house, built by the same emperor; it consists of apartments and galleries, all in a fine taste, with terraces down to the gardens on the river, commanding a glorious view of the Danube and country round, but all this noble building is in a ruinous condition

---

CHAP. VII.

Of some places in HUNGARY, near VIENNA; and from PRESBURG to BUDA.

WE made an excursion from Vienna to the south east, to see some antient places in Hungary. From Newstat we went to Oedenburg, thought to be Julia Scarabantia in the country called the deserts of the Bon. At Haina, a league to the east of Oedenburg, we saw an inscription on a stone coffin with these letters on it, MSCARB which seem to imply, that it was a municipium. There are several reliefs and inscriptions at Oedenburg, and they find many medals, and other antiquities. The Itineraries mention several ways, with different distances from this place to Vindebona, which have puzzled modern writers. Without entering into the dispute, I shall only observe, that we may very well account for three different roads to any place. The shortest only for horses, a summer road for carriages, and a longer round by the hills in winter, when the low grounds are not passible, and I have had experience in several places of a winter and summer road for carriages, and it is very common in all parts to have a short bridle road.

We

We went to Scharpin, where some would fix Scarabantia, but there are no fort of antiquities there, it had been a large town, and was burnt by the Turks Stenemanger is, without doubt, Colonia Claudia Sabaria, tho' some, on account of the name, would place it at Sarwar, where no antiquities are found, it is said that the præfect of Panonia resided here, and Aurelius Victor affirms, that Septimius Severus was proclaimed emperor at this place, but Spartian says it was at Carnuntum We saw at Steinemanger several pieces of granite pillars It is probable that Domitian was a benefactor to this town, for there are two infcriptions to him, with the name of Domitian erafed, as it was from all his infcriptions by an order of the fenate There are feveral other infcriptions, and fome curious reliefs about the town They have a ftory, which feems to be without any foundation, that Ovid was buried here It is faid, that St Martin was born at this town in three hundred and thirty-five, his father having been a tribune under Conftantine the great

The Newfidlerfee is the antient lake Peifo, the water of which was let out into the Danube by the emperor Galerius, that is, he probably cut a canal from it to the Rabnitz, which rifes in the morafly ground to the eaft of it, the water is falt, is fometimes very low, and there are but few fifh in it, the foil here is impregnated with nitre, and they make great quantities of falt petre at Newfidel At this lake Hunnimundus, king of Savia, was entirely defeated by Theodomir, brother of Walamir, king of the Goths At Wolf near the lake there is a fulphureous water which is heated and ufed for bathing, and there are iron mines at Eifenftatt which have not been lately worked, as it turns to better account to employ their hands in the vineyards Prince Efterhazi has a moft magnificent palace here This town was given to the emperor Frederick the third by Mathias Corvinus king of Hungary, as a pledge for the Hungarian crown, which the emperor delivered to him, as an infcription imports which is feen in the palace

When we departed from Vienna we went to the north of the Danube into Hungary, and croffed over thofe hills, which we thought to be the end of mount Carpites, that feparated this country and Dacia from Sarmatia When Buda was taken by the Turks, Prefburg was made the capital of Hungary, and the regalia are kept in it, this place having never been taken by the Turks

Going eaftward on the fouth fide of the Danube we paffed through Carlburg, thought to be Gerulata, and we faw figns of an old enclofure, part of which has been wafhed away by the Danube, and we obferved about it foundations of old buildings of Roman brick Altenburg is thought to be Ad Flexum, and two or three infcriptions have been found at Wifelburg, half a league to the eaft of it Near a firm houfe, called Brattoldtye, we faw a bank like the foundation of a wall, it feems to have been about a hundred paces fquare, three fides of it remaining We obferved feveral Roman bricks in fome earth lately thrown up, and they told us that they often found medals there, it is two Hungarian miles both from Rahab and Altenburg, and we concluded that it was Quadrata, which has not been obferved by any writer

Rahab

Rahab is the antient Arrabo, it was taken by the Turks in one thousand five hundred ninety-four, and retaken by stratagem four years after
Several inscriptions have been found here, but now there is only one to
be seen, and a relief in the north wall of the cathedral : We saw also a
relief and inscription at a village called Ais[a]. The citadel of Comorra
was never taken, there are three stone coffins in it, and several inscriptions about the town brought from Zeny. It has been commonly
thought that Bregetio was at Gran, but on considering the distances, and
from the inscriptions found at Zeny a league below Comorra, we discovered that this was the site of Bregetio About half a mile to the
west of Zeny we came to a spot enclosed with a slight fossee, where
there are some marks of old buildings ; and not so far beyond Zeny to
the east there is such another ruin, and between this and the site of the
antient town are some imperfect remains, which from the ground, we
judged to have been a theatre or amphitheatre Round the old town
there are signs of a double fossee, extending six hundred and forty paces
from east to west, and seven hundred and fifty from north to south,
these are joined by two other fossees on the north side, which extend
about two hundred paces to the river A little lower on the other side of
the river there is such another enclosure about a hundred and thirty paces
square, with an entrance on each side, and fossees drawn from it to the
river in the same manner This seems to have been for the defence of
that side of the river, and is now called Leanywar On both sides we
found many Roman bricks, but all the inscriptions have been carried
away chiefly to two churches, which are about a league to the east, at
a place called Futufy, they are in a kind of a peninsula, where the
small river Dotis falls into the Danube : To the south west of the
church, which is furthest to the east, we saw an inscription, in which
the first legion is mentioned that was quartered at Bregetio, and observing a large stone at the east end of the church, we employed men
to dig it out, and found an inscription on it, in which, as well as in the
other, mention is made of the third Thracian legion We saw in
the same church two or three other imperfect inscriptions on an altar, and
some reliefs. At the village of Zeny we found the top of a stone coffin,
and there is a stone at the door of the Calvinist church, on which we saw
part of an inscription, but could not prevail on the boors to dig it up, we
were informed also that there was an inscription a league to the south of
the village

We went four leagues a little way to the south east of the road to
Gran, to a small town called Dotis, which from some antiquities found
there is thought to be an antient place, and agrees best with the situation of Florian At the corner of the church there is a square pillar
divided into compartments three feet long, with a relief in each, as I
suppose, of a heathen god, with their emblems, though I could only
distinguish Juno with the peacock In the castle there is a relief of
Hercules encountering the lion, and a large marble coffin in a private

a Baia is two leagues to the south of Rahab,
where, they say, there are mines, and it may
be Ad munes, or Ad munos It is said, that
Justina, the widow of Valentinian, resided with

her son Valentinian in a village or house near
Bregetio, the expression is, "In Villa muro
cincta," which might be Ad munos I own
I'm not as to the country to the east of Arrabo

yard ; on each fide of an infcription on it is a Cupid refting upon an extin-
guifhed torch ; it appears to have been the tomb of the wife of a phyfician in ordinary to the firft legion Adjutrix, and that fhe was a lady
of Forum Hadriani in Lower Germany, which is thought to have been
Voorburg, oppofite to Ryfwick, within a league of the Hague. The
caftle here was in poffeffion of the Turks, who built a modern fortification round it, and blew up all, when they left it, in one thoufand five
hundred and fixty-five   They have quarries here of a red coarfe marble, as well as in the neighbouring mountains, and fome baths are mentioned near this place which we did not fee

Almas

From Dotis we went four leagues northwards under the hills, paffing
very near the two churches of Futufy, and came to Almas, which is near
four leagues from Comorra, and about three fhort leagues from old
Bregetio , here probably was Azao, which the Itinerary places between
Bregetio and Lacus Felicis, and may be the fame as Lepavift of the
Tables, placed fix miles from Bregetio ; but no antiquities are found
there   Half a league beyond this is Nefmid, the firft poft from Comorra, two long Hungarian miles diftant   We went two miles further by the Danube moftly under the hills, at one place where we were
obliged to go up the hill on account of the overflowing of the river,
and came to Neudorf   A quarter of a league to the north weft of the
town is a hill over the river, which commands a very fine profpect, and
might therefore be called Locus Felicis, of which Lacus Felicis of the
Itinerary is probably a corruption , and there is fuch another miftake as
to Walfee on the Danube in Germany, which is exactly fuch another
fine fituation   This place in the Itinerary is eighteen miles from Bregetio, which does not very much difagree with the diftance, as it is not
feven leagues from Zeny , Neudorf, which is further, being but four
miles off Hungary from Comorra   But what confirmed us in the opinion is a place called Gardellaca of the Tables, thirteen miles from Le-
pavo, which we thought muft be Almas, and fo the whole diftance
from Bregetio in the Tables is nineteen miles, which agrees better than
the Itinerary , the name alfo is another reafon, as it was probably a place
to guard the paffage of the Danube, for which it is very proper, and at
prefent there ftands a wheel on it as a fign that boats muft pay toll there.
But what puts it out of all difpute are the Roman infcriptions found
here, two of which are at the church of a Francifcan hermit on the hill,
a third on an altar fet into the wall, and another in the pedeftal of a ftatue erected on the hill out of devotion , and in the church-yard of
Neudorf we faw a piece of an altar, and another old ftone, with fome
letters on them   This hill was fortified by thofe who were in the rebellion of Hungary, and they were all cut to pieces here. We faw about the
ruins of the fort feveral Roman bricks, and in other parts foundations
of thick walls, which feemed to be Roman.

Gran

We arrived at Gran, and though the kings of Hungary formerly refided there, yet now it has more the appearance of a very large village
than of a city , and as they have no trade fo all the people are employed in hufbandry   It is the metropolitan fee of the province of Upper
Hungary, as Colocza is of the lower   And the archbifhop of Gran,
who refides at Prefburg, is primate of all Hungary   The caftle is very
ftrongly

strongly situated; which was taken by Solyman the second in one thousand five hundred and forty-two, and was soon retaken, but sultan Achmet possessed himself of it in one thousand six hundred and eighty-three. The armies of the emperor and king of Poland beat the Turks at the castle of Barcan on the other side of the river, and took the city and castle of Gran after it had been in the possession of the Turks eighty years. The Turks besieged it again in one thousand six hundred and eighty five, but the siege was raised by the dukes of Lorrain and Bavaria, who gave the Turks battle in the plain not far from the city, through which the road passes from Comorra to Buda, and defeated sixty thousand of them, who fled over the hills to Buda, leaving their baggage in the camp. The battle was to the north of a chapel where the Christians were buried; and this defeat made the Turks sue for peace. Stephen the third was buried somewhere in this city, and Bela the fourth was interred in one of the parish churches. St. Stephen king of Hungary was born here, and it is said was christened in a chapel near the cathedral, which probably was the old baptistry. The cathedral within the castle is in ruins, but the west door remains entire, which is a fine Gothic piece of architecture, of marble of different colours, adorned with figures of saints, made of large pieces of marble inlaid and marked out with lines. Over the door is king Bela, with the figure of the church in his hand, and the archbishop near him, that king, if I do not mistake, being founder of the cathedral. There is a chapel adjoining to the church of fine architecture, and lined with red marble, it was built by cardinal Bacocz in one thousand five hundred and seven. Some authors mention baths at this place, of which I could get no account. We passed over the spot of the famous battle, and by the chapel where the Christians were buried, and came into the high road to Buda, as we went on we had mount Pilis to the north of us, at the east foot of which there are ruins of a large monastery. We came to a village called Czaba, a little beyond the parish church there is another ruined church in the road, where they sometime ago dug up two inscriptions, which are now at the parish church, and probably others might be found by turning up the stones. Crumeros, it may be the same as Lusimari, might be here, and be a fort to guard the pass to the mountain. In one of the inscriptions the fourth legion is mentioned, which was probably quartered here.

Czaba

Beyond the village of Woreswar we left the road in order to go directly east to St. Andre on the Danube. We came to a cross opposite to a ruined church to the north, and found an antient miliary set up against it, and tho' the names of the emperors were much defaced, yet from the pedigree we concluded, that the names of Marcus Aurelius, Antoninus, and Lucius Verus were on it, at the bottom are these letters, AB AC MP the purport of the letters must have been so many miles from Acincum or Buda, but the number is not to be seen. We passed through two Rascian villages, Sobantza and Pomasz; to the east of the latter there are very great ruins of a castle entirely destroyed. We came to the small town of St. Andre, chiefly inhabited by Rascians, who have several churches, the Walachians also have two, and the Germans one. As there was no inn, we were accommodated with a

Andre

public

public houfe of the town, where we had not fo much as a bed; we fent to market, and got our provifions dreffed at one of their little wine houfes. Oppofite to this town there is a large ifland near two leagues broad, extending from Vifegrad almoft as far as Buda.

VifegradWe went four leagues northward to Vifegrad, paffing through Bogdani, oppofite to which we faw a fmall town called Vatz on the eaft fide of the Danube On a hill over Vifegrad there is a ruinous caftle very ftrongly fituated : The regalia of Hungary were kept in it till the Turks invaded this country, and then it was often taken and retaken by both armies Some of the kings of Hungary refided here, and particularly Matthias Corvinus Charles king of Naples being declared king of Hungary, and wounded in his head, was brought to this caftle under pretence of curing his wounds, and was ftrangled in it.

C H A P. VIII

Of BUDA, fome other parts of HUNGARY; and of CROATIA.

BudaBUDA has fuffered very much in the wars, there are two well built Turkifh mofques remaining in the town The fortrefs was taken and burnt by Soliman the magnificent in one thoufand five hundred and twenty-fix, and retaken the next year. Soliman took it again in one thoufand five hundred and twenty-nine, the Chriftians often attempted in vain to get poffeffion of it, till the duke of Lorrain took it by ftorm in one thoufand fix hundred and eighty, and in one thoufand feven hundred and twenty-three it was blown up by a magazine of powder which was fired by lightning, and now there remains but very little of the palace of the kings of Hungary, which was built by that encourager of arts and fciences Matthias Corvinus, who had here a valuable library, which has been fince difperfed Old Buda, to the north of the prefent city, is certainly the antient Acincum or Aquincum, and there are a great number of reliefs and infcriptions about it, in which the fecond legion Adjutrix is mentioned, which was quartered at Acincum, many of them are in the houfe of the counts of Schetfin We faw to the north of old Buda fome fign of the city walls, and remains of an amphitheatre, as we concluded from the manner in which the ground lay The water was brought to the old city about a league by an aqueduct which is a folid wall, that in fome places was ftrengthened by arches turned in it, this aqueduct has accidentally received an additional ftrength by the water running thro' it, which in feveral places has formed great rocks of petrifactions againft it, which I have feen in feveral other aqueducts There are many ruins to the north of old Buda, but we could form no judgment as to the nature of the buildings In the Rafcian fuburb there is a fragment of a fine ftatue fitting in long robes, the upper part of it being broken off Buda is famous for its hot baths, which are

faid

faid to be a compofition of gold, iron, calmi, fulphur, feveral falts,
allum, and fome other minerals, there are five baths of different qualities, and one of them makes a petrification, fomething like that of
Carlsbad

Pefth, which is probably Tranfacincum, is oppofite to Buda, and is **Pefth.**
a pleafant new town; fome infcriptions, and pieces of granite pillars remain in it; on the river to the north of the town there is a ruin,
which looks fomething like the end of a bridge, but as it is not probable that a bridge fhould be built at this place, both by reafon of the
difficulty of it, and becaufe there is no account of fuch a bridge, it may
be rather concluded to be the remains of a tower to defend the pafs of
the river   The chief fupport of Pefth are the two great courts of Hungary held here for civil difputes

We fet out from Buda for Stool-Weiffenberg; a league to the fouth
of the city thofe hills end, which go round part of the plain that is to
the fouth of Buda, this part is called Promontorium, and Marfili makes a
Roman work there; when we went to it we found feveral Roman
bricks about the fields, and there might be a fort here to defend the
pafs · There are feveral quarries of free ftone under the hill, and farther on we faw the remains of a Turkifh paved way, thofe who are
fkilled in the antiquities of Hungary, fay, that Attila and the firft kings
of the Hunns refided fomewhere in that large plain, which is to the eaft
of Buda, either at Yasberin or about it   Two Hungarian miles from
Buda, at a houfe of baron Banitzky, which is called Martinweifer,
we faw a relief of Hercules killing the Hydra; another of a fepulchral
kind, and a third which feemed to be an altar, with two reliefs on it,
one being a perfon holding a fimpulum; thefe were all brought from
Buda   We travelled over rich downs through an unimproved country,
very thinly inhabited, the nobility having a great number of oxen on
their eftates, which they fell moftly in Germany, and fend fome of them
even as far as Italy   The fheep here have twifted horns fomething like
the antelopes

We arrived at Stool-Weiffenburg; the air of this place is very bad, being **Stool Weif-**
fituated in a great morafs, which continues a confiderable way on each fide **fenburg**
of the river Sarwitz as far as Symontornya, a place famous for wines, which
are fold for Tokai, as well as thofe of Eperies and Cafchaw, which are
near Tokai   As many infcriptions and reliefs have been found here, fo
it is conjectured to have been fome antient town in the road from Sirmium, either to Lauriacum or Carnuntum, if the former, it agrees beft
with the diftances of Valco, if the latter, which feems more probable,
it anfwers the fituation of Cimbrianæ, they fay the kings of Hungary formerly refided here for fome time, and had their burial place in
the town, and that at firft it confifted only of the palace and the collegiate church, in which the kings were buried. This building from the
little that remains of it, appears to have been a magnificent ftructure, but
the Turks deftroyed it, and the bodies of the kings could never be
found, part of their monuments, with the reliefs in red marble, are feen
in the town wall, where moft of the infcriptions are placed   The Turks
took it in one thoufand five hundred and forty three; the emperor Matthias retook it in one thoufand fix hundred and one, but the next year

it was taken by the Turks again, who held it till one thousand six hundred and eighty-eight, and in one thousand seven hundred and three the emperor ordered the fortifications to be demolished. There is a Turkish mosque and a fountain remaining in the town, and some ruins of their bagnios.

In the way to Vesprin we had the morass to the south east of us, which seemed to extend towards the lake Balaton, and if so, probably the river Sarvitz rises out of the lake, whereas the maps make both the morass and the river to come from the north west. We passed by the village and castle of Palota, which held out some time against the Turks.

Vesprin. I saw fraxinella growing wild in the fields in these parts. Vesprin is situated on a rock about half a mile in circumference, there being a large suburb round it. It was taken and retaken in the first Turkish war, but in the last, the Turks did not get possession of it. There is a beautiful cathedral here, and a chapel under it, to which they say St. Emerick duke of Hungary used often to resort.

In the way to the lake Balaton, about a league from Vesprin, we saw them digging for stone, where there had been an antient building, I observed some Roman brick, and that the walls were very solid, probably it had been a fort to defend the passage this way. There is great

Lake Bala- plenty of coarse fish in the lake Balaton, which they catch in great
ton. abundance when the lake is froze over, by breaking holes, and letting down their nets. On the side of the lake there is a very spirituous mineral, which they drink, it tastes much like that of Piemont, and is laxative, they warm it likewise, and put it in tubs for bathing, they say sal nitre prevails in it, and I observed a very thick coat sticking to the vessels in which they boil the water. It is an extraordinary sight to see the peasants coming here every morning in waggons, to drink or bathe, some of the sick having their beds in the waggons. We crossed over the west end of the lake in a ferry boat. The river Sala falls into it there, which passes thro' the country of Salwar. Our carriage was conveyed over on a wooden floor laid on four boats, each of which were cut out of one piece of wood.

We travelled through the woods, and observed several ruinous churches, where there formerly had been villages, the country having been laid waste by the wars. The people here are mostly Calvinists, some being Romans and Lutherans. There is no manner of accommodation in these parts, except a very poor public house in the villages, and we commonly stopped every day in the woods to refresh
Canisha. ourselves and our horse. We came to Canisha, which was formerly fortified, and taken by the Turks in one thousand six hundred, it was frequently besieged, but was not retaken till the time of Leopold, who demolished both the town and fortifications, and now it is only like a large village.

We went over the Drave into Croatia, and crossing the old bed of the Drave, we came again into Hungary to Le Grad. Near forty years ago the Drave changed its channel, and Le Grad is between the old bed of the Drave and the present channel, a small stream now runs in the old bed, and falls into the Drave a quarter of a league below Le Grad, so that it makes an island about a league and a quarter in circum-

circumference Le Grad is like a large village, though there are five Le Grad hundred houfes in it, above a hundred of which are inhabited by Lutherans, but the people will not permit their minifters to come among them We were at a village called Stridona, where St Jerom was Stridona born, and they have built a chapel, which, they fay, is on the fpot, and his hiftory is painted in it. The grounds for their opinion is, that he fays he was born at Stridona on the confines of Dalmatia and Panonia But as Panonia extended much further, the place of St Jerom's birth is thought to be rather at Zerin in Croatia, and fome have conjectured that it was at Sdregna in Iftria

Czakathurn may be Alicanum, as it is in the poft road from Pettaw to Czakathurn Stenemanger, the antient Sabaria, and there is a fine ftone here with a Roman infcription on it, and fome reliefs, among them is Romulus and Remus fucking the wolf, and a Capricorn with the tail of a fifh. We left Hungary, and went into the kingdom of Croatia

The duke of Lorrain, as we were informed, was the firft viceroy of State of Hungary; the palatine before being the fecond perfon in the kingdom, Hungary and generaliffimo by his office, he is elected by the ftates of the greater and leffer nobility, and of the clergy, and by the deputies of the towns, and prefides in their affemblies The Roman religion is eftablifhed in Hungary, the Lutherans, Calvinifts, and Greek Rafcians are tolerated, and where there are no Romans they have the parifh church, tho' the minifters have not the tithes, but they enjoy them in Tranfylvania. The Lutheran minifters are moftly bred in the univerfity of Saxony, and the Calvinifts in Tranfylvania near Alba Julia There are a great number of Rafcians in Hungary who are of the Greek church, to which the Chingeners unite themfelves, who are like gipfies, and have the fame qualities, but they have a trade in making cutlery ware, and pitch their tents at the fkirts of the towns, they are not permitted in Germany

The air and climate of Hungary is looked on as very unwholfom, Nature in efpecially to ftrangers, occafioned by the nitre which is in the air, and ftory when it is hot by day, the nights are cold, and they have great dews, fo that it is very dangerous to be abroad at night, unlefs they are well cloathed Their wines have a fine flavour, but are heady, and are thought to caufe the ftone and gravel The foil is very fruitful, and many parts run fo much into wood that they bark the trees in order to kill them, and when they are rotten fet them on fire And at a diftance from towns, there is fuch a plenty of wood and pafturage that it is looked on to be in common to travellers, and they have a right to what they can ufe The mountains of Hungary, efpecially to the north weft, abound very much in minerals of gold, filver, copper, iron, lead, antimony, and cinnabar, the chief are to the north of Gran, at Neufoll, Altfoll, Kremnitz, and Schemnitz, to the north eaft of the laft they have mines of falt, which they ufe all over Hungary, and fome of it is fo fine that they make toys of it, which appear like tranfparent alabafter

They fay that the hawfom fifh in the Danube has been taken twentyone feet in length, they come up from the Euxine fea in the fpring as far as Buda to fpawn. We were informed of a very particular manner of catching

catching them, by encompaffing *them* with a net, and men go into the water, tickle them on the belly, and fo get them afhoar, and they muft not perceive the net before they are in fhallow water ; becaufe they are fo very ftrong, efpecially in their tails, that if they ftrike they certainly kill, it is a very fine fifh, and eats like a turbat.

Croatia.

The kingdom of Croatia is one of the five which were dependant on Hungary, the other four being Dalmatia, Sclavonia, Servia, and Bofnia: We went to Warafdin, which is a little way from the river, and is flightly fortified, there is nothing remarkable in the town. Croatia is governed by a ban, or viceroy, under the fovereign of Hungary; they pay no taxes, nor will they fubmit to any, but fend men to the war, and, if I do not miftake, they pay them At that time they fent fixteen thoufand, and the nobility go into the war as officers or voluntiers. The people are brave foldiers, and as they have always enjoyed their liberties, fo they have ever been faithful to their fovereign It is thefe people, if I have not been mifinformed, who in time of war fend one half of their men into the field one year, the others remaining at home to cultivate their lands, who go to the war the next year They fpeak Sclavonic, which is an oriental tongue, and of great ufe in the north eaft parts of the world, for, they fay, it is fpoken in different dialects as far as China, and may be looked on as a mother language, it is faid that the Hungarian is not derived from it, but from the Hebrew and other eaftern languages, the Hunns, being the antient Scythians, who without doubt originally came from the countries to the fouth eaft.

CHAP. IX.

Of STIRIA.

Stiria

STIRIA is called Steir Marck, that is, Stiria, on the bounds of Germany, for marck fignifies the bounds, and the countries on the bounds were called Margravates, and the governors Margraves, which feems to be much the fame office as that of the Duces Limitanei of the Roman empire, who prefided over the countries and provinces which were on the bounds, fo thefe countries feem to have been granted by the emperors to great men with the title of Margraves, that is, graffs, or counts of the boundary, on condition that they defended the bounds of the empire

Pettaw

Pettaw is the antient Petovn, which was fituated on the hill of the caftle, and on the high grounds to the north of it When the Romans befieged this city under Auguftus, a great number of the country came to their affiftance, but Auguftus led his army againft them, prevented their entering into the city, and received a wound in his knee by a ftone This city was made a Roman colony, and there are many infcriptions about the town, particularly at the church of Saint Martin, a mile out of the town, a mile further at Emffield, at the

houfe

houſe of count Saur. About half a league out of the town, in the garden of baron Cramp, there is a coffin of white alabaſter, which has ſome ornaments on it that ſeemed to be of the middle ages. There are ſeveral reliefs in the caſtle, and a very extraordinary one in the town; it conſiſts of the ſtory of Orpheus, and ſome other ſubjects, and is publiſhed by Montfaucon, the ſtone is of white alabaſter ſixteen feet long and ſix wide

At the caſtle of the biſhop of Seccau above Leibnitz, there are ſeveral inſcriptions and reliefs, ſuppoſed to have been dug up near, probably in the valley below. And it appears from an inſcription in the caſtle of Gratz, that in the time of the emperor Maximilian, a glaſs full of aſhes, bones, and a Roman medal were found at Leibnitz, and placed in that palace, on the whole it is to be concluded, that Muroela was ſomewhere near Leibnitz We came into the great road from Trieſte to Vienna, and arrived at the flouriſhing and beautiful city of Gratz, the capital of Stiria, ſuppoſed to have been firſt built by the ⟨Gratz⟩ Vindi or Sclavi, on the hill of the caſtle, about five hundred and ninety years after they had conquered Panonia Carnium, and Noricum; but when Charlemagne drove them out and made the Arab the bounds of Germany, they built Windiſh Gratz, or Gratz of the Vindi, and this place being inhabited by Bavarians, was called Bavarian Gratz.

The marquiſes of Stiria had reſided at Styre, and were made dukes by Frederick Barbaroſſa. On the death of Ottocarus that family was extinct, and the duchy of Stiria came to Leopold the virtuous, father-in-law of Ottocarus, and marquis of Auſtria, who firſt reſided at Gratz. From Charles of Gratz, ſon of Ferdinand the firſt, the Auſtrian family are lineally deſcended, that is, from his ſon Ferdinand the ſecond; this is called the Gratz line, for Maximilian the ſecond, being eldeſt ſon of Ferdinand the firſt, was ſucceeded by his eldeſt ſon Rudolph the ſecond, and he by his younger brother Matthias, in whom the line from Maximilian the ſecond was extinct, and then came in the line from the younger ſon of Ferdinand the firſt, that is Charles of Gratz, who being dead at the time of the deceaſe of Matthias his eldeſt ſon, Ferdinand the ſecond ſucceeded to the empire.

There are a great number of inſcriptions in the palace of the archduke of Auſtria, and alſo about the town, ſo that it is probable that Carrodunum was near this place We went a league to the church of Stranginy, which is on a hill, where we ſaw an inſcription and ſome reliefs, and there were other inſcriptions which have been removed, ſo that probably the antient city was there, for it is an old mother church, and there are ſeveral others dependant on it

We entered in between the mountains Cetius, which divided Noricum from Pannonia, and travelled northwards to Rettleſtein, oppoſite to a high mountain of that name, towards the top of which, they ſay, there is a grotto two miles long, and that what are called dragons bones are found in it, which probably are bones of animals carried in by beaſts of prey; for we could not croſs the river to go to it Pruck is in the road from Venice and Trieſte to Vienna We went from this place to Mari Zell, ⟨Mari Zell⟩ where there is an image of the Virgin Mary, to which they pay great devotion, the treaſury is rich in diamond rings, and cameos, and in ſtatues and vaſes of gold and filver, fome of which are adorned with precious ftones. In this road there are great iron works for making iron into bars, which is brought from the mines of Eifenarts to the weft; thefe, and the mines in the archbifhoprick of Saltzburg, without doubt are thofe which produced the iron of Noricum, fo famous among the antients. The common people in the mountainous parts of Stiria are very much troubled with fwelled necks, occafioned by drinking the fnow water

Seccau

Seccau is the fee of the only bifhopric in Stiria, in the cathedral there is a chapel wainfcoated with marble, and very richly adorned by Charles of Gratz, as a monument for his family, there being a vault under it, in which their bodies lie; from this place we went into Carinthia [a]

The county of Cilley is now looked on as a part of Stiria, it was governed by its own counts for three hundred years to the latter end of the fifteenth century, when it came to the houfe of Auftria, and the ftates of it meet at Gratz, with thofe of Stiria.

We went into that county from Laubach in Carniola; after traveling five miles we croffed the Save, which by an error in the Tables is made nine miles from Fmona Five miles from this place we paffed the Trifnitz [b] Trajaniburg, or Trajan's hill, is a village in this road at the foot of a hill, five German miles from Laubach; we found here three antient infcriptions; and this muft be the Manfio, called Hadrante or Adriante, thefe places are in Carniola.

County of Cilley

We came into the county of Cilley, and faw a grotto at Frantz, where there are fome curious petrifications; but we could not find that it had any communication with the rivulet below it· This place was probably Ad medias· Upellis was alfo fixteen miles from Cilley this way; and a village called Cuple feems to retain fomething of that name.

Cilley

Cilley is the old Cileia, which we found by an infcription was called Claudia Cileia, fo that probably Claudius brought a colony to this town We faw feveral heads with bulls or rams horns; which made us conjecture that Jupiter Ammon was worfhipped here, there are feveral antiquities and infcriptions in and about the town, efpecially at the churches of St. Maximilian, and St Andrew, as likewife of Okanick in the road to Vienna, and at a caftle called Ober-Cilley. The counts of Cilley are buried in the church of the Minorets; and the archduke of Auftria has a palace here, which was the habitation of thofe counts.

---

[a] I conjecture that Houndfmirk was Ad pontem mentioned in the Tables between Ovilabis and Petovio, and that Newmark is not Noreia, as fome have conjectured, of which I fhall have occafion to fay more

[b] About this place, Mutatio Ad quartodecimo of the Jerufalem Itinerary feems to have been, and Ad decimo of the Tables

CHAP.

CHAP. X.

Of CARINTHIA.

FROM Seccau in Stiria we went to Freisach in Carinthia, which Freisach seems to be Noreia, though it has been taken for other places; but this conjecture is confirmed by Strabo's testimony, that Noreia had veins of iron, and rivers with sands of gold : For there are iron mines half a league from the town, and there were mines of gold and silver in the hills to the east, which probably are exhausted, as they are not worked at present : There are several inscriptions and reliefs about the town I observed a hill near the town of a grey coarse marble of the Cippolino kind, of which all their hewn stone work is made here

At Gurck, which is a bishop's see, we saw an antient stone, with a Gurck defaced inscription, and a relief of a person holding a vase; some conjecture, with very little foundation, that this place was Graviacis At St. Veit we saw a bason of a fountain nine feet in diameter, which, St Veit they say, was dug out near the mill at Solfeld, and there is a small brass Gothic statue on it, which they affirm to have been found also at Solfeld, there are likewise several Roman reliefs and inscriptions here, all brought from that place.

We set out for Solfeld [c], the antient Solva or Flavium Solvense, sup- Solfeld posed to be a Roman colony, which might be planted by Vespasian, Solva and probably was a municipium, some are of opinion, that Attila destroyed this town, which does not appear, and as Odoacer ordered all the Romans to go out of Noricum, it is very natural to suppose that their towns should afterwards run to ruin, it is called Maria Sol from a church in the town, in which the font seems to be an antient vase · The old town was on the plain, and on the side of the hills; and probably extended from Arndorf church a league to a pit called Lindwurmb-Gruben: To the left it stretches to the river, and to the right up the hill to Rotzendorf church, and to Telshach wood

From Maria-Sol we went down into the plain, where there is a curious piece of antiquity, which is now called Kaisarstool, a large stone six feet long, and five broad is set up an end, on the west side a stone is put up against it; between this and the great stone there are two small ones, on one of which there is some part of a Roman inscription. The seat on the other side is a stone laid on an old Gothic capital, with a stone on each side of it for the urns to rest on, towards the top of the great stone on that side is cut RVDOLPHVS DVX, who was the first peaceable possessor of Carinthia Æneas Sylvius gives a

[c] In the way we found inscriptions at all the following places At the churches of Unter-Milbach, St Donatus, St Michael, and Prunner's Cross, at St Anthony, and the mill, where there are ruins of some antient building In a field to the south of the cross they say there was a temple of the sun, but I saw nothing but old Roman bricks scattered over the fields On the hill over the mill we observed the ruins of some building and going a quarter of a league to the east passed by the house of a nobleman near Meilelburg, and came to the churches of Possaw and Rotzendorf, and from that place to Lillhach, the palace of count Grobenich

very

very long account of an extraordinary ceremony performed here on invefting the duke in his dominions   We went up the hill to the weft to the palace of Tonfonberg; where they fhew many things in relation to Maximilian the firft, and have an opinion that he was born there, tho' Newftat was the place of his nativity   We faw here feveral reliefs and infcriptions.

Clagenfurt   Clagenfurt is one of the moft agreeable towns I have feen, it is well built, and ftreams of water run through all the ftreets [a]: There are no coins found here, and very few Roman antiquities to be feen in the town. A coloffal ftatue lies in the ftreet, the head of which is broke off, it has to the left what I took to be the Roman fafces, there is alfo a relief very ill executed of Hercules and a Centaur, his name being on it   We heard of an infcription in the town which we could not find, there were others formerly here, and we faw a relief, and copied an infcription at a ruined church on a hill called Spittalberg, half a league to the north weft. In the fquare there is a fountain fifty-five feet long, and over it is the ftatue of a dragon thirty-two feet in length, which is the arms of the town; it is made of a green fort of free ftone which is in this country, and before it is a coloffal ftatue of Hercules, with his club lifted up, as aiming at the monfter.   We travelled on the

Wurtfee   north fide of the Wurtfee, or lake, the waters of which are unwholefom, caufe pains in the bowels, and are laxative, they have plenty of trout, barbel, and cray fifh in it   We faw on a hill the palace of Landfcroon, where fome Roman medals had lately been dug up   Two

Offiaker lake   leagues to the north weft is the Offiaker lake   Many walnut-trees grow on both thefe lakes, of the nut of them they make an oil for painting; and the poor people eat the nut with bread after the oil is preffed out. Offiaker nuts are mentioned by fome authors under the name of Tribulus aquaticus, and that they make bread of them; on enquiry I found there is an aquatic plant here, which bears a nut or berry, of which they make a fort of bread that is unwholefom, and frequently caufes fevers.

Villach   Villach is thought by fome to be Julium Carnium, which cannot be, it is forty Italian miles from Volkmark, fuppofed to be Virunum; and as Graviacis was forty one miles from that city, it is probable it was at this place   We were told that there were fome ruins near the town between the Drave and the Guil, but we could not find any. Infcriptions have been publifhed which were copied about this place, and we met with feveral in the way to Spittal, which is eight leagues to the weft, particularly at St. Ann's church half a league from the town, at Hilleberg, Viftritz, at the church of St. Paternion, and at a palace on the hill belonging to a Venetian, Minuno might be about the laft of thefe places.   St Peter Hulft is on a fingle hill over the Drave, and is fup-

St. Peter Hulft

Teurnia   pofed to be Teurnia, which is fpoken of by Pliny among the towns of Noricum at a diftance from the Danube, and Gruter has an infcription, in which the Duumvir of Teurnia is mentioned, it was called Tiburnia in the middle ages, was a bifhop's fee, and the metropolis

[a] Cellarius thinks it was Claudia or Claudivum; but I rather conjecture that it was Beliandro, in the way from Varuno to Juvavia, though the diftances do not well agree, that road feems to have gone along by the Drave, which is now the high road from Saltzburg, and to have left that river fomewhere near Clagenfurt, and we were informed that there are remains of a Roman way over the vale of Heyden, about half a league to the eaft of Clagenfurt.

of

of Noricum ; there are some inscriptions here, and part of a stone coffin, and there is an account of one found here full of the horns of several sorts of beasts   We saw a relief of St. Peter and St. Paul, of a bishop with his pastoral, and another figure near it.   We observed foundations of walls round the top of the hill, and others within them, but the stones have been almost all carried away.

We returned to Villach, and travelled southward   A league from the town we passed by two warm baths at a place called Warmbad, they are of sulphur, lime-stone, and some other minerals, and being too laxative they are not drunk, but are used for bathing, and are good against knots in the joints, for strengthening the limbs after dislocation, and several other disorders

We went in between the mountains, antiently called Alpes Noricæ ; the south parts having the name of Alpes Carnicæ   There are two antient reliefs at the church of Arnoldstein, one is a sort of crocodile with the tail twisted, the other is a bust of a man and woman in mezzo-relievo ; the former has a roll in his hand, and the dress is very particular.

CHAP. XI.

Of the county of GORITIA, and the duchy of CARNIOLA.

THE county of Goritia was formerly governed by its counts, and afterwards became subject to the dukes of Carniola   The antient town of Goritia seems to have been on the site of the castle where the old counts lived , I was told there is a head of an antient statue in it, which we did not see.   We were shewn the tomb of the last count of Goritia , the cap or crown on his arms is something like the Phrygian tiara   We were at Comorns where seven or eight of the patriarchs of Aquileia resided in time of war, probably in a castle on the top of the hill, of which there are some small ruins. {.sidenote: County of Goritia. — Goritia — Comorns}

We came to Haydenshaft *, which is in the road from Vienna to Venice, the nearer way being that by Villach, but it is not the post road. The county of Goritia produces very excellent wine.   The country people talk Forlan, a corruption of Italian, French, and Sclavonic, but all people of condition, and those in the town, speak Italian {.sidenote: Hayddenshaft}

From Haydenshaft we came into Carniola, it was part of the country of the Carni, and because the Windi or Sclavi came and settled in under and middle Carniola, for that reason it is called Windisch March ; {.sidenote: Carniola}

* The name of this village signifies Heatheness, and it is called Idcuhna in Italian , so that the name, and also the coins, as well as other antiquities, which have been found here, give reason to think that it was an antient place, and probably the Mutatio, called Castra in the Journal demi Journey , the Alpes Julia being mentioned next after it   and from this place the old road went to Obrabuch over the mountain, till a new road was lately made, which is fourteen miles further round

and what they call the Windifch language is a dialect of the Sclavonic, which is talked all over this country   We came to the valley in which the river Vipao, the antient Frigidus, runs, at which Theodofius gained a fignal victory over Eugenius   Ad Frigidum amnem feems to be a place in the Itinerary in the way from Aquileia to Emona; the new road from Venice to Vienna goes along this valley and by Goritia, leaving the high road from Vienna to Triefte at Prewalt, fix leagues from Triefte   We croffed into the old road on the mountains which leads to Laubach, and after travelling two leagues we gained the top of the Alpes Carnicæ, or Juliæ, and coming to a pafs where there is an

Hydria inn, we left the high road to go to Hydria by a very difficult way, in order to fee the mine of quickfilver, which has been worked above two hundred years, and is efteemed the richeft in Europe, the mine is about eight hundred feet deep, and they were on a great work of turning arches through all the paffages, and making ftone fteps in many parts in order to defcend   The ore confifts of a black foft flate, mixed with a black clay, in which one fees the quickfilver in fmall globules, they pound the ftone, and wafh it as well as the clay, and it is fo rich that a hundred pound of the richeft cinnabar ore produces fifty pounds of quickfilver   There are particles of the pure native virgin quickfilver in the rivulet, which runs through the village, and the poor people collect it clandeftinely, though it is ftrictly prohibited

Laubach We went by Ober-Laubach to the city of Laubach the antient Emona. The town to the fouth of the river is the old town, which extended to the north fide alfo, where the old walls at prefent enclofe a fmall part of the town to the north   And as the church of St Peter is on the north fide, and half a mile out of the town, which is the old parifh church, fo they fuppofe the town antiently extended that way   There are feveral infcriptions in the city, and one a mile out of town at a church called Siftra   This city is faid to have been built by the Argonauts, after they had brought their veffel up the Ifter   The fteep hill on which the caftle is built is covered in a moft beautiful manner with trees, and probably was the fite of the firft town

Ober Lau bach We returned to Ober Laubach, the antient Nauportum, on the river Laubach, which is the Nauportus of the antients   Pliny fays, that the river received its name from the Argonauts bringing their fhip to this place   Tacitus mentions Nauportum as a town like a municipium, and

River Lau- bach we met with an infcription here   About a mile from Ober-Laubach the river comes out from under the hills in three large ftreams   In order to explain the nature of this river, it muft be underftood, that in the fouth parts of Carniola there are feveral rivers which are loft under ground, the neareft to this is a ftream called the Untz, which goes under ground, and is fuppofed to come out here   The river Poig, in the mountains of Carfo, to the north of Triefte, which in Homan's map appears in three ftreams that unite and feem to go under ground, is faid to enter a grotto at a place called Poffoina, and going under ground for five Englifh miles it comes out at a grotto not far from Planina, and near a caftle called Kleinhaufel, where it is called the Untz, and after having received another ftream which comes from the Czirnickferfee, it runs about three Englifh miles, and goes again under

ground

ground at Eibenschuſs, three miles further it comes out again near the Carthuſian monaſtery at Freudenthall, and is ſtill called the Untz, it runs near three miles furthei, and is loſt again, and in two miles comes out near Ober Laubach, and is called the Laubach, the ſources and courſe of all theſe ſtreams are very curious, and deſerve to be viſited by travellers

From Ober Laubach we went to the village of Planina, and ſtruck out of the road five Engliſh miles to the eaſt to the Czirnickſer-ſee, or Czirnickſer-lake, which is a great natural curioſity, it muſt be near twenty miles in circumference, and commonly empties itſelf about the month of July, if it is not a wet ſeaſon, and then the ground is ſown, and ſoon appears under corn, ſeven or eight rivulets run into it, and there are two great outlets at the weſt end of the lake. The baſon of the lake is a gentle ſlope on each ſide of a deep channel which is called the ſtream, in which there are about twelve holes, and there are others on the ſouth ſide of the lake, by ſome of which the water riſes or falls. The water ſinks in dry weather, and upon great froſts, and when the lake begins to fall, after two months dry weather, it is reduced to the channel, and in fourteen days more part of the channel begins to be dry, and the waters fall below the top of the higheſt hole, and then in fifteen days more the whole channel is dry; it commonly begins to go out in June, and generally returns in September, but this depends on the weather, for in a very dry year it has emptied three times in one year, and about thirty years ago the water had not gone out in ſeven years. There are ſeven principal holes out of which they have obſerved that the waters run regularly. The ground being higheſt to the north weſt the water runs out firſt by the holes which are on that ſide: Theſe holes are known by certain names, Vodonos, the higheſt hole, and likewiſe the largeſt and deepeſt is emptied in an hour after the water begins to fall, in an houi after that, Retia begins to run out, and the water leaves it in about the ſame time. Sixty hours afterwards the hole called Kreutz begins to empty, and is about two hours in running out. The third day after, Reſchetto begins to run out, and is dry in two hours and a half. On the third day after this Koten, runs out in four hours, theſe two laſt are in the ſouthern part of the ſea. On the third day after, Leuiſcha begins to empty, and is dry in ſix hours. When the water begins to retire within the channel a rock called Ribeſkakamen appears, and gives notice to the fiſhermen to prepare their nets for the firſt hole, and as ſoon as it begins to empty they put their nets into the hole, and catch the fiſh, which would otherwiſe be carried under ground, and ſome of the fiſhermen go a great way down into theſe holes after the fiſh. Many of theſe little fiſh alſo go into the holes, from which there are no ſubterraneous paſſages, and theſe are caught by the women. If a year or two paſſes, and the lake does not empty itſelf, it abounds very much in fiſh, but not ſo much if the water goes out every year. The fiſh of this lake are jack, tench, a ſort of eel, and a few large cray fiſh, one of which we ſaw nine inches long, and they informed us that there were ſome of them larger. The fiſhery belongs to the Carthuſian monaſtery near, but when the water goes out, the people obtain leave to fiſh for a ſmall ſum. If the lake empties itſelf early, they plough and ſow French wheat round

the

edges of it, and the inner parts become fine meadow, in which many uncommon plants grow, that are esteemed good for cattle And as reeds come up in some parts of the lake, and are a shelter for game; so they have plenty of hares, woodcocks, and snipes When the rains begin, the waters return by the holes very fast, if it empties in the summer, it remains dry about two months, if in the spring, a month, and in the winter about ten days The channel is filled in twenty-four hours, and the whole lake in about a week Sometimes it returns early, and overflows what they have sown In the winter there are on it great plenty of swans, wild ducks, and geese; and what they affirm as a great wonder is really true, that in a few days one may see on the same spot water fowl, fish, corn, grass, cattle, and all sorts of game and fowl There are four holes in the side of the lake where the banks are high, from which when it thunders they hear a great noise like a drum, and from two of them, at those times, a great quantity of water-fowl, particularly baldcoots are thrown out, the latter being blind, and most of their feathers are off, for retiring to these holes probably when the water falls, they are then forced out, and their feathers are torn off against the rocks, and having been in the dark, and being stunned, they cannot see when they first come out, and are easily caught or shot. We saw one of the holes, which is at the bottom of the rock, and only large enough for a man to creep in at, there is always water in it, and it was then full Two of these holes at the west end of the lake are the ordinary subterraneous outlets of it, the streams of which unite under ground, and run for about two miles, and come out in a small meadow, every way encompassed with wood, it runs about half a mile further, and then passes under a most extraordinary natural bridge of the rock, which is two hundred feet from the ground, and a hundred and twenty feet thick, the passage being a hundred feet above the water, and as many wide a hundred yards further the stream enters the grotto of S Kanzian, which is two hundred feet high, and a hundred wide, at the end of this, it runs through a narrower passage for three miles, comes out near Planina, and unites with the Untz, which I have already mentioned There was so much water in this passage that we could not go into it, but when the lake is dry, they can walk in it, and there are a great number of fine petrifications in this passage I mentioned before, the opinion concerning the passage of the waters, which run to the Laubach, but I think it is very probable that the Poig, and several other streams to the east, which are higher than the lake, go under ground, and having communication with the holes in the lake, consequently must fill the bason of it, and when they fail, this body of water must necessarily fall In Homan's map such rivers are laid down about Gottschee, Werxelberg, Guttenfelds, and Sneeberry

We went from Planina five miles to Fuck, to see a grotto, which is very curious, the entrance is romantick, being at a perpendicular rock, three hundred feet high, about half way up there is a large cavity, in which there is a castle built, with a passage to it by the rock From the side of the hill a little below it, there is a small entrance to the grotto, and there is a large cavity towards the bottom, which lessens at the lower end, so is to be only big enough to receive a small rivulet The grotto is

from

from ten to fifty feet high, and from five to fifteen paces broad, moſt part of the grotto is dry, but in ſome places the water drops, and makes beautiful petrifications, many of which are very curious, reſembling the antient Gothic canopies We returned to the high road at Poſtoina, where we ſaw a very curious grotto, it is not half a mile long, nor very high, what is much to be obſerved, a river paſſes through it, which is ſuppoſed to be the Poig I have mentioned, and there is a natural ſtone bridge over it, which ſeems partly to have been formed by the droppings of the water, and the whole grotto abounds in ſtalactites. We went two miles from this village to ſee the grotto called St Maria Magdalena, which, as to its petrifications, is the fineſt I ever ſaw, the whole being encruſted with the moſt beautiful natural groteſque works, and in the greateſt variety that can be imagined From Poſtoina we croſſed the deſolate mountains of Carſo to Trieſte

Trieſte was the Roman colony of Tergeſte Several inſcriptions and there antiquities have been found here, among them is a triumphal arch, adorned on each ſide with ſeveral Corinthian pilaſters, and a ſort of Attic ſtory, the ground is riſen up very high about it, this arch is engraved in Della Croce's hiſtory of Trieſte At the tower of the cathedral there are four fluted Corinthian pillars, which ſeem to be part of a portico of a temple, the entablature of them has been moved, the frieze is adorned with helmets, ſhields, and other ſorts of armour In the tower there is a coloſſal head of Auguſtus, and in the walls of the cathedral two fine reliefs of the battle of the Amazons, and on another ſtone are ſeveral heads of a family of the name of Barbius Within the preſent town walls are remains of a theatre which was of ſtone and brick, and at the port are ruins of a mole built by the Romans, ſeveral hundred paces into the ſea

Ten miles to the eaſt of Trieſte, between the mountains of Carſo, Aquædu? are remains of an aqueduct on which the waters run from a fountain to Trieſte, the channel is moſtly cut along the ſide of the mountains four feet ſix inches wide, and lined with brick, ſo as to contract it to one foot ten inches, and the whole was arched over At the caſtle of St Servolo there is a deſcent to a very curious grotto, which abounds in petrifications

Proſecco is ſituated on an eminence over the ſea, ſeven miles to Proſecco, the weſt of Trieſte, and muſt be the caſtle Pucinum of Pliny, mentioned alſo by Ptolemy Pliny ſays, that Livia attributed her great age to drinking the wine of Pucinum, of which then vineyards produced very little, and now this place is famous for an excellent muſcadine wine.

We came to the river Timao, which is the Timavus, that was ſo famous The Tima among the antients It is a river which affords ſome poetical thoughts, and it vus ſuited better for the poets in the ſtory of Antenor, to place it near Padoua, ſo that any one who looks for it according to their deſcriptions, would be very wide of it The antient geographers and writers of natural hiſtory, mention it as riſing a great way off, and going twenty miles under ground, and it does riſe in the mountain of Carſo, to the north eaſt of Trieſte, where it is called the Recca, it likewiſe paſſes under the mountains about the diſtance they mention, and comes out here in ſeven

mouths, which at different times may be more or less, they say it sometimes comes out with a great noise, on which account this place is called St Joanni Della Trumba [St John of the Trumpet], so that the
mouths mentioned by the poets, and the noise it makes are to be inter-
preted of its coming out from the mountain, it afterwards runs in three
streams of fresh water, though the antients speak of some of them as
being salt, and at length they unite and fall into the sea   There was a
temple of Diomedes near it, at which they yearly sacrificed a white
horse to Neptune, the port and grove being near it   We saw a Mosaic
pavement close to the springs, and in making the road they lately discovered foudations of walls, and at present there is a grove of trees near
the place   The air of this country is very bad, supposed to be occasioned by the noxious vapours of the waters, which are not fit for drinking   In the mountains a little above the place where the waters of the
Timavus come out, there are three deep pits, two of which have water
in them, but they are all so steep that it would be dangerous to venture
down, in order to see what communications they may have   There is a
small island at the mouth of the Timavus called Belforte, it is almost washed
away by the sea, and is very near being covered over at high water   The
antients mention hot waters here as rising and falling with the tide

---

CHAP XII.

Of Istria.

WE hired a boat at Trieste, in order to visit such places in Istria
as are on the sea   At Mudia we saw some stones, with antient work on them, and one inscription   Capo d'Istria is situated on an island, joined to the continent by a bridge and causeway,
and the water is not above three feet deep between the island and the
continent when the tide is out   It is the antient Ægida, called in the
middle ages Justinopolis, but it is agreed that the inscription was
forged which was said to be there, and mentioned the city as built by
Justinus, it is however said that the emperor Justinus did build a fortress here   We found no antiquities in this place except one vase, with
a short inscription on it

In the church of Pirano the font is an antient vase, with a relief on
it of a cupid on a dolphin   They conjecture that the town was built
after the time of Attila   We saw an inscription at Umago, which may
be Neugum of the Itinerary, as it agrees very near with the distances
of twenty-eight miles from Trieste, and eighteen from Parentium   The
port of Citta Nuova being very bad, it is in a most desolate condition,
we saw some inscriptions there, it may be an antient place, and possibly Mutila or Faveria mentioned by Livy   The see of Trieste being
at one time translated to this place, the bishops are still called in Latin
                                                                    bishop

bishops of Emona , but the authors of Istria would fix Emona about this place, and call the river Quiete the antient Nauportus, and say that the ruins of the old city are four miles higher up on the north side of the Quiete, which we went to see, and found the ruins of an old town or castle, that appeared plainly to be of the middle ages Cluver conjectures this to be Salvo of the Tables, tho' it cannot be, as it is placed between Parentium and Pola

Parenzo, the antient Parentium, was famous for a temple of Neptune , *Parenzo* the foundations and basement of which are seen at the west end of the town, and it seems to have been fifty feet broad ; there is a curious inscription in the square relating to it, and there are remains of the moles in the sea mentioned in that inscription, consisting of very large stones It is said that Otho emperor of Germany built the cathedral, with the materials of it, in which there are curious Mosaic works, and that which represents tridents and dolphins may be part of the pavement of the antient temple We saw some altars on the sea shoar, the inscriptions of which had been defaced by the weather Opposite to Parenzo is the island of St. Nicholas, covered with olive-trees, it belongs to the Benedictines of St George in Venice Orsera and its territory belongs to *Isle of S Nicholas Orsera* the bishop of Parenzo , the pope having the title of sovereign of it

Rovigno is a very populous town, and they have a great trade in *Rovigno* wine and oil · Opposite to it is the pleasant island of St Andrew, covered with wood, and there is a Benedictine convent in it Sailing towards Pola we saw the little town of Perdoli, inhabited by Greeks from *Perdo* Candia, settled here by the Venetians when that island was taken by the Turks There are some islands, before the port of Pola, one of which, St Nicola is near five miles in circumference, it is covered with sh and inhabited only by the men who work in the quarries of a grey marble, which is sent to Venice The island Brioni near it is also famous for its quarries There are some islands in the bay, in one of which we saw a very antient Greek church, and in that which is called Scoglio Grande there are ruins of a castle, and some stones which seemed to be the remains of an antient temple

Pola retains its antient name , it was called Julia Pietas, and is said *Pola* to have been built by the Colchians, who were afraid to return to king Ætetes when they could not find the Argonauts This city was made a Roman colony, probably in the time of Augustus , it was first destroyed by Attila, and afterwards by the Venetians, so that now it is a very poor place , but in relation to its antiquities it is to be regarded among the greatest The amphitheatre is to be esteemed as one of the finest in the world, and on the outside it is the most perfect remaining, for there are not so much as any ruins of the inside, except a very few remains of some walls, which must have been the foundation of the wood work , for the ground not being raised by any ruins, it is concluded that the seats must have been of wood , it is built of very large hewn stone, fastened together with cramps of iron There is a descent in the amphitheatre to a passage under ground three feet high, and eighteen inches broad, in which there are several runnings , but it seemed to point chiefly towards the sea, and was doubtless designed to carry off the

water from the plain: This building has been particularly deſcribed and
deſigned by the marquis Maffei. The temple of Auguſtus and Rome,
a plan and view of which may be ſeen in the hundred and firſt plate,
is near the ſea, and has been made uſe of as a dwelling houſe. Near it
is one end of another temple, which is ſo much like it, that probably it
was built to anſwer it, a view of it may be ſeen in the hundred and
ſecond plate. The ſepulchral arch in the hundred and third plate is
very near the walls at the ſouth end of the town, by the inſcription it appears to have been built by a lady of the family of the Sergii. This
arch is very much adorned with ſculpture, eſpecially with vines, on each
ſide of the entrances, and within on the arch itſelf, with roſes in
ſquare compartments, and an eagle with a ſerpent in the middle.
There are remains of a Roman cold bath near the theatre, it is a
ſemicircle twenty-five feet in diameter, has four ſteps round it,
and a ſpring of very clear water riſes in it, on the ſouth eaſt ſide of
the town on the ſide of a hill, are remains of a theatre called Zadro,
which was almoſt entire two hundred years ago, and there is a deſign of it in Serlio, it was deſtroyed by an engineer to build a fort on
the hill. This fortreſs was a very neat one, built of the fine hewn ſtone
of the theatre, but as it would be of no uſe, they cloſed up the entrance.
There are ſome very fine corniſhes of white marble near it, which probably belonged to the theatre. We copied the inſcription mentioned
by Mr Spon, which does not ſeem to imply that Pola was a republi-
ck, but only a Roman city governed by its own laws and magiſtrates,
and that their reſpublica or public-weal had erected ſuch an altar. Pola
is now a very poor town, and the air is reckoned unwholſom, the cathedral and other churches, appear to have been built out of the ruins of
the antient city. There are remains of a round pharos or light-houſe
on the bay two miles to the weſt of the town, it is called the tower of
Orlando, it is of brick, and, without doubt, is a Roman work.

C H A P. XIII.

Of FRIULI, and ſome other parts of ITALY.

A Little beyond the Timavus, already deſcribed, we croſſed over
the river S. Joanni into that part of Italy called Friuli, which is
ſubject to the Venetians, that river riſes in Lago di Pietra Roſſa,
and after it has run about a mile from the caſtle, it goes under a hill for
half a mile, and comes out again near two miles from the ſea, and is there
navigable. The water comes into the lake at the north eaſt part of it,
and is thought to come from a lake two miles higher, called Lago Do-
berdo. A ſmall rivulet called S. Antonio, falls into this river, it riſes
to the ſouth of Monte Falcone, not far from the ſea, near it are the
hot ſulphureous baths of Monte Falcone, the tide coming into them by
a communication under ground. We went to Lago di Pietra Roſſa, be-

ROMAE ET AVGVSTO CAESARI DIVI F PATRI PATRIAE

CII, p 264 N°2

A TEMPLE AT POLA

A SEPULCHRAL ARCH at POLA

cause it is thought to be the lake Timavus, mentioned by Livy, where the Romans encamped when they went against the Istrians. On a high hill to the south of it are signs of an entrenchment, which probably is the spot of the encampment, the hills to the north are called Vallone, and below the lake, at the foot of these mountains, are some houses, which go by the same name, this probably was the private place behind the hill where the camp of the Istrians was, and it may be from this obscure place they crossed over in the night, and marched behind the two hills to the east of the high hill, where the Romans were, and attacked them before it was light, without being seen by them from their camp, the entrenchment being on the side of the hill next the sea, this hill is about a mile and a half from the sea, which is near enough to justify the expression of the historian, that it was over the sea. We crossed the Lysonzo into the county of Gradisca, belonging to Austria, in the house of baron Delfin there are some inscriptions and antiquities chiefly brought from Aquileia. We came again into the Venetian territory. The fortifications of Palma are very beautiful, and the town is finely laid out, but it is not finished. In the way from Palma to Aqui-Palma leia, we saw some inscriptions and antiquities at Deal, Campolongo, Villa Michaelis, and Villa Vicentina, where we took up our quarters, went every day to Aquileia, and returned at night, in order to avoid the bad air of that place, the next day we went to Cervignan, St Martin's, and Murcis, and found inscriptions and antiquities at all of them. Terzo probably was at the third mile from Aquileia. As soon as we passed over the river Terzo, we saw foundations to the left, and soon came to a wall joining to it, which extends to Aquileia, and was an aqueduct built with arches, which are filled with a petrification made by the dropping of the water, the wall is seven feet thick, and it is about ten feet high, but seems to have been higher, we could make no discovery from what place the water was brought, though probably it was from the river at Terzo. The antient road from Aquileia to Concordia was by this aqueduct, crossed the marshes, and the river Arisa, the antient Alsa, on a bridge now called Ponte D'Orlando, about five miles from Aquileia, of which there are some remains, the road and bridge being mentioned in a curious inscription, which we copied at the nunnery, the name of the emperor, probably Domitian, being erased. We crossed several small streams on bridges of large hewn stone of Roman work, and observed some ruins at the church of St Stephen, and an inscription at a house near it. We arrived at Aquileia, a city very famous in antient history, being built by the Romans as a defence against the barbarians, it was made a Latin colony in the year five hundred and seventy of Rome, and three thousand foot had each fifty acres of land allotted to them, the centurions a hundred, and the equites a hundred and fifty, which is computed to take up a square of sixteen miles. They afterwards had the privileges of Roman citizens, and were inscribed into the Velonian tribe. The emperors frequently resided here, especially when they were in war with the Germans. The bravery of the ladies of this place is remarkable when they were besieged by Maximinus, for they cut off their hair in order to make strings to their bows, and the army observing the resolution of

the befieged, cut off Maximinus's head, and fubmitted to the fenate
The city was entirely erafed by Attila in the year four hundred and
fifty-three It was afterwards rebuilt by Narfes, but has never fince
flourifhed We found fome infcriptions which make mention of Bele-
nus, under which name the Aquileians, as well as the inhabitants of the
weftern parts of Gaul worfhipped Apollo It is thought that one of his
temples was at St Maria Belligne, where we faw the foundations of a
large building, and fix beautiful pillars of Ægyptian granite The old
walls of Aquileia built by fome of the patriarchs are moftly ftanding,
and are about two miles in circumference, the prefent town, or rather
village, is at the fouth eaft part on the river that falls into the Natifo.
There are feveral infcriptions about Aquileia, particularly at the convent
of the nuns, who in fummer live at Udine, and alfo in the houfe of
the learned canon Bertoli of this church, who has publifhed, with great
labour, the antiquities and infcriptions of Aquileia In the cathedral
there is a fmall chapel, in which they fay St Jerom was baptized ; and
there is a little round building in the church, in which they kept the
holy oil that was antiently diftributed from this church all over the pa-
triarchate In the antient church of St Felix there is a very antient
and fine Mofaic pavement, with the name on it of fome of the perfons
who contributed to the expence When Aquileia was deftroyed by Attila the patriarchs begun firft to refide at Grado, which in a fynod was
made the metropolis of Venice and Iftria They obtained great territories and privileges, which were loft in courfe of time. Afterwards the
Lombards fet up another patriarch, he and his fucceffors, as well as I
could be informed, refiding at Cormons and Cividal Friuli, but this
affair was fettled by the pope in a council held at Mantoua. The patriarchs came again to Aquileia, went to Udine, afterwards to Venice,
and then came to Udine again, and Venice was erected into a patri-
archate Some time ago they obtained a privilege of naming their fuc-
ceffor, which the archduke of Auftria not allowing, but requiring that
he fhould be acknowledged by him, and do homage to the emperor, as
Aquileia belongs to Auftria, on this account the revenues of the church
in the dominions of Auftria were feized on The patriarch cannot now
come to Aquileia, and the canons being put in by the Venetians, the
archduke of Auftria requires that they fhould be nobles, and chufe the
patriarch, and for this reafon has feized likewife on their revenues,
fo that the church of Aquileia is in a very miferable condition

From Aquileia we went to the iflands, and afterwards up the river
Timent the antient Romatinus to Porto Gruaro, we faw Concordia a
mile below it, where there are no remains of that city, which was a
famous Roman colony, except a few antient ftones and infcriptions We
at firft came into Friuli by Pontebi Veneta, and went to Venzone,
where fome bodies have been lately dug up uncorrupted, like thofe of
Bremen, and are feen in a room under the baptiftery. In the way
to Udine we faw an infcription at Spitaletto, mother at Gemona, and
fome relicts at the latter We came to Tricefimo, fuppofed to be at
thirtieth ftone or mile both from Aquileia and Julium Carnicum, it
was called Ad Tricefimum in the Tables, we faw an infcription in the

2   castle

Venzone

Tricefimo

caſtle Julium Carnicum is thought to be Zulio, which is in between the mountains, in the country now called Cargnia, where, they ſay, ruins have been found.

Udine is a very beautiful town, thought to be built when Aquileia Udine was deſtroyed, and ſome are of opinion that Attila was the founder of it. Paul the eremite was born here. There are ſeveral antiquities and inſcriptions at the palace of count Gorgi, particularly a great number of urns, and among them a large one of glaſs, they were almoſt all found about Aquileia, and at the church of the nuns of St Clare there is a very remarkable antient head of marble· The patriarch of Aquileia reſides here, and has a ſeminary and library at his palace. The town-houſe is a grand Gothic building, and oppoſite to it there is a very beautiful Ionic portico of the architecture of Palladio. In the way to Cividal di Friuli we paſſed the bed of the Torre, the antient Turrus, which below unites with the Natiſo, all the water of it in the ſummer is conveyed in two ſtreams to Udine. Cividal di Friuli is certainly Forum Julii, it was deſtroyed by Theodoric, and was afterwards rebuilt. The dukes of Friuli formerly reſided here, and the patriarchs of Aquileia alſo for ſometime. We found inſcriptions here, ſome of which make mention of the Scaptian tribe, to which it is ſuppoſed this colony belonged. Cornelius Gallus the poet, and favourite of Auguſtus, was a native of this place, and ſo was Paul the deacon of Aquileia. In the collegiate church, among other valuable manuſcripts, there is a very curious one of the four goſpels in Latin, written in large ſquare letters, and if it is not of the ſixth century, as they ſay, yet it muſt be very old, it belonged to the dukes of Friuli, and ſeveral of their names are writ in it, particularly thoſe of Anſelmus, Peter, and Urſus. At the Dominicans they have the hiſtory of Paul the deacon, which is thought to be writ in his own time. There is an extraordinary ceremony at the collegiate church on the day of Epiphany, in token of the antient temporal ſovereignty of the patriarch here. A deacon, after the goſpel is read, puts on a helmet of wood, and goes to the prieſt who celebrates with a naked broad ſword in his hand, and waves it before him.

CHAP. XIV.

Of the iſlands of GRADO, CORGLE, and ſome places in ITALY.

THE land between Aquileia and Grado is what they call lagune, or marſhes, covered by water when the tide is in. In the way to Grado we went to the iſland of S Coſmo, or Gorgo, to ſee an antient church. The town of Grado is near of the ſame extent as the Grado iſland. Tho' the cathedral is not very antient, yet the Moſaic pavement in it appears to be ſo, being near twelve hundred years old, and there are feveral infcriptions on it in Latin, and one in Greek of thofe who contributed to it, according to the vows they made, as it is expreffed in the infcriptions

Corgle.   From Grado we went to the ifland of Corgle, where there are fome antiquities, it is a bifhop's fee. Among the iflands of Venice, in Torcello the cathedral is a very curious old building, and it is faid to have been founded in fix hundred ninety-feven. At Venice we faw the Pifani library, and the collection of fignor Apoftolo Zeno, poet, and, if I miftake not, hiftoriographer of the late emperor, he has a very curious collection of antiquities, and efpecially of medals, and fignor Marc Antonio Diedo, a noble Venetian, with great politenefs, fhewed us himfelf his collection of antiquities, he has a great number of Greek medals, many of which are not publifhed, this collection was made when he was admiral in the Levant, and governor in Iftria, Dalmatia, Corfu, Zant, and Cephalenia. In the way from Venice to Trevifo at Altino, we vifited the fpot of the antient Altinum, deftroyed by Attila; we could fee only two infcriptions, and fome ftones fcattered over the fields. We faw at Baffano many pictures of the father and four fons, the famous painters of that place. At Feltri, the antient Feltria, we faw only one infcription, and three at Belluno, and a marble coffin finely adorned with reliefs, there is a beautiful tower at the cathedral, and the infide of that church is the defign of Palladio. The Piave here is very fhallow and rapid, they go down that river on floats eight miles an hour with the ftream. We arrived at Trent, and from that place I went by Mantoua to Leghorn, and embarked for Alexandria in Ægypt

A D b-

A
DESCRIPTION
OF
The *EAST,* &c.

BOOK the Sixth.
GEOGRAPHICAL OBSERVATIONS.

CHAP. I.

Remarks in relation to the antient GEOGRAPHY.

AS I mentioned in the Preface, I have followed the fea charts pub-lifhed by the order of Monfieur Maurepas, as to the fhape of the land, and the towns on the fea. The antient names are in Roman charaders, and the modern in Italic, and where the name of a town is only in Roman letters, it is the modern as well as the antient name. Except that in Syria, and it may be in fome other parts, I have inferted fome places according to the diftances in the Itineraries, which are fignified by the figures between them, though modern names are not known, but for the reft I have put in no antient names, where there is not reafon to conjecture that the antient places might be where modern names are now feen in the maps, except thofe of ports, capes, rivers or lakes, which may be certainly determined by their fituation.

In Candia, cape Saftofo is the fame as cape St Sebaftian, which was probably the old promontory Dion, and cape Croce is to the weft of it, fo that I was miftaken in confounding thofe two capes.

As to the map of Afia Minor, I found reafon to think that I was miftaken concerning my conjecture, in the road from Aleppo to Conftan-tinople, in relation to the river Hermus, and Ancyra in Phrygia, which

I have corrected in the map, and in that road Sis may be the same as Anawafy   Tocia also seems to be Ticua   I find that I took the island of St Andrew near Cyzicus for Calolimno, and did not see that island; the weather being bad when we made the voyage to Rodosto from Montagna   But the map of the Propontis places it opposite to the Rhyndacus, and consequently it agrees with the situation of the island Besbicus of the antients

In the map of Thrace and Greece I have chiefly followed Homan's map of the course of the Danube and of Greece, and that of Achaia, except that the Morea, as to the shape of the land and the rivers is chiefly according to Sanson, but for the names of the inland places and their situations, except on the west side, I have very much followed a map of modern Greece, printed at Venice by Jacomo Guftaldo, which feems to contain the modern names of places, probably from the observations which had been made in his time

With regard to places on the *Propontis*, both in this map and in that of Asia Minor, I have given them according to my own observations, whereas the map of the Propontis is exactly taken from Le Bonne's. The rout from Salonica to Constantinople was to have been a note, and I have inserted it here   It is most of it in the Roman road called Via Egnatia, which led to Constantinople from the two most frequented places of landing from Italy, Dyrrachium and Apollonia, it passed through Thessalonica and Milhturgis twenty miles from it, which was probably about Kirtly, twenty-six miles from Salonica, in the way to Constantinople, it then went through Apollonia seventeen miles further, somewhere about Orphano, which is nineteen miles distant, here St Paul was in his way from Amphipolis to Thessalonica   It after passed through Philippi thirty two miles further, the ruins of which are now known, St Paul wrote his epistle to the inhabitants of this place, it is about six miles to the north of Cavalla, the present road passing thro' Cavalla, twenty-three miles from Orphano, from which it is twenty-two miles to Carab Enfheh, probably the old Acontisma, twenty one miles from Philippi, and Neapolis was between Philippi and Acontisma   The next place in the present road is Carnoulago twenty-three miles, which might be about the stable of Diomedes, placed forty miles from it, and Topiro between them, only eighteen miles   This probably is at the lake, which in the sea chart is called Lago, and I suppose to be Lacus Stentoris   Eighteen miles further is a village of Bulgarians, which exactly answers to the distance of Impara or Pyrsohis, afterwards called Maximianopolis   Twenty-four miles further is Ohknch, which might be about Trajmopolis, placed indeed fifty seven miles off, and Brieze between them, twenty miles, this, is well as the other distances which follow in the Itinerary, being much too great   The next place in the modern road is Dercha twenty two miles, which one would imagine to be nearer Rodosto than Apris was, which is placed twenty six miles from it, whereas Dercha is only thirteen   It is put down eighty miles from Trajanople to Apris, but this plainly is not a direct road, as Cyplah is in it, which doubtless is the present Yplch, and must have been much to the south of Trajanople, and is about sixteen miles north of the mouth of the river Hebet   There was another road went from Trajanople

i

nople

nople to Heraclea, on which I have made some observations in another place.

On considering better the situation of Plotinopolis and Trajanople, it is probable that the former was at Ouzoun-Kupri, and Trajanople further to the east, it may be at Jeribol.

The account I have given of the rivers Ardah, Tounsah, and Meritcheh, are such as I apprehended at Adrianople, but I see others make the Tounsah run from the north, the Meritcheh by Philippopoli, and the Ardah from the west, and it is most probable that the Meritcheh should pass by Philippopoli. Ienegia near the Nestus retains in the Turkish language something of the name of Neapolis, and agrees with the situation of it. St Paul sailed from Troas to Samothrace, and the next day to Neapolis, and travelled from that place to Philippi, Acts xvi 11, 12. Stratonice probably was situated on the bay to the south west of mount Athos; Stephanus says, that it was near Caria, probably the town of mount Athos, now called Cares. Palaiocastro could not be Thronium, which was on the Boagrius, not far from the sea. The island Fornica is probably the antient Pharmacusa where Attalus was killed, and Julius Cæsar was taken by the pirates. I have a medal in brass which has a head with a beard on one side, and a bull like the Urus on the other, and these letters ΦΑΡΜΑ, from which it is conjectured to have been struck in this island.

As in Sanson's map of the Morea many antient places are put down, which seem to be only from conjecture, founded on the description of the antients, I have therefore very rarely regarded them, but have chose to make a conjecture in putting them at places where modern names are given. I find that to the west of Corinth the first river was the Nemea, and the second the Asopus.

On the whole, with regard to these maps I have endeavoured to make them as correct as I could, but there must be many mistakes as to the conjectures in relation to antient places, they will however shew for the most part that those places were somewhere in these situations. And if what I have done puts any one on considering this subject more exactly, I shall be extremely pleased to be corrected, and to be in any sense the cause of setting the antient geography in a better light.

CHAP. II.

An ITINERARY in EUROPE

AS many places which were vifited are not mentioned in the obfer-vations on Europe, it was thought that it might be agreeable to the reader to fee the rout that was taken after I landed from the eaft, to which I have for the fame reafon prefixed the other before I went into the Levant, the obfervations of which are the fubject of the laft book. I have likewife added another through France and Italy in 1733 and 1734, as all together, with the defcription of the eaft, con-tain the whole tour I have made.

SICILY	ECCLESIASTICAL	Pavia.	Freifing
Meffina	STATE.	Lodi	Pruck
Nov 13 1740.	Veletri	Crema	SWABIA.
	Marino.	Pizzighettone	Augsburg.
ITALY	Rome	Cremona	Burgaw
K of NAPLES	Citta Caftellana	Bozzolo	Ulm
Reggio	Otricoli	Goito	Nordingen
Scylla	Narni	VENETIAN TER	Oetingen
Bagnari	Terni	Villa Franca	FRANCONIA.
Palma	Spoletto	Buffolongo	Anfpach.
Rofarno.	Fuligno	Chiufa	Nuienberg.
Monte Leone	Spello.		Chriftian Erlang.
Caftiglione	Affife	GERMANY.	Bamberg
Lago	Perugia.	TRENT	UPPER SAXONY.
Cofenza	TUSCANY	Roveredo	Coburg
Tauvria	Cortona	Trent	Saalfield
Rovelo Nero	Arezzo	Salorn.	Rudelftat
Evoli	Florence	Bolzano	Uhlfadt
Salerno	Fiorenzola	TIROL	Orlamunda
Nocera	ECCLESIASTICAL	Claufen	Kala
L'Annonciti	STATE	Brixen	Iena
Naples	Bologna	Stertzingen	Weimar
Sorrento	DUCHY OF MO-	Matray	Erfurt
Capri	DINA	Infpruck	Gotha
Ifchia	Modena	Hall	Eifenach
Procita	Reggio	Schantz	Creutzburg
Bare	AUSTRIAN TER	Rotnberg	UPPER RHINE
Come	Parma	BAVARIA	Leichtenau
Puzzoali	Placenza	Reichenthal	Caftel
Portici	Marignano	Hall	Hirchsfeld
Noli	Milan	Saltzberg	Fuld
Benevento	Lago migore	Altenmukt	Hamelberg
Averfa	Aroni	Wifleburg	FRANCONIA
Capoua	Como	Munich	Wurtzburg
Fondi	Puiefini	Schleuham	Lohr.
Gaeti			LOWER

LOWER PALATI-NATE OF THE RHINE
Shaffenburg.
Hainau
Overback
Mentz.
Openheim.
Worms
Manheim.
Heidelberg
Spires
Philipsberg
Germeinsheim
ALSACE.
Strasburg.
Kehl
Marchelsheim
Huningen.
SWISSERLAND.
Basil.
Leichstal
Walbourg
Soloturn.
Arberg.
Morat
Avanche
Payerne
Moudon
Lausanne.
Morges
S Prex.
Rolec.
Nyon
Gex
Geneva
SAVOY.
Bonnevill.
Cluse.
Salanche
Chamoigny
Anecy
Thonon
Evian
St Gingou
SWISSERLAND.
Aigle
Villeneuf.
Vevay.
Fribourg
VOL. II. Part II.

Morat.
Neufchatel
Arberg
Berne.
Lucern.
Zug.
Zurich
Winterthur
Trawenfeld
Constance
Stein
Schafhouse.
Eglisau.
Kaiserstool.
Baden
Bruck.
Zurlach.
Waldshut
Lauffenberg.
Rhinfelden.
Augst.
Basil
ALSACE.
Altkirk.
Besort
Montbelliard
FRANCHE COMPTE.
Clerval
Baume.
Besançon.
ALSACE.
Cernai
Rusack
Hoburg.
Colmar
Guemar.
Schlestat
LORRAIN
St. Marieaux
Mines
S Diey
Neufville
Ar Isiad
St Nicolas
Nancy.
DUCHY OF BAR
Pont Mousson.
Toul.

Metz
Thionville
Kunigsmarken.
Syrk.
―――――
GERMANY.
D OF LUXEN-BURG
Remie
Grave Macheren
CIRCLE OF LOW-ER RHINE
Treves
Guemingen.
Creutznach.
Ingelheim
Mentz.
Bingen.
St Goar.
Coblentz
Andernah.
Bonn
Cologn.
Bergen.
Juliers
Aix la Chapelle.
HOLLAND.
Maestricht.
LIEGE.
Liege
Spaw.
LIMBURG.
FLANDERS.
Namui
Benche.
Mons
Valenciennes.
Cambray
Douay
St Amand
Tournay.
Lisle
Ypres
Beaumont
Steinberg.
Castl
St Omer.
Calais
LONDON,
Aug 30 1741
LLL

LONDON,
Aug 30 1733.
FRANCE.
Calais.
Boulogne.
Montrevil.
Abbeville.
Amiens
Clermont.
Chantilly
St Denis.
Vincennes.
Paris
St Cloud.
St. Germain.
Marly
Versailles.
Meudon.
Fontainbleau.
Sens.
Auxerre.
Dijon
Chalons.
Macon
Ville Franche.
Lyon.
Vienne.
Valence.
Viviers.
St Esprit.
Ville Neuve.
Avignon.
Nismes
Montpelier.
Ailes
Salon
Aix.
Marseilles.
Touloun
Frejus
Antibes

ITALY.
PIEMONT.
Onegha
GENOUESE.
Albenga.
Louano
Finale.
Savonne

Savonna
Utri.
Seſtri
St Pietro di Are-
na
Genoua.
　　TUSCANY.
Leghorn.
Piſa.
Lucca
Piſtoiya
Poggio Chiano.
Florence
Piatolino.
Fiele.
S Caſſiano
Pongibonzi.
Sienna
Redi coffani
ECCLESIASTICAL
　　STATE
Aquapendente.
Bolſena
Monte Fiaſcone
Viterbo.
Roncaglione.
Rome
Porto.
Oſtia.
Citta della Vigna
Nenii
La Ricca.
Genzano.
Albano
Caſtel Gandolfo.
Marino
Grotta Ferrata.
Froſcati
Tuſculum.
Paleſtrina.
Tivoli
Civita Caſtellana.
Falerium.
Caprarola.
Otricoli
Narni.
Termi.
Spoleto
Foligno.
Tolentino

Macerata.
Recanati.
Loretto.
Ancona
Sinigalia.
Fano.
Peſaro.
S Marino.
Rimini.
Cervia.
Ravenna.
Faenza
Imola
Bologna.
Fort Urbano
DUCHY OF MO-
　　DENA.
Modena.
ECCLESIASTICAL
　　STATE.
Ferrara.
　　VENETIAN.
Rovigo
Monte Felice.
Arquia.
Abano.
Padoua.
Fuſina.
Venice.
Lido
Murano.
Vicenza.
Verona
Peſchiera
Deſenzano
Breſcia
Palazzolo.
　　MILANESE.
Milan
Novara
　　PIEMONT
Vercelli.
Turin
Aveghiana.
Suſi
　　SAVOY.
Modane
S Andre.
S John Morienne.
Mont Melian.

Chamberry.
Pont Beauvoiſin.

_____

FRANCE

Burgoign.
Lyons
Ville Franche
Macon
Tornus
Chalons.
Chaigny.
Beaume.
Nuys.
Dijon.
Langres.
Chaumont.
Joinville.
S Dizier.
Vitry
Chalons.
Rheims.
Laon.
La Fere.
Ham
Peronne.
Arras.
Bethune.
Aire.
S Omer
Calais.
　　LONDON,
July 1 1734

_____

　　LONDON,
May 20 1736.
　　ARTOIS.
Calais.
FRENCH FLAN-
　　DERS.
Graveline.
Dunkirk.
　　FLANDERS.
Furnes
Newport.
Oſtend.
Gand.
Bruges.
Aloſt.
　　BRABANT
Bruſſells.

Lovain.
Mechlin.
Liere.
Antwerp.
Breda.

_____

HOLLAND.

Dort.
Rotterdam.
Tergow.
Delft.
Hague.
Loſdun.
Schevelling.
Leyden.
Katwych opzee.
Roomberg.
Haerlem.
Amſterdam
Monnikedam.
Edam.
Purmeren.
Hoorn
Encheyſen
Medenblick.
Alcmar
Beverwick.
Maarſen.
Batterſtein.
Utrecht.
Duerſtede.
Rhenen.
Nimeguen.

_____

DUCHY OF
CLEVES.

Cranenberg
Cleves.
Emerick

_____

HOLLAND

Schentzſcans.
Arnhem
Dieren
Zutphen
Joo.
Deventer

2

GERMANY

CIRCLE OF WESTPHALIA.
Benheim.
Rheine.
Ofnaburg.
Munfter.
Paderdorn.
Piermont
Hamalen

CIRCLE OF LOWER SAXONY.

ELECTORATE OF HANOVER.
Hanover
Hildefheim.
Lampfpring
Zellerfield.
Claufthall
Andersberg
DUCHY OF BRUNSWICK.
Gozlar
Wolfenbuttle.
Saltzdall
Brunfwick
ELECTORATE OF HANOVER
Zell
Ferden.
Delmenhoift
Bremen
Buxtehude
Harborough
Lunebourg
Lawenbourg.
Hamburg
DUCHY OF HOL-
SITIA
Altena
Bramefterde
New Munfter
Kiell
Preetze
Ploen.

BISHOPRICK OF LUBECK
Lubeck.

ELECTORATE OF HANOVER.
Ratzberg
DUCHY OF MECKLENBERG
Gadebuche
Swerin
Wifmar
Guftrow
Roftock
Ribnitz.

CIRCLE OF UPPER SAXONY.

POMERANIA
Damgard.
Stralfund
Ifle of Rugen
Grifpfwald.
Wolgaft
Ifle of Ufedom.
Penemunder.
Anclam
Ukermunde.
Stettin.
Peritz.
BRANDENBURG.
Soldin
Landsberg

POLAND.
Tribeche
Schewrin.
Blafe.
BRANDENBURG.
Sternberg
Reppen
Frankfurt
Berlin
Charlottenburg
Potfdam
Brandenburg
Wittenburg
Anhalt
Defau

Zerbft
Magdeburg
Bernberg
COUNTY OF MANSFIELD.
Mansfield
Eifleben.
Hall.
ELECTORATE OF SAXONY.
Mersberg.
Leipfick
Altranftad
Hubertsbourg
Meiffen
Drefden
Moritzberg
Pillnitz
Koningftein

BOHEMIA
Budyn
Welburn
Prague
Carlsbad
Shonbach.
Egra.

UPPER PALATINATE OF BAVARIA
Ratisbon
Straubing.
Deckendorf
Vilfhoven
Paffaw

CIRCLE OF AUSTRIA
Afchaw
Altenfhiym
Lantz.
Inns
Ips
Melk.
Sten
Mauten
Gotwich.

Calenberg
Cloyfter Neuburg
Vienna
Shoenbrun.
Mauibach.
Laxenburg
Baden
Neyftatt

HUNGARY.
Oedingburg
Scarpin
Steneminger
Guntz
Locahoufe
Ekenmart
Wolf
Schidendorf
Eifenftatt
Manersdorf

AUSTRIA.
Bruck.
Haynburg.
Altenberg.
Petronel
Vifchmund.
Swechat
Eberfdorf
New Gebaw.
Ekerfau
Schlofhoff

HUNGARY.
Prefburg
Carlburg
Altenberg
Raab
Comorra
Dous
Neudorf
Gran
Worcfman.
S. Andre
Vitegrad.
Buda
Pefth
Sool Weiffenburg
Vefprin

Lake

Lake Balaton.
Toplocza.
Canifha.
Le Grad.

CROATIA.
Warafdin.
STIRIA.
Pettau.
Fridau

HUNGARY.
Strigona
Czakathurn

GERMANY.
STIRIA.
Luttenberg
Racklesberg.
Murcgg
Leibnitz.
Gratz.
Frowenleitten
Pruck
Kapfenberg
Maria Zell
Loiben.
Seccau
Knittlefield
Judenburg
Newmark

CARINTHIA.
Freifach.
Strasberg
Gurk
St Veit

Solfeld.
Clagenfurt.
Villach.
S Paternion.
Spittal.
S. Peter Hulft.
Arnoldftein
Tarvis
Ponteba Imperiale.

ITALY.
FRIULI
Ponteba Veneta
Venzone
Gemona
Artegno
Tricefimo.
Udine
Cividal di Friuli.

GERMANY
COUNTY OF GO-
RITIA.
Cormons
Goritia
CARNIOLIA.
Hydria
Ober Laubach.
Laubach
Cilcy
Returned to
Ober Laubach.
Planina
Czirnicz
Leuk
Poftaina
Triefte.

ISTRIA.
Muglia
Capo d'Iftria.
Ifola
Pirano.
Umago.
Citta Nuova
Parenzo
Ifle of S. Nicola.
Orfera
Rovigno.
Pola
CARNIOLA
Triefte.
S Servolo.
Profecio
Duino.

ITALY.
FRIULI
Monfalcone.
Gradifca
Palma.
Aquilea
Ifle of S Cofmo
Ifle of Grado.
Ifle of Corgle
Concordia
Porto Gruaro
VENETIAN.
Venice.
Ifle Murano
——S. Chriftopher
——S Michael.
——Burano.
——Torcello.

Ifle Mazorbo.
——Francefco del Deferto
——New Lazaretto.
——Lido
——La Gratia
——S Clemente.
——S Spirito.
——Palegia
——Malocomo.
——S Servolo
——S Nicola di Lido
Altino.
Trevifo.
Baffano.
Primolano.
Feltri
Belluno.

GERMANY.
Trent
Roveredo.

ITALY.
Buffolongo
Villa Franca.
Mantoua
S Benedetto.
Mirandola
Buon Porto.
Modena
Bologna.
Fiorenzola.
Florence
Leghorn

CHAP. III.

Conclusion, with reflections on travelling, on customs and manners, and the great change of things.

WHEN I first resolved on travelling into the east, as I foresaw that it would be a journey attended with great danger and difficulty, it was very natural to propose to make my observations as extensive as I could, particularly with regard to antiquity, natural history, customs, and manners: For there are different ends of travelling, which is of great use for young persons in order to learn the modern languages, especially if they are to be concerned in public affairs, they also go through their exercises, and not only gratify their curiosity, but by seeing different countries, often acquire a taste for antiquity, for architecture, sculpture, and painting; and it may be for the history of those countries they pass thro'. Some, who turn their travels to the greatest advantage, endeavour to mix with the people of the country, and with all strangers, in order to make proper observations on customs and manners, get over the prejudices of education, of being bigotted to their own, and learn to conform to such as are either innocent or convenient in the several countries they visit; and by making proper reflections on national virtues and vices both at home and abroad, they imitate and improve the one, avoid and root out the other, and, when they return, introduce such useful customs, as are suited to our climate and dispositions

From observing the many inconveniences which attend different sorts of government and manners, they learn to value their own, which is a real happiness, and whatever they have suffered abroad, makes them enjoy with greater pleasure that liberty, ease, and affluence which falls to their share when they are settled in their own country In this manner they improve their minds, which otherwise will receive but little advantage from travelling, and may be rather impaired; there being in reality no great difference in the countries themselves, and rambling makes little alteration in the mind, unless proper care be taken to improve it by the observations that are made.

There is use also in seeing the works of nature and art, in admiring the power and wisdom of the Creator, who has made such a wonderful variety of things, and given so much invention and ingenuity to mankind for the use and ornament of life

A knowledge of antiquity and geography is of great service with regard to history, and adds an infinite pleasure to the study of it. A taste for architecture has had effects very much to the honour of our country Painting and sculpture are such embellishments as are not without their use, circulate the money of the great among the ingenious, and from them to the lower rank of people, and encourage arts and sciences· A picture or a statue too may be a moral or political lecture, as well as a poem.

The great revolution of things, which they obferve in the feveral countries they pafs through, may alfo afford matter for ufeful reflection. When they fee the changes which have been made in governments, they may confider if there is not reafon to think that they are the effects either of their virtue or immorality. When they obferve countries laid wafte and uninhabited, and famous cities, like the antient Babylon, deftroyed and become the habitation of wild beafts, they may be fenfible, that public vices are the natural caufes and forerunners of the downfal of empires. And when they fee great ftates and cities, which have rifen up in their ftead from a low beginning, it may lead them to the confideration of thofe virtues, which contributed to their rife, not without a view to that power which directs the motions of the univerfe. And if they are convinced that the extraordinary revolutions of great empires have certainly been foretold, and have come to pafs accordingly, this may be a fure proof, that they are neither the effect of chance, nor even of natural caufes alone, but muft be wifely directed by that being who has this foreknowledge, which cannot be done without an influence of every thing from the leaft to the greateft, by that hand which wonderfully protects them in all dangers, and brings them home in fafety to a fweet enjoyment of their experience in agreeable and ufeful reflections.

F I N I S.

INDEX.

Assise,

H

Hill.

M

S

Vol II Part II
H h h h

E R R A T A

Of Part I omitted

Page	Line	for	read
84	2	South	North

Of Part II omitted

Page	Line	for	read
188 Plate 82		Thyrsus orientale	Thyrsus orientalis
	14	Nimsleberg	Nymphenberg
212	41	That beautiful model	An ex voto in the form of a Portico
214	48	Shaffenburg	Afhaffenburg
220	41	Canferus	Caferns

Page	Line	for	read
226	40	Lampfring	I amfpring
228	27	Butchude	Buxtehude
234	27	Lirzen	Lurzen
237	6	Galeafti	Gallafch
	8	Tfchemen	Tfchernin
239	28	Third	Fourth
243	11	Hauforn	Haufon
244	30	Haska	Harka
	1	Scharpin	Schapring
246	17	Nefmid	Nefmiel
257	28	Comorry	Cormons

Lightning Source UK Ltd.
Milton Keynes UK
UKHW050952100822
407113UK00007B/1464